THE
TECHNOLOGY
OF TEXT VOLUME TWO

PRINCIPLES FOR STRUCTURING, DESIGNING, AND DISPLAYING TEXT

THE TECHNOLOGY OF TEXT VOLUME TWO

PRINCIPLES FOR STRUCTURING, DESIGNING, AND DISPLAYING TEXT

DAVID H. JONASSEN
Editor
University of North Carolina at Greensboro

EDUCATIONAL TECHNOLOGY PUBLICATIONS
ENGLEWOOD CLIFFS, NEW JERSEY 07632

Library of Congress Cataloging in Publication Data
(Revised for volume 2)
Main entry under title:

The Technology of text.

   Includes bibliographies and indexes.
   1. Information display systems. I. Jonassen, David H.,
1947-
TK7882.I6T4   1982   001.55   81-22167
ISBN 0-87778-182-6 (v. 1)

ISBN (v. 2): 0-87778-191-5.

Printed in the United States of America.

Library of Congress Catalog Card Number:
81-22167.

International Standard Book Number:
0-87778-191-5.

First Printing: January, 1985.

To Ted Hines,
a pioneer in the information age,
whose vision and tenacity inspired many of us.

The Contributors

Thomas H. Anderson is associate professor of educational psychology at the Center for the Study of Reading, University of Illinois. After completing his doctorate at Illinois in the psychology of learning and instruction, he joined the faculty at Arkansas Polytechnic and then Indiana State universities before returning to Illinois. His current research interests are text features that affect studying and computer-based instruction.

Bonnie B. Armbruster is a visiting assistant professor at the Center for the Study of Reading, University of Illinois. She received her doctorate at Illinois in educational psychology. Her current research interests include content area reading/studying/writing and instructional development.

Bruce K. Britton is associate professor of psychology and a Fellow of the Institute of Behavioral Research at the University of Georgia. He received his Ph.D. from the University of Iowa. He was co-founder of the Text Design and Learner Strategies special interest group in A.E.R.A. and has co-edited *Understanding Expository Text.* His research and writing interests are in cognitive psychology, especially on the cognitive demands of reading.

John F. Carter is currently associate professor and chairman of the Psychology Department, Southern California College. After completing his Ph.D. at Illinois, he served as assistant professor at Syracuse University, research psychologist at the Navy Personnel R & D Center, educational consultant with Educational Radio and Television of Iran, and director of instructional development for the International Correspondence Institute in Brussels. His major research interests are instructional design and text design.

Phillipe C. Duchastel is an instructional researcher interested in learning theory applications, especially in textual learning situations. He received his graduate training at Florida State University and has worked in instructional design and research in Europe, the USA, and Canada. He is currently director of the INRS-Education, a research center in Quebec City, Canada.

Thomas M. Duffy is associate professor of English and psychology and a member of the Communications Design Center at Carnegie-Mellon University. As a research scientist at the Navy Personnel R & D Center, he studied the technical manual development and design process as well as the basic skills required to use the manuals. He is currently focusing on the design and use of training and reference documents and has recently co-edited *Designing Usable Texts.*

James E. Eisele is associate professor of education and has served as director of the Office of Instructional Development and the Division of Educational and Technical Support at the University of Georgia. He received his doctorate from the State University of New York at Buffalo. His major research and writing interests combine instructional uses of computers and instructional design and development.

Shawn M. Glynn is associate professor of educational psychology at the University of Georgia. He received his Ph.D. in educational psychology from Pennsylvania State University. He has published extensively in the areas of text comprehension and design, and he is past chairman of the Text Design and Learner Strategies SIG of the American Educational Research Association.

James Hartley is reader in and head of the psychology department of the University of Keele, England. He completed his doctoral work at the University of Sheffield and has published widely in the fields of programmed learning, educational technology, university teaching methods, and designing instructional text. His major publications include *Strategies for Programmed Instruction* (1972), *Contributions to an Educational Technology* (1978), *The Psychology of Written Communication* (1980), and a second edition of *Designing Instructional Text* (1985).

Parmalee Hawk is assistant to the dean of the School of Education, East Carolina University. As a teacher and administrator committed to putting learning theory into practice, she works with public school classrooms to develop effective teaching procedures for all school personnel.

Rudy J. Joenk has been involved with technical text for more than 20 years—as author, editor, and information manager. After receiving his Ph.D. in physics and doing theoretical research in magnetism at the IBM Research Center, he migrated to the field of technical information and became editor of the *IBM Journal of Research and Development*. Since 1979, he has been manager of information development—customer and service information manuals and internal technical documentation—for IBM. He has served also as the editor of the *IEEE Transactions on Professional Communication*.

P. Kenneth Komoski has worked as Director of the Collegiate School Automated Teaching Project, the Center for Programmed Instruction, and the Institute for Educational Technology. Since 1967, he has been Executive Director of the Educational Products Information Exchange Institute and is an adjunct associate professor at Teacher's College, Columbia. His numerous papers and addresses have concerned improving the selection and use of all forms of instructional materials, integrating technology into the learning process, learner verification and revision, and recently, achieving equity in the area of microcomputers.

F.W. Lancaster is professor in the Graduate School of Library and Information Science, University of Illinois. He has served also with two information consulting companies, two industrial information services, and the National Library of Medicine as well as numerous consultancies with the U.N. and other governmental agencies throughout the world. His major research interests are the design and evaluation of information services, paperless information systems, and the future of electronic publication. He has written numerous influential books, including *Libraries and Librarians in an Age of Electronics, Information Retrieval Systems*, and *Toward Paperless Information Systems*.

Reinhard W. Lindner is presently a Ph.D. candidate in educational psychology at the University of Connecticut. His primary interests include cognitive development, cognition and instruction, and the philosophy of science, and he is working on a critique of cognitive psychology applied to education.

Nancy P. McLeod is coordinator of curriculum and instruction at Lee-Scott School in Auburn, Alabama. As a former seventh and eighth grade teacher of social studies and science, she has assisted in the development of graphic organizers and has used them extensively.

Bonnie J.F. Meyer is professor of educational psychology at Arizona State University. She received her Ph.D. from Cornell University and has published widely in the areas of prose learning, discourse analysis, and reading comprehension, including *The Organization of Prose and Its Effects on Memory*. During the past five years, her research on learning and memory from text by adults (ages 18 to 85) has been funded by the National Institutes of Mental Health and the National Institute of Aging.

Ann Jaffe Pace is assistant professor of educational psychology at the University of Missouri-Kansas City. She obtained her doctorate in learning and cognition at the University of Delaware. Her major research interests concern reading comprehension and student-initiated strategies for studying and learning from text. She recently co-authored a major textbook in educational psychology.

John Rickards received his Ph.D. from Pennsylvania State University. Since then, he has taught at the State University of New York-Albany, University of Victoria, and Purdue University, where he was an associate professor for ten years. He is currently professor of psychology at the University of Connecticut, Storrs. His major research interests are cognition and instruction, and he has published widely in the areas of study strategies and aids to comprehending and recalling text.

Murray H. Tillman is professor of curriculum and instruction at the University of Georgia. His teaching and research interests are the design of self-instructional materials, particularly textbooks and training manuals and their associated use with computers. He has authored several texts, developed courses for human service agencies, and constructed evaluation plans for school agencies.

Robert H.W. Waller is currently lecturer in Textual Communication Research with the Institute of Educational Technology at the Open University, Milton Keynes, England. A typographer by

training, he has been increasingly employing psychological principles to research in the design and comprehension of text materials.
He is also editor of the *Information Design Journal* and co-editor
of *Designing Usable Texts*.

Amy Warner received an M.A. degree in Hispanic linguistics
from Indiana University in 1978 and an M.S. degree in Library and
Information Science from the University of Illinois in 1981. She is
currently enrolled in the Ph.D. program at the Graduate School of
Library and Information Science, University of Illinois. Her
research interests include interdisciplinary studies in the fields of
linguistics, artificial intelligence, and information science.

Arthur Woodward, prior to receiving his Ph.D. in curriculum
studies from the University of Illinois in 1982, joined the staff of
the Educational Products Information Exchange. He has worked
on and directed a number of projects, including the Teacher
Information Exchange Project and the Carnegie-funded Degrees of
Reading Power project. As Associate Director of EPIE, he has
assumed responsibility for a broad range of projects, including
EPIE's extensive programs for the analysis and evaluation of
educational software and textbooks. His writing has focused on
the evaluation, selection, and integration of instructional materials
into the school curriculum.

Kieth C. Wright is professor and chairman of the Library
Science/Educational Technology Department at the University of
North Carolina at Greensboro. After completing his Ph.D. at
Columbia University, he served as an assistant professor at
Gallaudet College and Dean of the College of Library and
Information Science, University of Maryland. His major research
and writing interests are in information retrieval, indexing, and
library services to the handicapped, leading to the publication of
two editions of *Library and Information Services for Handicapped
Individuals*.

Patricia Wright is a member of the scientific staff of the Medical
Research Council, working at the Applied Psychology Unit in
Cambridge, U.K. Her research interests concern the ways in which
people interact with written technical information, both as readers
and writers. Her publications cover such topics as diverse as

people's comprehension of instructions and tables, the design of forms and manuals, people's problems with computer-assisted communication systems, and empirical methodologies for design and evaluation.

Preface

This is the second volume in a series of as yet undetermined length devoted to examining issues, principles, and procedures for designing informational and instructional text. As in the first volume, most of the authors and I use the term text in its broadest sense. Essentially, text is simply a collection of original written words—without regard to the context for their use or the form of their delivery.

Historically, text has been equated with textbooks or more generally *print-on-paper*. The prevalence of this association is not difficult to understand, since Gutenberg and his movable type had at least a 500-year jump on integrated circuits and microwave transmissions. Indeed, for most people, print-on-paper represents their only experiences with text. Therefore, their schema for text includes only words-on-paper associations. This schema is changing for most people as our society grows increasingly computer-dependent and computer-literate.

The expansion of computer applications in all facets of our existence will eventually make *computer-based text* as common or even more common than paper-based text. Becoming inured to magazines on disk, electronic mail, and teletext-adapted television sets, all of which are now generally available, will accelerate our redefinition.

Text should no longer be defined by its delivery device. Assent for that proposition leads directly to the hypothesis that non-verbal information (graphics) also constitutes text (Jones, Walker, and Martin, 1984). If we consider the range of graphics that supports content texts, their function can be described according to existing prose text structures. So text, according to these authors, becomes any meaningful information presented as text.

Graphics often constitutes a majority of the information presented in text. In these cases, the verbal text is supplemental to the graphics, rather than the more common obverse. For example, most forms of online or computer-based text present a more graphic display. There is no reason to believe that tomorrow's electronic text (e.g., encyclopedias) will resemble the verbally-laden text of today. More likely, it will consist of a voice-activated sequence of still and moving computer-enhanced images. So, our concept of text needs to expand to accommodate an increasingly graphic orientation.

In this text (which happens to be print-on-paper), the term text will refer to almost any method for structuring and designing visual information displays. Since all of the authors in this book (as well as all its readers, I suspect) developed their schema for text around print-on-paper, some of the authors include more print-oriented examples of their design principles. However, electronic text examples and an online orientation are frequently included, and in the case of the fifth section, these are the subject of the chapters. There is no question that our conception of text is evolving, often despite our willingness to adapt. That evolution is reflected in this book.

Macrostructure of the Book

Just as the *macrostructure* of a passage of text is important to its comprehensibility, it is also important to the coherence and comprehensibility of a book. Based roughly on the model of text comprehension proposed by Kintsch (1974), this book possesses an overall macrostructure that I will explain or (to use the terminology of the second section) explicitly signal.

The book is divided into seven sections, each a *macroproposition* representing the reasoning behind the techniques or principles for designing text described in the sections. The overall structure of this text is one of comparison within sections and contrast between sections (a typical sort of scheme). In each section, the authors focus on a central theme that is previewed in the Introduction. The themes or propositions represented within each section will be contrasted with each other on two overall issues—process vs. content and learner-controlled vs. text-controlled.

The first issue, process vs. content, refers to the purpose of text design techniques. Should text design reflect or instigate specific text *processing* activities on the part of the reader? Or should text design concentrate on clarifying the content's overall *structure*, coherence, or cohesion? Which approach yields better text comprehension? Should text designers be more concerned with how readers will be processing the text or with adequately explaining the content, assuming that clearer content necessarily will be better comprehended? We know that awareness of *top-level passage information* produces better recall of text, but so does learner use of specific organizational strategies. Not surprisingly, a very recent study (Slater, 1984) suggests that a combination of structural cues and organizational processing strategies produces the greatest recall of text propositions.

The second issue, *learner vs. text control* of processing, refers to the executive control of text processing. Learner control assumes that learner-generated strategies account for differences in comprehension, whereas the latter contends that text design features, such as signaling, produce greater effects on text comprehension. As with the first issue, there is empirical support for both views. The intent of this book is to expose the issue in a contrastable manner to allow you to decide for yourself.

In the Introduction to each section, I will classify the proposition represented by the chapters in the section according to the two-dimensional array shown in Figure 1. That is, text design principles or techniques presented in each section may be learner- or text-controlled and reflect either content- or learner-processing concerns. You should compare each author's interpretation of the proposition within each section and then contrast the propositions between each section when deciding your approach to text design.

Text in most forms, including this book, is presented in a linear sequence. One chapter or block of text necessarily follows another. That does not mean that it has to be accessed and read sequentially. Follow your own interests or information needs to generate your own strategy for accessing the chapters, or use the graphic outline in Figure 2 to follow the flow of arguments in the

Figure 1

Text Design in the Book

	Process	Content
Learner-Controlled		
Text-Controlled		

book. You may want to create your own arguments that will suggest yet a different organization.

It is necessary, according to at least two sections of this book, to provide access structures that facilitate access to information in the book, such as contents lists, headings, and so on. In doing so, however, the author or editor imposes his or her own organizational structure on the reader. Unfortunately, publishing conventions would not allow me to leave the Table of Contents blank for you to fill in or to replace it with the Index, to provide for random access to information, but those might be very useful strategies, from the point of view of constructing arguments. See the section of the Lancaster and Warner chapter on *hypertext* to see how it might work. The argument goes that you should access text in the sequence that best reflects how you relate ideas. This argument provides a good transition into the first section of the book, which contends that by imposing your own knowledge structures on text, you will better comprehend the material it presents.

Figure 2

Flow of Macropropositions in the Book

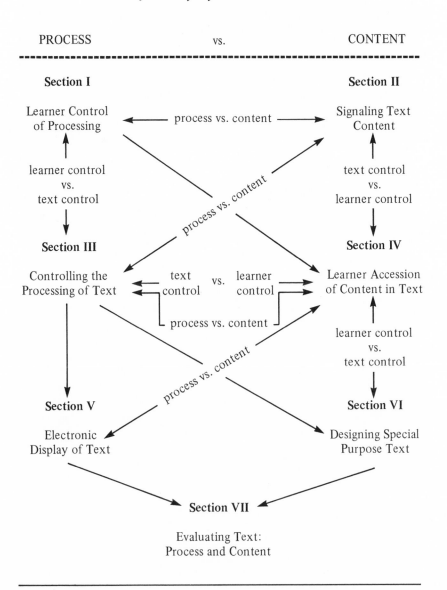

PROCESS   vs.   CONTENT

Section I   **Section II**

Learner Control   ← process vs. content →   Signaling Text
of Processing   Content

learner control   text control
vs.   *process vs. content*   vs.
text control   learner control

Section III   **Section IV**

Controlling the ← text vs. learner → Learner Accession
Processing of Text ← control   control → of Content in Text
          └── process vs. content ──┘

learner control
vs.
text control

Section V   **Section VI**

Electronic   *process vs. content*   Designing Special
Display of Text   Purpose Text

→ **Section VII** ←

Evaluating Text:
Process and Content

References

Jones, B.F., Walker, B.J., and Martin, B. Graphics as text. Paper presented at the annual meeting of the American Educational Research Association, New Orleans, LA, April, 1984.

Kintsch, W. *The representation of meaning in memory.* Hillsdale, NJ: Lawrence Erlbaum Associates, 1974.

Slater, W.H. Effects of structural organizers on ninth grade students' comprehension and recall of four patterns of expository prose. Paper presented at the annual meeting of the American Educational Research Association, New Orleans, LA, April, 1984.

Table of Contents

I. Learner Processing of Text: Introduction 3

   1. Generative Learning vs. Mathemagenic Control
      of Text Processing
      David H. Jonassen 9

   2. Learning to Learn Through Text Design: Can It
      Be Done?
      Ann Jaffe Pace 46

II. Signaling the Structure of Content: Introduction 59

   3. Signaling the Structure of Text
      Bonnie J.F. Meyer 64

   4. Frames: Structures for Informative Text
      Bonnie B. Armbruster and Thomas H. An-
      derson 90

   5. Using Typography to Structure Arguments: A
      Critical Analysis of Some Examples
      Robert H.W. Waller 105

III. Controlling the Processing of Text: Introduction 127

   6. Questions Inserted in Text: Issues and Implica-
      tions
      Reinhard W. Lindner and John Rickards 131

7. Graphic Organizers in Texts, Courseware, and
    Supplemental Materials
    *Parmalee Hawk, Nancy P. McLeod, and David H.
    Jonassen* 158

IV. **Providing Access to Information in Text: Introduc-
     tion** 187

8. Typographical Cues in Text: Management of the
    Reader's Attention
    *Shawn M. Glynn, Bruce K. Britton, and Murray
    H. Tillman* 192

9. Marginalia
    Philippe C. Duchastel 210

10. The Role of Headings in Printed and Electronic
    Text
    James Hartley and David H. Jonassen 237

11. Designing Contents Lists and Indexes for Access
    Kieth C. Wright 264

V. **Electronic Display of Text: Introduction** 287

12. Electronic Publication and Its Impact on the
    Presentation of Information
    F.W. Lancaster and Amy Warner 292

13. Computer-Based Authoring Systems
    James E. Eisele 310

VI. **Designing Special Purpose Text: Introduction** 325

14. Considerations in the Development of Distance
    Education Texts
    John F. Carter 329

15. Engineering Text for Engineers
   R.J. Joenk 346

16. Preparing Technical Manuals: Specifications and Guidelines
   Thomas M. Duffy 370

VII. **Evaluating Textual Materials: Introduction** 393

17. The Continuing Need for Learner Verification and Revision of Textual Material
   P. Kenneth Komoski and Arthur Woodward 396

18. Is Evaluation a Myth? Assessing Text Assessment Procedures
   Patricia Wright 418

Index 437

THE
TECHNOLOGY
OF TEXT VOLUME TWO

PRINCIPLES FOR STRUCTURING, DESIGNING, AND DISPLAYING TEXT

Section I

Learner Processing of Text

Introduction

One of the key issues that we will examine throughout this book is the degree to which text processing and comprehension are a function of the learner's processing skills and knowledge base or the structural and display characteristics of the text base. To what extent can the text affect comprehension by use of structural or typographic means? A book with a title such as this one certainly avers the probability. Yet, we know intuitively that without readers and their processing activities, there is no comprehension. One of the purposes of this book, as indicated in the Preface, is to explore both options—to provide a forum for proponents of each.

In the first section of this book, Ann Jaffe Pace and I will state the case for processing differences. Text processing and comprehension constitute a complex interaction of cognitive tasks, each of which introduces variance into comprehension performance. These tasks and the differences in comprehension they produce can occur at three general levels of text processing: (1) micro-processing, (2) macro-processing, and (3) meta-processing.

At the micro-processing level, differences in verbal coding and short-term memory account for differences in reading (Perfetti and Lesgold, 1977). When words are encoded into working memory and further processed, differences in memory span may also account for differences in comprehension (Daneman and Carpenter, 1980).

The most consistent differences in comprehension result from

macro-processing variations. Macro-operators transform propositions contained in the text base into the gist of text that a person
constructs—processes that are determined by the schemata that
the reader uses in generating his or her own propositions (Kintsch
and van Dijk, 1978). The schemata that are available and used to
assign meaning to text are a function of the reader's world
knowledge, that is, how much the learner knows in general as well
as how much he or she knows about the subject content of the
text. Comprehension of meaning from text is generally a function
of the knowledge that a person already possesses and, specifically,
the schemata that the reader applies to any text (Anderson *et al.*,
1977, 1978). These are the important propositions of the first
chapter.

At the meta-processing level, differences in comprehension
result from a combination of metacognitive processes (Flavell,
1979), cognitive strategies (Brown *et al.*, 1981; Weinstein and
Underwood, 1983), and executive control processes (Wagner and
Sternberg, 1983). While these undoubtedly describe many of the
same processes, the point that most of them make is that learners
who consciously employ various processing strategies in processing
different kinds of text almost invariably comprehend it better.
This is the important point of the second chapter.

In this section of the book, we are going to look primarily at
the top two levels, leaving micro-processing concerns to more
traditional reading texts. In the first chapter, I will examine
macro-processes—those involved in generating meaning from text.
In the second chapter, Ann Jaffe Pace will focus on meta-processes
in comprehension and if they can be fostered by text.

Mathemagenic vs. Generative Processing:
Text Control vs. Learner Control

Who is in control of text processing—the reader or the
author/text designer? The answer is simple, you say—the reader—
since the reader elects to read the text or not. That is undeniable,
but who determines the ideas generated by the reader from text?
Well, the text does, since the reader is processing the author's
words. That is, the author controls the sequence and combination of
schemata of words, graphics, or typographics included in the text. It

is somewhat of a circular argument—obviously without any definitive resolution. The same argument can be applied to all three levels of text processing.

In the first chapter in this section, I will look at learner vs. text control of macro-processing of text, the processing used in deriving meaning from text units and relating that meaning (or gist) to other ideas in text or in memory. I will cast the argument in terms of concepts more familiar to education and psychology, contrasting the mathemagenic hypothesis, representing text control, with the generative hypothesis of learning, representing learner control. I contend, based on several principles of cognitive psychology reviewed in the chapter, that a stronger rationale can be made for the generative model. The argument is then exemplified by contrasting mathemagenic and generative approaches to underlining and notetaking. These are common text design techniques that provide good examples of the argument contrasting generative and mathemagenic processing of text. More meaningful and exemplary applications of generative processing result from the use of such strategies as questioning, elaboration, imagery, and organization of the text base by the learner. After reviewing those, I review the effects of generative processing on text comprehension, with some suggested generative activities. Finally, I summarize the design implications of the generative hypothesis.

In the chapter, my purpose was not really to set up mathemagenic processing as a straw man. I do believe that arguments (even straw-men arguments) provide an excellent top-level structure for text. In setting up the argument, an author intends to influence your macro-processing of text. Whether or not you believe the argument does not matter as much as whether you accept that the *argument* itself is valid. Both supporting and rejecting the position taken by the author leads to deeper processing. So the question is whether or not the argument that the text presents controls the way you structure the text, or whether you impose your own arguments or hypotheses on the text. If you accept the author's argument, then the text is controlling (to a limited extent) your processing. If you do not, it has at least stimulated your generative processing of ideas by generating your own argument (text structure). The argument in this chapter is not meant seriously as a test of either text or learner control of text processing. I merely wanted to raise the argument.

Learning to Learn Through Text

Ann Jaffe Pace's chapter, to a degree, argues with my chapter. While both chapters argue that learner processing of text is more important to comprehension than the arrangement or structure of the content of the text, she tentatively concludes that the author can exercise more control over that processing. The generative model of text processing, on the other hand, contends that learners are controlled largely by their own integrative processing of text rather than by any features of text.

Pace begins by distinguishing between reader-based texts and writer-based texts—the former describing her assumptions and the latter the assumptions of the second section of this volume. The intent of a text, she claims, should be "to assist readers to become independent and skilled processors of informative text." One of the important ways in which this may be accomplished is through the application of metacognitive skills—"knowing how" rather than "knowing that" (with no intended relationship to Gilbert Ryle's similar, nominal distinction). Skilled learners normally employ metacognitive processes in their reading, including monitoring and self-regulation of processing strategies. The remainder of her chapter is concerned with how to get all learners to employ these strategies in their processing of text. Using research in reader-generated questions as support, she concludes that metacognitive behavior can be produced by text. She provides us with a list of suggestions for designing "self-conscious" text to help readers learn how to learn from text. Her conclusions are tentative because of the newness of the issues and the lack of definitive research support available. However, this in no way affects the implicit rationality of her conclusions.

Summary

How the learner processes text determines ultimately what gets comprehended. From the initial perception, association, and decoding of individual graphemes to the executive control of comprehension processes, the learner most affects what gets learned or comprehended. This does not mean that the processes cannot be controlled, guided, or at least stimulated. This first section argues that text may stimulate or even exemplify to learners the processing that most effectively leads to comprehension. But we also argue that the higher the level of learner control over those processes, the more that will be comprehended and the better able learners will be to comprehend what is in text.

References

Anderson, R.C., Reynolds, R.E., Schallert, D.C., and Goetz, E.T. Frameworks for comprehending discourse. *American Educational Research Journal*, 1977, *14*, 367-381.

Anderson, R.C., Spiro, R.J., and Anderson, M.C. Schemata as scaffolding for the representation of information in connected discourse. *American Educational Research Journal*, 1978, *15*, 433-440.

Brown, A.C., Campione, J.C., and Day, J.D. Learning to learn: On training students to learn from texts. *Educational Researcher*, 1981, *10*(2), 14-21.

Daneman, M., and Carpenter, P.A. Individual differences in working memory and reading. *Journal of Verbal Learning and Verbal Behavior*, 1980, *19*, 450-466.

Flavell, J.H. Metacognitive and cognitive monitoring. *American Psychologist*, 1979, *34*, 906-911.

Kintsch, W., and van Dijk, T.A. Toward a model of text comprehension and production. *Psychological Review*, 1978, *85*, 363-394.

Perfetti, C.A., and Lesgold, A.M. Discourse comprehension and sources of individual differences. In M. Just and P. Carpenter (Eds.), *Cognitive processes in comprehension.* Hillsdale, NJ: Lawrence Erlbaum Associates, 1977.

Wagner, R.K., and Sternberg, R.J. Executive control of reading. Paper presented at the annual meeting of the American Educational Research Association, Montreal, Quebec, Canada, April, 1983.

Weinstein, D., and Underwood, V.L. Learning strategies: The *how* of learning. In J. Segal, S. Chapman, and R. Glaser (Eds.), *Relating instruction to basic research.* Hillsdale, NJ: Lawrence Erlbaum Associates, 1983.

Chapter 1

Generative Learning vs. Mathemagenic Control of Text Processing

David H. Jonassen

Introduction: Form vs. Process

For over 60 years, media research has compared the effects of media on learner performance, usually without finding any consistent advantage for any delivery system (text, television, slides, film, programmed instruction, and now computers). This is partly because "countless studies have conducted exhaustive examinations of the wrong questions" (Wilkinson, 1980, pp. 38-39). Early researchers assumed that the medium directly affects learning without regard to the characteristics or codes of the medium and the cognitive processes instigated by these characteristics. More contemporary researchers, embracing the mathemagenic hypothesis, believed that certain design attributes of any medium give rise to learning. The form or structure of the display induces the necessary cognitive processes to produce learning. The focus of mathemagenic aids has been on the instructional stimulus. "They cue or otherwise encourage learners to cognitively operate on some information in a way that they would not under natural, i.e., non-instructional, conditions" (Winne, 1982, p. 15). Yet, research has failed to confirm any consistent relationship between what learners do and that which was supposed to result from exposure to the instructional stimulus. Causal propositions about such relationships are, according to Winne, black boxes. The underlying question I will pose in this chapter is whether control of cognitive processes is beyond instructional stimuli, specifically textual materials.

This question necessarily will refocus attention from the instructional stimuli to the learner—from the structure or the form of instruction to the process of comprehending and retaining information presented in text. In doing so, I assume that what gets learned is more a function of the mental processes in which the learner engages than any attribute of the text display, because learning is a <u>generative</u> process—an act of constructing knowledge. I will compare the definitions, purposes, and assumptions of the mathemagenic and the generative hypotheses, concluding that the generative is a more useful model of text comprehension for text designers. To support that conclusion, I will present a rationale for the generative model of learning that justifies it in terms of the most popular, current theories of cognitive psychology. Next, I will review research on various text features that compares the generative and mathemagenic assumptions about text processing, and finally, state some implications of the generative model for designing text.

Mathemagenic Model: Definition

Mathemagenic activities "are those student activities that are relevant to the achievement of specified instructional objectives in specified situations or places" (Rothkopf, 1970, p. 327). The concept of mathemagenic activity is well-known. Essentially, an instructor identifies the specific combination of orienting, acquisition, and translation processes that most efficiently result in the acquisition of a specific skill or unit of knowledge. Instructional activities and sequences that model those processes are said to "give birth to learning." The mathemagenic model of instruction assumes that learners are better led to learning than allowed to determine the relevance or meaning of material themselves.

Generative Model: Definition

The generative model of learning (Wittrock, 1974a, 1974b, 1978) is the synthesis of a melange of principles, models, and theories of cognitive psychology, some of which will be offered later in support of the model. The generative model asserts that learners, when faced with stimuli (text, illustrations, conversation, etc.), construct and assign meaning to that information based upon prior learning. That is, existing knowledge structures are activated for the purpose of interpreting that incoming stimuli, which are in turn encoded as distinctive features of memory that may be later accessed to explain new information. When we encounter text, we try to find connections between what we know and what is presented in the text. The more connections that we make, the more meaningful the text becomes.

The comprehension process involves the proactive transfer of existing knowledge, which functions as a context for interpreting newly-encountered information. This transfer process depends upon a set of cognitive transformations and elaborations that are performed on stimuli (see Figure 1.1).

Understanding relies on:

- attention to stimuli;
- motivation (the need to understand);
- the existence of schemata and more elaborate knowledge structures;
- semantic memory processes that abstract knowledge into structures;
- episodic memory for events and/or situations in the form of imagery or verbal processes; and
- processes for selecting, accessing, and relating these memories to the stimuli.

So, human learning requires both the construction of organizational structures for storing and retrieving memories as well as the cognitive processes for relating new information to stored information (Wittrock, 1974b). Knowledge structures include the various concrete, abstract, and/or distinctive associations that we have formed. These associations are the result of prior interactions with the environment. The ability to retrieve prior experiences from memory and relate them to current stimuli are the most important cognitive processes involved in learning, according to most contemporary models of learning.

Figure 1.1

Generative Process of Interpreting

NOMINAL STIMULI	Cognitive Transformations and Elaborations	FUNCTIONAL STIMULI
Combination of spatial, ortho- graphic, auditory characteristics	(e.g., verbal-semantic, imaginal, inferential, referential processes)	Distinctive associations, semantic associations

Mathemagenic Model: Purpose

The mathemagenic model of instruction and the generative model of learning begin with a similar assumption about the cognitive processing of instructional stimuli. Both assume that meaning is not implicit in the instructional material. The nominal stimuli (text, illustrations, etc.) are interpreted by the learner as functional (Wittrock, 1974a) or effective (Rothkopf, 1970) stimuli (see Figure 1.1). There is even some agreement regarding what makes the latter functional or effective, namely, the cognitive transformations performed on the nominal stimuli. The intent presumably is the same–to stimulate learner involvement and facilitate those transformations necessary for determining the effective or functional stimuli. How do we get the learner to think about information in the right way?

The explicit purpose of the mathemagenic model, though, is the control of the transformations and elaborations performed on the nominal stimuli (see Table 1.1). Mathemagenic behaviors seek "the effective management of instructional processes," controlling student behaviors "that are relevant to the attainment of instructional objectives" (Rothkopf, 1970, p. 326). Mathemagenic aids to text, such as adjunct questions, overviews, and organizers, seek to orient the learners to the text, to show them what is

Table 1.1

Cognitive Characteristics of Processing Strategies

Generative Strategies	Mathemagenic Strategies
Learner-generated	Text (instructor) provided
Individually-constructed knowledge	Text (instructor) controlled
Constructive	Reproductive
Intrinsic motivation	Extrinsic motivation (Class I mathemagenic)
Personally relevant	Content relevant
Stimulates metacognition	Supplants metacognition
Activates appropriate knowledge structures	Identifies/supplants knowledge structure
Learner-referenced	Objective-referenced

Degree of learner control ⟷ Degree of text control

relevant and important, and finally, to insure the proper translation and encoding of that information in memory. The emphasis is on controlling what learners acquire and how they relate to it. Such control implies a reductive approach to learning as opposed to a constructive or generative approach. Mathemagenic aids attempt to elicit the same orienting responses from each learner. The effective stimuli relevent to the content are provided and/or identified for the reader. The purpose is to represent or supplant the necessary cognitive processes as well as functioning as "substitutes for the metacognitive aspects of instruction" (Anderson, 1980, p. 497) so important to studying from text (see Pace chapter, this volume). Readers do not have to know if they understand the content, according to Anderson; the materials tell them whether or not they understand.

Generative Model: Purpose

Generative strategies for text learning, on the other hand, are individual and learner-generated. Learning is not "a passive reception of someone else's organizations and abstractions" (Wittrock, 1974b). Meaning in text is learner-constructed rather than text-controlled, conceptually-driven as opposed to data-driven, to use the popular psychological jargon. The text learner is responsible for activating the appropriate knowledge structures and using them to interpret meaning from text. Motivation to understand depends upon the learner's intrinsic need to know, rather than on orienting activities embedded in text. Metacognition is an essential feedback process in generative learning. If learners do not understand, they attempt to access additional knowledge structures capable of explaining information. The generative learning model emphasizes not only learner involvement, as does the mathemagenic model, but also learner control of the processes that produce comprehension.

Mathemagenic Processes

Mathemagenic behaviors can be sub-divided into reproductive and constructive strategies (see Table 1.2). Text characteristics that produce reproductive learning include those designed to directly affect specific encoding processes through producing attending behaviors (critical to the mathemagenic model). Typographic cuing such as highlighting or underlining are meant to call attention to specific information. Mechanical, linear forms of programmed instruction in effect do the same by having learners practice specific associations, that is, attend repeatedly to specific stimuli. Reproductive characteristics, though, do not purport to make information more meaningful, just more obvious.

Constructive, mathemagenic strategies address meaningfulness by attempting to orient the learners to the textual content or by affecting the way they process it. Objectives, organizers, overviews, headings, and so on attempt to signal the structure of the content in the text. Crowderian or branching programmed instruction is an example of a constructive mathemagenic strategy that attempts to influence the way that learners process information. Aspects of these strategies, such as the position of questions or the context, are better described as orienting directions (Frase,

Table 1.2

Examples of Processing Strategies

Generative Processing	Mathemagenic Processing
Selective	Reproductive
Scanning	Linear programmed instruction (copy frames)
Underlining/highlighting	Underlining/highlighting
Mnemonics	
Constructive	Constructive
Notetaking	Instructional objectives
Paraphrasing/summarizing	Branching programmed instruction
Synthesizing	Advance organizers
Generating questions	Inserted questions (pretest)
Imaging/illustrating	Titles/headings/markers
Mapping/networking	Graphic organizers
Learner control	Text control

1970). They attempt to control the cognitive processes that a learner employs in processing text.

Generative Processes

Generative processing can also be described in terms of the type and depth of processing. Table 1.2 lists selective, generative processes, such as scanning or skimming, learner underlining or highlighting, or mnemonic activities. These are individualistic processes for selecting information or content from text, depending upon their purpose for learning, i.e., the task requirements or their information needs. Their major function, like that of the reproductive mathemagenic activities, is attentional—to increase one's awareness of specific materials. The difference is that the learner determines what is important as a result of testing the information in the text against what he or she already knows in order to decide what is important enough to be cued.

Constructive, generative processes, on the other hand, are primarily intended to increase the meaningfulness of textual content. Notetaking (which often represents selective processing for lack of processing depth), paraphrasing/summarizing, generating questions, imaging, and mapping are all individual methods for interpreting material based upon prior knowledge and subsequent alteration of that knowledge base. Meaningfully encoding those interpretations is the essence of generative learning. Techniques such as outlining, mapping, or pattern-noting are means by which individuals can describe their knowledge structures. I will describe all of these techniques in greater detail later in the chapter.

Generative Model: A Rationale

A number of currently viable theories and principles of cognitive psychology lend support to the use of various learner strategies that rely on generative processing to derive meaning from text. I will review the major theories briefly, showing how each is related to the generative model of learning.

Ausubel's Theory of Cognitive Psychology. Meaningful learning, as distinguished from rote learning, occurs only when ideas can be related to an individual's cognitive structure (Ausubel, 1963, 1968). That is, information becomes meaningful insofar as we are able to relate it to something that we already know (prior learning), which is the basis for generative processing. By anchoring new ideas in text to existing concepts, we set up the conditions for meaningful processing, which will make the information processed more stable. These conditions are established by providing advance organizers in text as a bridge between new information and existing knowledge structures. Organizers generally facilitate learning and retrieval (Hartley and Davies, 1976; Luiten *et al.*, 1980).

Assimilation Encoding Theory. Mayer (1979a) reinterpreted Ausubel's ideas in terms of assimilation encoding theory, which contends that meaningful learning depends upon reception of material, availability of relevant, past experiences, and activation of that context during learning. The key to the comprehension process is the integration of new information with prior learning, which is also the basis for generative learning.

Mayer (1979b) refined Ausubel's research paradigm, finding organizers most effective for instruction using conceptual material and requiring transfer of learning. We can conclude from Ausubel's and Mayer's work that generative learning strategies—those in which the learner uses prior knowledge to interpret new information—will improve comprehension and recall.

Levels of Processing. Craik and Lockhart (1972) contended that what gets encoded into memory depends on the level or depth of processing of information occurring during encoding. Only deeper, semantic processing of information, that is, forming meaningful associations between the instructional stimuli and existing knowledge, would produce memory traces resistant to forgetting.

Decoding words during reading may only stimulate orthographic (spelling) and auditory or phonological (pronunciation) processes. You no doubt remember having finished "reading" a page of text only to realize that you do not have the slightest notion of what any of it was about. You were not semantically processing the information in the text. You were only processing the words—not their meanings. So, leading readers to encode meaningfully what they read (e.g., by asking them to paraphrase what they have read) produces better comprehension (Andre and Sola, 1976).

Generative processing of text necessarily entails deeper processing of text. To the extent that types and sequences of questions or directions in text can control the depth of processing, it is reasonable to infer that text processing strategies that induce generative learning should provide the deepest processing possible. As with organizers, though, this depends upon the availability of relevant prior knowledge structures in the learner capable of subsuming the ideas presented in the text.

Schemata and Scripts. A lot of people studying comprehension have referred to knowledge in terms of schema or the plural schemata. What people comprehend depends on their structure of existing knowledge (a person's network of schemata) and how they are able to relate new information to that structure. If this sounds similar to the rationale presented so far, that is because there is a rough conceptual cohesion to all of cognitive psychology. The concept of schema, whether attributed to Kant, Bartlett (1932), Bobrow and Norman (1975), or Rumelhart and Ortony (1977), is generally considered to be the basic unit for representing knowledge. Mental constructs or schemata are developed to represent objects, actions, events, settings, or abstract ideas. An individual's schema (representation in memory) for any object, say a fire truck, consists of the amalgam of associations and relationships possessed about that object (e.g., siren, shiny red truck, hoses, ladders, pumps, water, Dalmation dogs, etc.). We also develop schemata or scripts (Shank and Abelson, 1975) for situations or events that help us determine how to behave. For instance, most of us have a script for a restaurant. We walk in, are seated, a person (often uniformed) takes our order, brings our food (which we eat), and waits for a tip. These scripts or schemata are automatically activated in comprehending text.

Schemata also allow us to make inferences about information. The question, "Over easy or sunny-side up?," activates our schemata for eggs and, by schematic inference, breakfast. Schemata are arranged heterarchically in different types of knowledge structures, which in turn control the way we comprehend and interpret text. For instance, given passages with intentionally ambiguous interpretations, physical education majors and music majors constructed distinctly different interpretations of the passage consistent with their backgrounds (Anderson, Reynolds, Shallert, and Goetz, 1977). That is, meaning for the text is generated while we are processing it, based upon what we already know about the subject.

As with the previous theories, differences in prior knowledge among learners (different schemata in memory) will produce different interpretations of text. When schemata in learners are not as well developed (sparse or poorly elaborated), comprehension will suffer. Given two passages containing the same information in alternative settings (restaurant vs. supermarket), comprehension was better for the passage that activated the better-developed schema (restaurant) (Anderson, Spiro, and Anderson, 1978). The level of prior knowledge (schemata) that can be generated is "the principal determinant of the knowledge a person can acquire from reading" (Anderson *et al.*, 1977). Text processing is a generative process based upon existing schemata.

Achievement Treatment Interactions. A useful method for investigating how different people generate associations by using their prior learning and abilities is aptitude-treatment interaction research (Wittrock, 1974a). A part of that research has focused on the interaction of instructional treatments with prior learning (achievement). The general hypothesis of these studies has been that the higher the level of prior achievement (which presumably is reflected in more elaborate knowledge structures), the lower the level of instructional support required to learn (Tobias, 1976). Restated, the higher the achievement level of the learner, the more elaborate the knowledge structures (schemata or scripts) that can be evoked for subsuming new information, so deeper semantic processing will require less effort. This hypothesis has been repeatedly supported, and it is consistent with the generative model of learning.

Summary. The generative model conceives of learning as an active, constructive process, which is consistent with most contemporary theories of cognitive psychology. The meaning that a learner assigns to text results from the activation of the network of specific associations and relations that an individual has encoded into memory. These knowledge structures also determine the nature of the interpretive, elaborative, transformational, and inferential processes that an individual can activate when trying to understand material. Learning is a process of constructing and reconstructing mental representations of events or ideas. Text designers need to consider how these processes can be exploited in the arrangement and writing of text.

Text Processing Strategies

In this section, I will review common text design features in terms of the mathemagenic and generative processes they stimulate. The contemporary research paradigm for these strategies compares experimenter-provided vs. learner-generated text characteristics. Experimenter-provided text characteristics are more mathemagenic, most often as forms of cuing intended to control the learner's orientation to the text. Learner-generated strategies are those in which the learner overtly assigns some form of meaning to the text as it is being processed. Table 1.2 lists these text vs. learner strategies classified by type of process. While each technique may not be exclusively mathemagenic or generative, its primary purpose or effect is better described by one model of learning.

Underlining

The highlighting or underlining of text is the strategy that has received the most research attention. The primary distinction in underlining is whether passages are underlined by the author to create arousal and attention to the material underlined or by the reader as a locational signal for important information. The former represents typographic cuing and is largely mathemagenic, while the latter represents a potentially generative activity.

Underlining as Typographic Cuing (Mathemagenic). Authors will often underline or highlight in different color type sections of a passage in order to call attention to that information. The effect of such typographic alterations is to cue the reader's attention, which in turn should result in better retention of that information. Such orienting stimuli are mathemagenic, defining an acquisition target for the reader, which should increase scanning of both the highlighted and the adjacent text (Kulhavy, 1972).

Increased scanning or reading has resulted in increased retention of target or core material (Cashen and Leicht, 1970; Foster, 1979; Kulhavy, 1972). Unfortunately, more intense focusing on cued (intentional) material tends to depress recall of incidental (non-cued) material, which is consistent with the effects of most mathemagenic activities. The extent of this effect depends upon the kinds of directions given the learner relative to the underlining. Crouse and Idstein (1972), for instance, told readers that test-relevant information was underlined. So the fact that underlining produced twice-as-good performance is not surprising. When readers are not specifically directed to attend to cuing prior to reading, no advantage occurs (Coles and Foster, 1975).

The effectiveness of underlining as typographic cuing is also a function of the amount of cuing. Using five different types of cues to signal the categories of lesson content, Hershberger and Terry (1965) only managed to befuddle the readers, while a simpler cuing scheme using only two categories did enhance learning of core material.

Summary. The typographic cuing (mathemagenic) hypothesis of underlining assumes that encoding by underlining is effective only if done by the researcher/writer, but not if done by the reader, since he or she must guess the contents of the retention test (Crouse and Idstein, 1972). While the writer should better understand the material and therefore be better able to identify and cue the most important information in a passage, the effectiveness of cuing (underlining) "may ultimately depend upon the amount of faith they (the readers) have in the judgment of the person who did the highlighting" (Fowler and Barker, 1974, p. 358).

Underlining as Generative Strategy. Underlining may also be reader-generated. Rather than calling attention to cued portions of a passage, the generative model of underlining contends that active highlighting or underlining by the reader improves retention of the material selected and is therefore superior to passive reading of highlighted material (Fowler and Barker, 1974). What they found was a great deal of variation in the choice of material that was highlighted by different readers. Although learners retained material that they had highlighted, no overall performance differences occurred because of the variation. Other studies (Kulhavy, Dyer, and Silver, 1975; Stordahl and Christenson, 1956), where reader underlining was unconstrained, also found that underlining was no more effective than repetitive reading. What is important to one learner is understandably different from what is important to another. That is consistent with the generative model of learning.

Underlining effects often depend upon the way in which the

underlined material is used, not what gets underlined. Idstein and Jenkins (1972) argued that underlining should facilitate review of material—not initial encoding. Unfortunately, providing additional review did not affect the performance of students who possessed underlined material in their study.

If underlining is to be considered a generative activity, the basis on which portions of a passage are selected for underlining must be better understood. Unrestrained highlighting produces too much diversity, so Rickards and August (1975) restricted learners to underlining only one sentence per paragraph. When restricted, students tended to underline high-level material capable of serving an assimilative function. In fact, allowing students to underline the sentences of their choice yielded greater assimilation and better recall than learners who were explicitly directed to underline high-level sentences. Schnell and Rocchio (1974) found that two hours of underlining instruction failed to produce greater learning than instructor-provided underlining. The directions were too explicit. Learners should have been allowed to decide, perhaps with some constraints, what was important to them. Underlining is a generative strategy that cannot be controlled but can be constrained (Rickards and August, 1975).

Summary. Underlining can be a generative activity. Given the opportunity, learners underline material that has more meaning to them than material they do not underline. While constrained underlining may involve some aspects of generative processing (viz. testing prose for meaningfulness), the level of generative processing is limited. As indicated in Table 1.2, underlining represents a selective, generative activity, which requires only that the learner confirm existing knowledge. Because the learner is only selecting information and testing it based upon its personal relevance, less knowledge construction is occurring. The generative hypothesis contends that it is only through constructing new knowledge structures that new information is effectively integrated with existing knowledge. Mathemagenic cuing calls attention to material during initial encoding.

But orientation to material does not by itself generate knowledge construction. Learner-generated underlining also acts as an orienting device for review. The level of generativity depends upon the degree to which learners actually relate material that they are highlighting to existing knowledge. Highlighting, especially the mechanical process practiced by most students of recoloring pages of text with felt-tipped markers, represents shallow processing of information. Deeper processing (in this case, semantic selectivity, if you will) is necessary for assigning any additional meaning to new information. The next level of generative activity, notetaking, involves more interpretive and integrative processes and is therefore more generative.

Notetaking

One of the most common study strategies in learning from text and from lectures is notetaking. In this chapter, I will deal only with notetaking from text and not from lectures, since text design is the topic of the book. Learners have always been encouraged to take notes, examine them, and learn to improve their strategy (Hartley and Davies, 1978). Yet, research has sometimes failed to support the effectiveness of this strategy in terms of the amount recalled (Todd and Kessler, 1971), even after extensive training in marginal notetaking and summarizing (Arnold, 1942). A clear majority of the studies, however, has concluded that notetaking, both during lectures and from text, can aid learning as well as provide a useful tool for review (Hartley, 1983). A larger proportion of studies favored notetaking from text than from lectures. These findings about the effectiveness of notetaking clearly distinguish the purpose for which notes are taken and the cognitive processing entailed by those purposes. DiVesta and Gray (1972), who first analyzed the function of notetaking, proposed that notes acted either as external storage devices or as facilitators for encoding information in memory.

External Storage Hypothesis

The external storage function implies that notetaking is merely a memory aid—a form of off-line storage. Since humans, like computers, cannot keep all their information in working memory, some of it has to be "written off to disc" or to a long-term memory store. Notes are a means for storing information that can on demand be loaded back into working memory (the very popular study strategy of cramming) for purpose of review. Notetaking as such is more of a mathemagenic activity, serving to call attention to or orient to relevant, new material (Frase, 1970). As an attentional device, though, the cognitive effort invested in storing the material can interfere with acquiring meaning from new information, especially among lower-ability learners (Peters, 1972). Attention theory, on which the external storage hypothesis is based, limits the depth of information processing to attending (selecting) and copying (recording) so, comprehension of material is not necessarily implied by this function. The external storage function is useful, though, for notetaking has been concluded to be more effective when notes can be reviewed prior to a test (Carter and Van Matre, 1975). In fact, a case study analysis of the notetaking research concluded that encoding was less important than the effects of review (Ladas, 1980). Information is more likely to be retained if it is in notes. So we know that notes do function as off-line storage.

Encoding Hypothesis (Generative)

According to the encoding hypothesis, when information is written in notes, some memory encoding is naturally entailed. The information in the passage is transformed in some way, rather than merely being recorded. When learners take notes, they arrange or modify the passage to meet their own organizational scheme (Shultz and DiVesta, 1972). When directed to reorganize a passage through notetaking, immediate and free recall and retrieval improved (Shimmerlik and Nolan, 1976). This reorganization or reconceptualization occurs at input (encoding). So, the deeper the semantic processing involved in notetaking (paraphrasing or summarizing), the better a passage is recalled (Bretzing and Kulhavy, 1979). While the findings related to the encoding hypothesis are divided (Hartley and Davies, 1978), it is generally accepted that what is recalled (at least from a lecture) is highly contingent on the content of the notes (Aiken, Thomas, and Shennum, 1975) and that skill and efficiency in notetaking also determine what gets recalled (Howe, 1970).

Notetaking serves an encoding function. The way a learner

processes and thinks about information is therefore affected by the act of notetaking. This becomes more evident when the specific purpose for notetaking is considered, that is, when learners are oriented by advance knowledge of the criterial task. For example, the test mode expectancy research related to notetaking has concluded that the type of test expected affects the kinds of information externally stored in notes (Rickards, 1979). When learners expected an essay test, they noted information higher in the content structure of the passage (more general) than those expecting a multiple-choice test (Rickards and Friedman, 1978).

Encoding or Storage?

Although a recent study comparing the functions of notetaking concluded that it primarily serves an encoding function (Barnett, DiVesta, and Rogozinski, 1981), the relationship of notetaking to learning cannot be accurately described as either encoding or storage. Both functions facilitate learning. Notetakers may recall more ideas than readers only, but we know that rehearsal (review) enhances their ability to recall (DiVesta and Gray, 1972; Fisher and Harris, 1973). The function of notetaking can also interact with the level of content recorded in the notes, with review of high-level information enabling learners to reconstruct the details associated with it (Rickards and Friedman, 1978). "Hence, notetaking *per se* may not be especially productive of recall, but notetaking plus reviewing of notes is productive of recall" (Rickards, 1980, p. 5). What is obviously more important is the kind of information that is included in notes, which is indicative of the level or depth of processing of information included in notes. How much the learner thinks about the information before recording it implies that notetaking is a generative process rather than an attentional device, as suggested by the external storage and hence the mathemagenic hypothesis.

Generative Notetaking

Too often learners merely encode information as it is presented in text, rather than relating it to prior learning. Meaningfulness, according to the generative hypothesis, is the <u>key to effective</u> <u>memory</u>. Attempts to make incoming information meaningful by activating appropriate knowledge structures improve recall. So it should be with notetaking. That is, if notetakers are encouraged to actively integrate the information they are reading or hearing with past experiences and prior knowledge, by paraphrasing, organizing, or elaborating on it, the quality of learning should improve (Peper and Mayer, 1978). The generative hypothesis of notetaking is an elaboration of the encoding hypothesis. It predicts that the benefits of notetaking occur on the encoding end of the memory process. It more clearly specifies the nature of the cognitive processing that should occur during encoding. If notetaking is generative, the information in a text needs to be transformed and elaborated on in terms of distinctive memory traces. A series of studies conducted by Peper and Mayer (1978) supported the generative model of notetaking. When generative notetaking strategies were employed, learners consistently performed better on interpretive (transfer-type) questions. They acquired broader learning outcomes that integrated new material with old at the expense of some detail, while non-notetakers simply tried to catch the main ideas. Generative notetakers are active learners who try to interrelate knowledge, which results in a more coherent pattern of recall, according to Peper and Mayer.

Cognitive Learning Strategies

The role of various cognitive and affective learning strategies in instructional situations has received a great deal of recent attention (e.g., O'Neil, 1978; O'Neil and Spielberger, 1979). This interest has produced comprehensive learning strategies curricula (Dansereau *et al.*, 1976; Dansereau *et al.*, 1979; Weinstein, 1978). The strategies are mental operations, not necessarily present in the learner prior to training, that the learner uses to acquire, retain, and retrieve different kinds of knowledge and performance (Rigney, 1978). They may direct cognitive information processing or be cognitively controlled. Further, they may be <u>detached</u> (independent of subject matter) or <u>embedded</u> (within subject content) in order to orient learners to it. More recently, a lot of attention has been given to learner's self-monitoring and control of learning strategies (Bovy, 1981; Brown, Campione, and Day, 1981). Concern with such metacognitive awareness and control of learners' strategies has focused on mental ability. While low-ability learners exhibit a more consistent need for learning strategy, instruction, and modeling (Bovy, 1981), research has indicated that all learners can profit from learning to use strategies, since even high-ability learners vary in their use of strategies. Higher-ability learners normally employ a greater variety of appropriate strategies, as well as being metacognitively aware of why they use them (see Pace's chapter, this volume, for an extended discussion of metacognition and text processing).

Student-Generated Questions

The most popular mathemagenic aid to text is the adjunct question. Questions are inserted into the text in order to control the way that the learner attends to and processes the content of the passage (see Linder and Rickards' chapter, this volume, for a discussion of adjunct questions). The generative counterpart to adjunct questions requires learners to generate their own questions about a passage. Andre and Anderson (1978/79) found that training students to generate questions produced good comprehension questions and improved reading performance of lower verbal ability learners, precisely the group that needs such training. On the other hand, Frase and Schwartz (1975) found that when unrestricted, learners tended to generate only verbatim recall questions (perhaps a case of modeling), so no advantage over inserted questions was found. When directed to produce more difficult questions, recall improved because the activity stimulated by the questions was more integrative. Improvement in all cases was confined to information targeted by the questions the students generated, suggesting an attentional function rather than a generative function for the student-generated questions. When asked to generate questions related to passage objectives, Duell (1974) found that writing low- and high-level questions resulted in better learning of both recognition and application-type test questions. The results generalized better. Yet, the activity was still largely mathemagenic, since the specific nature of the questions generated, and by inference the cognitive processes used, were controlled by the objectives. The question-generating issue is not sufficiently developed to be considered an adequate test of the generative model of learning.

Elaborational Strategies

Elaborations require the learner to relate new information to what one already knows, that is, putting new information in the context of semantically congruous knowledge (Stein and Brans- ford, 1979). Elaborational strategies and generative strategies are closely related, if not synonymous. Generative processing by definition entails a series of transformations and elaborations performed on new stimuli. So it seems logical that intentionally manifesting these transformations should be generative. Subject- generated elaborations improved performance on a variety of memory tasks across a variety of conditions in clinical settings (Bobrow and Bower, 1969; Slamecka and Graf, 1978). Weinstein (1978) investigated the application of a variety of strategies, including sentence elaboration, imaging, using analogies, and drawing inferences from material presented in text, to a broad range of curriculum materials. Over a five-hour training period, ninth graders created elaborators or mediational aids for 20 learning tasks. Immediate posttesting produced significant effects for free recall and a paired-associate task. Delayed testing produced improved performance on reading comprehension and paired-associate tasks. What is most significant about this study is the extent of intervention necessary to produce consistent results (Anderson, 1980). Most elaboration strategies are detached, i.e., adjunct strategies required by the experimenter or writer. In- creased experimenter control reduces learner control, calling into question the level of generative activity. Additionally, elaboration will improve retention only if it clarifies the precise significance of information during acquisition (Stein and Bransford, 1979). That is, the effectiveness of subject-generated elaborations is related to the quality of the elaborations. When experimenter-provided elaborations are more precise, they will produce better recall. Since elaboration strategies are the most conceptually related to generative processing, they are probably the best test of the generative hypothesis available.

Imagery

Imagery in the form of idiosyncratic drawing or generating images while reading is an important facilitator of long-term retention of information (Paivio, 1971). For instance, directing the learner to form a mental picture of the events or ideas in text has produced much better recall, particularly on delayed tests measuring paraphrase-type questions as opposed to verbatim recall (Kulhavy and Swenson, 1975). Imagery is actually a form of elaboration strategy that has received such consistent support as to be considered separately. One important reason for its effectiveness is that the use of imagery entails dual coding of information in two distinct memory stores. This bilateral processing provides more distinct and precise elaborations of text material, resulting in better retention of information.

Organizational Strategies

The ability to interpret and encode passage structure is integral to generating meaning from text. The mathemagenic approach is to attempt to manipulate the reader's processing activities by providing the reader with information about the text's structure (Dee-Lucas and DiVesta, 1980). By making the relationships between units of text explicit, text structure should be encoded in memory, which should function as a framework for associating ideas in a passage. Graphic organizers have been used extensively to portray the relationships among key concepts in text in the form of tree diagrams. A recent meta-analysis of graphic organizer research (Moore and Readance, 1983) shows that they are effective, even after a single passage, as an integrative device. They mostly affect longer term retention of vocabulary (concept) learning rather than comprehension. But that suggests an attentional (mathemagenic) function, since the diagrams are constructed using passage vocabulary. Such explicit signaling of passage structure was found to be most effective for older, skilled learners.

To test the generative hypothesis, we need to ask whether experimenter-provided structural cues, such as graphic organizers, are less effective than reader-generated structural cues. Dee-Lucas and DiVesta (1980) found that by having learners generate topic sentences, they generated and remembered better structural information, while experimenter-provided contexts resulted in better recall of subordinate information. This result is corroborated by research on titles and headings (see Hartley and Jonassen chapter, this volume, on headings).

Believing that meaning is a function of the relational links between concepts, one of the learner strategy programs discussed earlier (Dansereau *et al.*, 1979) taught different types of learners how to select key concepts, interrelate them, and elaborate on them by using imaginal or episodic memories, and by comparing newly-presented concepts with existing knowledge (the Node Acquisition and Integration Technique—NAIT). While total overall recall did not improve in a series of studies, the knowledge structures (arrangement of ideas in memory) of trained learners became more similar to the structures of experts (Diekhoff, 1977), not because the learners were induced to think like experts (mathemagenic), but because this organizational strategy is one that higher-ability learners naturally tend to use. Organizational strategies appear to affect assimilation activities as much or more than any other strategies. In another study (Holley *et al.*, 1979), learners trained to map concepts and their relationships in a passage outperformed untrained learners on all measures, but especially on essay and concept cloze activities designed to assess performance on main ideas. Recall of subordinate information is not facilitated by this mapping technique, which is consistent with Mayer's assimilative encoding hypothesis (discussed earlier in the chapter) and various elaborational strategies that focus processing on structural knowledge. Such processing does not tend to provide anchoring for subordinate information, which further distances the technique from any mathemagenic activity.

Summary. If the types and sequences of adjunct questions in text can control the depth of information processing, it is a reasonable inference that the type of generative strategy may also control the level of processing. The lack of consistent, facilitative effects for underlining, notetaking, and other allegedly generative strategies is that the levels of processing engendered by them were insufficiently deep, whereas elaboration, organization, and other more constructive strategies better facilitate comprehension, because the processing levels are more consistent with those required by the generative hypothesis.

Generative Learning and Text Design

A fundamental assumption of a generative model of text processing, regardless of the display mode, is that meaning is not implicit in words, sentences, paragraphs, or passages; language is merely a "skeleton" for the construction of meaning (Spiro, 1980). Language stimulates the cognitive processes that generate meaning, which results in comprehension. It is the learner's interpretation and processing of stimuli, not their nominal characteristics, that determines what is comprehended. Text consists of words, pictures, cues, and spatial characteristics, which are merely the media—not for conveying ideas, but for activating cognitive processes. These verbal, semantic, memorial, and inferential processes transform or recode text into associative meaning specific to the individual learner. If the text comprehension process is generative, then the text medium has less to do with the message than with the learner. If that is so, the assumption that a text designer can explicitly display text structure and that such a display will affect the meaning encoded from text is compromised by the experiential idiosyncracies of each and every reader. If existing knowledge structures and the ability to accommodate new knowledge exert the greatest influence on the meaning generated from text, then to what extent are text designers capable of affecting meaning? Well, the text designer can employ mediational strategies to control processing. Or detached learning strategies can be instigated by directions to engage in certain generative activities during text processing.

Mediational Strategies

Two arguments can be made for text-based, mediational strategies. First, without the text, there would be no processing.

Linguistic conventions make text universally interpretable. Typographic conventions also convey some information, even if only to increase arousal. Perhaps the equivocal results of typographic research are attributable to the absence of conventional interpretations for various cues (see Glynn *et al.* chapter, this volume, for a further discussion of typographic functions). Second, there is too much evidence (Kintsch and van Dijk, 1978; Meyer, 1975, and her chapter in this volume; Thorndyke, 1977; to name but a few) that indicates that both content and text structure play important roles in comprehension, that is, that comprehension is at least partially data-driven. Signaling text structure, as suggested by Meyer or Armbruster and Anderson in their chapters, exemplifies embedded text strategies. However, the relative contributions of text structure and the reader's knowledge structure is dependent on the nature of text, the purpose for reading, and the ability of the reader. Comprehension is best represented as an interaction of content in text and the reader's prior knowledge (Spiro, 1977). If text content can be directly related to prior knowledge, it seems logical to presume that the interaction would be more productive.

What Should Generative Strategies Do?

The other option is to embed or include detached learning strategies in your text. But why?

Truly generative learning is learner-controlled and instigated. It therefore must possess aspects of metacognitive processing (covered more extensively by Pace in the next chapter) as well as cognitive processing. Self-directed learning necessitates internal feedback mechanisms in the learner. That is, once a learner accesses schemata to explain information in text, he or she must analyze those knowledge structures in terms of how meaningful they make the text. If the learner realizes that he or she does not understand, alternative memories may be retrieved. If adequate or appropriate schemata do not exist, the learner realizes that no way exists for understanding the text, so he or she gives up. Learners with an adequate repertoire of metacognitive skills will use this feedback to employ an alternative strategy, e.g., rereading, seeking alternate explanations, or quitting.

Generative strategies stimulated by text devices are in effect an interaction of mathemagenic control and metacognitive skills. The text designer who is interested in stimulating generative processing by including detached strategies tries to control or supplant metacognitive behavior. The integrative and relational strategies activated by techniques such as NAIT, discussed earlier, force the learner to identify key concepts, build a structure to accommodate them, and search memory for experiences that explain them. These are generative processes that higher-aptitude learners, who are sensitive to organizational structure (a metacognitive orientation), normally perform (Meyer, 1975). So tasks that force such activities may be superfluous for that type of learner (Dee-Lucas and DiVesta, 1980). These learners are aware of their preferences for and ability to impose their own structure on material, that is, they are metacognitively aware of their generative strategies. Text designers, however, cannot take such skills for granted, since lower-ability learners infrequently possess such metacognitive awareness. So designers attempt to control them. Which generative text processing strategies might be mathemagenically controlled?

Generative Text Strategies

Techniques for stimulating generative processing in text can be classed in three groups: (1) producing distinctive memories, (2) accessing and relating prior knowledge, and (3) organizing information.

(1) Producing Distinctive Memories

Imagery. As learners read through a text, they should be provided with directions to pause after every important sentence or other unit of text so as to create a clear image of what they have just read. An alternative is to provide space after each unit of text (size of unit to vary with type of text and capabilities of learners) and direct learners to draw an image of the ideas presented in the text. The images will doubtlessly be distinctive, providing a concrete, experiential retrieval cue for the information. This can be much more effective than providing illustrations to explicate textual information (Bull and Wittrock, 1973). The use of high-imagery language also stimulates imaginal processing, which results in greater retention (Wittrock and Goldberg, 1975). So try to use concrete language or analogies that refer to concrete objects with which the learners are apt to be familiar. These effects will understandably improve with the developmental level of the learner. Older, more capable learners will create more meaningful images, because they have a greater wealth of experiences on which to draw.

Mnemonics. Occasional directions to produce mnemonics for blocks of information presented in text will also stimulate low-level generative processing. The methods of loci and pegword systems entail imaginal processing, which should by itself improve learning. However, the images generated by mnemonic techniques are not semantic interpretations of the textual information. Rather, they are arbitrary imaginal associates of the information in text. Therefore, they are low-level (reproductive) generative activities, which are probably not as effective as other imagery instructions, although no direct comparisons have been made. Mnemonics should probably be used only with list-type (serial) information. As with imagery instructions, do not provide the mnemonic, just the directions to generate one. The only difficulty is that students must have been trained in creating and using mnemonics, a task too complex to include as an adjunct to most texts.

(2) Accessing and Relating Prior Knowledge

As suggested by elaborational strategy training (Holley *et al.*, 1979), such as the Node Acquisition and Integration Technique (Diekhoff, 1977), direct the learner to elaborate and compare concepts, that is, to look for verbal-associative or episodic links to information presented in text. Provide the stimulus and the space along with some sort of criterial feedback for the learners to generate examples from memory of the ideas being presented in text. "Meaningful Elaboration of the Material" is a strategy that asks learners to think about and provide personal examples of relevant experiences, beliefs or attitudes, ideas you have, implications, what you already know, etc. (Weinstein, 1978). Students need to describe the similarities between their examples and the examples or definitions provided by the text. It is only through this comparison process that they will integrate new information into memory. It would also be useful for learners to identify the nature of the relationships between examples and definitions. According to Holley and his colleagues (1979), these links can be mapped, and the nature of those links described by classifying them as one of six types of links, such as example or characteristic relationships between concepts. This "networking" technique forces the learner to concentrate on the macrostructure for the passage.

Summarizing. Summarizing in your own words will be generative only if the ideas are truly constructed by the learners from their experiences and in their own words. Provide space at the end of chunks of text or a response form cued to the text (perhaps in outline form with the same headings used in text) and have the students write "in their own words" the meaning they ascribed to the unit of text they have just read. A separate form would force learners to look away from the text while paraphrasing their answers. In computer-displayed text, simply prompt the learner to strike a paraphrase key when ready, which clears the screen, so the paraphrasing must come from memory. The individual learner's summary could be saved in a file, which could be printed out at the end of the session—sort of an electronic notebook.

Two potential problems exist with summarizing. Preventing reproductive behavior (discussed above) is the major problem The other problem is how to provide meaningful feedback. Since summaries are individually constructed, it would be difficult at best to let the learner know that the summary or examples he or she provided are appropriate descriptions of the textual content. This is normally the purview of the live teacher. Text, both print and electronic, is limited to providing models of correct interpretations. So, you may want to direct the summarization with questions that prompt the readers to ask questions which clarify the significance of the target information (e.g., "Why might the main character be involved in the actions?" rather than "What else happened?"), which have been found to improve retention of material (Stein and Bransford, 1979).

Adjunct Questions. The form in which summarizing, elaborating, or interpreting behaviors can be stimulated is through questions posed to the learner by the text. The key here is to phrase the question in a way that stimulates a constructive response (e.g., "What other ideas have you read about which relate to . . . ." or "Can you think of examples of . . .?"). You want to avoid questions requiring convergent answers characteristic of mathemagenic-type, adjunct questions. With divergent answers, the feedback problem persists. Try suggested answers, criteria for evaluation in algorithmic form, aspects of a response to look for, etc.

(3) Organizing Information

Integrating new knowledge entails accommodation of new information to existing knowledge structures. In order to accommodate, some understanding of the structure of knowledge in memory vis-à-vis the structure of content is essential. To facilitate this understanding, methods for showing both content and cognitive structure are needed.

Structural Maps. A number of techniques for mapping content structure exist—digraph analysis (Harary, Norman, and Cartright, 1965) or active structural networks (Norman *et al.*, 1975). Digraphs have been used to describe content structure (Shavelson, 1972). These structural networks also function as models of cognitive structure. Another, more readily implementable technique is provided by pattern notes (Buzan, 1974; Fields, 1982). Pattern notes use free association and two simple rules to create representations of cognitive structure (Jonassen, 1983). Space should be provided after or adjacent to each unit of text for the learner to quickly generate a pattern note connecting the ideas presented on the page with ideas presented in other units. The learner is thereby creating a visual map of ideas in memory. Comparing individual pattern notes with an author-produced pattern of content provides the feedback mechanism. As a diagnostic tool or a means for confirming poor organization, pattern notes offer us a powerful design tool. I am currently working on a method for describing the links in pattern notes, similar to that in NAIT, in order to better describe the structure and interrelationships of ideas in memory (Jonassen, 1984) Since patterning is so much easier to learn than other strategy systems, it offers a useful comprehension/memory strategy.

The presentation of maps has been found to improve knowledge of high-level text structure (Eggan, Kauchuk, and Kirk, 1978), as well as the ability to elaborate and make inferences during retrieval (Glynn and DiVesta, 1977). A selective mapping process is used by Clifford (1981) in the "Ed Syke Game" that accompanies her foundations text in educational psychology. Blank maps of chapter content, specifying only the relational links or propositional connectors, require the learner to integrate the ideas presented in each chapter in order to complete the map.

Outlining. Outlining provides another well-established procedure for stimulating integrative processing of information. Not much support exists for this procedure, probably because the results are not that distinctive. Outlines too often represent only list structures of information, which do not indicate the nature of the interrelationships of ideas. Outlines are hierarchical, yet knowledge in memory is not always represented hierarchically.

Design Implications of Elaboration Strategies

- Retention is affected by elaborations that specify the relevance or significance of concepts relative to events in which they are embedded.
- The effects of elaboration are dependent on the specific activities the learner engages in, which may depend on the specific instructions included in text, especially for less able learners.
- If there is a match between elaboration activities and criterion measures, then elaboration stimulated by directions to use a detached strategy will facilitate performance on the task.
- Therefore, instructional designers must produce elaborative strategies that are consistent with test items (task characteristics) required by the content.
- The effectiveness of such strategies will be enhanced if

students are made aware of the goals of the material they are studying.

The goal of including elaborative learning strategies in text is that learners should be capable of matching appropriate processing strategies to instructional situations. A considerable amount of research is needed to correctly match the appropriate types of detached and embedded strategoes with the learning task requirements, content types, and learner characteristics before we realize the goal of more automatic generation of appropriate learning strategies when presented with text.

Summary

Generative learning is something that cannot be controlled; but it can be stimulated. It will occur to some degree with or without our intervention. That is, learners will construct some meaning for material they read in text. But the association activated or constructed by the learner is up to the learner. Even when learners quit, unable to activate any appropriate knowledge structures, they are assigning some meaning to the material—that it is recondite nonsense that no one needs to know. An important task for text designers is to instigate, encourage, even guide generative processing of textual material. Sixty years of media research have finally convinced us that the delivery medium matters less than how the learner interacts with and processes information in determining what gets learned and remembered! Using mathemagenic aids, you can control how a learner orients to text, but the meaning derived from it is ultimately a personal construction based on an interaction of prior learning, cognitive strategies, and textual content. That interaction is instigated every time someone begins to read. It can be fostered and even enhanced, but it cannot be controlled.

References

Aiken, E.G., Thomas, G.S., and Shennum, W.A. Memory for a lecture: Effects of notes, lecture, and information density. *Journal of Educational Psychology*, 1975, *67*, 439-444.

Anderson, R.C., Reynolds, R.E., Shallert, D.C., and Goetz, E.T. Frameworks for comprehending discourse. *American Educational Research Journal*, 1977, *14*, 367-381.

Anderson, R.C., Spiro, R.J., and Anderson, M.C. Schemata as scaffolding for the representation of information in connected discourse. *American Educational Research Journal*, 1978, *15*, 433-440.

Anderson, T.H. Study strategies and adjunct aids. In R.J. Spiro, B.C. Bruce, and W.F. Brewer (Eds.), *Theoretical issues in reading comprehension: Perspectives from cognitive psychology, linguistics, artificial intelligence, and education.* Hillsdale, NJ: Lawrence Erlbaum Associates, 1980.

Andre, M., and Anderson, T.H. The development and evaluation of a self-questioning study technique. *Reading Research Quarterly*, 1978-79, *14*, 605-623.

Andre, T., and Sola, J. Imagery, verbatim, paraphrased questions, and retention of meaningful sentences. *Journal of Educational Psychology*, 1976, *68*, 661-669.

Arnold, H.F. The comparative effectiveness of certain study techniques in the field of history. *Journal of Educational Psychology*, 1942, *33*, 449-457.

Ausubel, D.P. *The psychology of meaningful verbal learning.* New York: Grune and Stratton, 1963.

Ausubel, D.P. *Educational psychology: A cognitive view.* New York: Holt, Rinehart, and Winston, 1968.

Barnett, J.E., DiVesta, F.J., and Rogozinski, J.T. What is learned in notetaking? *Journal of Educational Psychology*, 1981, *73*, 181-192.

Bartlett, F.C. *Remembering.* Cambridge: Cambridge University Press, 1932.

Bobrow, S.A., and Bower, G.H. Comprehension and recall of sentences. *Journal of Experimental Psychology*, 1969, *80*, 455-461.

Bobrow, D.G., and Norman, D.A. Some principles of memory schemata. In D.G. Bobrow and A. Collins (Eds.), *Representation and understanding.* New York: Academic Press, 1975.

Bovy, R.C. Successful instructional methods: A cognitive information processing approach. *Educational Communications and Technology Journal*, 1981, *29*, 203-217.

Bretzing, B.H., and Kulhavy, R.W. Notetaking and depth of processing. *Contemporary Educational Psychology*, 1979, *4*, 145-153.

Brown, A., Campione, J.C., and Day, J.D. Learning to learn: On training students to learn from text. *Educational Researcher*, 1981, *10*(2), 14-21.

Bull, B.L., and Wittrock, M.C. Imagery in the learning of verbal definitions. *British Journal of Educational Psychology*, 1973, *43*, 289-293.

Buzan, T. *Use both sides of your brain.* New York: E.P. Dutton, 1974.

Carter, J.F., and Van Matre, N.H. Note taking versus note having. *Journal of Educational Psychology*, 1975, *67*, 900-904.

Cashen, V.M., and Leicht, K.L. Role of isolation effect in a formal educational setting. *Journal of Educational Psychology*, 1970, *61*, 484-486.

Clifford, M.M. *Practicing educational psychology.* Boston: Houghton Mifflin, 1981.

Coles, P., and Foster, J. Typographic cueing as an aid to learning from typewritten text. *Programmed Learning and Educational Technology*, 1975, *12*, 102-108.

Craik, F.I.M., and Lockhart, R.S. Levels of processing: A framework for memory research. *Journal of Verbal Learning and Verbal Behavior*, 1972, *11*, 671-684.

Crouse, J.H., and Idstein, P. Effects of encoding cues on prose learning. *Journal of Educational Psychology*, 1972, *63*, 309-313.

Dansereau, D.F., Collins, K.W., McDonald, B.A., Holley, C.D., Garland, J., Diekhoff, G., and Evans, S.H. Development and evaluation of a learning strategy training program. *Journal of Educational Psychology*, 1979, *70*, 64-73.

Dansereau, D.F., Long, G.L., McDonald, B.A., Atkinson, T.R., Ellis, A.M., Collins, K., Williams, S., and Evans, S.H. Effective learning strategy training program: Development and assessment. *Catalog of Selected Documents in Psychology*, 1976, *6*, p. 19.

Dee-Lucas, D., and DiVesta, F.J. Learner generated organizational aids: Effects on learning from text. *Journal of Educational Psychology*, 1980, *72*, 304-311.

Diekhoff, G.M. The node acquisition and integration technique: A node-link based teaching/learning strategy. Paper presented at the annual meeting of the American Educational Research Association, New York, April, 1977.

DiVesta, F.J., and Gray, C.S. Listening and note-taking. *Journal of Educational Psychology*, 1972, *63*, 8-14.

Duell, O.K. Effect of type of objective, level of test questions, and the judged importance of tested material upon posttest performance. *Journal of Educational Psychology*, 1974, *66*, 225-232.

Eggan, P.D., Kauchuk, D., and Kirk, S. The effect of hierarchical cues on the learning of concepts from prose materials. *Journal of Experimental Education*, 1978, *46*(4), 7-10.

Fields, A. Getting started: Pattern notes and perspectives. In D.H. Jonassen (Ed.), *The technology of text: Principles for structuring, designing, and displaying text.* Englewood Cliffs, NJ: Educational Technology Publications, 1982.

Fisher, J.L., and Harris, M.B. Effect of notetaking and review on recall. *Journal of Educational Psychology*, 1973, *65*, 321-325.

Foster, J.J. The use of visual cues in text. In P.A. Kolers, M.E. Wrolstad, and T.H. Bouma (Eds.), *Processing of visible language*, Vol. 1. New York: Plenum Press, 1979.

Fowler, R., and Barker, A. Effectiveness of highlighting for retention of text material. *Journal of Applied Psychology*, 1974, *59*, 358-364.

Frase, L.T. Boundary conditions for mathemagenic behaviors. *Review of Educational Research*, 1970, *40*, 337-347.

Frase, L.T., and Schwartz, B.J. Effect of question production and answering in prose recall. *Journal of Educational Psychology*, 1975, *67*, 628-635.

Ganske, L. Note-taking: A significant and integral part of learning environments. *Educational Communications and Technology Journal*, 1981, *29*, 155-175.

Glynn, S.M., and DiVesta, F.J. Outline and hierarchical organization as aids for study and retrieval. *Journal of Educational Psychology*, 1977, *69*, 89-95.

Harary, F., Norman, R.Z., and Cartright, D. *Structural models: An introduction to the theory of directed graphs.* New York: John Wiley, 1965.

Hartley, J. Note-taking research: Resetting the scoreboard, *Bulletin of the British Psychological Society*, 1983, *36*, 13-14.

Hartley, J., and Davies, I.K. Pre-instructional strategies: The role of pretests, behavioral objectives, overviews, and advance organizers. *Review of Educational Research*, 1976, *46*, 239-265.

Hartley, J., and Davies, I.K. Note-taking: A critical review.

Programmed Learning and Educational Technology, 1978, *15*, 207-224.

Hershberger, W.A., and Terry, D.F. Typographical cueing in conventional and programmed texts. *Journal of Applied Psychology*, 1965, *49*, 55-60.

Holley, C.D., Dansereau, D.F., MacDonald, B.A., Garland, J.C., and Collins, K.W. Evaluation of a hierarchical mapping technique as an aid to prose processing. *Contemporary Educational Psychology*, 1979, *4*, 227-237.

Howe, M.J.A. Using students' notes to examine the role of the individual learner in acquiring meaningful subject matter. *Journal of Educational Research*, 1970, *64*, 61-63.

Idstein, P., and Jenkins, J.R. Underlining versus repetitive reading. *Journal of Educational Research*, 1972, *65*, 321-323.

Jonassen, D.H. Patterns for mapping cognitive structure. Paper presented at the annual meeting of the Association for Educational Communications and Technology, New Orleans, LA, January, 1983.

Jonassen, D.H. Developing a learning strategy using pattern notes: A new technology. *Programmed Learning and Educational Technology*, 1984, *21*(3).

Kintsch, W., and van Dijk, T.A. Toward a model of text comprehension and production. *Psychological Review*, 1978, *85*, 363-394.

Kulhavy, R.W. Effects of embedding orienting stimuli in a prose passage. *Psychonomic Science*, 1972, *28*, 213-214.

Kulhavy, R.W., Dyer, J.W., and Silver, L. The effects of notetaking and text expectancy on learning of text material. *Journal of Educational Research*, 1975, *68*, 363-365.

Kulhavy, R.W., and Swenson, I. Imagery instructions and the comprehension of text. *British Journal of Educational Psychology*, 1975, *45*, Pt. 2, 47-51.

Ladas, H. Summarizing research: A case study. *Review of Educational Research*, 1980, *50*, 597-624.

Luiten, J., Ames, A., and Ackerson, G.A. A meta-analysis of the effects of advance organizers on learning and retention. *American Educational Research Journal*, 1980, *17*, 211-218.

Mayer, R.E. Twenty years of research on advance organizers: Assimilation theory is still the best predictor. *Instructional Science*, 1979(a), *8*, 133-167.

Mayer, R.E. Can advance organizers influence meaningful learning? *Review of Educational Research*, 1979(b), *49*, 371-383.

Meyer, B.J.F. *The organization of prose and its effects on memory.* Amsterdam: North Holland, 1975.

Moore, D.W., and Readance, J.E. Meta-analysis of organizer research. Paper presented at the annual meeting of the American Educational Research Association, Montreal, Canada, April 11-15, 1983.

Norman, D.A., Rummelhart, D.E., and the LNR Research Group. *Explorations in cognition.* San Francisco: W.H. Freeman, 1975.

O'Neil, H.F. *Learning strategies.* New York: Academic Press, 1978.

O'Neil, H.F., and Spielberger, C.D. *Cognitive and affective learning strategies.* New York: Academic Press, 1979.

Paivio, A. *Imagery and verbal processes.* New York: Holt, Rinehart, and Winston, 1971.

Peper, R.J., and Mayer, R.E. Notetaking as a generative activity. *Journal of Educational Psychology*, 1978, *70*, 514-522.

Peters, D.L. Effects of notetaking and rate of presentation on short-term objective test performance. *Journal of Educational Psychology*, 1972, *63*, 276-280.

Rickards, J.P. Notetaking: Theory and research. *Improving Human Performance Quarterly*, 1979, *8*(3), 152-161.

Rickards, J.P. Notetaking, underlining, inserted questions, and organizers in text: Research conclusions and educational implications. *Educational Technology*, 1980, *20*(6), 5-11.

Rickards, J.P., and August, G.J. Generative underlining strategies in prose recall. *Journal of Educational Psychology*, 1975, *67*, 860-865.

Rickards, J.P., and Friedman, F. The encoding versus the external storage hypothesis in notetaking. *Contemporary Educational Psychology*, 1978, *3*, 136-143.

Rigney, J.W. Learning strategies: A theoretical perspective. In H.F. O'Neil (Ed.), *Learning strategies.* New York: Academic Press, 1978.

Rothkopf, E.Z. The concept of mathemagenic activities. *Review of Educational Research*, 1970, *40*, 325-336.

Rumelhart, D.E., and Ortony, A. The representation of knowledge in memory. In R.C. Anderson, R.J. Spiro, and W.E. Montague (Eds.), *Schooling and the acquisition of knowledge.* Hillsdale, NJ: Lawrence Erlbaum Associates, 1977.

Schnell, T., and Rocchio, D. A study of the relative effectiveness of various underlining strategies on reading comprehension. Paper presented at the meeting of the College Research Association, Bethesda, MD, November, 1974.

Shank, R.C., and Abelson, R.P. *Scripts, plans, goals, and understanding.* Hillsdale, NJ: Lawrence Erlbaum Associates, 1975.

Shavelson, R.J. Some aspects of the correspondence between content structure and cognitive structure. *Journal of Educational Psychology*, 1972, *64*, 225-234.

Shimmerlik, S.J., and Nolan, J.D. Reorganization and recall of prose. *Journal of Educational Psychology*, 1976, *68*, 779-786.

Shultz, C.B., and DiVesta, F.J. Effects of passage organization and notetaking on the selection of clustering strategies and on recall of textual materials. *Journal of Educational Psychology*, 1972, *63*, 244-252.

Slamecka, N.J., and Graf, P. The generation effect: Delineation of a phenomenon. *Journal of Experimental Psychology: Human Learning and Memory*, 1978, *4*, 592-604.

Spiro, R.J. Remembering information from text: Theoretical and empirical issues concerning the "state of schema" reconstruction hypothesis. In R.C. Anderson, R.J. Spiro, and W.E. Montague (Eds.), *Schooling and the acquisition of knowledge.* Hillsdale, NJ: Lawrence Erlbaum Associates, 1977.

Spiro, R.J. Constructive processes in prose comprehension recall. In R.J. Spiro, B.C. Bruce, and W.F. Brewer (Eds.), *Theoretical issues in reading comprehension: Perspectives from cognitive psychology, linguistics, artificial intelligence, and education.* Hillsdale, NJ: Lawrence Erlbaum Associates, 1980.

Stein, B.S., and Bransford, J.D. Constraints on effective elaboration: Effects on precision and subject generation. *Journal of Verbal Learning and Verbal Behavior*, 1979, 769-777.

Stordahl, K.E., and Christenson, C.M. The effect of study techniques on comprehension and retention. *Journal of Educational Research*, 1956, *49*, 561-570.

Thorndyke, P.W. Cognitive structures in comprehension of memory of narrative discourse. *Cognitive Psychology*, 1977, *9*, 77-110.

Tobias, S. Achievement treatment interactions. *Review of Educational Research*, 1976, *46*, 61-74.

Todd, W.B., and Kessler, C.C. Influence of response mode, sex, reading ability, and level of difficulty on four measures of recall of meaningfully written material. *Journal of Educational Psychology*, 1971, *62*, 229-234.

Weinstein, C.E. Elaboration skills as a learning strategy. In H.F. O'Neil (Ed.), *Learning strategies.* New York: Academic Press, 1978.

Wilkinson, G. *Media in instruction: 60 years of research.* Washington, DC: Association for Educational Communications and Technology, 1980.

Winne, P.H. Minimizing the black box problem to enhance the validity of theories about instructional effects. *Instructional Science*, 1982, *11*, 13-28.

Wittrock, M.C. Learning as a generative process. *Educational Psychologist*, 1974(a), *11*, 87-95.

Wittrock, M.C. A generative model of mathematics learning. *Journal of Research in Mathematics Education*, 1974(b), *5*, 181-197.

Wittrock, M.C. The cognitive movement in instruction. *Educational Psychologist*, 1978, *13*, 15-29.

Wittrock, M.C., and Goldberg, S.M. Imagery and meaningfulness in free recall: Word attributes and instructional sets. *Journal of General Psychology*, 1975, *92*, 137-151.

Chapter 2

Learning to Learn Through Text Design Can It Be Done?

Ann Jaffe Pace

The purpose of this chapter is to explore the issue of whether instructional texts can be designed so as to induce readers to *learn how to learn* from them. This is a concern that goes beyond that of designing texts to help readers learn specific content. In a sense, the answer to the question posed by the chapter title—whether this broader purpose can be achieved by text design—has to be "no," if the design and structure of texts are taken to be the sole means by which this goal is to be accomplished. On the other hand, if the question is interpreted to mean whether texts can be designed to assist in this process, then the answer presented here will be, "Very probably. So let's try it and see." What follows, then, is a proposal for designing texts in a way that will help the reader—the learner—learn how to use them, along with arguments for why this is important.

The Goal: "Self-Conscious," Reader-Based Texts

A recent article in *Simply Stated*, the monthly newsletter of the Document Design Center of the American Institutes for Research, drew the distinction between "writer-based" and "reader-based" approaches to the design of instructional manuals (*Simply Stated*, 1983). A writer-based approach, it noted, focuses on the explanation of content. By contrast, a reader-based approach ". . . tells the reader very specifically what to do to use the system, not

46

merely what the system does" (*Simply Stated*, 1983, p. 3). Further, as part of the reader-based approach, a document is tested with representatives of the intended audience in order to alert designers to aspects of the document that may be difficult for the potential user (see the Komoski and Woodward chapter, this volume). In general, the reader-based approach is one that appears to be sensitive to who is using a document, why he or she is using it, and how. I would like to urge that instructional texts be designed with the same kind of awareness of the potential audience, so that the reader can be helped to understand how to use such a text most effectively and, in the process, acquire skills that can be used to learn from similar kinds of instructional materials.

Instructional text differs from other kinds of writing in that its purpose is explicitly didactic. It aims to *instruct*—whether about some subject, as in a textbook, or about a procedure, as in an instructional manual. Many of the chapters in this volume (see, for example, those by Duchastel, Glynn *et al.*, Hartley and Jonassen, and Waller), as well as several of those in the first volume of this series (e.g., Duchastel, 1982; Hartley, 1982; Jonassen and Kirschner, 1982; Sari and Reigeluth, 1982), describe ways by which text can be structured, designed, or displayed so as to facilitate the reader's acquisition of the information being presented. Such recommendations are made with the understanding that features of the medium by which information is conveyed affect the ease with which the reader receives, interprets, and remembers the message. In addition, the text itself can be written so as to enhance the reader's ability to perceive important ideas and significant relationships. (See the chapter by Meyer, this volume, and that by Pace, 1982, in Volume I.)

To serve its primary purpose, instructional text certainly should be well-structured, and the best elements of design should be incorporated within it. However, the contention of this chapter is that more can—and should—be done to assist readers to become independent and skilled processors of informative text. The text's didactic function should be made explicit, as should the means employed to achieve this end. In other words, readers should be told *how* to use the medium and how to benefit from the elements of text structure and text design that have been employed to enhance their learning of the content. Texts should, in effect, become "self-conscious" and reveal how they were designed and why. The argument will be made below that such an open declaration may not only be needed to help insure that the text design is being used effectively by readers, but also to make readers more aware of the nature of instructional text itself and of the means at their command to monitor and regulate their understanding of it.

Metacognition and Learning How to Learn

Monitoring and regulating one's accomplishment of a cognitive task, whether understanding some complex principle of theoretical physics or following the plot of a Baroque novel, are aspects of *metacognition*, a term used to refer to a cluster of related phenomena that have been the focus of increasing study and attention during the past decade. In general, the term metacognition encompasses both the knowledge people have about their own cognitive processes and abilities (for example, what they can remember under given circumstances), as well as their ability to employ appropriate procedures or strategies to control their performance of some task, such as studying a chapter in a psychology textbook.

Brown (1981), in distinguishing between these two kinds of metacognitive knowledge, describes the former as "knowing that" and the latter as "knowing how." The first kind of knowledge— "knowing that"—she suggests, may be easier to talk about but harder to acquire. The ability to reflect upon and describe how one functions cognitively seems to be a late-developing achievement. The second aspect of metacognition—"knowing how"—is of more immediate concern here. It involves, among other things, sensitivity to the requirements of a particular task, planning how to accomplish it through the identification and selection of task-appropriate strategies, checking to see whether adapted procedures are working effectively, knowing what to do if they are not, and evaluating one's current state of understanding or success with regard to the task (Brown, 1981; Paris, 1982). The essence of metacognition from this perspective, then, is self-regulation or self-control of the cognitive task at hand. Such self-regulation requires that a person possesses a repertoire of resources that can be used for this purpose, a knowledge of how and when to employ these resources and the intention to utilize these resources toward a desired goal. Over time, such processes may become more-or-less automatic, so that a person might not be aware of utilizing them unless a problem is encountered in a particular situation, in which case, conscious effort may be required (Brown, 1981; Flavell, 1981). In addition, whether or not a person will engage in this kind of self-regulatory behavior may be less a function of age than of such factors as the task domain, the specific demands of a particular task, that person's degree of expertise, regardless of age (Brown, 1981, 1982; Brown, Campione, and Day, 1981), and the individual's purpose or motivation for engaging in the task (Pans, Lipson, and Wixson, 1983).

Training Metacognitive Skills

A major reason for the growing interest in metacognitive processes is the conviction on the part of a number of investigators in this area that such behaviors are a crucial part of learning how to learn (Bransford, Stein, Shelton, and Owings, 1980; Brown, Campione, and Day, 1981). That is, the kind of self-regulatory skills encompassed by the term metacognition may be important for the accomplishment of independent learning tasks. If one of the goals of schooling, or of instruction in general, is to produce self-directed learners, then perhaps the development of metacognitive skills actively needs to be fostered. Until recently, though, there was little evidence that these were being taught deliberately.

However, a number of attempts are now being made to train students to be more self-aware learners and to utilize a number of self-regulatory procedures appropriately and knowledgeably (Brown, 1981; Brown, Campione, and Day, 1981; Lipson, 1982; Palinscar, 1984). Many of these efforts have been aimed directly at exploring how such instruction can be incorporated into ongoing classroom practice, particularly in the area of reading comprehension (Duffy and Roehler, in press; Lipson, 1982; Paris, 1982). Although this literature is comparatively new, effective training procedures seem to have had several characteristics in common. For one, the attempt is made to analyze carefully the exact nature of the task to be accomplished. Second, and usually on the basis of such an analysis, explicit instructions (often with modeling) or the procedures to be followed are provided. Frequent feedback is also given in most cases. Additionally and importantly, explanations included reasons why the procedures are being taught so that students will not just apply them mechanically. By being given a rationale for these practices, students presumably will come to understand when and how to employ them and then be able to use them independently in appropriate circumstances. They would, in effect, have transferable skills at their command that had become part of their cognitive repertoire. Lipson (1982) has provided evidence that children as young as nine or ten cannot only learn such procedures but also demonstrate that they know how and why to use them several months following the end of the training program.

These results, while preliminary in some respects, are impressive. They show that instruction aimed at helping students learn how to learn can be effective, even with quite young children. The question of interest here is whether instructional texts can be designed so as to facilitate this process. Before addressing this concern directly, however, it will be useful to consider related efforts to enhance learning through written supplements to text content.

Use of Within-Text Adjunct Aids to Promote Learning

The idea that material included with text can influence the way readers process it and thus learn from it is not, of course, new. Adjunct questions in text were meant by Rothkopf (1970) to affect the reader's *mathemagenic* activities, or those behaviors that lead to increased learning. However, as Macdonald-Ross (1979) has indicated, most adjunct or inserted pre- and postquestions have been directed at the informational content of the text rather than at the processes readers employ while reading. Processes have been inferred from patterns of readers' responses to test questions. One recent study (Schumacher, Moses, and Young, 1982) did attempt to explore readers' processes by monitoring the eye movements of two groups of students. One group read texts with inserted questions, the other texts without questions. Although the authors found that those reading text with questions tended to look back at text information more often than the other group, the groups did not differ on their performance on a passage recall test. Several authors, though (e.g., Anderson, 1980; Andre, 1979; Frase, 1971; Watts and Anderson, 1971), have commented that the use of higher-level questions, or those demanding more than the recall of factual information, has produced more thorough learning of the text material. Such conclusions suggest that inserted questions can enhance readers' text-learning strategies. Still, the primary purpose of adjunct questions has been to facilitate the learning of a particular text's content rather than to help readers acquire generalizable strategies that can be used, as appropriate, with any written instructional material. Since they are designed for specific texts, different sets of adjunct questions have to be produced for each text, and, as Anderson (1980) points out, developing good, instructionally useful questions is very difficult. For this reason, among others, he does not believe that adjunct questions can be readily adapted for use with instructional texts. Some other approach may have wider applicability. The form such a direction could take is suggested by some recent studies.

Use of Reader-Generated Questions and Written Instructions

One promising possibility, the use of student-generated questions, has been explored by André and Anderson (1978-79). These authors found that high school students who ranked in the lower range of verbal ability on a standardized vocabulary test, and who had been given training and instructions to generate their own questions about the main ideas in a text, scored higher on a criterion test covering the passages read than comparable students who had received instructions simply to reread the passages or those who were instructed to generate questions without practice. Those who received training as well as question-generation instructions saw model questions provided by the experimenters and had the opportunity to practice producing their own. Although students of high verbal ability achieved higher scores overall on the posttest than did the other students, the question-generation instructions and training did not significantly affect their performance. This result plus similar findings from other studies suggest that high-ability students, once they have reached the upper-secondary grades or college, have developed reading and study procedures that work well for them, and intervention measures may only lead to marginal improvement. André and Anderson did find, however, that across ability levels, the questioning with training group produced a significantly higher percentage of good comprehension questions than did the untrained questioning group. The authors suggest that the self-generation of questions induces readers to take an active role in the monitoring and control of their comprehension, or, to be more metacognitively aware while reading.

In addition to showing the potential utility of reader-generated questions for learning from and about texts, the André and Anderson study (1978-79) is interesting for its demonstration of the role of written instructions in text processing. Ellis, Konoske, Wulfeck, and Montague (1982) also examined the effect of instructions on the recall of text information. In two experiments, they compared the posttest scores of four groups—those reading texts with adjunct postquestions, those receiving written instructions with the passage, those receiving both adjunct questions and instructions, and those simply given directions to read the experimental passage. Both groups receiving instructions were given a sample passage, shown the type of question they would have to answer, and told to study the test passage so they would be able to answer similar factual questions. Persons in the instructions-only condition also read written reminders at points within the passage (where adjunct questions would have been inserted) to stop and think about the material they had just read. In both experiments, the three experimental groups had higher scores on the posttest than the controls. Additionally, in the first experiment, both groups receiving instructions did better on incidental test questions than the adjunct-question group. Thus, this study demonstrates that within-text instructions can, apparently, influence studying behavior and subsequent test performance and that they can, in some cases, be as or more effective than adjunct questions. Taken together, the André and Anderson (1978-79) and Ellis *et al.* (1982) studies offer useful suggestions for ways in which instructional texts might be designed both to facilitate readers' use of effective text-processing strategies and to make them more aware of how and when to use them.

Designing "Self-Conscious" Text to Help Readers Learn How to Learn

How, then, could instructional text be designed so as not only to help readers learn text information but also to promote the readers' use of reading or study procedures that could be utilized with similar kinds of instructional material? Based on the literature and issues discussed above, the following recommendations are offered.

1. The text should "talk about itself." That is, it should contain an introductory section that explains the purposes it serves, how it is designed, and why. Let us assume that the text has been designed according to the kinds of principles recommended by Duchastel (1982) and Hartley (1982). Then this introductory section should describe the design features that have been used, such as, possibly, boldface for important concepts, marginal notes for explanations, etc. Additionally, the reader should be told how best to use these features to learn and understand the text content. Examples should be provided and discussed.

2. Likewise, general aspects of text structure (Kintsch and van Dijk, 1978) should be described in a manner appropriate for the level of the text. Special attention should be focused on how major points are presented and then developed through supporting details, examples, or arguments. Armbruster and Anderson (this volume) recommend the use of frames for this purpose. Suggestions should be provided for how readers can utilize the text structure to aid comprehension and learning. Again, examples should be given.

3. This introductory section should also contain guidelines for procedures readers could use to monitor their comprehension and retention as they study the text. For example, readers should be instructed how to formulate questions to

ask themselves at appropriate junctures in the text, samples of good questions should be presented, and explanations of when such questions would be useful should be given. Recommendations for procedures to follow when comprehension is not occurring should also be made.

4. In addition, the traditional kind of text introduction should be included in order to place the text content within the context of the broader discipline it represents.

5. At appropriate places within the text itself, remarks should be addressed directly to the reader to call attention to special features of the text or to remind the reader to use one of the recommendations contained in the introductory section. These remarks could be set off from the text content itself by a different type face, color, or both.

An example of such a reminder might be:

> *NOTE TO THE READER*: Can you identify the major conclusion drawn by the authors in the preceding section, as well as the evidence they have used to support their viewpoint? If so, see if you can write and answer your own question about the principal argument presented here. If you are having trouble, go back and reread paragraphs 2.02 and 2.03, keeping in mind the above question as you read.

Will It Work?

An answer to this question is premature at this time. However, given certain limitations, a response might be, "it should." Two characteristics, especially, of potential readers should be kept in mind when considering the kind of proposal presented here. One of these is ability; the other is age or grade. As mentioned above in reference to the André and Anderson article (1978-79), several studies have shown that older students of lower ability tend to benefit more from instructional interventions than higher-ability students. This is understandable and presumably a result of better students at the upper secondary and collegiate levels already having acquired effective study habits. But there is no good reason to believe that text designed according to these recommendations would interfere with the learning of higher-ability students. Better students may not need these text modifications, but they may still find them useful.

The issue involving age is somewhat different. Studies of students' sensitivity to text structure and effective use of study strategies have shown marked developmental trends (Brown and Smiley, 1977, 1978). Compared with junior and senior high school or college students, elementary-school pupils exhibited little awareness of the relative importance of text segments and minimal appropriate use of study strategies. Does this pattern, then, suggest that elementary students would not benefit from the use of "self-conscious" text? The results of the Lipson (1982) study indicate otherwise. As mentioned, these findings showed that third- and fifth-grade students could learn and retain effective procedures for monitoring and improving their comprehension of text. What this does suggest, though, is that younger children may need a more comprehensive instructional program for learning how to learn, of which text designed to facilitate this process would be one part. Since children seem to profit from explicit training in text-processing skills, instructional text that promoted such development could well be a component of this training. It may be particularly important for students to have well-designed texts in the upper-elementary grades when written instructional material becomes a significant part of the school curriculum.

In conclusion, there are several reasons to believe that instructional text designed to help readers learn how to study and learn from them could be effective and beneficial. The effort seems worth trying.

References

Anderson, T.H. Study strategies and adjunct aids. In R.J. Spiro, B.C. Bruce, and W.F. Brewer (Eds.), *Theoretical issues in reading comprehension.* Hillsdale, NJ: Lawrence Erlbaum Associates, 1980.

André, M.E.D.A., and Anderson, T.H. The development and

evaluation of a self-questioning study technique. *Reading Research Quarterly*, 1978-79, *14*, 605-623.

Andre, T. Does answering higher-level questions while reading facilitate productive learning? *Review of Educational Research*, 1979, *49*, 280-318.

Bransford, J.D., Stein, B.S., Shelton, T.S., and Owings, R.A. Cognition and adaptation: The importance of learning to learn. In J. Harvey (Ed.), *Cognition, social behavior, and the environment.* Hillsdale, NJ: Lawrence Erlbaum Associates, 1980.

Brown, A.L. Metacognition: The development of selective attention strategies for learning from texts. In M.L. Kamil (Ed.), *Directions in reading: Research and instruction.* Thirtieth Yearbook of the National Reading Conference. Washington, DC: National Reading Conference, 1981.

Brown, A.L. Learning and development: The problems of compatibility, access, and induction. *Human Development*, 1982, *25*, 89-115.

Brown, A.L., Campione, J.C., and Day, J.D. Learning to learn: On training students to learn from texts. *Educational Researcher*, 1981, *10*, 14-21.

Brown, A.L., and Smiley, S.S. Rating the importance of structural units of prose passages: A problem of metacognitive development. *Child Development*, 1977, *48*, 1-8.

Brown, A.L., and Smiley, S.S. The development of strategies for studying texts. *Child Development*, 1978, *49*, 1076-1088.

Designing reader-based computer manuals. *Simply Stated*, June-July 1983, 1, 3.

Duchastel, P.C. Textual display techniques. In D.H. Jonassen (Ed.), *The technology of text: Principles for structuring, designing, and displaying text.* Englewood Cliffs, NJ: Educational Technology Publications, 1982.

Duffy, G.G., and Roehler, L.R. Direct explanation of comprehension processes. In G. Duffy, L. Roehler, and J. Mason (Eds.), *Comprehension instruction: Perspectives and suggestions.* New York: Longman, Inc., in press.

Ellis, J.A., Konoske, P.J., Wulfeck, W.H., II, and Montague, W.E. Comparative effects of adjunct postquestions and instructions on learning from text. *Journal of Educational Psychology*, 1982, *74*, 860-867.

Flavell, J.H. Cognitive monitoring. In W.P. Dickson, *Children's oral communication skills.* New York: Academic Press, 1981.

Frase, L.T. Effect of incentive variables and type of adjunct questions upon text learning. *Journal of Educational Psychology*, 1971, *62*, 371-375.

Hartley, J. Designing instructional text. In D.H. Jonassen (Ed.), *The technology of text: Principles for structuring, designing, and displaying text.* Englewood Cliffs, NJ: Educational Technology Publications, 1982.

Jonassen, D.H., and Kirschner, P.A. Introduction to section two: Explicit techniques for structuring text. In D.H. Jonassen (Ed.), *The technology of text: Principles for structuring, designing, and displaying text.* Englewood Cliffs, NJ: Educational Technology Publications, 1982.

Kintsch, W., and van Dijk, T. Toward a model of text comprehension and production. *Psychological Review*, 1978, *85*, 363-394.

Lipson, M.Y. Promoting children's metacognition about reading through direct instruction. Paper presented at the annual meeting of the International Reading Association, Chicago, 1982.

Macdonald-Ross, M. Language in texts. In L.S. Shulman (Ed.), *Review of research in education* (Vol. 6). Itasca, IL: F.E. Peacock Publishers, Inc., 1979.

Pace, A.J. Analyzing and describing the structure of text. In D.H. Jonassen (Ed.), *The technology of text: Principles for structuring, designing, and displaying text.* Englewood Cliffs, NJ: Educational Technology Publications, 1982.

Palinscar, A.S. Reciprocal teaching: Working within the zone of proximal development. Paper presented at the annual meeting of the American Educational Research Association, New Orleans, April, 1984.

Paris, S.G. Combining research and instruction on reading comprehension in the classroom. Paper presented at the annual meeting of the International Reading Association, Chicago, 1982.

Paris, S.G., Lipson, M.Y., and Wixson, K.K. Becoming a Strategic reader. *Contemporary Educational Psychology*, 1983, *8*, 293-316.

Rothkopf, E.Z. The concept of mathemagenic activities. *Review of Educational Research*, 1970, *40*, 325-336.

Sari, I.F., and Reigeluth, C.M. Writing and evaluating textbooks:

Contributions from instructional theory. In D.H. Jonassen (Ed.), *The technology of text: Principles for structuring, designing, and displaying text.* Englewood Cliffs, NJ: Educational Technology Publications, 1982.

Schumacher, G.M., Moses, J.D., and Young, D. Students' studying processes on course related texts: The impact of inserted questions. *Journal of Reading Behavior*, 1982, *15*, 19-36.

Watts, G.H., and Anderson, R.C. Effects of three types of inserted questions on learning from prose. *Journal of Educational Psychology*, 1971, *62*, 387-394.

Section II

Signaling the Structure of Content

Introduction

The overall informational structure of any text is represented by its macrostructure (Kintsch and van Dijk, 1978). Research has shown consistently that readers make more use of and are therefore better able to retain and retrieve this super-ordinate or top-level information in text (Kintsch and van Dijk, 1978; Meyer, 1975; Yekovich and Thorndyke, 1981), what Kintsch (1974) earlier referred to as the *gist* of a passage. The gist, or *general ideas*, are more likely to be recalled than specific supporting details. In fact, an important reading-comprehension skill is the ability to follow the organization of a passage (Carroll; 1972; van Dijk, 1977). Knowledge of the structure of a passage is important, because in it the author is depicting his or her *plan* for the passage, as Bonnie J.F. Meyer explains in her chapter. Readers must ultimately construct their own meaning for a passage, but if the author successfully conveys content, the reader's constructed meaning will accurately reflect the *intent* of the author. It is therefore helpful to most readers (except for the very skilled reader) to know just what the author intends. These intentions usually constitute the top-level structure or organization of a passage. So, the better organized the passage, the easier it will be for the reader to interpret the intent of the author, and the better will be the reader's comprehension of the text.

The premise of Section II is that the more clearly and explicitly we indicate the overall structure of a passage, the more likely readers are to comprehend the content of the passage. If we activate the right schemata, or scripts, in the readers, they will better follow the flow of a passage and anticipate what will come next, as well as providing ideational anchors that will help readers retrieve information that they have read and remembered.

The three chapters in this section explain and illustrate the belief that in order to reduce ambiguity and misunderstanding, the author needs to explicitly *signal* the structure of a passage. The intent of signaling is to clarify the content of the passage. While learner processing of text material is essential to comprehension, the focus of these chapters is on the content of the passage, which is under author control. Since information high in the passage structure is better recalled, and since recall of it facilitates recall of information of lower structural importance (details), it is important to explicate the overall structure of the passage for the reader. The comprehension process, according to this belief, is more *text-controlled*. The ideas presented in this section stand in contrast to the convictions of the first section—that comprehension is primarily learner-controlled. The contrast, as explained in the Introduction, merely represents an argument that I am using as the macrostructure for the book. Text comprehension is doubtlessly both text-controlled (data-driven) and learner-controlled (conceptually-driven). Which plays a greater role in the comprehension of any given text depends upon the type and cohesiveness of the text base as well as the world knowledge, encoding, and conceptual ability of the reader.

Signaling the Structure of Text

Bonnie J.F. Meyer begins this section by illustrating ways that writers can signal their intentions through the text structure. The section owes more to her than that which is in her chapter, as she is largely responsible for popularizing the notion of signaling. She first explains and illustrates five major ways to organize text and suggests that one may be (in proper text bases) more appropriate. Next, she identifies and provides examples of four methods for signaling the organizational structure of a passage, as well as discussing who profits most from such devices. Her summary distills a prodigious amount of research into a very useful list of suggestions for organizing and designing text that any text designer will find useful.

Frames and Slots

The context for the second chapter in this section, as well as a considerable body of research and writing by Bonnie B. Armbruster and Thomas H. Anderson, has been the goal of designing and writing *considerate* content text. Considerate text, according to the authors, is well-organized, and the structure of the organization is clearly communicated to the reader. Unlike the basic, content-independent text structures discussed by Meyer, Armbruster and Anderson describe *content-specific text structures*. They describe content structures as *frames* that are defined by main ideas called *slots*. These represent the macropropositions in the text. Numerous examples from diverse disciplines clarify a variety of these text structures. They conclude by providing suggestions for organizing text content and signaling that organization.

Typographic Signaling of Text Structure

While Meyer and Armbruster and Anderson focus on linguistic methods for signaling the structure of the passage, Robert H. Waller contends that typography can be used for the same purpose. In order to enable the reader to keep track of the arguments in a text, the text must function as a diagram to clarify the structure of a passage. This chapter includes numerous examples to support its arguments, which are clearly and typographically signaled.

Summary

It is generally accepted that the better organized a passage is, the more likely it is that it will be comprehended by the reader. Skilled readers, though, are able to comprehend even poorly-organized text by hypothesizing the author's intended structure or by imposing their own structure on the passage. As text designers, we cannot be assured that only skilled readers will access our books, articles, online messages, or courseware. So it is necessary for us to organize the text in some coherent manner. In order to increase the likelihood that average-and-below readers will interpret correctly the structure we impose on text, we need to devise an emphasis plan that will highlight our organization. The type of structure that we impose depends upon our purpose. We might wish to emphasize general arguments or characteristics, as Meyer has suggested, or focus on the structure of the content that we are presenting, as Armbruster and Anderson have suggested. Understanding content depends upon understanding the arguments represented by that content. In order to insure that readers comprehend and use the appropriate structure for comprehending the text, this section contends that those structures need to be signaled or made explicit. The signaling may include linguistic connectives or typographic conventions. The important point is that the reader becomes aware of how the text is organized and how the subordinate information in the text fits together. For many readers, recall and retrieval of information from text will improve, since the organization of text recapitulates the organization of memory.

References

Carroll, J.B. Defining language comprehension: Some speculations. In J.B. Carroll and R.O. Freedle (Eds.), *Language comprehension and the acquisition of knowledge.* Washington, DC: V.A. Winston, 1972.

Kintsch, W. *The representation of meaning in memory.* Hillsdale, NJ: Lawrence Erlbaum Associates, 1974.

Kintsch, W., and van Dijk, T.A. Toward a model of text comprehension and production. *Psychological Review*, 1978, *85*, 363-394.

Meyer, B.J.F. *The organization of prose and its effects on memory.* Amsterdam: North Holland, 1975.

van Dijk, T.A. Macrostructures and cognition. In P.A. Carpenter and M. Just (Eds.), *Cognitive processes in comprehension.* Hillsdale, NJ: Lawrence Erlbaum Associates, 1977.

Yekovich, F.R., and Thorndyke, P.W. An evaluation of alternative functional models of narrative schemata. *Journal of Verbal Learning and Verbal Behavior*, 1981, *20*, 454-469.

Chapter 3

Signaling the Structure of Text

Bonnie J.F. Meyer

A plan consists of a goal and steps to achieve that goal. Plans are a central component of the processes of communicating and understanding. A writer must evolve some general plan of what to communicate, and a reader must somehow be able to follow that plan. For a writer, the plan is similar to a set of directions about how to present one's information. In this chapter, I will discuss two important functions of writing plans. First, their topical function—they help a writer conceive and organize main ideas on a topic. Second, their highlighting function—they help the writer show the reader how some ideas are of greater importance than others.

Writer, Text, and Reader: A Conversation Etched in Ink

Figure 3.1 (taken from Meyer, 1981) presents a scheme for examining the conversation (Grice, 1967) between writers and readers. The writing variables identified in the Figure determine the quality of the text. The writing process involves planning, transcribing, and editing (Flower and Hayes, 1980). In the planning phase, a mental representation of the prose to be written is generated. The quality of this mental representation is dependent on the writer's knowledge of topics, audiences, and writing plans, and how this knowledge can be integrated with task demands and the purpose for writing. The editing process

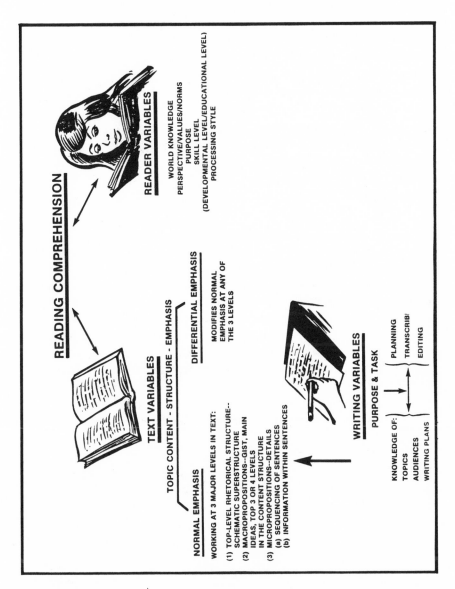

Figure 3.1. Writer, text, and reader variables that influence comprehension of text (from Meyer, 1981, reprinted with permission of Praeger Publishers).

compares the prose written with the writer's mental representation of the topic, audience, and writing plan to detect and correct errors.

The reader, however, has only the final edited form of the text and is without access to the writer for further clarification. Texts often contain sections where writers have not clearly specified their plans and leave ambiguous relationships among ideas. Readers are required to use their knowledge of text structures and the world to construct parallel or similar interpretations of the text to that intended by the writer. In this chapter, I will suggest ways for writers to signal their plans (or text structures) to their readers, and thereby reduce the possibility of misunderstanding by readers.

A topic can be viewed as a network of interrelated ideas. Due to readers' limited capacity to remember everything in text and their need to selectively forget some information, writers must cue readers into viewing some information as more important to remember than other information. The use of writing plans accomplishes this goal. Writing plans cue readers into the writer's perspective by the way they structure topic content and the emphasis they place on certain aspects of it. More specifically, they explicitly or implicitly suggest the type of overall (top-level) structure or schema to use in interpreting the topic. In addition, they highlight and superordinate the main ideas or message of the writer. They also subordinate major details that support these main ideas and further subordinate, interrelate, and sequence the very specific details on the topic. Thus, after a writer combines writing plans and information on the topic, the structure of a topic no longer looks like a network. Instead, it has been pulled out into a hierarchy representing the writer's perspective of the topic.

Psychologists have explored the role of hierarchical subordination in recalling what people read (Kintsch and van Dijk, 1978; Mandler and Johnson, 1977; Meyer, 1975; Meyer and McConkie, 1973; Thorndyke, 1977). My own work centers around methods for modeling reading and comprehending in terms of a hierarchy of text content. Figure 3.2 (taken from Meyer, in press) shows a tree diagram for a passage about the problems caused by oil supertankers (such as spilling oil and destroying wildlife) and

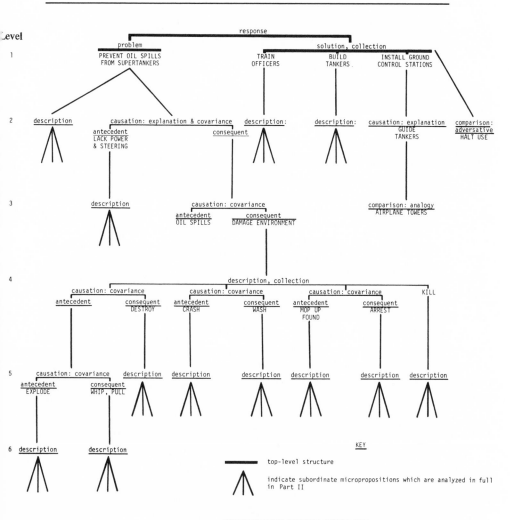

Figure 3.2. Content structure for a text on supertankers (from Meyer, B.J.F. Prose analysis: Purpose, procedures, and problems. In B.K. Britton and J. Black (Eds.), Analyzing and understanding expository text. Hillsdale, NJ: Lawrence Erlbaum Associates, in press, courtesy of the publisher.

about the possible solutions for these problems (training officers, redesigning ships, installing control stations on land, discontinuing use). This tree, called the content structure, is postulated as a representation of the hierarchy, so that main ideas are above subtopics and details.

The relationships among the items in the tree are stipulated along the lines of recent work on semantic relations like "cause of" or "description of." Some of these relations indicate moving down a level in a hierarchy, e.g., "description of." Some of the subordination is due to how a topic is organized according to more or less important constituent topics. I have gathered some support for these hierarchies by having independent judges make informal outlines of the content elements of text.

Research with various materials, learners, and tasks generally indicates that content at the top of the hierarchy is better recalled and retained over time than content at the lower levels. One explanation of this effect is that readers make heavier use of this top-level content, calling it to mind frequently and integrating it with large amounts of material coming from the text (Kintsch and van Dijk, 1978). Hence, this content is better practiced and easier to access.

A correlate to the content structure in composition methodology is the use of outlining. Less skilled writers profit from an outline precisely because it returns them periodically to high levels of their content hierarchy. However, outlining is often vague regarding how the various entries further down in the hierarchy are (or should be) related to the top level. For example, some of our tests found that confusion arises about whether events are related causally or temporally; by signaling the exact nature of these relationships, we were able to eliminate the confusion. Perhaps student writers might enrich their outlining by trying to label the relations among the various entries in the outline.

The normal order appears to be presenting the superordinate materials before the subordinate. Such a procedure is helpful because it provides easy means to integrate new content into what is already known. Unskilled writers may depart from this normal order and thereby obscure their content hierarchies. In that case, it could be helpful to rearrange their statements or paragraphs in accordance with some hierarchical outline made after the act of writing. Superordinate materials could then be moved to earlier stages of the presentation and placed in proper highlighting.

An important reading skill is to be able to view the topic from the writer's perspective. Evidence for this assertion comes from a study conducted by my research group (Meyer, Brandt, and Bluth, 1980). In this study, 102 ninth-graders each read two texts and wrote down whatever they remembered, first right after reading and then one week later. The recall protocols (the documents thus obtained) were examined to see if the readers were organizing their reports along the same type of plan (top-level structure) as the writer of the texts. We then correlated the results of this analysis with the amount that the readers could recall.

Forty-six percent of the students organized protocols written right after reading along the same plan as was used by the writer of the text; one week later only 30 percent of the 102 students organized their protocols according to the writer's plan. Those who did remembered far more information, retaining main ideas especially well, even a week after reading. They recovered more details, too. These students performed much better on a true/false test on the content of the passage; and they were also the students who had shown good reading comprehension skills on standardized tests and through appraisals by teachers. Conversely, students who did not use the author's plan tended to make disorganized lists of ideas, so that they could not recover either main ideas or details very well. These were also the students who had lower scores on standardized reading tests.

There are two sides to this kind of evidence. First, it indicates a need to gear reading instruction around identification of writing plans, so that readers can effectively learn and remember the materials they study. Second, it indicates a parallel need in methods for writing texts, so that writers can offer readers this support in some recognizable way. Schooling involves a confrontation with many topics about which students are not yet knowledgeable. In that situation, organizational plans are far more crucial to reading than they would be otherwise, because unfamiliar content (Meyer, 1984, a) must be thoroughly organized in order to be learned (e.g., Bower, 1970; Mandler, 1967).

As indicated by the purpose factor under reader variables in

Figure 3.1, readers can read for purposes other than communicating with the writer, and may read for certain types of information that better fit their purpose or perspective. However, it seems that they may first need to acquire the skill of identifying a writer's plan and knowledge about different types of plans. In the study with ninth-graders, those students who did not use the writer's plan did not impose some other systematic plan, but instead simply listed ideas from the passage with no overall structure or plan. In cases where readers can bring an alternative plan to impose on the text (e.g., Meyer, 1984, b; Meyer and Freedle, 1984), the network on a topic is pulled out into a hierarchy of importance that differs from the hierarchy based on the writer's perspective.

An analogy can be drawn from a typical kitchen steel-wool scouring pad. Let the scouring pad represent a network of information on a topic. If you pull up the scouring pad from one edge, you get a hierarchy of relationships representing the writer's perspective. If you pull it out in another way, you get another hierarchy representing what a reader with a different perspective or purpose believes to be important. However, we do not know if pulling up the network from the reader's perspective obliterates the hierarchy from the writer's perspective. It may be that the two hierarchies combine in some way (Flammer and Tauber, 1982). For example, a hierarchy based on a reader's perspective may have an upward bump in it caused by the writer's perspective that elevates certain subtopics above other subtopics at the same level in the reader's hierarchy.

Text Structure: Evidence of Planning by Writers

Research shows that a communication is vastly more efficient (it saves effort) and effective (it gets results) if it follows a plan instead of being a miscellaneous sequence of sentences or paragraphs (Frase, 1969; Mandler and Johnson, 1977; Stein and Nezworski, 1978; Thompson, 1960; Thorndyke, 1977). That is, people remember more and read faster information which is logically organized with a plan than they do when the same information is presented in a disorganized, random fashion. For example, Kintsch, Mandel, and Komzinsky (1977) compared readers' ability to comprehend paragraphs in normal sequences with their comprehension of the paragraphs arranged in a scrambled order. Students read a narrative passage of 1,400 words and then wrote summaries. The scrambled versions were much more time-consuming to read. Interestingly, the summaries produced by the two groups were much the same; no doubt the readers were using the extra time to unscramble the content and reorganize the story. Under severe time limitations, they were no longer able to do so and produced inferior summaries.

Such findings suggest that the presence of a visible plan for presenting information plays a crucial role in assuring the interpretability of a passage. Differences in text types are, in part, a result of differences in writing plans. The same information can be recast in various plans, and the impact on communication will vary. For example, a boldface caption for an advertisement in *Better Homes and Gardens* magazine stated, "I switched from clay litter to Litter Green when my husband said 'get rid of the odors, or ged rid of the cat.' " There is a causal relationship between the two clauses or propositions; she switches as a result of what her husband said. An article could expand on this plan, describing the consequent more fully and going into details about the husband's threat. However, this advertisement, or an expanded discourse on the topic, could also be written with a problem/solution plan: problem = cat odor, solution = Litter Green; a comparative plan: favored product = Litter Green, inferior product = clay litter; or a plan comprised of a collection of descriptions: Litter Green and its extolling qualities. Thus, the plan of a discourse can be considered apart from topic content, and deserves separate consideration from those who are planning text.

Drawing upon linguistics (Grimes, 1975) and rhetoric (Aristotle, trans. 1960; Fuller, 1959), Meyer (1975, 1982, in press) has gathered evidence for five basic ways to organize discourse. These five types of organization are designated as follows: *collection, description, causation, problem/solution*, and *comparison*. Figure 3.3 (taken from Meyer and Freedle, 1984) specifies the organizational components of the structures that correspond to the five basic plans for discourse.

The collection structure is a list of elements associated in some

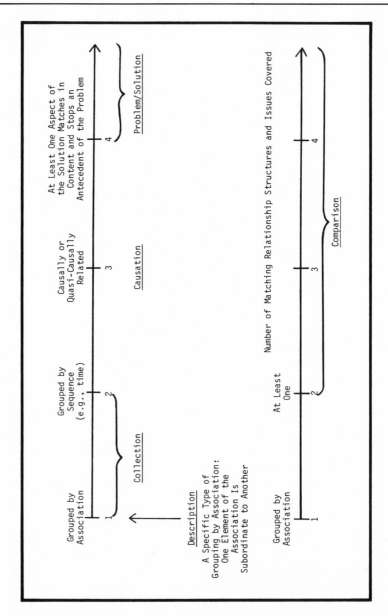

Figure 3.3. Type and number of specified organizational components required for the different discourse types (from Meyer and Freedle, 1984, courtesy of American Educational Research Association).

manner. This listing becomes more organized when it is sequenced and particularly when it sequences events or ideas according to chronology (e.g., a history listing events in chronological order). The scale in Figure 3.3 is cumulative; that is, ordered historical events with dates as specific time markers would represent a collection structure between two and three on the scale: (1) grouped by association (e.g., Civil War battles), (2) sequenced by time of occurrence, and (2+) the sequence explicitly plotted by dates.

As seen in Figure 3.3, the description plan has only one organizational component. It is a specific type of grouping by association: One element of the association is subordinate to another (the topic). The description gives more information about a topic by presenting an attribute, specific, or setting. For example, on the topic of whales, descriptive texts could be generated by describing the physical characteristics of whales as a group, by describing one particular type of whale, by describing the environment of whales, etc. The structures of collection and description often combine when a number (collection) of attributes, specifics, or settings are given about a topic.

The causation schema surpasses the collection and description plans in organization. Elements in a causation structure are (1) grouped, (2) before and after in time, and (3) causally or quasi-causally related. This structure is aimed at presenting causal relationships (like the "if/then" of antecedent/consequent statements in logic).

The problem/solution structure is at the most organized end of the first cumulative scale shown in Figure 3.3. It has all of the organizational components of causation with the addition of overlapping content between propositions in the problem and solution and at least one element of the solution able to block an antecedent of the problem. For example, in a passage with a problem/solution organization on the environmental damage caused by oil spills from supertankers (Meyer, Brandt, and Bluth, 1980), an antecedent for this problem was lack of power and steering equipment in emergency situations. One solution in a collection of three was the installation of backup power and steering equipment on supertankers. A requirement of the problem/solution organization is at least one such relationship between an antecedent of the problem and a posed solution. The passage on supertankers contained more than one of these ties; thus, its organizational scheme would be placed on the far end of the cumulative scale in Figure 3.3.

In contrast, the comparison plan is on a separate scale from causation and problem/solution (see Figure 3.3). It does not organize on the basis of time nor causality, but organizes on the basis of similarities and differences. The number of matching relationships and issues compared varies with the complexity and kind of comparative discourse (e.g., comparison of deodorant brands, to beliefs about God, to highly-structured legal arguments).

These five basic plan types are familiar in various contexts. Political speeches are often of the comparison type, and, in particular, its adversative subtype where one view is clearly favored over the other. Newspaper articles are often of the description type, telling us who, where, how, and when. Scientific treatises often adhere to the problem/solution type, first raising a question or problem and then seeking to give an answer or solution. The typical article in a psychological journal follows a quite specific version of the problem/solution plan, having well-marked sections for "problem," "method," "results," and "discussion." History texts frequently follow the collection plan with chronological ordering.

Many texts will reflect more than one of these basic five plans. For example, folktales contain much description, causation, and events sequenced in time (collection) within an overall problem/ solution organization where the protagonist confronts and resolves a problem. Folktales may carry an overall comparison organization, such as demonstrating the contrast between good vs. evil (e.g., Meyer, Haring, Brandt, and Walker, 1980).

We gave a group of ninth graders a week of training in identifying and using the four plan types of causation, problem/ solution, description, and comparison. This group read and recalled texts on three occasions; before training, a day after training, and three weeks after training. A control group did the same tasks, but received no instruction about the plans. The trained group could remember nearly twice as much content from the texts after their instruction (both one day after and three weeks after) than they could before; and they outperformed the control group by twice the amount recalled. Moreover, those students in both groups who found and used the author's plan remembered more information from texts than those who did not find the plan (Bartlett, 1978).

These and similar studies (Cook, 1982; Hurley, 1982) may provide support for composition teachers who assign papers that describe, compare, raise problems, and so forth. These plans need to be taught effectively; teaching would include identification of the plans apart from content as well as practice with plans on a variety of topics. Such plans can be shown empirically to provide benefits for both writers and readers. Content is better integrated and organized during writing, and readers retain more with less time and effort.

However, we still need to inquire further whether one plan type is more or less effective than another. Niles (1974), a reading specialist, examined some of these same types of discourse in terms of frequency of occurrence, rather than memorability. She claimed that the collection of descriptions was the most frequently-used organization in factual writing. In our ongoing studies of the memorability of the different reading plans, we have expected that the plans with more organizational components, as shown in Figure 3.2, would result in better memory of texts. In several of our studies (Meyer, 1984, a; Meyer and Freedle, 1984), we have found the comparison plan particularly useful in contrast to a plan comprised of a collection of descriptions. For example, when two passages with the same topic and detailed content, but with different plans, were read aloud, listeners for the comparison version did better on recall and question-answering than listeners for the descriptive version. The superiority of both the comparison and causation plans over the collection/description plan for facilitating memory has been shown with young adults in graduate programs with high scores on vocabulary tests (Meyer and Freedle, 1984). These adults could identify and utilize the organizational components of the more structured causation and comparison plans. However, studies with older adults with lower vocabulary performance indicated an inability to take advantage of these more organized structures, and even an advantage for memory in using the collection/description plan (Ellis, 1982; Meyer, 1983).

The simpler plan may be a more frequently used and better mastered organizational strategy for this population of adults. More research is needed on this issue. At this point, it would be unwise for writers to compose texts with only comparison structures; clearly, the function of the communication and the population for which it is written must be considered.

Signaling the Writer's Plan to the Reader

Authors show their perspective on a topic by the plan (or top-level structure) employed to organize the text, the main ideas or macropropositions that fill the slots of this structure, and the structure of propositions at lower levels in the text (see text variables in Figure 3.1). In addition, perspective is shown by the order of sequencing words, sentences, and paragraphs (e.g., Clements, 1975). It is also shown by adjunct techniques that highlight and repeat propositions through signaling, illustrations, questions, and objectives.

I identified four types of signaling in Meyer (1975). I took Halliday (1968) and Grimes' (1975) notion of theme and staging in sentences and applied these non-content aspects of text to passages. Signaling is information in text that does not add new content on a topic, but that gives emphasis to certain aspects of the semantic content or points out aspects of the structure of the content (see Bradley, 1981; Crismore, in preparation; Williams, 1981, for other discussions of signaling in composition). The four types of signaling identified included (1) specification of the structure of relations in the content structure, (2) preview statements, prematurely revealed information abstracted from content occurring later in the text, (3) summary statements, and (4) pointer words, such as "an important point is . . . ." Under type four would fall underlining, italics, and similar techniques. Examples of each type of signaling follow.

Specification of the structure of relations in the content structure. This type of signaling includes words that explicitly cue the writing plans discussed in the previous section of this chapter. For example, the signals "problem" and "solution" cue the problem/solution structure, and "one," "two," and "another" cue the collection structure. An example combining these two is: Two problems are evident. One is the problem of an energy shortage, and another is the problem of pollution. Table 3.1 lists the five basic writing plans and signals that can be used by writers to alert readers to these plans.

Preview statements. This type of signaling prematurely reveals information abstracted from content occurring later in the text. It uses the same words or paraphrasing to state information toward the beginning of a passage or paragraph that is developed more fully later in the text. It is often seen in titles and introductory sentences of passages or paragraphs. This superordinate information is abstracted out and presented prior to its discussion in detail in the text. There appear to be two subtypes of preview statements. The first is the prior enumeration of topics to be discussed later in the text. An example can be found in the first paragraph of this chapter: Two functions of writing plans are their topical function and their highlighting function. The first half of this chapter, on text structure, dealt with the topical function, and the last half of this chapter deals with their highlighting or signaling function. The second subtype of preview statements prematurely states ideas or interrelationships among them that are pointed out later in the text. An example would be: "These problems must be resolved over the next few decades." The text would develop the 30-year-time period later on, perhaps several paragraphs or more away from the prior mention of the time.

Summary statements. This type is similar to the type discussed above, except that the information is not given prematurely. Instead, the same words or paraphrased wording for information already presented is stated again at the end of a paragraph or passage. It is often seen in summary statements at the end of a paragraph or passage summarizing the main points made. An example is: "In conclusion, a wonderful pet, the parakeet, is available for those with little extra capital, space, and time."

Pointer words. Pointer words are signaling words that explicitly inform the reader of the author's perspective of a particular idea. An author may use this type of signaling when he or she explicitly states that an idea is important, or gives an opinion about an assertion or fact given in the text. Examples are: "*My first important point* is that God's creation of the universe is a

Table 3.1

*Five Basic Writing Plans and Signals
that Cue Readers to These Plans*

Writing Plan		Signals
Collection	—grouping	and, in addition, also, include, moreover, besides, first, second, third, fourth, etc., subsequent, furthermore, at the same time, another
	—sequence	before, after, soon, more recently, afterwards, later, finally, last, early, following, to begin with, to start with, then, as time passed, continuing on, to end, years ago, in the first place
Description		for example, which was one, this particular, for instance, specifically, such as, attributes of, that is, namely, properties of, characteristics are, qualities are, marks of, in describing
Causation		as a result, because, since for the purpose of, caused, led to, consequent, thus, in order to, this is why, if/then, the reason, so, in explanation, therefore
Problem/ solution		problem: problem, question perplexity, puzzle, enigma, riddle, issue, query, need, to prevent, the trouble solution: solution, answer, response, reply, rejoinder, return, comeback, to satisfy the problem, to set the issue at rest, to solve these problems
Comparison		not everyone, but, in contrast, all but, instead, act like, however, in comparison, on the one hand, on the other hand, whereas, in opposition, unlike, alike, have in common, share, resemble, the same as, different, difference, differentiate, compared to, while, although

reasonable explanation of the origin of man. *Unfortunately*, few educators and psychologists appear to agree with me."

In summary, signaling can clarify both hierarchical and semantic relationships. If we encounter "thus," "therefore," "consequently," and the like, we know that the next statement should follow from whatever has already been presented. If we see "nevertheless," "still," "all the same," or the like, we must be prepared for a statement that does not follow. On a larger scale, signaling can indicate how whole blocks of content are related, e.g., as "illustrations," "evidence," "further details," or the like. Or, a "summary," "conclusion," "preview," or whatever may be announced. It should be expected that signaling would operate as a significant support for clear writing and effectual reading.

To probe this expectation, we carried out a study of signaling with a version of the passage about supertankers (Meyer, Brandt, and Bluth, 1980). One group of ninth graders read the passage as shown below—it follows a problem/solution plan—with the signaling words (italics added here). A control group read the same passage with the signaling deleted.

> A *problem of vital concern is* the prevention of oil spills from supertankers. A typical supertanker carries a half-million tons of oil and is the size of five football fields. A wrecked supertanker spills oil in the ocean; this oil kills animals, birds, and microscopic plant life. *For example*, when a tanker crashed off the coast of England, more than 200,000 dead seabirds washed ashore. Oil spills *also* kill microscopic plant life, which provide food for sea life and produce 70 percent of the world's oxygen supply. Most wrecks result from the lack of power and steering equipment to handle emergency situations, *such as* storms. Supertankers have only one boiler to provide power and one propeller to drive the ship.
> *The solution to the problem is* not to immediately halt the use of tankers on the ocean, since about 80 percent of the world's oil supply is carried by supertankers. *Instead, the solution lies in the training of officers of supertankers, better building of tankers, and installing ground control stations to guide tankers near shore. First*, officers of supertankers must get top training in how to run and maneuver their ships. *Second*, tankers should be built with several propellers for extra control and backup boilers for emergency power. *Third*, ground control stations should be installed at places where supertankers come close to shore. These

stations would act like airplane control towers, guiding tankers
along busy shipping lanes and through dangerous channels.

Intriguingly, the deletions had no effect on the ability to recall
content for readers at both ends of the proficiency scale on
reading comprehension, i.e., those who scored either quite high or
quite low on standardized reading tests (notably the Stanford
Achievement Test). Apparently, the very good readers could
recognize and use the author's problem/solution plan, whether or
not the signaling was present. The poor readers, on the other hand,
could not use the plan either way.

However, the signaling expression did make a difference for
readers whose comprehension scores on the Stanford Achievement
Test fell into a category below their vocabulary scores. With the
signaling, these readers recalled more and produced better-planned
protocols. A similar effect was found for students in junior
college, but not for those in regular college (Marshall and Glock,
1978).

It would be wrong to conclude from such findings that signaling
does not matter. True, if you write for an audience of skilled,
well-informed readers, you can dispense with signaling, because
they will have no trouble identifying and applying the proper
highlighting plan. Indeed, much scientific writing is poorly
organized and yet understood by the target audience. But to reach
the much larger audiences of average, non-expert readers, a writer
ought to include signaling at strategic points, in correspondence
with the major hierarchy of superordination and subordination. In
this manner, the facets of highlighting support each other instead
of acting at cross purposes (Kintsch and Yarborough, 1982;
Kozminsky, 1977).

Signaling, as well as other emphasis devices, can be applied in a
normal or differential manner (see Figure 3.1). Normal emphasis
reflects a correspondence between the organizational plan or
content structure of a text and the deployment of signaling or
emphasis. In contrast, differential emphasis highlights information
above its normal level in this content structure (Meyer, 1981,
1984, b; van Dijk, 1979).

A recent study by Meyer and Rice (1982, 1983) examined the
effects of normal and differential emphasis on the recall of two

topics. Overall, there was some facilitation in total recall for passages following normal emphasis plans rather than differential plans, but the most dramatic effects related to the different types of information recalled (Meyer and Rice, 1983). We had young, middle, and old adults read and immediately recall a version of the supertanker passage and a passage of comparable length, hierarchical levels, number of ideas, and number of details on the topic of railroads. The railroad passage explained that businessmen favored the early development of the railroad and took steps to promote its development. Then, a brief description was given about different groups of people who opposed railroad development. Five versions of each passage were written (see Table 3.2, taken from Meyer, in press, a). Two versions followed normal emphasis plans with type one (signal structure) and type two (title previews organizational plan and important ideas to that plan) signaling. One of the versions with normal emphasis contained 22 specific names, dates, and numbers at the lowest level in the content structure and the other did not; for the version without specific details, general terms were substituted (e.g., thousands for 200,000 and years ago for 1975). The next two versions listed in Table 3.2 followed differential emphasis plans; the writing plans and major structures relating sentences and paragraphs were not signaled with explicit cues in the text nor the title. These two versions both contained the 22 specific details designed to attract attention low in the content structure and away from the structure of the text; one of these two versions with differential emphasis also had pointer words (signaling of type four) aimed at these specific details (e.g., notable year of 1829). The final version had no explicit emphasis plan: no signaling of the structure and no specific details placed low in the structure (see Meyer, in press, for copies of the texts and a model of text memory relating to these text variations).

For the supertanker topic, signaling increased recall of the ideas and relationships most central to the problem/solution plan used to organize that text; signaling also facilitated high use of the problem/solution structure by subjects to organize their recall protocols. Information high (H and MH in Table 3.2) in the content structure was remembered better by all age groups than was low-level information (ML and L); thus, levels effects were

Table 3.2

Signal Logical Relations	Add Specific Dates & Details	Comparison, History of Railroads Text		Problem/Solution Supertanker Text	
		Levels Effect	Use of Comparison Top-Level Structure in Ss' Recall Protocols	Levels Effect	Use of Problem/Solution Top-Level Structure in Ss' Recall Protocols
Signal	Details	Some Levels Effect (Y^2: H > L > MH > ML / M: L > H = MH > ML / O: H > ML = L = MH)	Moderate Use (72%)	Levels Effect (H^1 > MH > ML > L)	Very High Use (93%)
Signal	No Detail	Levels Effect (H > MH > ML > L)	High Use (80%)	Levels Effect (H > MH > ML > L)	Very High Use (92%)
No Signal	Signal Details	No Levels Effect (L > H = MH = ML)	Low Use (60%)	Some Levels Effect (H = MH > ML > L)	Moderate Use (78%)
No Signal	Details	No Levels Effect (L > H = ML = MH)	Low Use (68%)	Some Levels Effect (H = MH > ML > L)	High Use (85%)
No Signal	No Details	Some Levels Effect (Y: H = MH = ML > L / M: H > ML = MH > L / O: H > MH > ML > L)	Moderate Use (78%)	Some Levels Effect (H = MH > ML > L)	High Use (88%)

[1] H = Highest Levels in Content Structure, Levels 1-4
MH = Medium High, Level 5
ML = Medium Low, Level 6
L = Low, Levels 7-9

[2] Y = young adults 18-32
M = middle adults 40-54
O = old adults 65-up

Changes in Levels Effect and Organization
of Recall Protocols with Variations in Signaling
the Text's Logical Structure and Emphasis and Addition of Details
(from Meyer, in press, courtesy of
Lawrence Erlbaum Associates).

present for all versions. The versions with normal emphasis resulted in superior recall of levels 1-4 in the structure and the signaled relationships over the versions with differential or no emphasis plan. Evidently, having to make inferences to identify the structure in text reduces the probability of finding and recalling it, which, in turn, reduces recall of main ideas in the text. The detail manipulation appeared to have little effect on the levels effect or organization of recall protocols for the supertanker passage.

In contrast, both the signaling and detail manipulations have large effects on the type of information recalled and how it is organized for the railroad topic. Only the version with normal emphasis and no details shows a strong levels effect and high use of the comparison plan to organize recall. Moderate use of the comparison plan and some levels effects occur for versions that change either one of these conditions; that is, signal the structure and contain specific details or no signals and no specific details. No levels effects and lower use of the comparison plan result for the two versions with differential emphasis. In fact, for these two versions, the details (levels 7-9) from the comparison plan are recalled better than the main ideas (levels 1-6).

The different effects of varying emphasis plans for these two topics result from the specific details providing an alternate writing plan, an historical time sequence plan, for the railroad text and no such alternative plan for the supertanker text. For the supertanker text, signaling helped readers identify and focus on the structure of the text and its main ideas; differential emphasis for this text reduced the readers' ability to focus on these superordinate aspects of the author's plan, but did not give them an alternative plan for viewing the topic.

In contrast, the differential emphasis plans for the railroad topic cued readers into viewing the topic from a different perspective, a history of railroad development, rather than different views on railroads and the outcomes of these views. There was a small difference favoring normal emphasis in the total amount of information recalled when we varied the features of text that influenced which plan was identified as the overall topical plan. However, there was a big difference in the kinds of information remembered; if readers identified and used the comparison plan, the readers remembered causal and comparative relationships and related the content in this manner, but recalled few historical events and facts. In contrast, readers who recognized and used the time-sequence plan remembered these specific facts very well, but recalled less of the information that was closely related to the comparative and causal logic in the text. This study can serve as a warning to writers to: (1) identify the critical information they want to communicate, (2) use a writing plan that directly incorporates the critical information, and (3) employ signaling and other emphasis devices that highlight their selected text structure and main ideas.

Summary and Implications

I have briefly reviewed some findings about text structure and signaling that are relevant for the design of text. These findings lend support to the use of organizational techniques for planning a text in such a way that it can be read and remembered by wide audiences without undue effort. Planning can fulfill the strategic functions of organizing data and ideas and highlighting them and their interrelationships. Different plan types, such as collection, description, causation, problem/solution, and comparison, can be introduced so that they can be used by both writer and reader, and so resources like attention and memory are deployed to best advantage.

Explicit instruction in the identifying and using of plans can be included in the curriculum for both reading and writing. For example, composition classes could be devoted to analyzing prose passages in terms of the types of plan and plan function that the writer has selected. Students might gain insights by applying such an analysis to their own writings (or that of fellow students) in order to determine if the plan and plan function are clear and consistent in a particular case. If not, guides should be established for revision: presenting concepts high in the hierarchy before lower ones; inserting explicit signalings; and so on.

Deliberate attention to plans in composition training is, indeed, well-justified, in view of our research. (Of course, there is a difference between consciously using a plan, as writing students will do if so instructed, and unconsciously using one, as expert writers presumably will do on their own.) As was already proposed above, plans are particularly crucial if the topic is not a familiar one. Perhaps the tendency of beginning writers to fall back on trite, commonplace topics is a defense mechanism resulting from insufficient ability to use writing plans and thus to develop original topics.

In designing texts, the following list of suggestions should prove helpful.

1. After identifying a potential topic, select an organizational plan that best organizes the critical ideas for communication (see Figure 3.3).
2. Explicitly signal writing plans and major structural relationships (see Table 3.1).
3. Use preview statements to highlight upcoming major propositions.
   a. Use titles and subtitles to focus on main ideas and explicitly signal the structure; e.g., a text with a problem/solution plan explaining how breeder reactors can solve the energy crisis should be titled "Nuclear Breeder Reactors: A Solution to the Energy Crisis" rather than "Fast Breeder Reactors."
   b. Use abstracts, introductions, or figures to explicitly preview the main ideas.
4. Use summary statements to review major points.
5. Use pointer words to emphasize the structure (e.g., a critical problem) and highlight the main ideas.
6. Check to be sure that important ideas are not buried at low levels in the structure of the text.
7. Check to be sure that signaling complements the structural plan.
8. If after working with a topic you change your perspective on what is important, be sure you systematically change your organizational and highlighting plans.

References

Aristotle. *The rhetoric of Aristotle* (L. Cooper, trans.). New York: Appleton-Century-Crofts, 1960.

Bartlett, B.J. *Top-level structure as an organizational strategy for recall of classroom text.* Unpublished doctoral dissertation, Arizona State University, 1978.

Bower, G.H. Organizational factors in memory. *Cognitive Psychology,* 1970, *1,* 18-46.

Bradley, A. *Principles and types of speech communication.* Glenview, IL: Scott, Foresman, 1981.

Clements, P. *The effects of staging on recall from prose.* Doctoral dissertation, Cornell University, 1975.

Cook, L.K. Effects of reading strategy training on learning from science text. Paper presented at the 90th annual convention of the American Psychological Association, Washington, DC, August, 1982.

Crismore, A. *Metadiscourse in social studies texts: Its effects on student performance and attitude.* Urbana, IL: University of Illinois, doctoral dissertation, in preparation.

Ellis, J.P. *Hemispheric specialization for the processing of prose and maps.* Unpublished doctoral dissertation, Arizona State University, 1982.

Flammer, A., and Tauber, M. Changing the reader's perspective. In A. Flammer and W. Kintsch (Eds.), *Discourse processing.* Amsterdam: North-Holland, 1982.

Flower, L.S., and Hayes, J.R. The dynamics of composing: Making plans and juggling constraints. In L. Gregg and E. Steinberg (Eds.), *Cognitive processes in writing: An interdisciplinary approach.* Hillsdale, NJ: Lawrence Erlbaum Associates, 1980.

Frase, L.T. Paragraph organization of written materials. The influence of conceptual clustering upon level of organization. *Journal of Educational Psychology,* 1969, *60,* 394-401.

Fuller, D.P. *The inductive method of Bible study* (3rd Ed.). Pasadena: Fuller Theological Seminary, 1959. Mimeo.

Grice, M.P. *Logic and conversation.* The William James Lectures, Harvard University, 1967.

Grimes, J.E. *The thread of discourse.* The Hague, Holland: Mouton, 1975.

Halliday, M.A.K. Notes on transitivity and theme in English. *Journal of Linguistics,* 1968, *4,* 179-215.

Hurley, P.B. *The correlation of standardized, cloze, and schema related reading scores with holistic writing scores of adult community college students.* Unpublished doctoral dissertation, Indiana University of Pennsylvania, 1982.

Kintsch, W., Mandel, T.S., and Kozminsky, E. Summarizing scrambled stories. *Memory and Cognition*, 1977, *5*, 547-552.

Kintsch, W., and van Dijk, T.A. Toward a model of text comprehension and production. *Psychological Review*, 1978, *85*, 363-394.

Kintsch, W., and Yarbrough, J.C. Role of rhetorical structure in text comprehension. *Journal of Educational Psychology*, 1982, *74*, 828-834.

Kozminsky, E. Altering comprehension: The effect of biasing titles on text comprehension. *Memory and Cognition*, 1977, *5*, 482-490.

Mandler, G. Organization and memory. In K.W. Spence and J.T. Spence (Eds.), *The psychology of learning and motivation: Advances in research and theory.* New York: Academic Press, 1967.

Mandler, J.M., and Johnson, N.S. Remembrance of things parsed: Story structure and recall. *Cognitive Psychology*, 1977, *9*, 111-151.

Marshall, N., and Glock, M.D. Comprehension of connected discourse: A study into the relationships between the structure of text and information recalled. *Reading Research Quarterly*, 1978, *14*, 10-56.

Meyer, B.J.F. *The organization of prose and its effects on memory.* Amsterdam: North-Holland, 1975.

Meyer, B.J.F. Basic research on prose comprehension: A critical review. In D.F. Fisher and C.W. Peters (Eds.), *Comprehension and the competent reader: Inter-specialty perspectives.* New York: Praeger, 1981.

Meyer, B.J.F. Reading research and the composition teacher: The importance of plans. *College Composition and Communication*, 1982, *33*, 37-49.

Meyer, B.J.F. Text structure and its use in studying comprehension across the adult life span. In B. Hutson (Ed.), *Advances in reading/language research* (Vol. 2). Greenwich, CT: JAI Press, 1983.

Meyer, B.J.F. Prose analysis: Purposes, procedures, and problems. In B.K. Britton and J. Black (Eds.), *Analyzing and understand-*

ing expository text. Hillsdale, NJ: Lawrence Erlbaum Associates, in press (a).

Meyer, B.J.F. Organizational aspects of text: Effects on reading comprehension and applications for the classroom. In J. Flood (Ed.), *Reading comprehension*. Newark, DE: I.R.A., 1984(a).

Meyer, B.J.F. Text dimensions and cognitive processing. In H. Mandl, N. Stein, and T. Trabasso (Eds.), *Learning and understanding texts*. Hillsdale, NJ: Lawrence Erlbaum Associates, 1984(b).

Meyer, B.J.F., Brandt, D.M., and Bluth, G.J. Use of top-level structure in text: Key for reading comprehension of ninth-grade students. *Reading Research Quarterly*, 1980, *16*, 72-103.

Meyer, B.J.F., and Freedle, R.O. Effects of discourse type on recall. *American Educational Research Journal*, 1984, *21*, 121-143.

Meyer, B.J.F., Haring, M.J., Brandt, D.M., and Walker, C.H. Comprehension of stories and expository text. *Poetics: International Review for the Theory of Literature*, 1980, *9*, 203-211.

Meyer, B.J.F., and McConkie, G.W. What is recalled after hearing a passage? *Journal of Educational Psychology*, 1973, *65*, 109-117.

Meyer, B.J.F., and Rice, G.E. The interaction of reader strategies and the organization of text. *Text*, 1982, *2*, 155-192.

Meyer, B.J.F., and Rice, G.E. Interaction of text variables and processing strategies for young, middle-aged, and older expert readers. Paper presented at the annual meeting of the American Educational Research Association, Montreal, Canada, April, 1983.

Niles, O.S. Organization perceived. In H.H. Herber (Ed.), *Perspectives in reading: Developing study skills in secondary schools*. Newark, DE: I.R.A., 1974.

Stein, N.L., and Nezworski, T. The effects of organization and instructional set on story memory. *Discourse Processes*, 1978, *1*, 177-193.

Thompson, E. An experimental investigation of the relative effectiveness of organizational structure in oral communication. *Southern Speech Journal*, 1960, *26*(1), 59-69.

Thorndyke, P.W. Cognitive structures in comprehension and

memory of narrative discourse. *Cognitive Psychology*, 1977, *9*, 77-110.

van Dijk, T.A. Relevance assignment in discourse comprehension. *Discourse Processes*, 1979, *2*, 113-125.

Williams, J. *Style: Ten lessons in clarity and grace.* Glenview, IL: Scott, Foresman, 1981.

Chapter 4

Frames: Structures for Informative Text

Bonnie B. Armbruster and Thomas H. Anderson*

This chapter is about organizational patterns, or structures, in text, particularly textbooks designed to inform the reader about a particular discipline or content area. We address the topic of structure for two reasons. First, it is important. Research has shown that structure makes a difference in learning from text (for example, Goetz and Armbruster, 1980; Meyer, 1979; Shimmerlik, 1978). In general, the better organized the text and the more apparent the structure to the reader, the higher the probability that the reader will learn from reading. The second reason we are addressing this topic is that structure seems to be a particular problem in the many textbooks we have examined. Elsewhere, we have written about "inconsiderate" text, in which poor organization plays a leading role (Anderson and Armbruster, 1984; Armbruster, 1984; Kantor, Anderson, and Armbruster, 1983).

In this chapter, we try to clarify what is meant by text structure by defining two kinds of structures—basic, *content-independent* structures, and *content-dependent* structures, which we call "frames." Our particular focus is frames—what they are and how they might be used in the design of textbooks.

Basic Text Structures

A few text structures are fundamental; they reflect some of the basic patterns of human thought and logic. These structures are

*The research reported in this chapter was supported in part by the National Institute of Education under Contract No. NIE 400-81-0030.

content-independent because they describe the nature of the relationships among ideas without reference to the content of the ideas. They can be instantiated with content from many different subject matter areas. These basic text structures have been identified by rhetoricians, linguists, and psychologists. They are discussed in everything from high school English composition textbooks to books on methods of teaching reading (for example, Herber, 1978; Readence, Bean, and Baldwin, 1981). The most common structures are:

1. *Description*—a listing of properties, characteristics, or attributes where the order of presentation of the items is not significant.
2. *Compare/contrast*—a description of similarities and/or differences between two or more things.
3. *Temporal sequence*—a sequential relationship between ideas or events considered in terms of the passage of time.
4. *Explanation*—an interaction between at least two ideas or events. One idea (the effect) is to be explained, and the other is(are) the reason(s) or cause(s) for the effect.
5. *Definition/example*—a concept is defined, and examples of the concept are given.

Virtually any textbook in any field will contain some or all of these basic structures. However, pure forms of these fundamental structures do not account for all, or even many, of the patterns of ideas found in textbooks. Rather, bits and pieces of the basic text structures are spliced together to form what we call content-dependent text structures.

Content-Dependent Text Structures: Frames

Different disciplines or content areas have different conceptual structures (e.g., Schwab, 1962). Text that informs the reader about the discipline usually reflects the underlying conceptual structures. The text itself assumes a generic structure containing set categories of information. We call these generic, content-dependent structures *frames* and the content categories within frames *slots*. The slots of content-area frames are filled with critical information about the topic. In other words, slots define the "main idea" of the content.

We recognize two types of frames: static and dynamic. A *static frame* is a Description Basic Text Structure that is applied to a specific content, like geology or economics. The critical characteristics or properties of the concept are labeled and become the slots of the frame. However, as with Description, there need not be a particular order to the slots. Just as static frames are more specific versions of Description Basic Text Structures, so *dynamic frames* are more specific versions of Explanation Basic Text Structures. Dynamic frames specify causal, or at least directional, relationships among the slots.

Since frames can best be understood through examples, we turn next to a description of some frames in the areas of science/technology and social studies/history. Some of the frames mentioned in science/technology and all of the frames in social studies/history we ourselves derived in two different but complementary ways. One way was by knowing the definition of the target concept—the critical attributes that define the particular concept and make it distinctive from other concepts. The second way was by examining what authors typically write about the concept. Authors writing about a particular concept seem consistently to include certain kinds of information; these categories of information became the frame slots.

Examples of Science/Technology Frames

Other researchers have worked with frames or frame-like constructs in the natural sciences. For example, Dansereau (in press) describes a cognitive counterpart of frames, which he calls *knowledge schemata*. Knowledge schemata consist of the set of categories of information a well-informed learner should know about a particular topic. An example is a knowledge schema related to Scientific Theories, derived by asking a sample of college students what they considered to be the important categories of information relevant to understanding a scientific theory. The major resulting categories were *Description, Inventor/ History, Consequence, Evidence, Other Theories*, and *Extra Information*, each having its own subcategories. Although knowledge schemata are meant to describe cognitive rather than text structures, it is easy to imagine text structured in a similar way in a static frame.

Lunzer, Davies, and Greene (1980) have proposed several static frames for secondary science texts. For example, Lunzer *et al.* propose frames for Structure, Mechanism, Process, and Hypothesis-Theory, each with its own set of slots. The Process frame, for instance, describes or explains transformations or sequential changes over a period of time. The Process frame has slots for the *State* or *Form* of the phenomena at different stages, the *Properties/Structure* of the phenomena, the *Stage* or *Steps* or *Time* of change, the *Instrument* or *Agent* of change, the *Action* that causes transformation, the *Location* of change, and the *Transformation*.

We have identified two other science/technology static frames. One is the Systems frame (Armbruster and Anderson, 1984). The Systems frame is applicable to biological systems (digestive, circulatory, etc.) as well as technological systems (hydraulic brakes, electrical, etc.). The Systems frame has slots for *Function/ Uses* (the function or use of the system within the whole), *Parts and Their Functions* (a description of each part of the system and the function performed by that part), *How It Works* (an explanation of how the system works or operates), and *Problems/ Preventions/Solutions* (problems that can impede the performance of the system, ways to prevent the problems from occurring, and/or solutions to problems once they have occurred).

An example of a Systems frame might occur in a health textbook. For example, a chapter titled "The Respiratory System" begins with a discussion of the necessity for exchanging gases in the human body (*Functions/Uses*). The text continues by describing the six major parts of the air passage (nose, pharynx, trachea, bronchi, bronchial tubes, alveoli) and the part they play in respiration (*Parts and Their Functions*). Then the text describes the process of breathing, including the relationship between the movement of the diaphragm and inhalation/exhalation, and the exchange of gases between capillaries and alveoli (*How It Works*). Finally, the text talks about diseases and disorders that affect the respiratory system (including the common cold, pneumonia, asthma, etc., and mentions some ways of treating these illnesses (*Problems/Solutions*).

Another science/technology frame is a static frame for biomes. The Biomes frame has slots for *Location, Climate, Plant Life*, and *Animal Life*. For example, a science textbook might contain a chapter on biomes, comprised of sections on the tundra, taiga, deciduous forest, tropical rain forest, grassland, desert, and ocean. The section on the tropical rain forest, for example, explains that the rain forest is in areas near the equator—Central or South America, Asia, Africa, and Australia (*Location*). Then, the section describes the *Climate* of the rain forest—warm, heavy rainfall. The dense layers of vegetation are discussed next (*Plant Life*), followed by a description of the wild pigs, leopards, monkeys, bats, snakes, insects, etc., (*Animal Life*) found in the tropical rain forest. The textbook might even include a systematic comparison among the features or slots of the various biomes.

Our developmental work on frames has not required us to generate any dynamic science/technology frames. As causality plays an integral role in all science, we feel that innumerable such frames are possible.

Examples of Social Studies/History Frames

An example of a static frame in social studies is the Cultures frame. The slots of the Cultures frame are *Technology* (Tools and Machines, Food, Clothing, Shelter); *Institutions* (Family, Political, Economic, Religious, Educational); *Language*; and *Arts*. Although textbook versions of cultures at different grade levels may not include information in all slots, these slots seem to represent the major categories of information needed to define a particular culture and differentiate it from other cultures.

Another example of a static frame is the People frame. Social studies and history textbooks are replete with biographical sketches of noteworthy individuals. Information about individuals usually contains some or all of the following slots: *Background* (when they lived and significant "shaping" events of their lives); *Traits* (distinctive personality traits); *Goals* (motivating beliefs and ideas); and *Accomplishments* (significant actions or accomplishments of their lives; why they are "famous"). For example, a textbook sketch of Frederick Douglass might mention the fact that he was born a slave, and the unusual circumstance of his being taught to read as a child (*Background*). The account might go on to describe his desire for personal freedom and his hope of abolishing slavery (*Goals*). The sketch would probably mention Douglass's intelligence, his talents as a public speaker and newspaper editor, and his leadership abilities (*Traits*), which enabled him to become one of the great leaders of black abolitionists (*Accomplishments*).

An example of a dynamic frame is what we call the Goal frame. We believe the Goal frame can capture the "main ideas" associated with the explanation of an historical event. The Goal frame is depicted in the following diagrammatic representation, which we call a frame-map.

The *Goal* is the desired state sought by an individual or a group. The *Action* is the action taken in order to attain the Goal. The *Outcome* is the consequence of the Action, which may either satisfy or fail to satisfy the Goal.

Many explanations of historical events fit the Goal frame: the search of Cortés for gold and silver and the subsequent conquest of the Aztec empire; the need for improved transportation to link the East and West and the building of the transcontinental railroad; Hitler's desire to preserve the "master race" of "Aryans" resulting in the murder of six million European Jews; and so on.

A variation of the dynamic Goal frame is the Problem/Solution frame. In this frame, the Problem is an event, a condition, or a series of events or conditions resulting in a state that is an obstacle to the attainment of the Goal. The Problem prompts a Solution, which takes the form of the Action and Outcome of the Goal frame. The Outcome of the Solution either solves or fails to solve the Problem; that is, the Outcome either satisfies or fails to satisfy the Goal.

As an example of a text for which the Problem/Solution frame is appropriate, consider typical accounts of "voyages of discovery." Such accounts usually begin with a statement of the Goal—the desire of Europeans for goods from the East, including silks and spices. The accounts then explain the Problems of obtaining goods from the East, including the difficult and dangerous journey and the high prices paid to Italian merchants. Then the texts discuss the Solution. The Action slot consists of the actual voyages by various explorers, and the Outcome slot includes the early disappointing outcomes of the quest for an all-water route, as well as the resulting discoveries of the explorers.

The Goal and Problem/Solution frames described so far are appropriate for explaining events perpetrated by a single individual or a group of people acting as a single entity. These dynamic frames can be modified to accommodate the more typical case involving interactions among two or more individuals (or groups), each attempting to achieve his or her own goals. For example, a common Problem is that the Goals of two parties are different or incompatible. Two common solutions to this type of Problem are *compromise* and *war*. As one more illustration of a dynamic frame, consider the following Compromise frame-map:

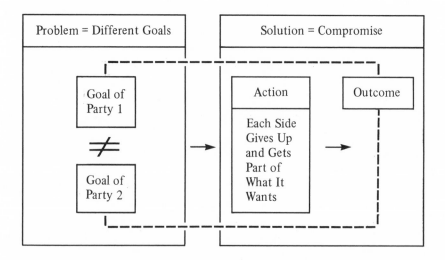

The Problem is that the Goals of the two parties are different and apparently incompatible. The Solution is standard—a compromise. The Action slot is also standard—each side gives up and gets something of what it wants. The Outcome includes the specific result of the compromise—what each party obtained with respect to its Goals.

For example, consider the "Great Compromise" involved in framing the U.S. Constitution. Two groups had different Goals or plans for determining representation in the new Congress. Proponents of the "New Jersey Plan" wanted a system of equal representation for all states. Advocates of the "Virginia Plan" wanted each state's population to determine the number of representatives it would send to Congress. The "Great Compromise" combined the main features of both Goals. The Outcome was a Congress having two houses; in the Senate, the representation from each state would be the same, while in the House of Representatives, representation would be based on population.

So far in this chapter we have defined frames as generic conceptual structures and presented a few examples of static and dynamic frames in very different content areas. Our thesis is that the conscientious use of frames in designing content-area textbooks will facilitate student learning from reading. Text written from frames will have a clear, consistent structure, which we know enhances learning outcomes. Text written from frames will also highlight the "main ideas" of the content that should be the focus of student attention and study. We turn next to some suggestions for *how* frames might be used in designing textbooks.

Using Frames in Designing Textbooks

Organizing the content. First, of course, the author or content-matter expert must determine the relevant frames for the textbook. Basically, this involves analyzing the content for the major concepts to be taught, and then analyzing each concept to determine its important attributes. These attributes become the slots of the concept frames. Once the frames have been determined, the difficult problem of organizing the text has been solved. Since frame slots are the equivalent of main headings in an outline, the author only has to fill in the "details"—the particular information to be included for each instance of the concept. Use of the frame as an outline will help ensure even and consistent content coverage. Consider how the author of a health textbook might use frames. With the Systems frame, she has a ready-made outline for several chapters of the textbook. The generic, frame-based outline will help her avoid chapter outlines like the following:

The Respiratory System   **The Circulatory System**
- Structure and Function   Your Heart
- How You Breathe   Your Circulation
- The Common Cold and Pneu-   Your Blood
  monia   Diseases and Disorders
- Influenza
- Hay Fever
- Asthma
- Emphysema and Bronchitis

(Meeks and Heit, 1982)

Clearly, these chapters were meant to cover the same kinds of information about the two systems, but from the Table of Contents, at least, they appear to do so in an inconsistent and uneven manner.

Signaling the Structure and Content

Besides providing a generic structure for authors to use in writing the text, frames suggest appropriate signaling (see chapter by Meyer, this volume). Some of the signaling devices Meyer discusses are explicit statements of the structure or organization; previews or introductory statements, including titles and summary statements. As Meyer points out, the use of signaling can improve reading comprehension, particularly of middle-ability readers. We recommend the following guidelines for including signaling in frame-based text.

First, we recommend that authors introduce a section of frame-based text by describing the frame to the reader. For example, in the Introduction to the unit on "Your Body Systems," the author could state,

> In this unit, you will read about four systems of the human body: the circulatory, respiratory, digestive, and nervous systems. For each system, you should be able to answer the following important questions:

1. What is the function of the system? What part does it play in keeping the body living and growing?
2. What is the structure of the system? What are its parts?
3. How does the system work to accomplish its functions?
4. What can go wrong with the system? What disorders can attack the system?
5. How can disorders be prevented? How can they be treated once they have occurred?

The text is organized to help you learn the answers to these questions. Each chapter of the unit covers one of the four systems. Each chapter has five sections: The Function of the .... System; The Structure of the .... System; How the .... System Works; Disorders of the .... System; and Prevention and Treatment of Disorders in the .... System.

If specific uses of the frame are spread throughout the textbook, the author should describe the frame before the first use and then tell the reader each time the frame is to be used again. For example, "In Chapter 5, 'We the People,' you learned about the Compromise frame and saw several examples of compromises in the writing of the Constitution. Now we will use the Compromise frame again in discussing the Missouri Compromise."

Second, we recommend using frame and slot labels as headings and subheadings in the text. Our impression from examining many textbooks is that the choice of headings and subheadings is willy-nilly. Ambiguous or misleading headings make it difficult for the reader to use them as the comprehension and studying aids they could and should be. Here is an example. The intention of this fourth-grade textbook is to have the readers use a "frame" for reading and studying "Regions." The textbook begins,

This year you are going to study different *regions* of our earth ... As you study each region, you should try to answer these questions.
1. What does the land of the region look like?
2. What is the climate like?
3. How do the people make a living?
4. In what kinds of houses do they live?
5. What do they eat?
6. What do they wear?
7. How do they get an education?
8. What games do they play?

9. How do they travel and send messages?
10. What is the story of early days in this region?
11. How do the people live and work together in peace and friendship?

(Gross, Follett, Gabler, Burton, and Nilsen, 1980)

The questions correspond to slots of a Region frame. Unfortunately, the authors did not use the frame in writing the text. Here is part of the outline for one unit:

Forest Regions

The Twins Save the Forest
A Giant Tree Falls
Living in Evergreen City
Early Days in the Forest
The Twins Visit Some Big Mills
Christmas in Evergreen City
The Green Guards Plant a Tree
Camping in the Forest
.
.
.

Although the information to answer the frame slot questions is probably somewhere in the text, the headings are no clue. We suspect that fourth-grade readers would have an easier time learning about forest regions if headings reliably signaled where the information relevant to each slot could be found.

Finally, we recommend that authors use frames to write summaries. Since frame slots define the "main ideas" of the concept, it is a relatively simple process to generate a summary from a frame. For example, the summary of text about a compromise could consist of two sentences: one sentence describing the conflicting goals, and another sentence describing the outcome of the compromise and relating it to the original goals. Such a summary will certainly capture the most important information about the compromise.

Using Frames in Adjunct Exercises

In addition to aiding the writing and signaling of the prose itself, frames can be used as the basis for adjunct exercises in the textbook or student workbook. For example, instead of the random-appearing questions that are at the end of most textbook chapters, publishers could substitute questions generated from frame slots. This practice would ensure that students were being asked about "main ideas."

Frames could also be used as the basis for two-way tables in which the rows correspond to slots and the columns to instances of the generic concept. The student's task is to fill in the cells and then perform various comparative analyses of the categorized information. Figure 4.1 presents an example of a possible frame-based exercise to accompany a unit on biomes.

Concluding Remarks

In this chapter, we tried to clarify what is meant by text structure by defining two types of structures. One type is content-independent structures that are likely to be found in many types of content-area textbooks. We listed five major types of content-independent structures: description, compare/contrast, temporal sequence, explanation, and definition/example. The second type of text structure is content-dependent. The focus of this chapter was on this second class of text structures, which we call frames.

Our reason for introducing the notion of frames was the need to capture the structure of "real" text of longer than a paragraph or two. We found that before the text organization became clear to us, we had to analyze the underlying organization of the content itself. Frames represent our attempt to capture those patterns of content. With frames, we think we have a neophyte technology that can be used by textbook writers to accomplish two important goals: (1) ensuring an appropriate match between structure and underlying content, and (2) helping students learn by providing a clear, consistent structure.

Figure 4.1

*Example of Frame-Based Exercise
to Accompany a Textbook Unit on "Biomes"*

Directions: Fill in the following table and then answer the questions below.

Biomes

	Tundra	Taiga	Deciduous Forest	Tropical Rain Forest	Grassland	Desert	Ocean
Location							
Climate							
Plants							
Animals							

Questions
1. Contrast the climate of the tropical rain forest and the grassland.
2. Which has more species of large animals—the deciduous forest or the desert?
3. Which biomes are located in the middle latitudes (20°-40° N or S)?

References

Anderson, T.H., and Armbruster, B.B. Content area textbooks. In R.C. Anderson, J. Osborn, and R.J. Tierney (Eds.), *Learning to read in American schools: Basal readers and content texts.* Hillsdale, NJ: Lawrence Erlbaum Associates, 1984.

Armbruster, B.B. Learning from content-area textbooks: The problem of "inconsiderate text." In G.G. Duffy, L.R. Roehler, and J. Mason (Eds.), *Comprehension instruction: Perspectives and suggestions.* New York: Longman, Inc., 1984.

Armbruster, B.B., and Anderson, T.H. Structures for explanations in history textbooks or so what if Governor Stanford missed the spike and hit the rail. *Journal of Curriculum Studies*, 1984, *16*(2), 181-194.

Dansereau, D.F. Learning strategy research. In J. Segal, S. Chipman, and R. Glaser (Eds.), *Thinking and learning skills: Relating instruction to basic research* (Vol. 1). Hillsdale, NJ: Lawrence Erlbaum Associates, in press.

Goetz, E., and Armbruster, B. Psychological correlates of text structure. In R.J. Spiro, B.C. Bruce, and W.F. Brewer (Eds.), *Theoretical issues in reading comprehension.* Hillsdale, NJ: Lawrence Erlbaum Associates, 1980.

Gross, H.H., Follett, D.W., Gabler, R.E., Burton, W.L., and Nilsen, W.D. *Exploring our world: Regions.* Chicago: Follett Publishing Co., 1980.

Herber, H.L. *Teaching reading in content areas* (2nd Ed.). Englewood Cliffs, NJ: Prentice-Hall, 1978.

Kantor, R.N., Anderson, T.H., and Armbruster, B.B. How inconsiderate are children's textbooks? Or, of flyswatters and alfa. *Journal of Curriculum Studies*, 1983, *15*(1), 61-72.

Lunzer, E., Davies, F., and Greene, T. *Reading for learning in science* (Schools Council Project Report). Nottingham, England: University of Nottingham, School of Education, 1980.

Meeks, L.B., and Heit, P. *Health: Focus on you.* Columbus, OH: Charles E. Merrill, 1982.

Meyer, B.J.F. *A selected review and discussion of basic research on prose comprehension* (Prose Learning series: Research Report No. 4). Tempe: Arizona State University, Department of Educational Psychology, Spring, 1979.

Readence, J.E., Bean, T.W., and Baldwin, R.S. *Content area reading: An integrated approach.* Dubuque, IA: Kendall/Hunt, 1981.

Schwab, J.J. The concept of the structure of a discipline. *The Educational Record*, 1962, *43*, 197-205.

Shimmerlik, S.M. Organization theory and memory for prose: A review of the literature. *Review of Educational Research*, 1978, *48*, 103-120.

Chapter 5

Using Typography to Structure Arguments: A Critical Analysis of Some Examples

Robert H.W. Waller

This chapter is about the relationship between the typography of a text and the content it displays. Its purpose is to amplify an argument set out in the first volume of this series (Waller, 1982) and to demonstrate it through a series of critiques of typographic examples.

Good communication design is transparent. We are disturbed by its absence, but rarely notice its presence. Thus, the most comprehensible texts (or other media) have usually been invested with the most elaborate preparation, while those to which little attention is paid by the writer cause the most problems to the user. To those who mainly read and rarely write or design, the transparency of good communication can be both misleading and mysterious—misleading if no problem is perceived, and mysterious when the solution depends on some esoteric professionalism that others seem to have but never explain. Guidelines can be given and research results reported, but the history of practical education in writing, editing, and designing suggests that demonstration is still the best way of conveying insight. Hence the examples.

Text as Diagram

This metaphor, used as the title to the earlier chapter, was designed to focus on the written-ness of text. A minimal definition of prose is the transcription of spoken language. In physical terms, it is little more than a linear string of sentences that is cut into lines and divided into pages in an arbitrary way, determined by the manufacturing process and of little concern to either the writer or the reader. Some—perhaps even most—prose is like that (though, I suspect, not the best), but there are too many exceptions to leave it there. There is a sense in which the physical shape of prose adds something to its meaning. Poets and advertising copywriters testify to this through their extensive use of indention and line breaks; but paragraphing is a more ubiquitous example (Nash, 1980).

Diagrams are essentially graphic—they use space and graphic marks to display concepts and the relationships between them, and they have no equivalent in speech (although a case might be made for analogy and spatial metaphor). For many diagrams, particularly the more complex ones, the precise nature and quality of the graphic marks used (lines, tints, captions, and so on) are part of its essence—a diagram redrawn by another artist to suit a different printing process no longer says quite the same thing. In exactly the same way, text-as-diagram has no life apart from its realization in print. The exact choice of printing process, typeface, format, paper, and binding—even of printer, at times— can determine success or failure.

Diagrams carry meaning not only in the way particular components are drawn and linked but also in the overall pattern or shape that results. The importance of the pattern is the reason why diagrams that cross page boundaries are rarely satisfactory. Text-as-diagram shares this characteristic, too—typographically-structured pages must be seen in their wholness, must operate within the artifactual limitations of the print medium in a way that contrasts with our normal view of prose.

Text and speech both use language, but deliver it in different ways. Text is realized in space not in time, in visual marks not in sounds. Consequently, the move from oral to literary discourse frees the author from the limitations of pre-allotted time periods and the listeners' attention span. For many authors, then, the length of a traditional text is determined solely by the nature of their argument, since readers can leave and re-enter as they please. This is important—our culture depends on this ability to develop complex, comprehensive, rational lines of thought—but in some circumstances, it is inappropriate. The perception of larger patterns can easily be obscured by the interpretation of the detail. Unless the author takes care to make the text accessible (through both linguistic and typographic means), there is little hope of a busy reader keeping track of long and complex arguments encountered over a succession of separate engagements. The text-as-diagram metaphor proposes that readers who cannot see the wood for the trees may benefit from a map—that typographic and spatial factors can be used to clarify the larger structural relationships in a text, easing the cognitive burden that long, featureless texts impose on the reader.

Some authors—of scholarly and scientific texts, for example—can assume an able and committed readership, but where the readers' commitment and stamina are less reliable, the accessibility question becomes more significant. Newspapers and magazines are perhaps the best example of text-types that have developed the graphic structure of their content. Reference books and technical manuals, too, have always recognized the need for graphic clarity—their content and conditions of use very obviously demand it. The examples that follow are taken from three such publications, typical of a genre of highly-structured and illustrated manuals that has emerged in recent years. Pages from them have been selected fairly randomly—it would have been possible to generate similar critiques of many others. They are intended for a general market, but their content is similar in nature to the sort of technical and instructional material of interest to readers of this book. Two characteristics in particular represent a departure from earlier traditions of such texts.

First, they are produced by large teams of writers, editors, artists, designers, and researchers, instead of a single author assisted later by publishing staff. Indeed, such teams have largely replaced the old style author in some areas of publishing, although a well-known name is usually recruited to front the team, and appear on the book jacket. Book packaging, as it is called, is a highly professional new wing of the publishing industry; books are planned, designed, and sold to publishers before they are actually written. When the text is finally drafted, then, it is the product of a lengthy period of research into the subject area and the needs of the target audience.

Second, typography is treated as an integral and primary part of the discourse. The two factors are closely related: the team approach represents a shift of emphasis from the author's to the readers' needs, with a consequently greater priority given to the accessibility of the content to readers with different goals. In these examples, typography works alongside the normal lexical and syntactic methods by which the writer ensures structural cohesion among the disparate components of an argument; and it adds the diagrammatic quality that can make such a structure accessible to the browsing or less committed reader.

It is also significant that all the examples use a multi-column layout (typographic designers refer to them as "grid systems"). The grid has become a necessary feature of texts with a high level of typographic structure—for the designer, it combines consistency of typesetting with flexibility of spatial arrangement. For the reader, however, multi-column texts can be problematic. As several of the examples illustrate, the grid does not by itself define the relationship between the components of the page. Typographic and spatial cuing is still needed to display information structures and sequences.

The Examples

The examples start with a simple grid and progress to more complex and problematic systems. This may reflect the historical development of the technique—although grid systems were initially used somewhat rigidly, designers have felt able to bend the rules as this style of layout has become more familiar. Whether they have carried their readers with them is an open question. Recent research on reading behavior with multi-column texts casts some doubt (Schumacher and Waller, in press).

Wood/Types of finish

Transparent coloured polyurethane

Coloured polyurethane finishes will allow the natural grain of the wood to show. They give a tough surface which resists chipping, scratching and even boiling water.

They are excellent for use on new wood that has few blemishes and fillings. When choosing whitewood furniture to be finished with coloured polyurethane, select pieces with a good, unbroken grain.

Old wood that has been treated with paint, varnish or any other finish must be cleaned right down to the bare wood. **Application:** clean off all grease and wax with an abrasive and white spirit; do not apply the finish in humid conditions.

Apply the first coat, preferably of clear Hardglaze, with a cloth pad. Leave this to dry for at least six hours, then apply further coats with a paint brush. If you wait for longer than 24 hours between coats, rub down the previous coat with fine glass-

paper or a medium grade of steel wool.

Obtain a matt finish, if preferred to the normal glossy finish, by giving a final coat of clear Ronseal Mattcoat.

Clean treated surfaces with a damp cloth. In areas of heavy wear, apply a wax polish for added protection. Cloths used for application are highly inflammable, so destroy them after use.

Do not use these finishes on linoleum, thermoplastic PVC or rubber.

Coloured polyurethane paint

One-pack opaque polyurethane paints are extremely tough and scratch-resistant and give an ideal finish for nursery and kitchen furniture. They withstand temperatures up to 100°C (212°F) without discolouring, and table tops in these finishes are not harmed by contact with hot plates.

Polyurethane paints are durable when used outdoors. They are available in gloss and eggshell finishes.

Application: no special preparation of the

timber is necessary. After a coat of polyurethane primer, apply with a brush or spray unit in the same manner as ordinary paint.

For best results, lightly sand between coats, taking care to remove all dust and allowing not more than 24 hours between applications of successive coats.

Previously painted surfaces do not require priming but do need careful cleaning, to remove dirt and grease, followed by a

light rubbing down with abrasive paper. Exposed surfaces need at least two coats; a single coat may suffice indoors if the new paint is much the same colour as the one it is covering.

Most polyurethane paints are touch-dry in about three hours, are ready for sanding within six to eight hours, and are fully hard after three or four days.

Clean brushes or spray equipment immediately after use with white spirit.

Floor sealers

Some floor sealers on the market, such as Bourne Seal, are also suitable for finishing general woodwork and some furniture. They are, in many ways, a compromise between oil and lacquer finishes and are well suited for wood finishing in the home.

They are applied in the same way as oil finishes. They penetrate deep into the timber and, like oil, tend to darken it. With successive coats, a fairly resistant film can be built up if required. This will not have the toughness of two-pack lacquers, but it can be repaired and recoated fairly easily;

and with average wear and use it will require little maintenance.

Application: apply with a brush or a pad of non-fluffy cloth to the unfilled timber, working across the grain and well into it. Finish by brushing out or wiping off any surplus, this time working with the grain, before allowing to dry.

Drying is slow, and the surface is best left overnight. Lightly sand between coats to remove high spots.

On all vertical surfaces, such as panelling, and on shelving, one or two coats are

sufficient. Leave the final coat for a few days before rubbing down, with the grain, with steel wool, grade 00 or 000. Remove dust and apply a thin coat of wax polish.

Horizontal surfaces, likely to have to withstand harder wear, may require three coats. Further coats can be applied periodically, but only after all traces of wax or grease have been removed.

These finishes can be applied to any timber and are well suited where the extreme hardness of two-pack lacquers is not essential.

French polish

This is a traditional finish and is applied to many valuable antiques. The basic material is shellac dissolved in methylated spirit.

There is little point in French polishing at home except on repair work and when matching existing furniture—although it provides an excellent finish, it is easily marked by heat and liquids.

Various proprietary brands of French polish make the job simpler for the amateur and, applied with care, give a satisfactory result.

Garnet polish, button polish, white polish and transparent polish are all forms of French polish, having a base of shellac and differing only in colour; true French polish is a rich brown, the others being degrees lighter, down to near-transparent.

Techniques in application vary according to the type of polish and the user's skill. The following serves as a general guide to polishing procedure and should be within the capabilities of a careful amateur.

Preparation: the timber must be well sanded and clean, and the grain filled with a grain filler. Choose the shade of polish you require, bearing in mind that darker polishes darken wood considerably. When

matching colour, experiment first on sample pieces of timber. Any staining must be done before applying the polish.

Equipment: the most important implement in French polishing is the polishing rubber; it is with this simple tool that the best work is produced. It consists of a pad of cotton wool, which acts as a reservoir for the polish, and a cover of soft white linen or cotton fabric, similar to a well-worn handkerchief, which acts as a filter.

The rubber must never be dipped into the polish; it is charged by pouring the polish on to the pad with the cover removed. Avoid over-soaking the rubber; the polish should ooze slightly through the cover when a light pressure is applied.

Application: work evenly over the surface with a slow figure-of-eight motion until the timber is coated with a thin layer of polish. The object is to apply a series of thin coats, allowing only a few minutes for drying between coats. Make sure that corners and edges get their full share of polish.

When you have obtained a level and even-bodied surface, the work is ready for the second stage, spiriting off.

Allow the work to stand for at least

eight hours, then take a fresh rubber with a double thickness of cover material and charge it with methylated spirit. Wring out until practically dry—the cover of the rubber should feel damp and no more. This is vital, as too much spirit will simply dissolve the polish.

The object of spiriting off is to remove the rubber marks and to give that brilliance of finish associated with French polish. The motion of the rubber should be the same as before, figure-of-eight, with increasing pressure as the rubber dries out. Replace the covers with fresh pieces of cloth from time to time.

Finally, work in the direction of the grain and continue until the surface is free from smears and rubber marks. Leave to harden off. French polish dries quickly but takes several days to acquire maximum hardness.

Shellac-based polishes can also be applied by brush, each coat being allowed to dry thoroughly and rubbed down lightly with fine abrasive paper.

The finish obtained in this way, whilst being satisfactory for many uses, does not compare with French polishing in quality of film and finish.

141

Figure 5.1. This simple page from a home maintenance manual (*Reader's Digest Book of Do-It-Yourself Skills and Techniques*, 1977, London: Reader's Digest Association, Ltd.) contains only prose. It clearly establishes the three-column grid. Although its content is all prose, certain diagrammatic decisions nevertheless underlie its composition:

○   The four sections, each divided exactly into three columns, accurately fill the page. This is no coincidence, since it is a feature of every other page in the book—the pattern of the page is clearly such a priority that the text has been extended or cut to fit.

○   The four sections are stacked vertically, so that each occupies a distinct rectangle. The headings stretch across the column breaks to emphasize the horizontal arrangement of each section. Further sub-headings are underplayed in order not to detract from the integrity of the rectangles.

○   The position and type style of the "Wood/Types of finish" heading link it to similar headings of the same genre on other pages. It is placed at the outside edge of the page for ease of access.

Wood/T-joints

Overlap joint using supporting blocks

The overlap T-joint combines simplicity and strength for general-purpose jobs such as framing, fencing, shelving racks and lightweight gate construction.

It can be screwed, nailed or bolted and, for strongest results, should also be glued.

To make a screwed overlap joint, cramp both pieces of wood together with a G-cramp (see p. 54) while drilling holes.

Drill a clearance hole through the top piece and a pilot hole in the lower piece with a twist bit small enough to allow the screw thread to bite firmly.

Countersink the holes in the top piece, coat both inner surfaces evenly with glue, fit the pieces together, and screw.

A simple glued and screwed T-joint, using supporting blocks, makes effective shelving units or bookcases.

Glue and screw blocks to each side of the casing, and then glue and screw the

shelving to the blocks. On heavier shelving, —say, over 200 mm. (8 in.) wide—use the housing joint, described opposite.

A firmly fixed support block restricts shrinkage or expansion across the grain, which can be considerable.

Overlap T-joint: position screws diagonally to avoid splitting the wood.

Shelf-support blocks can also be screwed or masonry-nailed direct to the walls of alcoves (see p. 149).

To make a neat job, chamfer the exposed edges of the support blocks, or chamfer their front corners on the underside.

Support block: first screw the block to the upright, then screw in the shelves.

Full lap and half lap T-joints

These joints are far stronger and neater than the simple overlap construction. Use them for fitting cross-rails flush into frames which are to be covered in with panelling.

In a full lap joint the side rail is cut out to accommodate the whole of the cross-rail.

To make it, mark the exact shape of the cut-out on both faces of the side rail and across its top edge.

Cut out the waste with a tenon saw and chisel, paring away gradually from each side until the base of the cut-out is level.

Check the fit, glue all mating surfaces, and complete the joint by pinning or screwing.

In a half lap or T-halving joint, the cross-rail and the side rail are both cut away to give a flush fit when they are mated.

Mark the width of the cross-rail across the face of the side rail and half-way down both edges [1].

On the back of the cross-rail, mark a shoulder line across at a distance from the end a little greater than the width of the side rail.

Continue the line half-way across the edges. Set a gauge to half the thickness of the wood and gauge lines from the face of both pieces.

Saw a centre slot in the cross-rail, skimming the gauge line on the waste side [2]. Remove the waste block by cutting across the shoulder line.

Saw just inside the lines marking the side rail cut-out [3]. Saw an extra cut in the centre to make waste removal easier. Pare away the waste from both sides to complete the cut-out, check for fit [4], fix and trim.

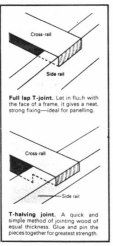

Full lap T-joint. Let in flush with the face of a frame, it gives a neat, strong fixing—ideal for panelling.

T-halving joint. A quick and simple method of jointing wood of equal thickness. Glue and pin the pieces together for greatest strength.

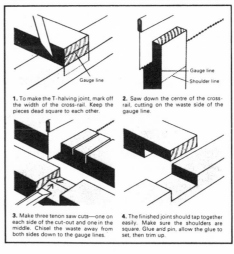

1. To make the T-halving joint, mark off the width of the cross-rail. Keep the pieces dead square to each other.

2. Saw down the centre of the cross-rail, cutting on the waste side of the gauge line.

3. Make three tenon saw cuts—one on each side of the cut-out and one in the middle. Chisel the waste away from both sides down to the gauge lines.

4. The finished joint should tap together easily. Make sure the shoulders are square. Glue and pin, allow the glue to set, then trim up.

122

Figure 5.2. The division of this page (from the same manual) into just two sections again shows how some structural features of the argument have been underplayed in order to simplify the page.

○ Each of the two sections actually divides into two ("overlap joint using supporting blocks" and "full lap/half lap T-joints"). This is shown in each section through two contrasting diagrams, but it is otherwise not graphically signaled in the prose. As Figure 5.3 shows, it would be theoretically possible to include several more hierarchical levels in the system of headings, but typographic texts cannot be as relentlessly logical as true diagrams. At some point, traditional prose must take over. The decision about when, like so many other matters of prose composition, is a judgment of rhetorical effect and literary style.

○ In another context, the bold rules around the two sets of diagrams at the bottom might seem to separate them from the section above. Here, though, we are in no doubt that they are part of that section (headed "Full ... T-joints"); their purpose is simply to divide the six diagrams into two sets. Every heading in this book remains "in force" until the next heading of equal or larger status. This rule is unspoken, though, and only works if used with total consistency.

○ Again notice how each column of type is precisely aligned. The captions to the middle and bottom rows of diagrams all happen to come to the same number of lines of typesetting. This results in a neat page whose graphic structure is clear, but the question arises: Has the integrity of the message been compromised for the sake of appearances? In this case, it is hard to fault the captions—it is a well-crafted page, where the logic and the aesthetics of the text work together to produce coherent and readable communication. In less skilled hands, though, the practice of adjusting the content to fit the design could be disastrous. However, there is little difference in principle between this practice and the demands of normal prose composition. There is rarely only one right way to express something—more often there are many alternatives, the one used being chosen on the basis of the rhetorical design of the text as a whole as much as the exactness of its reference.

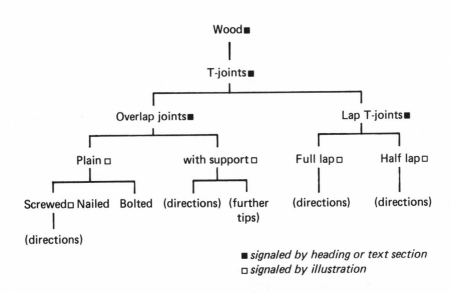

Figure 5.3. A structural analysis of the content of Figure 5.2. Although the typographic signals cease at the third level of the hierarchy, certain other features have been highlighted by the selection of illustrations.

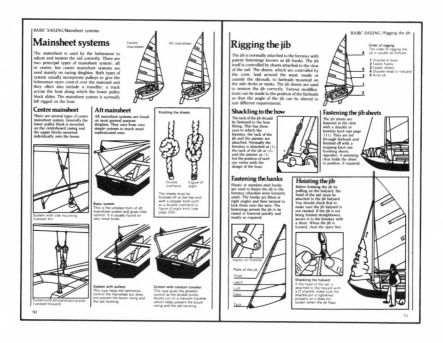

Figure 5.4. These two pages from a sailing manual (Bob Bond, *The Handbook of Sailing*, 1980, London: Pelham Books, Ltd.) use a more flexible grid which gives them a choice of two or three columns.

○   Although the pages represent separate topics, they are related by the similar layout of the heading and introduction at the top—not unlike the use of rhythm or parallelism in prose. Like several other pages in the book, each has a main heading and a standard outline sketch of a dinghy on which the subject of the page is highlighted. Seen in this light, there is some logic to their placing on the page, which could otherwise be seen as problematic: on the left-hand page, the two sketches at the top seem to belong more correctly with the two sub-sections below; on the right-hand page, readers might assume that the sketch belongs to the prose in the column below to which it is slightly closer in distance.

○	There is slightly greater use of typographic style to identify the genre of text components—like the home maintenance manual, sans serif type is used to identify picture captions, but a larger type is also used for the introductory paragraphs, and there are two levels of main heading in addition to the small running heads at the top of each page. In the maintenance manual, the running heads were enlarged to combine with the function of main heading for the page.

○	The small boxed item ("Knotting the sheets") on the left-hand page is an interpolation that relates to both pages—it is placed where space is available. "Hoisting the jib" on the right-hand page, however, is different. It is just the fourth sub-section of that page, and is boxed in an attempt to alleviate a rather clumsy shift from two-equal columns to a one-third/two-thirds arrangement. Although ideally we may prefer items of equal status to be signaled equally, in practice we have no empirical evidence about the effect of inconsistency on the reader—it may not be a problem. In prose punctuation, after all, we accept that for stylistic reasons alternative marks exist to achieve the same function—commas, dashes, and parentheses, for instance.

○	Vertical rules between columns are used to specify the sequence of components on the page. On the left, there is a rule between the first two columns, which represent different components, but not between the second two columns—they are part of the same sub-section. On the right-hand page, the vertical line is presumably meant to prevent us from moving to the right after reading "Shackling to the bow." By the same token, it is the absence of such a line that should cue us to relate the sketch at the top right to the introductory paragraph to its left; however, research on similar layouts suggests that the cuing is too subtle to affect reading strategies reliably (Schumacher and Waller, in press).

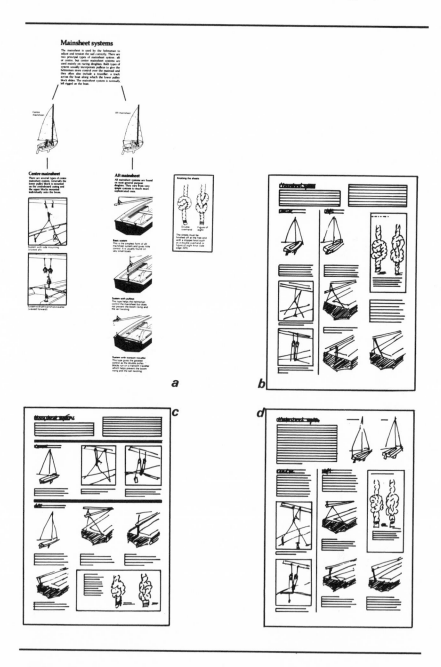

Figure 5.5. The interaction of syntax and artifact: how the "ideal"
text-diagram is constrained by the page boundary.

○   At the layout stage of production, the editors might have been faced with several alternative designs for the left-hand page of Figure 5.4. Sketches (b) and (c) are alternative ways in which (a) could have been shoe-horned into the page area; (d) is the design chosen. The first (b) is similar to the final choice (d), but relates the two introductory sketches more closely to the sub-sections they illustrate. The second (c) uses the stacked arrangement also seen in Figure 5.1 to give equal status to components of different size. Both of these alternatives would require some adjustment of the prose—but so, presumably, did the original choice.

○   This exercise illustrates three categories of functional imperative, introduced in the previous volume (Waller, 1982), which must inform the parsing of typographic displays. The stylization and disposition of components on the page results not only from their *syntactic* relations, but also from *artifactual* effects of the print medium and *usability* requirements of the reader. The designer of this page has attempted to maintain the correct syntactic relations between the components, within the artifactual (and linguistically arbitrary) constraint of the page size; the use of a larger page size, with more generous use of space, has presumably been rejected as unwieldy for the user. It is notable that the Swiss school of typographers, the originators of the grid system in the 1950s, typically use small sizes of type, arranged in many columns (often six or more) on relatively large formats; this enables a more generous use of space and great flexibility of layout, but at the expense of economy and legibility.

118   *Technology of Text II*

Pile and pontoon berths

Some marinas use pairs of piles instead of finger pontoons to secure the boat to the pontoon. Most permanent berths have permanent lines attached to the piles and the pontoon, for making leaving and arriving easier. If there are no permanent lines attached you will have to rig your own warps and remove them as you leave. Although boats with strong engines will be able to berth stern-to, most sailing boats with weaker engines will find it easier to berth bow-on.

Leaving

When leaving a berth between marina piles, the method you use depends on the effect of the wind on the boat. If it is from ahead or astern, assuming the boat is berthed bow-on, the stern lines are taken forward to the shrouds and rigged as slip lines, and the bow lines cast off. By pulling on the stern lines, the boat can be taken smoothly straight out. As the bow comes level with the piles the lines are released. With permanent lines at the pontoon and piles, simply let them go as necessary. With strong cross-wind blowing, assuming you are berthed bow-on, you will first have to ease out the windward bow and stern lines, letting the boat drift to leeward until you can reach the leeward pile, letting go the leeward stern and bow lines. Then pull the boat back up to windward and rig an extra line as a slip from the windward pile to a point near the bow.

The windward bow and stern lines (whether they are permanent lines or ones you have rigged yourself) are then released and the boat motored out astern. If the bow starts to blow to leeward, tighten the slip line briefly to pull the bow back to windward. As the bow passes clear of the piles, the slip line is released. If the boat is berthed stern-to, reverse the instructions for bow and stern and motor forwards out of the berth.

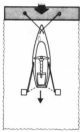 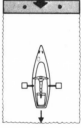 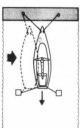 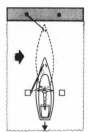

Wind ahead or astern
1 Rig stern lines as slips and cast off bow lines.

2 Reverse boat out of berth, and when level with piles, release slip lines.

Cross-winds
1 Ease windward bow and stern lines to release leeward lines.

2 Rig slip line from bow to windward pile. Reverse out using slip line to guide you.

Arriving

The crew should rig two bow lines and two stern lines, the ends of which are led forward to the shrouds. If there is a cross-wind come in close to the windward pile. As you reach the piles the crew members attach your lines to the mooring rings (see page 176). Motor in while the crew pay out the lines. If the wind is on the beam, keep the bow up to windward. As you reach the pontoon, two bow lines are taken ashore, and the lines adjusted to keep the boat just away from the pontoon and between the piles. Permanent lines are rigged in the same way.

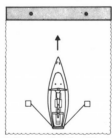 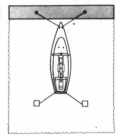

1 Rig stern and bow lines. Bring stern lines to shrouds and attach stern lines to piles.

2 Motor forward, paying out stern lines and fasten bow lines on pontoon.

191

Figure 5.6. Although a fairly straightforward page, the syntax breaks down in two respects:

○ The sub-headings ("Leaving" and "Arriving") are given the same typographic status as the main heading ("Pile and pontoon berths"). There might appear to be three equal sections if it were not for two additional factors: the use of two columns for the introduction has the effect of bracketing the rest of the page under the introduction; and the titles of the two sub-sections, being opposites, form an obvious sub-group.

○ The diagrams in the middle are equally spaced and so appear to form a single series. In fact, they are two pairs showing alternative wind conditions. Extra space in the middle, or the use of rules, would clarify their relationship (compare with Figure 5.1). Also, the incorporation of the diagram headings in the captions disrupts their rhythm. The caption numbers ("1" and "2") now appear on different lines.

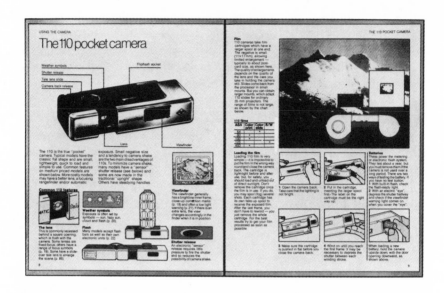

Figure 5.7. This basic photography manual (Michael Langford, *Pocket Camera Handbook*, 1980, London: Ebury Press) also uses a flexible grid, allowing the use of one, two, three, or four columns. However, the combination of low-key typography and complex layout casts doubts on its effectiveness.

○   The main components of the left-hand page are: the main heading; the introductory illustration; the introductory text; and a list of "common 110 features."

The articulation of the first three is clear enough, but two problems arise with the fourth: first, the typographic distinction between the section heading ("Common 110 features") and the slightly smaller sub-headings ("The lens," etc.) is too subtle; second, the intrusion of the illustration belonging to "Viewfinder" into the space beside the introductory paragraph disrupts the shape of the section. The combined result is that the graphic argument of the page is blurred.

○ The right-hand page is clearer. In two instances, though, aesthetic judgments may have prevailed over clear syntax. First, the small table in the left-hand column has been aligned with the foot of the photograph to its right. This squares up the top half of the page neatly, but with the result that the table appears to be more closely related to the next section ("Loading the film") than with the paragraph it follows. Second, tension has been introduced into the relationship between the right-hand column ("Batteries") and the section to its left ("Loading the film"). They are correctly separated by a vertical rule, but needlessly linked by the alignment of their diagrams.

Figure 5.8. Although some of the rules, implicitly adhered to by most of the previous examples, have been broken here, this spread may still work: Its subject is relatively simple, and the consequences of misunderstanding are not severe. More positively, the inclusion of such layouts might add interest to the text.

o   The left-hand page contains a clear structure which is disrupted by the two illustrations in the center column. Since they are duplicated elsewhere (at the top right and top left), they have no new information to contribute, but confuse the tabular arrangement of the other four illustrations (which form a matrix of horizontal/vertical formats and 35mm/110 cameras).

o   The right-hand page breaks down into an introduction ("Avoiding shake") and three sub-sections. Once again, the typographic distinction between their headings is hardly noticeable. The two sub-sections in the bottom corners ("Press the shutter gently" and "Support the camera") form tightly defined groups, while the other sub-section ("Find a support") spreads into every available space on the page. Although the resultant shape is unusual, the overlapping illustrations enable it to cohere reasonably well as a group.

Conclusion

These examples focus our attention on the interconnectedness of the text as an artifact—a physical and graphic object—and the text as an argument—a system of ideas expressed in linguistic strings. To the reader, the artifact is primary—it is the route through which the argument may be discerned. To the writer, it is the other way around.

As well as perpetrating a tautology, it is true to say that text is a mediating medium—it comes between the two communicants in a way that speech appears not to. Instead of a single relationship (speaker/listener), there are two separate relationships (writer/text and reader/text) (Waller, 1979; Sless, 1982).

To the traditional writer, a text is first and foremost a means of expression—to him or her, the various devices and techniques suggested in books like this one are primarily ways of constructing a coherent argument. Whether the reader can use the text-as-arti-fact to reach the text-as-argument, although important, is second-ary to such a writer. In effect, the text itself acts as a surrogate reader—it is the thing to which the author relates, and which reflects an objective and concrete representation of his or her thoughts for examination and modification.

In the case of a graphically-structured text, however, the linear sequence of language is still dominant, but neither the writer nor the reader is bound by it. The readers' view—the text-as-artifact—is as important a design determinant as is the argument to be expressed. In all of the examples shown, each topic took up a whole page or spread; no page contained more than one topic. The complete production process—the planning of the content, the composition of the prose, the design of the illustrations, and the choice of printing process—was treated as a holistic design exercise.

It is doubtful that effective instructional texts can be routinely produced in the traditional way; "the technology of text" has been suggested to describe the approach that replaces it. However, its progenitor's justification for the term (Jonassen, 1982) might happily be moderated—the idea that "a scientific approach to text design" is "a counterpoint to the artistic and unsystematic approach ... that has prevailed since petroglyphs were first inscribed on walls" flatters science and undervalues art. Scholars of many persuasions have tried for centuries to systematize the communication process, and it is surely naive to suggest that a few experiments will improve upon all scholarship since the Greeks. Rather I am with Steinbeck when he commented, "A strange and mystic business, writing. Almost no progress has taken place since it was invented."

An alternative conception of technology, though, is as the articulation and evaluation of reliable techniques in some practical arena, whether their source be science or craft. It was in this spirit that the role of the "transformer" was suggested by the great social philosopher and graphic communicator Otto Neurath (Neurath, 1974) and revived in the modern context by Macdonald-Ross and Waller (1976). If a technology of text can articulate some of the hidden skills of those who have mastered the arts of teaching and writing, can inform us with data on reading, cognition, and learning, can widen our definition of literacy to include the visual alongside the verbal, and can suggest procedures for the management and monitoring of such quality, then it is to be welcomed. It has been the purpose of this chapter to contribute in a small way to the critical tradition of such a technology.

References

Jonassen, D.H. *The technology of text: Principles for structuring, designing, and displaying text.* Englewood Cliffs, NJ: Educational Technology Publications, 1982.

Macdonald-Ross, M., and Waller, R.H.W. The transformer. *The Penrose Annual*, Volume 69. London: Northwood Publications, 1976.

Nash, W. *Designs in prose.* London: Longman, 1980.

Neurath, M. Isotype. *Instructional Science*, 1974, *3*, 127-150.

Schumacher, G., and Waller, R.H.W. Observing reading behaviour: A comparison of procedures. In T. Duffy and R. Waller (Eds.), *Designing usable text.* New York: Academic Press, in press.

Sless, D. *Visual communication and learning.* London: Croom-Helm, 1982.

Waller, R.H.W. Four aspects of graphic communication: An

introduction to this issue. *Instructional Science*, 1979, *8*, 213-222.

Waller, R.H.W. Text as diagram: Using typography to improve access and understanding. In D.H. Jonassen (Ed.), *The technology of text: Principles for structuring, designing, and displaying text.* Englewood Cliffs, NJ: Educational Technology Publications, 1982.

Section III

Controlling the Processing of Text

Introduction

It is generally accepted that text comprehension results from the interaction of the reader's knowledge base with the text base. The words function to activate the reader's schemata for those ideas. The sequence of those words determines the relationship between those schemata, based upon an accepted syntax. So at even the lowest level of text organization (micro-structural), the author of the text controls the comprehension process. In the second section, we looked at text design techniques for structuring the overall content (macro-structural) and relating that structure to the reader. Those techniques exercised a greater degree of text control over the content.

In this section, we will briefly examine two *mathemagenic techniques* for controlling the reader's *processing* of text rather than the content of text, as examined in the first section. Mathemagenic techniques, the subject of the chapters in this section, are reading or study behaviors stimulated by adjunct textual inclusions that seek to control the information processing activities of the learner. For an in-depth analysis of mathemagenic processing, see the first chapter in the book. Briefly, though, their purpose is to orient the reader to the text and determine what is to be comprehended, including the translation and elaboration processes leading to comprehension. The intent of these mathemagenic activities, when applied to text, is to *control text processing*.

Another key difference between the techniques presented in

this section and the text organization techniques presented in the second section is the maturity of their literature bases. Our knowledge of the relationships between text bases and readers' knowledge structures is still developing. Most of the research has been generated in the last decade. The mathemagenic literature, on the other hand, began, emerged, and matured in the sixties and early seventies. Less research has been generated in the last decade. Most of the operational issues have been exhausted. As Lindner and Rickards claim in their chapter, that is because it has yet to develop a sound theoretical foundation. The mathemagenic hypothesis is grounded in neo-behavioral theory, while the text organization literature emerged from accepted, cognitive theory. The mathemagenic literature for the past decade has been in a transitional stage, moving toward the use of cognitive constructs for explaining learning processes. These comparisons are not intended to disparage either literature base. Both have obvious implications for designing text, as is obvious from the chapters in each section.

Inserted Questions in Text

Reinhard W. Lindner and John P. Rickards provide us with a comprehensive and critical examination of the adjunct question literature. The adjunct inclusion of questions in text is the best established, most popular, and most heavily researched of the mathemagenic techniques. This examination begins with an historical perspective, tracing the concerns of researchers through the paradigm shift in psychology to its current cognitive orientation. While they argue that this transition has manifested more concern for the *level of processing* activity required by the question, the literature still lacks a firm theoretical foundation. Operationally, the major criticism concerns our inability to define questions at various levels. Perhaps the neo-behavioristic model of mathemagenic activity was more useful. Similar operational deficiencies have plagued most of the mathemagenic techniques. Additionally, adjunct question research suffers from equivocal results and ecological validity problems. The authors review other concerns, such as the interaction of inserted questions with task directions and individual learner differences. The authors conclude that computer courseware provides a better medium for using adjunct questions than print text. Just when we thought that exegesis was a lost art, Lindner and Rickards apply the techniques to one of the most deserving literatures in all of instructional psychology.

Graphic Organizers

Next to inserted questions, the inclusion of *advance organizers* in text is probably the most common mathemagenic technique employed. Advance organizers are introductory material presented in advance of instruction or text at a higher level of abstraction than information presented in text. They function, according to Ausubelian cognitive theory (operationally, they tend to function neo-behavioristically), as conceptual anchors in the reader's knowledge structure for subsuming new information presented in text. For a more detailed review of the conceptual foundations and technology of advance organizers, see the chapter in the first volume of *The Technology of Text*.

Graphic organizers function in much the same way as advance organizers, except that they do it visually. The added modality presumably results in additional coding of the information, making it more memorable. In this chapter, Parmalee Hawk, Nancy P. McLeod, and I review the conceptual foundations of and the procedures for producing and using graphic organizers in various forms of text (print and courseware). While the technique is in the early stages of verification, it represents a potentially valuable technology of text.

Summary

The equivocal research findings that plague educational research, discussed by Lindner and Rickards in their chapter, result largely from individual differences in learner processing. At the beginning of this Introduction, I reiterated that comprehension is a consequence of an interaction of the reader's processing strategies and knowledge base and the text base. If we accept that all knowledge is constructed, then the knower is largely responsible for what comes to be known. The text designer can exert only so much control over the reader's processing. Presenting inserted questions does not assure that they will be answered or even attended to. Accessing text in the first place is usually volitional. So comprehension ultimately begins with the reader's disposition to learn. The ability of the author/text designer to influence the way that the reader organizes information (see the second section of this book) or processes text (as represented by this section) is limited to individual differences in decoding skill, world knowledge, and so on. While the techniques in this section have proven to be useful, it is incumbent on text designers to realize the limits of their techniques and to consider the process more holistically, rather than basing their designs on some myopic and self-serving advocacy.

Chapter 6

Questions Inserted in Text:
Issues and Implications

Reinhard W. Lindner and John P. Rickards

Introduction

Historical View

For nearly two decades, a great deal of research has examined the process of learning from text. One such process, about which a considerable body of literature has grown, involves the use of inserted or *adjunct questions* designed to facilitate learning from textual material.

The investigation of the effects of inserted questions upon the retention of textual material dates back to 1929 and the work of J.N. Washburne. While Washburne's work differs in certain respects (he, for example, allowed his subjects to refer to passage material while reading the inserted questions) from recent efforts as well as suffering from a certain statistical innocence, it has nevertheless proved amazingly farsighted. Not only did his investigation include the major variables that have occupied the interest of more recent investigators (frequency, position, and level of question), but it also considered individual differences. Furthermore, Washburne was the first to distinguish between *intentional* and *incidental learning* in regard to adjunct questions.

Despite Washburne's farsighted and pioneering effort, it is E.Z. Rothkopf who must be credited for stimulating most of the current interest in adjunct questions. It was Rothkopf, in the middle sixties, who resurrected the investigation of adjunct question effects and developed it into an experimental paradigm designed to explore their *mathemagenic* potential.

The Paradigm

Although a number of variations exist, the typical adjunct question study consists of text segments and questions usually appearing on separate sheets of paper. The reader is neither allowed to turn back to a page once he has turned it, nor allowed to take notes while reading. Questions may appear before (pre) and/or after (post) a related segment of text. After completing the total text passage, including the inserted questions, a posttest designed to assess the effects of the adjunct questions is given. The results are normally compared to those of a read-only control group. Both the amount questioned (intentional) and non-questioned (incidental) material the reader is able to recall are of interest. However, it is the mathemagenic (Rothkopf, 1965) or indirect (Anderson and Biddle, 1975) effect, evidenced by the amount of incidental material recalled, that is generally considered of greater educational significance.

Theoretical Orientation

Rothkopf began his investigations under the theoretical banner of neo-behaviorism. Thus, inserted questions were first viewed as potentially discriminative and/or reinforcing stimuli that could be used to shape the reader's learning behavior. However, over the last decade and a half, most of the subsequent research involving adjunct questions has assumed a cognitive perspective, which emphasizes the active and constructive role of the learner. According to Rickards (1979), both the shift of interest from the effects of factual, verbatim-level questions to those of higher, conceptual-level questions and the attempt to examine precisely and in detail the *nature of the processing activities* generated in the reader through the use of adjunct questions are indicative of the change from a behavioristic to a cognitive orientation.

However, as we shall point out, the adjunct question paradigm like so much of educational research, continues to suffer from the lack of any solid theoretical foundation.

Nevertheless, a great deal of effort has been expended and a number of tentative conclusions are, at least from a pragmatic perspective, possible. We intend to review and examine these conclusions and to examine as well the direction research in this area is presently taking. We shall also explore both the potential and limitations of the adjunct question paradigm in general. Finally, we will discuss the need for a stronger and more coherent theoretical foundation to guide both investigations and practice regarding inserted questions.

Review of Adjunct Question Research

Several comprehensive and recent reviews have appeared that have examined the effects of adjunct questions as aids to text comprehension (Andre, 1979; Anderson and Biddle, 1975; Rickards and Denner, 1978, Rickards and Denner, 1979; Rickards, 1979; van Hout-Walters, 1980). While these reviews make the task of sifting through the many publications in this area for conclusions somewhat less demanding, we shall see that disagreements exist among certain authors as to what we can claim as conclusive. Overall, it appears that too much of what we know is less than certain. In 1978, Rickards and Denner comprehensively reviewed the development of research in this area beginning with the early efforts of Washburne. These authors suggest that the critical factors in adjunct question studies are the variables (position, type, frequency, level of question) examined as well interactions among these variables, the process induced in the reader as a result of various types of questions, and individual differences in cognitive processing associated with adjunct questions.

According to Rickards and Denner, the earliest work in the modern era dealt largely with verbatim-level questions requiring only literal recall of specific textual information. Regarding the *position of questions* (pre or post), the general conclusion has been that verbatim postquestions lead to better performance than prequestions, and only postquestions lead to better performance than read-only controls. Some studies have shown a poorer performance when using prequestions.

The results for *frequency of question* have been inconclusive; some have found that as the amount of text between questions increases, the degree of intentional and incidental learning increases for the prequestion group but decreases for the postquestion group. Others have found no interaction between frequency and position. Rickards and DiVesta (1974) also found no interaction between frequency and position of questions for verbatim-level questions. However, they did find *meaningful learning* postquestions to be more effective when occurring more frequently in text.

As the theoretical orientation of researchers has moved from behavioristic to cognitive, the *level of processing* required to answer questions has become more important. Since educators have generally concluded that rote learning of facts alone is of a little educational value, earlier studies employing verbatim-level questions came to be criticized as lacking significance (Carver, 1972; Watts and Anderson, 1971).

Both the level of processing of questions (verbatim vs. conceptual) and the *interaction of level and position of question* have been investigated. See Appendix (pp. 155-157) for examples of inserted questions at various levels. Generally, higher-level (conceptual) questions produce more and better organized recall of passage material than lower-level questions. However, results concerning the best position for higher-level questions have been inconclusive. For example, while Felker and Dapra (1975) found conceptual postquestions leading to better performance than conceptual prequestions, Rickards (1976) arrived at the opposite conclusion. On the other hand, Mayer (1975) found both positions to be equivalent. As Rickards and Denner (1978) point out, the problem is that we are, as yet, unable to clearly differentiate the various levels of processing associated with different higher-level questions that will enable us to operationally define questions at each level with the proper degree of precision. Chiefly responsible for this state of ambiguity is the continuing lack of a strong theoretical foundation on which to base such distinctions and issues. Nevertheless, most educators and educational researchers appear to believe that higher-level questions hold the most promise as adjunct aids to text comprehension.

General Conclusions

Before analyzing the mental processing produced by adjunct questions and investigating the current issues, we would like to offer some tentative conclusions about their effects. In general, *factual adjunct postquestions* have been found to facilitate performance of learners receiving them, beyond that of either prequestion or read-only control groups. However, exceptions to this conclusion have appeared, particularly where verbatim-level questions have been used. *Higher-level questions* appear to facilitate both the amount and organization of information recalled from text. However, the optimal position likely depends on the type of higher-level question asked. Frequency (pacing) appears to affect higher-level questions more critically than it does lower-level questions.

Processes Produced by Adjunct Questions

In order to understand the effects of adjunct questions, we must first understand the type and nature of the cognitive processes they produce. Frase (1967) first suggested the notion of *forward and backward processes* as potentially responsible for the effects of adjunct postquestions. What Frase had in mind was both a general review (backward) process and a general test-taking orientation (forward) process. Extending Frase's original insight, Rickards (1979) concluded that four intertwined yet distinct processes are probably involved (see Figure 6.1): (1) *a general backward process* including the mental review of material either adjacent to and/or thematically related to questioned material; (2) a *specific backward process* involving review of only that material actually questioned; (3) a *general forward process* resulting in heightened attention to all subsequent passage material; and (4) a *specific forward process* whereby the learner adopts a learning set attuned solely to the particular type of information questioned. It is possible that the specific forward effect, by overfocusing the reader's attention to a specific type of information, may be responsible for the depressive effect on incidental learning that has appeared (see, for example, Rickards, Anderson, and McCormick,

1976). Negative effects are more commonly associated with prequestions.

Rickards and DiVesta (1974) investigated these processes by dividing their experimental passage into two paragraph text segments, with one paragraph related (questioned) and one unrelated (non-questioned). They also employed different levels of questions (rote learning of facts, rote learning of ideas, meaningful learning) that examined the types of processes engendered by the different levels of questions. The results indicated that factual postquestions induced a specific backward process while rote learning of concept questions produced a general backward process. In addition, meaningful learning questions produced both a specific forward effect and a specific backward effect. It seems that different types of postquestions result in different types of processing activities varying in both direction and kind.

Figure 6.1

Processes Produced by Adjunct Questions

	Forward	Backward
Specific	Search for questioned material	Review of questioned material only
General	Increased attention to all material	Review of related material

---

Backward Effects

Several recent experiments examined more closely the kinds of processes adjunct questions induce. Sefkow and Meyers (1980) sought to specify the locus of the backward review effect (specific vs. general) of postquestions. In addition, they sought to determine whether the backward review effect was dependent on what is stored at the time of answering the question or triggered at the time of the posttest, i.e., at retrieval. Using materials developed by Frase (1969), which required learners to draw inferences on the basis of passage material, they presented text and material via tape, with learners responding to true/false questions. The results, based on a free-call posttest, indicated that a backward review effect of a specific nature was used, since memory was selectively enhanced for only those statements for which learners were required to respond to questions.

In a second experiment, Sefkow and Myers sought to establish the reliability of the backward effect and to *distinguish between the storage and retrieval hypotheses.* In this instance, a backward review effect occurred which indicated that the effect of the review is to strengthen storage, rather than to trigger retrieval only.

Forward Effects

Contrary to the results of Sefkow and Myer's study, Reynolds, Standiford, and Anderson (1979) and Reynolds and Anderson (1982) found that enhanced performance as a result of adjunct postquestions could be attributed to a *specific forward* rather than a specific backward effect. In the former study, they presented text passages and questions via a computer that allowed for accurate measurement of the amount of time subjects spent viewing each text segment. This allowed the experimenters to determine if learners spent a disproportionate amount of time on questioned versus non-questioned segments of text. Subjects showed both a steady decline in reading time per text segment over the course of the experiment and spent a disproportionate amount of time on those segments containing target (questioned) material.

In the latter experiment, Reynolds and Anderson sought to establish the existence of a *general forward effect* using a more precise measure of attention. Both the amount of time spent per segment of text and reaction time to a secondary (probe) task were measured to assess what the authors term the *volume of attention* (duration and intensity). The general assumption behind the experiment was that the amount (or volume) of attention related directly to the amount of learning. They argued that relatively slow reaction time to the probe coupled with increased reading time for related text segments would indicate a specific forward effect, which is exactly what they found.

No support for a general heightening of attention (general forward effect) was found. Interestingly, while reading time decreased over the course of the experiment, probe reaction time increased. Hence, the total "volume of attention" remained the same, providing support for the importance of this two-dimensional concept of attention. Unfortunately, both experiments employed only factual level (lower-level) adjunct questions. It remains to be seen if the same type of result would appear with the use of higher-level questions.

So far, we reviewed the history and traditional issues in adjunct question research. We then provided a conceptual framework for this research by considering the mental processes instigated by the questions. However, a newer and perhaps more useful set of issues has emerged which we shall now take up.

Levels of Processing

Perhaps the most important issue related to adjunct question research and practice relates to the level of cognitive processing required by questions inserted in passages. (Again, see examples, pp. 155-157.) What level of processing is necessary to produce knowledge or understanding of passage information? Andre (1979) provided a lengthy review of the subject, concluding that while the levels of processing hypothesis has received some support in verbal learning research, such studies have generally compared superficial levels of processing to deeper semantic levels of processing for meaning. Little or no research has compared various levels of meaningful processing, whereas it is such comparisons that are truly educationally relevant.

compared various levels of meaningful processing, whereas it is such comparisons that are truly educationally relevant.

Since no clear-cut typology of higher-level questions exists, Andre offers the following classifications: (1) application questions that require subjects to choose from among various alternatives a new example of a concept or principle encountered in text; (2) meaningful learning or inference questions requiring readers to identify relationships between elements of a passage which are implied but not explicitly stated; and (3) higher-order analysis and/or evaluation questions, defined as being above the knowledge or memory level on any taxonomy of learning. In addition, Andre divides level-of-question studies on the basis of the type of posttest employed—whether the posttest requires factual or verbatim recall of passage material vs. higher-level questions.

Andre criticizes factual recall questions because they can only demonstrate a quantitative effect on learning. Hence, factual questions cannot distinguish between *learning of* and *learning from* a passage. By the same token, if higher-level questions lead to improved recall of facts contained in a passage, as they sometimes have, he argues that this may simply be because they direct the reader's attention to more of the material in text. Having to attend to more, these readers are able to recall more facts than those who have to answer factual-level questions that focus on specific items only. He calls this the *directed attention* hypothesis or model (DAM). If directed attention alone explains the facilitative effects of higher-level questions, Andre states, then we ought to be able to achieve the same results by simply asking more factual questions per passage. At any rate, directed attention is all that we can argue for on the basis of using posttests that require only factual recall.

Andre's argument is not entirely compelling. Level of question studies have not only demonstrated better but more organized recall (see Rickards and Denner, 1978). It appears that higher-level questions affect not only the level at which material is processed but the manner in which such material is organized in memory. That is, higher-level questions may affect the quality as well as the quantity of recall. For example, Andre criticizes the work of Rickards and associates (Rickards and DiVesta, 1974, and Rickards, 1976) for only requiring factual recall on the posttests of his experiments, yet in both of the above-mentioned experiments, higher-level questions resulted in more organized and structured recall than the verbatim-level counterparts. These effects were shown through correlational and clustering analyses. In the case of Rickards (1976), higher-level questions led to greater long-term retention than lower-level questions. Simply providing more frequent factual-level questions would not achieve similar results.

Andre also concluded that different types of questions, by directing the reader's attention to particular types of information, ultimately result in inducing different processing strategies in the reader. We might call this the *directed strategy hypothesis* or model, which seems a more reasonable explanation for the facilitative effect of higher-level questions than DAM.

But what about those studies that employed higher-level questions not only as adjunct questions but on the posttest as well? According to Andre, the results of these studies may be summarized in the following manner:

(1) When provided adjunct application questions concerning concepts and principles as opposed to adjunct factual questions, the subjects' ability to apply their knowledge of the concepts and principles in order to recognize new examples or solve problems involving the same concepts or principles is enhanced.

(2) Such effects are apparently specific to the concepts and principles directly questioned. In other words, evidence for learning of concepts or principles not directly questioned has failed to emerge.

(3) The effects of higher-level questions other than application questions are less clear. But even these results are cast in doubt by conclusions gleaned from Andre's own experiments.

The results of a series of studies conducted in Andre's laboratory appear to suggest that students given *factual-level questions* vs. those given *application-level questions* actually perform better when tested with new application items. Andre concludes that other variables must be affecting the results. In particular, he points to the higher difficulty level of adjunct application questions vs. factual-level questions, and variations in the ability level of subjects. Consequently, he recommends that future research examine the possibility of trait by treatment interactions. Overall, his general conclusion is that "questions may well have different effects on different learners in different situations."

Other researchers have explored the *level of question issue* with mixed results. Friedman and Rickards (1981), for example, presented readers with three different types of questions: (1) verbatim; (2) paraphrase; and (3) inferential They reasoned that only inferential questions would lead subjects to process passage material by relating it to their existing cognitive structure. Since this should result in a deeper (semantic) level of processing than that produced by either verbatim or paraphrase questions, inferential question subjects should elicit superior learning of both questioned and non-questioned material. In order to insure the production of *deeper processing*, learners either read a paragraph twice before answering an inserted question (RRQ) or read the paragraph, answered the question, and then re-read the paragraph (RQR). The latter (RQR) sequence, due to its potential facilitation of forward processing, was hypothesized to prove superior to the RRQ sequence (see also Andre and Sola, 1976). In addition, they examined the effect of using the answers to the inserted questions as review cues. Half of their learners were allowed a ten-minute mental review prior to the posttest while the other half received the answers to the inserted questions for the same period of time. It was believed that the cued group would outperform the mental-review-only group. A posttest was given 24 hours after the experimental procedure (to more closely approximate school conditions).

The results of the experiment indicated that both paraphrase and inference questions proved superior to verbatim questions for both direct and indirect learning. Paraphrase and inference questions also resulted in superior performance on target (questioned) items at all levels, implying that a transfer of level effect was facilitated by these questions. In addition, subjects receiving inference questions outperformed those receiving paraphrase questions in both direct and indirect learning. Only the read-question-re-read groups exhibited the transfer or level effect, possibly indicating that this sequence results in improved learning across cognitive levels. As would be expected, cuing subjects with the answers to the adjunct questions served to improve performance on target items only. Overall, the results of this experiment support the conclusion that the *level of processing of text* can be manipulated by varying the level of postquestions.

Andre *et al.* (1980), in a series of experiments designed to investigate the potentially facilitative effect of adjunct application (higher-level) questions over that of adjunct factual questions, were unable to demonstrate any positive influence for higher-level questions. In fact, these investigators found that factual-level questions, in some instances, led to better performance on a posttest than application questions. In the same report, Andre *et al.* sought to compare the directed attention hypothesis discussed earlier with the *representation hypothesis*, which states that different kinds of processing, ostensibly induced by different levels of questions, result in different representations in memory which then influence later performance. Unfortunately, they failed to find support for either hypothesis.

Two final experiments were undertaken to examine the effects of variations in the level of difficulty of adjunct questions. Learners received either easy or hard factual questions and/or easy or hard application questions. Results indicated only that easy questions (of either type) led to better performance than difficult questions. On the basis of their investigations, Andre *et al.* concluded that level of adjunct question is not a powerful determinant of learning to apply concepts presented in prose, and that, therefore, current conceptions of school learning and memory based on the levels of processing metaphor are cast in doubt.

Conclusions related to level of processing issue

Like so many areas of educational research, manipulating the levels of processing required by adjunct questions has produced inconsistent results. Some researchers have been able to obtain powerful learning effects for higher-level questions, while some have not. Generally, questions that require learners to relate textual information to what they already know—that require them to interpret and infer from textual material—make the textual material more meaningful and therefore more memorable.

Individual Differences

Traditionally, adjunct question research has recapitulated so many other investigations of instructional technique—the search for a generalizable methodology of instruction, or the holy grail, as it were. Recent developments in differential psychology have convinced us that all learning from instruction is mediated by individual differences. Each learner applies his or her unique set of skills and experiences to comprehending text. With what we know about cognitive development, we cannot expect adjunct questions to have similar effects for different age or ability groups of learners.

Some recent adjunct question research has shown increased awareness of the role of *individual differences*. Rickards and Hatcher (1978), for example, divided their subjects into good and poor comprehenders on the basis of reading comprehension scores. Each group received either meaningful or rote learning postquestions or no questions at all. While good comprehenders performed equally well regardless of condition, poor comprehenders benefited significantly more from meaningful learning postquestions in regard to recall of subordinate facts. In addition, poor comprehenders receiving meaningful learning postquestions did not differ significantly in the recall of subordinate facts from good comprehenders. Rickards and Hatcher concluded that poor comprehenders benefited to a greater extent from high-level questions than do good comprehenders, who more commonly engage in meaningful learning.

Loosely employing a Piagetian framework and dividing poor from average comprehenders on the basis of reading scores on the California Achievement Test, Wilson (1979) looked at the effects of question position, question level (factual vs. inferential), and the differences in processing strategies used by readers of different ability in probed recall tasks. Factual questions dealt with matters of "who," what," "when," or "where," while inferential questions inquired as to "how," "why," "if-then," or "because." All subjects read three stories each of approximately 1500 words in length. Eight questions (four factual, four inferential) were massed together either before or after each story or interspersed within the text. Responses to questions were given orally by the subjects who were also asked to explain how they arrived at their answers. The results indicated that average readers performed better on either type of question. Inferential questions produced the greatest differences between reading levels, while factual questions contributed most to the distinction between question position. Interspersed questions led to better performance on factual questions for either group. The average readers showed more organized recall, were more sensitive to text order, and proved better able to synthesize the material. In this instance, better readers simply performed better on questions than poor readers, a not altogether surprising result. Unlike the Rickards and Hatcher subjects, the poor comprehenders did not appear to disproportionately benefit from the higher-level questions.

Both Wilson (1979) and Rickards and Hatcher (1978) employed *subjects of younger ages* than has been typical in adjunct question experiments (sixth and seventh graders and fifth graders, respectively). Hudgins, Dorman, and Harris (1979) sought primarily to extend the technique to intermediate grade children (fourth, fifth, and sixth graders). They divided their subjects into two groups on the basis of reading comprehension. The division of good from poor comprehenders was, in this case, accomplished by use of a pretest employing the same reading material (the first seven paragraphs) to be used in the experiment. Since both repeated and new questions appeared on the posttest, both intentional and incidental learning effects could be examined. For *intentional learning*, all three main effects (for comprehension level, location, and pacing) proved significant. In short, high comprehenders performed best, post questions proved most effective, and interspersed questions, as opposed to massed questions, proved most facilitative. The interaction between comprehension ability and question location also proved significant. The facilitative effect of postquestions disproportionately favored the higher comprehenders. Regarding *incidental learning*, significant main effects appeared for comprehension level and for question position. No other significant results were obtained. High comprehenders performed best on new questions, and postquestions proved more facilitative. Again, postquestions were most beneficial for high comprehenders.

Limitations of Adjunct Question Research

Another issue of importance concerns the *artificiality of the adjunct question paradigm*. In the real world, students do not face the restrictions that are normally applied in adjunct question experiments. A study by Gagné *et al.* (1979), which was designed to explore the usefulness of different types (identify, give, summarize, list) of adjunct postquestions in improving accuracy of concept classification, allowed subjects to refer to the passage after reading the questions and provided feedback as to the correctness of their answers to inserted questions. This experimental arrangement seems to more closely parallel study behavior in the real world than the standard adjunct question method. While the results of this experiment were somewhat inconclusive, it does demonstrate the need for adjunct questions to be explored in a more ecologically valid setting.

Ellis, Wulfeck, and Montague (1980) attempted to extend the paradigm to a potentially more *realistic learning situation* by examining the effects of adjunct postquestions on learning in an individualized technical training course. The subject matter was composed largely of facts. Learners were asked to proceed through a seven-lesson sequence with each lesson being followed by a posttest which had to be successfully completed before moving on to the next lesson. The experimental groups received workbooks containing practice questions that differed only in terms of the number of questions in the workbooks. The workbooks, in turn, contained questions identical to those included in either the lesson tests or the final test (Group 1 = 100 percent identical; Group 2 = 50 percent identical; Group 3 = 0 percent identical; and a no-workbook control group). This constitutes a procedure unlike that which is typically used in adjunct question studies. We should also point out that all groups were tested after each lesson prior to the final test, and so all groups in effect received questions of some sort prior to the test.

The results indicated that the facilitative effect of adjunct questions was limited to directly questioned material. Not surprisingly, the 100 percent group outperformed all other groups, with none of the latter differing significantly from each other. No incidental learning occurred. Also, the 100 percent group, having the opportunity to see the same questions most often, required the least study time. Once again, however, the results must be qualified by the fact that only factual-level questions were employed. It is admittedly easier to provide and control experimental materials at a factual level, but in lieu of the now long-standing opinion of educators that purely factual, rote learning is of limited educational value and given that higher-level questions have in a number of cases seemingly engendered multi-stage learning (learning of facts as well as concepts), the persistence of the use of factual-level questions in recent studies seems rather unfortunate.

It is readily apparent that the limitations placed on the learner in adjunct question studies in no way resemble the normal reading and/or study behavior of students. Subjects can neither re-read nor underline nor take notes in the typical experiment, nor are they allowed to review text passages once they have encountered a question. *Generalizations to real-life settings* from the results of adjunct question experiments are, consequently, rather limited. It is also not the case that when questions appear in text, they are normally presented intermittently on separate pages from associated textual material. Such an arrangement would prove costly and impractical to textbook publishers.

Summary and Conclusions

Experimental Evidence

What, in summary, does the most recent research on the uses of adjunct questions tell us? The *level of question issue* remains somewhat unresolved. Both Friedman and Rickards (1981), and Lee (1980) found higher-level questions resulted in the facilitation of learning at several levels. Andre, however, was unable to support the unresolved. Both Friedman and Rickards (1981), and Lee (1980) found higher-level questions resulted in the facilitation of learning at several levels. Andre, however, was unable to support the facilitative effect of higher-level questions at least on immediate retention tests. In a more recent experiment (Andre and Reiker, 1983), application-level questions were found to be superior to factual-level questions on a delayed test but not on an immediate test.

A heightened awareness of the role of *individual differences* is apparent in much of the recent work. Whereas some researchers have simply attempted to control for this factor, others have explored it directly. It is clear, to no one's surprise, that better comprehenders (readers) outperform poor comprehenders, whether or not they receive adjunct question. However, some evidence exists to indicate that poor comprehenders benefit disproportionately more from the use of high-level adjunct questions.

Concerning the *type of processes* induced by adjunct questions, there is some recent evidence to suggest that higher-level questions appear to facilitate a *specific backward review process* while lower-level questions seem to produce a *specific forward process*.

Finally, some researchers are becoming aware of the need to alter the adjunct question paradigm, so it will fit more ecologically valid situations. This is apparent in the Gagné *et al.* study and in the training study of Ellis, Wulfeck, and Montague. At present, these kinds of studies serve to underscore the dangers of leaping from the psychological laboratory to the real world.

Theoretical Void

Despite the shift in theoretical orientation of psychological research due to the cognitive revolution, there is a considerable *lack of theory in adjunct question research*. Specifically, there has been little in the way of model building and model testing other than the quite general notions of forward and backward effects (Frase, 1967; see also Rickards, 1979), which have been most recently examined in a clever and well-executed study by Reynolds and Anderson (1982). There has been some post-hoc theorizing, as in the information processing model proposed by Andre (1979), but such work has not yet led to experimental testing.

Methodological Concerns

In addition to the paucity of theory in educational research, there seems to be at least two other concerns that pertain to adjunct question research. First, we seem to be willing to make generalizations on the basis of too few investigations. Second, we seem all too willing to apply these generalizations to school settings that bear only a slight resemblance to the experimental paradigm on which they are based.

Regarding the first issue, there does not seem to exist in educational research a sufficient appreciation of the need for *long-term systematic research* of a particular phenomenon from many different researchers examining the same and different variables before any generalizations from the research are attempted. For example, in the research on levels of questions, different investigators have used different "models," if you will, in distinguishing higher-order from lower-order questions. These have included everything from calibrations on the basis of inferential distance (Frase, 1969), distinctions between verbatim and paraphase processing in the manner of Anderson (1972), to differences in level of processing using Bloom's taxonomy or Ausubel's assimilation theory. The result of this has been a potpourri of studies with no discernible systematicity from which it is difficult to draw any generalizations. It is just as difficult to draw conclusions from levels of questions investigations that examine the position effect. Quite naturally, the best position for higher-order questions will depend on the particular kind of high-level question being asked, for with each kind of question a different type of processing is invoked.

It would seem to be academic anarchy to attempt to draw any firm generalization from these levels of questions studies, not to mention the disquieting fact that "levels" is defined differently in different studies. Future researchers might explore the possibility of using some text analysis system as a basis for distinguishing between levels of questions. Surely, as cognitive educational researchers, we must go beyond the vague distinctions offered by the forefathers (Bloom and Ausubel) of the levels of processing framework.

Regarding the problem of *overgeneralization in educational research*, it is important to realize that the vast majority of research on questions has been done using the standard adjunct question paradigm, which does not conform to the way in which in-text questions are presented in more natural situations. There are virtually no textbooks that consistently present material and associated questions on separate pages. Furthermore, few if any students would not turn back to a page of text after reading the postquestions in order to confirm their answers. This artificial arrangement of passages and questions, of course, restricts generalizations to situations similar to the standard paradigm.

Limitations

We do not intend to suggest that the adjunct question paradigm and the associated research is without any practical usefulness. We merely suggest that there are boundary conditions for its application and the implications we have suggested. For example, given the standard paradigm, it seems gratuitous to expect the adjunct question effect to occur when questions are inserted in a textbook after every two pages of text and the textbook is to be read as part of the assigned reading for a university course, as in Shavelson *et al.* (1974). Other than the obvious fact that questions were inserted in text, none of the other conditions of the original paradigm were met. That is, there is no indication that the students actually answered the questions. If they answered them, they may have used them as prequestions not postquestions as intended. Furthermore, if they were used as postquestions, it seems likely that the students would have re-read the material to answer the questions rather than simply relying on mental review of their knowledge of the text for answers, as in the standard paradigm. In any case, they may have concentrated their attention on the answers to the inserted questions rather than on the whole text, thereby leading to what Shavelson termed a "mathemathanic (death of learning) effect."

Future Paradigm

In contrast, the work of T.H. Anderson (see Anderson *et al.*, 1974) represents an excellent example of the adjunct question research paradigm applied to the real world. These researchers developed a computer-assisted study management system (CAISMS), which, in part, involved asking students questions after they had studied short segments of text that were read as part of a college-level introductory economics course. The material was presented via computer (CAI setting), and the conditions of the standard question paradigm were not violated in any significant way. The experimental evaluation revealed that the CAISMS group scored significantly higher ($p<.05$) on the economics final test than the control group (Anderson *et al.*, 1975). These results suggest that computer-based instructional systems are more conducive delivery systems for applying adjunct questions than print-on-paper text, at least using the traditional adjunct question paradigm. Not only do computers enhance experimental control, but they also fit the model better.

While the CAISMS developed by Anderson *et al.* does represent good "educational engineering," we can ill afford to rely on such inventiveness occurring with sufficient frequency without the formal development of a set of heuristics for application. Such heuristics or guidelines should form the base of instructional psychology as it is the field that bridges the gap between theory and research, on the one hand, and practice, on the other. At the moment, there is little in the way of development of these engineering principles going on in instructional psychology. With few exceptions (such as Gagné and Glaser), much of the current work in the field is too highly circumscribed to particular applications.

The potentially facilitative effects of adjunct questions as aids to comprehension should be kept in perspective. Educators have a dangerous habit of expecting too much from new methods or technologies that appear on the scene with auspicious portention. However, the research seems to indicate clearly that adjunct questions do facilitate intentional, and to a lesser extent, incidental learning of both facts and concepts. That they may prove of greater consequence for some student populations than others should not be overly surprising. The fact remains that we do not, as yet, know enough to come to a final verdict. One of the things we need to know more about is the kinds of processes that adjunct questions induce in the learner. Such knowledge would benefit not only our understanding of the effects of adjunct questions but our understanding of the learning process as well.

Cognitive Analysis of Adjunct Aids

While no comprehensive theory to guide the structure of adjunct question research has been forthcoming, there do exist some metatheoretical frameworks which can be applied towards the evaluation of past studies as well as an aid to future empirical investigations. For example, Von Hout-Walters (1980), in a comprehensive cognitive analysis of methods designed to facilitate learning from text, provides a framework of variables critical to understanding the outcomes of research on adjunct aids to text comprehension. She considers the following variables as critical: (1) *text variables*, for example, content (easy/difficult), structure or organization of information, length, format, representations, etc. (2) *test variables* including type, size, content (conceptual level), situation (immediate vs. delayed), whether or not a pre-test was given, (3) *personal variables* such as reading ability, personality factors (I.Q., interest, cognitive style), age, level of education, goals, etc., (4) *procedural variables*, for example, type of instructions given, study time, and (5) *interactions* among the above.

A somewhat similar but more compact framework, applicable to analyzing research on learning and cognition in general, is provided in Bransford's (1979) adaptation of Jenkins' (1978) tetrahedral model of memory experiments. Four factors are viewed as critical from Bransford's perspective: (1) characteristics of the learner, (2) learning activities (attention, rehearsal, etc., (3) criterial tasks (recognition, recall, problem-solving, etc.) (4) the nature of the materials (modality, conceptual, difficulty, topical structure, sequencing, etc.). Whichever framework one adopts, the complexities and difficulties inherent in attempting to answer the deceptively simple question of whether or not adjunct questions facilitate learning or comprehension are readily apparent.

References

Anderson, R.C. How to construct achievement tests to assess comprehension. *Review of Educational Research*, 1972, *42*, 145-170.

Anderson, T.H., Anderson, R.C., Alessi, S., Dalgaard, B., Paden, D., Biddle, B., Surber, J., and Smock, H. *A multifaceted computer based course management system.* Unpublished manuscript, University of Illinois, Urbana-Champaign, 1974.

Anderson, T.H., Anderson, R.C., Dalgaard, B., Paden, D., Biddle, W., Surber, J., and Alessi, S. An Experimental evaluation of a computer-based study management system. *Educational Psychologist*, 1975, *11*, 184-190.

Anderson, R.C., and Biddle, W.B. On asking people questions about what they are reading. In G. Bower (Ed.), *Psychology of learning and motivation* (Vol. 9). New York: Academic Press, 1975.

Andre, T. Does answering higher-level questions while reading facilitate productive learning? *Review of Educational Research*, 1979, *49*, 280-318.

Andre, T., and Reiker, T. Type of question, delay interval, and learning from prose. Paper presented at the meeting of the American Educational Research Association, Montreal, April, 1983.

Andre, T., and Sola, J. Imagery, verbatim and paraphrased questions and retention of meaningful sentences. *Journal of Educational Psychology*, 1976, *68*, 661-669.

Andre, T., Mueller, C., Womack, S., Smid, K., and Tuttle, M. Adjunct application questions facilitate later application, or do they? *Journal of Educational Psychology*, 1980, *72*, 533-543.

Bransford, J.D. *Human cognition: Learning, understanding, and remembering.* Belmont, CA: Wadsworth, 1979.

Carver, R.A. Critical review of mathemagenic behaviors and the effect of questions upon the retention of prose material.

Journal of Reading Behavior, 1972, *4*, 93-119.

Ellis, J.A., Wulfeck, W., and Montague, W. The effect of adjunct and test question similarity on study behavior and learning in a training course. *American Educational Research Journal*, 1980, *17*, 449-457.

Felker, D.B., and Dapra, R.A. Effects of question type and question placement on problem-solving ability from prose material. *Journal of Educational Psychology*, 1975, *67*, 380-384.

Frase, L.T. Learning from prose material: Length of passage, knowledge of results, and position of questions. *Journal of Educational Psychology*, 1967, *58*, 266-272.

Frase, L.T. Structural analysis of the knowledge that results from thinking about text. *Journal of Educational Psychology*, 1969, *60* (Monogr. Suppl. 6, Pt. 2).

Friedman, F., and Rickards, J.P. Effect of level, review, and sequence of inserted questions on text processing. *Journal of Educational Psychology*, 1981, *73*, 427-436.

Gagné, E.D., Broughton, S., Eggleston, P., Holmes, S., Hawkins, P., and Sheldon, K. Type of postquestion and accuracy of concept classification in learning from text. *Journal of Experimental Education*, 1979, *46*, 302-306.

Hudgins, B.B., Dorman, J., and Harris, M. Some effects of adjunct questions on intermediate grade children with differing reading comprehension abilities. *Journal of Educational Research*, 1979, *72*, 259-265.

Jenkins, J.J. Four points to remember: A tetrahedral model of memory experiments. In L.S. Cermak and F.I.M. Craik (Eds.), *Levels of processing and human memory*. Hillsdale, N.J.: Lawrence Erlbaum Associates, 1978.

Lee, H. The effects of review questions and review passages on transfer skills. *Journal of Educational Research*, 1980, *73*, 330-336.

Mayer, R.E. Forward transfer of different reading strategies evoked by test-like events in mathematics text. *Journal of Educational Psychology*, 1975, *67*, 165-169.

Reynolds, R.C., Standiford, S.N., and Anderson, R.C. Distribution of reading time when questions are asked about a restricted category of text information. *Journal of Educational Psychology*, 1979, *71*, 183-190.

Reynolds, R.E., and Anderson, R.C. Influence of questions on the allocation of attention during reading. *Journal of Educational Psychology*, 1982, *74*, 623-633.

Rickards, J.P. Interaction of position and conceptual level of adjunct questions on immediate and delayed retention of text. *Journal of Educational Psychology*, 1976, *68*, 210-217.

Rickards, J.P. Adjunct postquestions in text: A critical review of methods and processes. *Review of Educational Research*, 1979, *49*, 181-196.

Rickards, J.P., Anderson, M.C., and McCormick, C.G. Processing effects of common-word and number questions inserted in reading material. *Journal of Educational Research*, 1976, *69*, 274-277.

Rickards, J.P., and Denner, P.R. Inserted questions as aids to reading text. *Instructional Science*, 1978, *7*, 313-346.

Rickards, J.P., and Denner, P.R. Depressive effects of underlining and adjunct questions on children's recall of text. *Instructional Science*, 1979, *8*, 81-90.

Rickards, J.P., and DiVesta, F.J. Type and frequency of questions in processing textual material. *Journal of Educational Psychology*, 1974, *66*, 354-362.

Rickards, J.P., and Hatcher, C.W. Interspersed meaningful learning questions as semantic cues for poor comprehenders. *Reading Research Quarterly*, 1978, 538-553.

Rothkopf, E.Z. Some theoretical and experimental approaches to problems in written instruction. In J.D. Krumboltz (Ed.), *Learning and the educational process.* Chicago: Rand McNally, 1965.

Sefkow, S.B., and Myers, J.L. Review effects of inserted questions on learning from prose. *American Educational Research Journal*, 1980, *17*, 435-447.

Shavelson, R.J., Berliner, D.C., Loeding, D., Porteus, A., and Stanton, G. Adjunct questions, mathemagenics and mathemathanics. Paper presented at the meeting of the American Psychological Association, New Orleans, 1974.

van Hout-Walters, B. *Improving learning from texts: An analysis of research articles.* Unpublished manuscript, University of Nijmegen, The Netherlands, 1980.

Watts, G., and Anderson, R.C. Effects of three types of inserted questions on learning from prose. *Journal of Educational Psychology*, 1971, *62*, 387-394.

Wilson, M.A. The processing strategies of average and below average readers answering factual and inferential questions on three equivalent passages. *Journal of Reading Behaviors*, 1979, *11*, 235-247.

APPENDIX

Example 1. Sample Text Passage and Questions

Rainfall is less than two inches per year in southern Mala. The soils in this area are either rocky or sandy. Vegatation covers only about two percent of the land of southern Mala. In the summertime, temperatures have been recorded as high as 135 degrees in southern Mala.

Verbatim Question (requiring only verbatim recall of part of single text sentences): How many inches of rain fall per year in southern Mala?

Conceptual Question (requiring the learner to abstract concepts from the whole paragraphs of text): What geographical term best describes southern Mala?

Adapted from Rickards, J.P. *Journal of Educational Psychology*, 1976, *68*, 210-217.

Example 2. Sample Text Passage and Questions

The southern area of Mala can best be described as a desert. Rainfall is less than two inches per year in southern Mala. The soils in the southern area of Mala are either rocky or sandy. In the summertime, temperatures have been recorded as high as 135 degrees in southern Mala.

Rote Learning or Fact Question (requiring literal recall of a specific detail from a text sentence): How many inches of rain fall per year in southern Mala?

Rote Learning of Ideas Question (requiring verbatim recall of the general idea presented in the topic sentence): What geographical term best describes southern Mala?

Meaningful Learning Question (requiring organization of specific details around a general idea): Why can it be said that southern Mala can best be described as a desert?

Adapted from Rickards, J.P. and DiVesta, F.J. *Journal of Educational Psychology*, 1974, *66*, 354-362.

Example 3. Sample Text Passage and Questions

The study of similarities and differences among the various species clearly demonstrates that whenever there is a behavioral resemblance, there is a resemblance of brains. The actual size of the brain is not in itself of great psychological significance, for several animals have brains much larger than man's. The human brain has an average weight of about three pounds compared with ten pounds for an elephant and fourteen pounds for a whale. The ratio of brain weight to body weight is much more significant psychologically than mere brain weight. This ratio is 1/50 for man, 1/500 for the elephant, and 1/10,000 for the whale.

Verbatim Question: Which of the following is an exact duplicate of one sentence in the passage you just read?
   a. Psychologically, the ratio of brain weight to body weight is much more significant than mere brain weight?
   b. The ratio of brain weight to body weight is much more significant psychologically than mere brain weight.
   c. The ratio of brain weight to body weight is much more significant than mere brain weight psychologically.

Inference Question: Which of the following is a correct inference based on a sentence in the paragraph you just read? An inference requires you to extend your thinking beyond the information contained in the passage.

a. Man is smarter than other animals because he has a lower ratio of brain weight to body weight.

b. Man is smarter than other animals because he has a higher ratio of body weight to brain weight.

c. Man is smarter than other animals because he has a higher ratio of brain weight to body weight.

Adapted from Freidman, F. and Rickards, J.P. *Journal of Educational Psychology*, 1981, *73*, 427-436.

Chapter 7

Graphic Organizers in Texts, Courseware, and Supplemental Materials

Parmalee Hawk, Nancy P. McLeod, and David H. Jonassen

Introduction

Books, during their history in education, have provided the conceptual and practical basis for instruction. From the variety of techniques available to instructors, the most often chosen procedure continues to be the lecture-discussion method with an accompanying textbook for the student to read:

> Didactic exposition has always constituted the core of any pedagogical system, and probably always will, because it is the only feasible and efficient method of transmitting large bodies of knowledge. (Ausubel, 1978, p. 547)

Thus, the elements present in the majority of classrooms are students, teachers, textbooks, and supplementary materials, plus lecture-discussion strategies. In this chapter, we consider each of these in turn, plus the technology and implications of *graphic organizers* for each of the components. (See Figure 7.1.)

The Student

"Perhaps the most basic thing that can be said about human memory, after a century of research, is that unless information is

Figure 7.1

Relationships Between Student,
Teacher, and Text Material

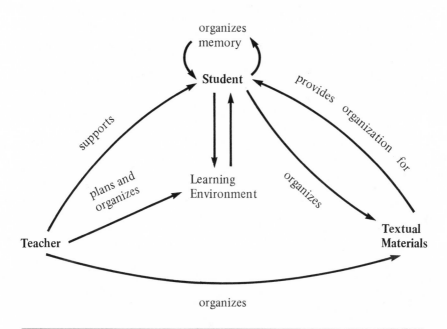

placed in a structured pattern, it is rapidly forgotten" (Bruner, 1960, p. 24). Children and adults perform better on a test when they are instructed to organize the material in some logical manner prior to the test (Hall and Pierce, 1974). Most memory researchers maintain that a person's ability to retrieve information is dependent on the organization imposed on the material during the time it is encoded into memory (the abstractive trace hypothesis).

> To organize is, to a considerable extent, to remember. Active and consistent categorization is sufficient to yield a high level of recall, and additional instructions to recall do not facilitate performance further (Ornstein, Trabasso, and Johnson-Laird, 1974, p. 1017).

What students of any age want and need from an instructor, a text, and a course is planning and organization (Balch, 1981). Humans possess an innate tendency to impose order on their environment. By reducing disorder and disorganization, we seek to structure our perceptions in such a way as to make them more meaningful, which in turn facilitates learning and problem-solving. It is our responsibility, therefore, as educators and educational materials producers to foster the internal organization of ideas in learners.

The Teacher

A successful teacher possesses a blend of interpersonal, strategic, and organizational skills that interact with local conditions. First, teachers must be concerned with each student's self-concept. A teacher who encourages a student to share his or her thoughts, who helps a student to become more sensitive to himself or herself and others, and who frequently directs reassuring and supportive comments to an individual or whole class is viewed by students and evaluators as an effective instructor.

Second, an effective teacher dedicates most of the class time to the subject content, making sure that students stay on task. In order to accomplish the first two, teachers need organizational skills. Teachers who are organized, who have a structured classroom, who have their presentations well-planned, and who consistently monitor student behavior are repeatedly considered highly effective and efficient teachers. This chapter, thus, focuses on the organization of instruction—specifically text-oriented instruction.

Textual Materials

Textbooks and other text-based materials provide the basis of instruction and the focus for instructional tasks in both schools and non-school settings. While computer display is gradually displacing print materials as the prominent focus of instruction, most of the same organizational and text design concerns remain.

Since most of this material, print and electronic, historically has been poorly designed and organized, a lot of recent attention has been given to instructional designs and strategies for text materials (Duffy and Waller, in press; Jonassen, 1982 (a, and this volume); Kolers, Wrolstad, and Bouma, 1979, 1980). This interest has led to the suggestion that text become the product of a team rather than the traditional subject matter expert as author, and that an instructional designer become an integral part of any text writing team (Sari and Reigeluth, 1982). This volume and the others are dedicated to designs for text construction.

But what about texts currently in use that lack adequate structure and organization? To overcome deficiencies, we need to create organized supplemental material. So, in the remainder of this chapter, we will present a strategy, *graphic organizers*, that has been developed to provide structure and organization to textbooks and the information they contain.

The Strategy: Graphic Organizers

Rationale

Getting the material to be learned into a structured, organized manner is the responsibility of the instructor. Jerome Bruner (1969) offered a theory of instruction to guide and help teachers, suggesting that students explore a subject, organize the principles of the subject, and relate the newly organized material to prior learning. This process he called *discovery learning*. The teacher's responsibility is to structure the learning situation so that discovery can take place. Bruner believes that any body of knowledge can be organized so that it can be transmitted efficiently and understood by students. The most efficacious presentation is one that is well-organized and simply stated.

Another cognitive psychologist influential in the evolving theory of instruction is David Ausubel (1963, 1978), who favors expository teaching (presenting, explaining, and discussing material), which entails *reception learning* (material presented to the learner in final form) as opposed to discovery learning. Ausubel believes that the most important function of a school is to impart

Figure 7.2

Graphic Outline
of Types of Organizers

* Advanced
     prior to material

* Verbal
     sentence
     paragraph
     question

* Abstract

   or

* Inclusive

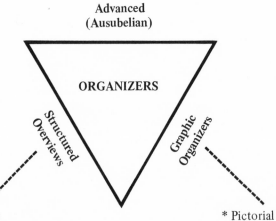

Advanced
(Ausubelian)

ORGANIZERS

Structured Overviews   Graphic Organizers

* Tree diagrams   * Pictorial

* Spatial relationships   * Key concepts

* Key vocabulary terms   * Graphic relations

subject information to students. The most recent research on schools supports his contention that the acquisition of subject content and skills takes precedence in schools. Because it is not possible for every student to discover every principle and skill, the presentation of the information in final form is most often preferred. Expository teaching is most beneficial with lecture and text material, and it must be presented in a structured, organized manner.

In order for reception learning to be meaningful to the learner, material needs to be related to knowledge already possessed by that learner. In order to do this, Ausubel advocates the use of advance organizers to aid in knowledge acquisition. Organizers represent introductory material presented in advance of instruction at a higher level of abstraction or inclusiveness than information presented in text or by the instructor. Organizers function as conceptual anchors or links between the material and the learner's knowledge structure. In essence, the instructor who uses organizers is stating explicitly where new information fits in relation to the general knowledge associated with the material or in relation to what the learner already knows (for an overview of the technology of advance organizers, see Jonassen, 1982b). Ausubel's organizers are normally in sentence, paragraph, question, or other prose forms, as indicated in the graphic overview of organizers in Figure 7.2. Organizers, as shown in the figure, can also be graphic.

Traditional Graphic Organizers: Structured Overviews

Because many students have difficulty reading and comprehending text, Barron (1969) modified Ausubel's concept of organizers by designing tree diagrams utilizing the new vocabulary in a passage. These diagrams, referred to as *structured overviews* or *graphic organizers*, used the spatial characteristics of diagrams to indicate the relationships and distances between key terms in a passage. This method for explicitly signaling the organization of important concepts in a learning task has been a widely recommended comprehension aid.

A recent meta-analysis of the 23 known studies (mostly theses) related to this form of graphic organizer (Moore and Readance, 1983) has concluded that:

- Post-organizers benefit learners more than advance.
- Graphic organizers benefit specific passages more than courses of study.
- Vocabulary learning is most positively affected.
- Effects sizes are much greater for university students, probably because they are better able to utilize the strategy properly.
- Teachers believe they improve their own performance when they construct graphic organizers.

Moore and Readance concluded that more research is needed, especially regarding how graphic organizers fit into the interaction depicted in Figure 7.1. Such explicit graphic statements of passage structure has the greatest effects on productive (elaborations/inferences) or transfer tasks over longer periods of time (retrieval) (Eggan, Kauchuk, and Kirk, 1978; Glynn and DiVesta, 1977; Moore and Readance, 1983). These conclusions are generally consistent with the results of advance-organizer research.

Graphic Organizers as Introduced in this Chapter

The form of the graphic organizer that we advocate evolved from both Ausubel's and Barron's work. Like verbal organizers, graphic organizers attempt to link new material to prior learning. Like structured overviews, the key concepts and terminology are graphically or spatially related. However, graphic organizers, such as the one in Figure 7.3, are more pictorial than structured overviews. Instructional objects may be represented along a continuum from verbal to pictorial (Wileman, 1980). Using this continuum as a point of comparison, then, advance organizers employ verbal symbols, structured overviews are graphic, and graphic organizers are pictorial/graphic.

To rationalize a more pictorial form of graphic organizer, we must consider both modality of perception (visual, auditory) and the form, code, or sign system used to present information. Graphic organizers contain both pictorial (iconic sign) and verbal (digital sign) information. The dual coding hypothesis (Paivio, 1971) contends that these different sign systems are processed in distinct ways and encoded in different parts of the brain. So

Figure 7.3

Final Form Graphic Organizer

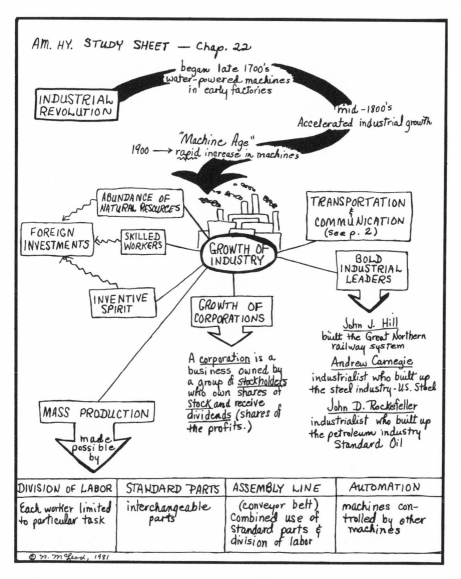

graphic organizers in text presumably will result in dual coding of information. The technique of illustrating concepts in diagrams, as in graphic organizers, has been shown to be especially helpful to learners of low verbal ability (Holliday, Brunner, and Donais, 1977). In other words, graphic organizers should be of most benefit to poor readers.

Next, we need to consider the processing modality of the learner. The pathway a person uses to integrate the external stimuli into the brain is called perceptual modality. This term is used to discuss an individual's preference to learn through a particular sensory system. One person may learn best through the visual pathway, another through the auditory channel. The use of more than one sensory pathway to transmit information to a person's brain is not a recent idea. Wolpert (1971) contended that:

> The rationale underlying the use of several modalities is that each sensory experience reinforces the other sensory experience and gives the learner a better understanding of what he has learned. (p. 640)

The graphic organizer is a technique that provides both digital and iconic signs (words and images) and is processed visually and combined with auditory processing (the lecture/discussion) of digital signs (words).

Constructing a Graphic Organizer

There are two kinds of graphic organizers, participatory and final form.

Participatory Organizers. On the participatory organizer, space is left for the student to fill in the definition of key terms and details (see Figure 7.4). Other forms of participation may include filling in values or identifying parts of a graph or chart, or sketching illustrations. Many teachers believe the use of fill-in organizers facilitates student learning, because the writing of the material involves another modality—the haptic (kinesthetic) sense. In responding to open-ended activities, learners are called upon to generate their own meaning from text or lecture material, a

Figure 7.4

Participatory Graphic Organizer

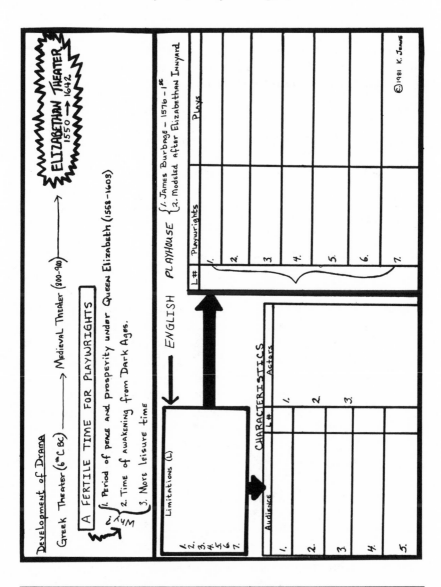

process that activates their prior knowledge structures in the interpretation of what they see or hear, resulting in deeper processing of material (see Jonassen's chapter on generative strategies).

Final Form Organizers. The final form organizer (see Figure 7.3, for example) has all the information already filled in on the organizer. The learners do not participate in their completion. There is no difference in the conceptual basis nor in the procedure for developing the two types. Which type is more appropriate is left to the teacher and his or her interpretation of the material.

A graphic organizer should cover one chapter of instructional program material. On occasion, graphic organizers that encompass the material of an entire unit (several chapters or several programs) may be developed.

We suggest the following ten steps for constructing graphic organizers:

Step 1. *Read the chapter, or work through the computer courseware, making lists of the terms, people, and concepts to be included on the graphic organizer.*

Step 2. *Analyze the lists.* Trim the initial lists until they contain only the most important terms and concepts found in the text. At this point, additional material not found in the text may be added to the lists for inclusion on the graphic organizer.

Step 3. *Check text and courseware or workbook activities.* This is to ensure that the presentation of existing published material is not replicated.

Step 4. *Block off new terms under the instructions "Define" as shown in Figure 7.5.* Before students can successfully study new material, they must have a working knowledge of the terms to be used. Blocking of terms is done to provide an additional visual cue. This visual compartmentalization provides students with a physical placement of the term on the page. This placement may later facilitate retrieval of information from memory. If terms are related in some way, they should be grouped accordingly (Figure 7.5), that is, by class. Also note in Figure 7.5 that the box sizes vary to accommodate the length of the definition.

Step 5. *Organize the concept into some graphic presentation.* In reviewing the concept material, some logical structure will evolve. This structure may take the form of chronological order (Figure 7.6), simple to complex, cause and effect (Figure 7.7), or a variety of other organization schemes (Figures 7.8a and 7.8b). The graphic presentation using arrows, brackets, figures, or charts stimulates student interest and gives the concept a reasonable, orderly form.

Step 6. *Repeat steps 4 and 5 for each concept to be studied in the chapter/program or unit.* The organizational structure for each concept will not necessarily be the same. Different material lends itself to different organization. Often, it is advisable to use different structures because the variations help sustain student interest.

Step 7. *Evaluate the rough draft.* Ask the following questions:

(a) Is the organizer visually appealing?

(b) Is the organizer self-explanatory? Are the directions clear?

(c) Is the information decided upon in Step 1 included on the organizer?

(d) Is the organizer concise?

Generally, information can be depicted on one or two pages. However, on rare occasions, a third page may be needed. More computer screen pages will be required.

Step 8. *Make the final copy for reproduction purposes.* The graphic organizer should be reproduced in hand-printed form. A graphics tablet is useful when including graphic organizers in computer courseware. Extensive use of this strategy has shown that typed or professionally-printed organizers are not as effective as those that are hand-lettered (thus the somewhat "rough" nature of the Figures in this chapter).

The heading of the final copy should include the chapter number, chapter title, and student identification blank. If the organizer has more than one page, the chapter number and page number should appear in the top right-hand corner of subsequent pages.

Step 9. *Supply the answers on the teacher's copy of the graphic organizer in a contrasting color of ink.*

Step 10. *Make a rough draft of the evaluation instrument to be used at the completion of the chapter/unit.* A graphic organizer does not limit testing to the knowledge level. In fact, the strategy is most appropriate for facilitating higher levels of thinking. The graphic organizer presents facts that are recalled by the student to answer knowledge-level questions; however, this knowledge is prerequisite to any kind of critical thinking required in answering higher-level questions.

The rough draft of the test is not put into final form at this time because it is essential that any predetermined test material be adjusted to reflect actual classroom activities, emphases, and time involvement. This test adjustment should be completed near the end of the chapter/unit.

A graphic organizer constructed in this fashion presents the important material not only in an orderly, structured manner but also in small, manageable pieces. A common error made by instructors in presenting new material is trying to include everything—every detail—as if it all were of equal importance. The process just described will aid instructors in determining what information is most important, and it provides an effective procedure to organize that information.

Using a Graphic Organizer

Once the graphic organizer is constructed, it is reproduced and presented as a handout sheet (discussion of organizers in courseware follows) to each student at the beginning of an instructional chapter/unit. When a graphic organizer is used initially, students

Figure 7.5

Participatory Graphic Organizer with Definition Blocks

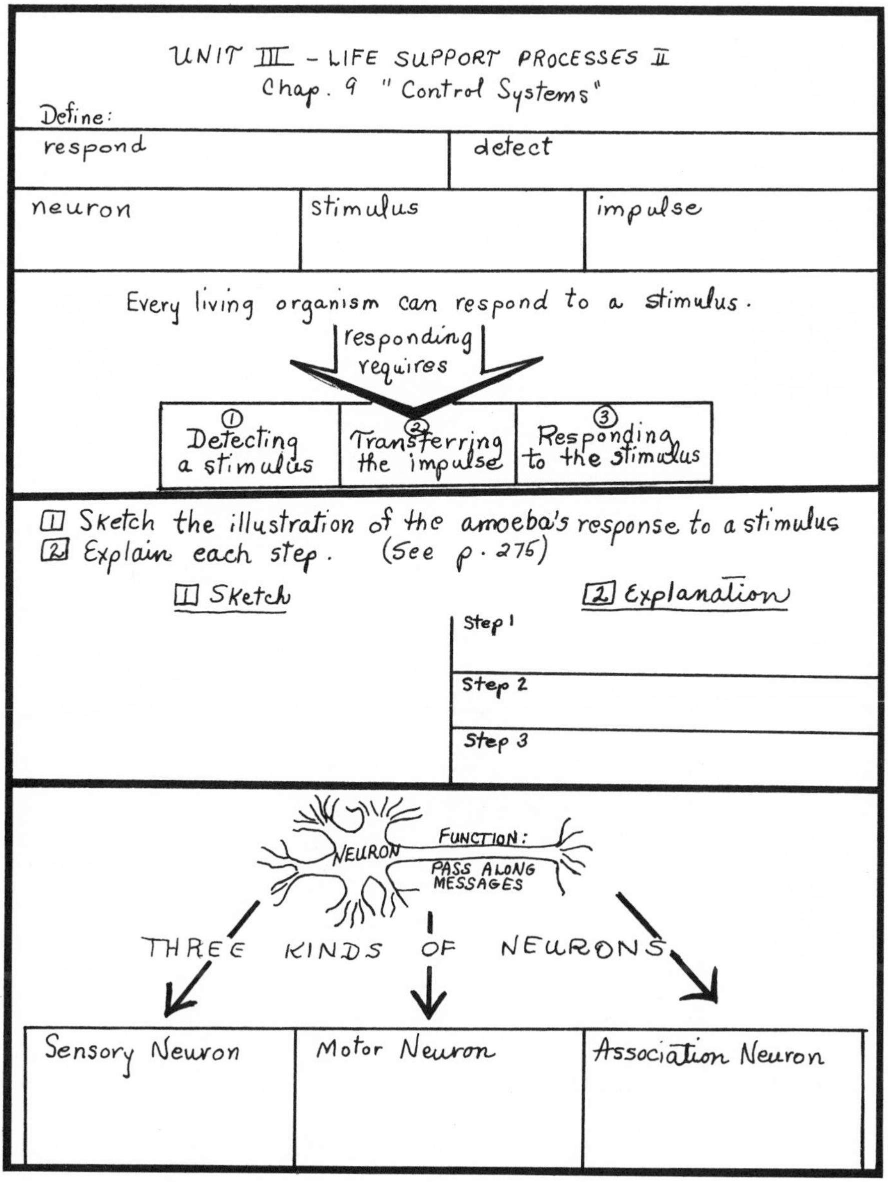

Figure 7.6

Graphic Organizer with Chronological Structure

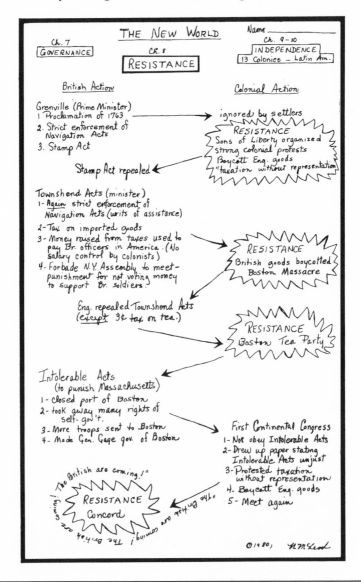

Figure 7.7

Graphic Organizer with Cause-Effect Structure

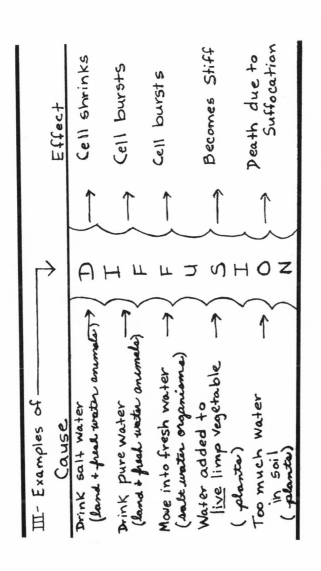

Figure 7.8a

Graphic Organizer with a Variety of Organizational Structures

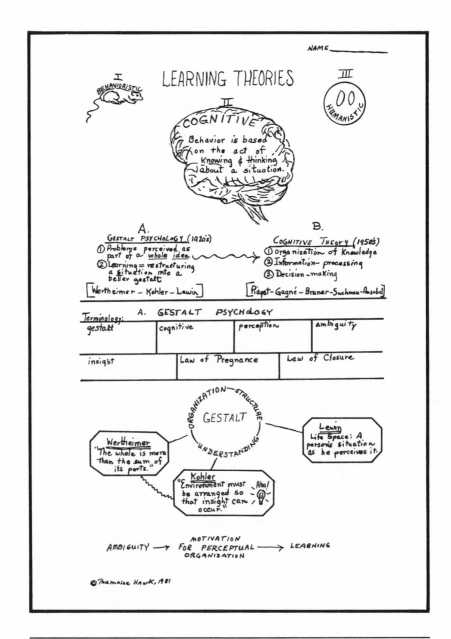

Figure 7.8b

Graphic Organizer with a Variety of Organizational Structures

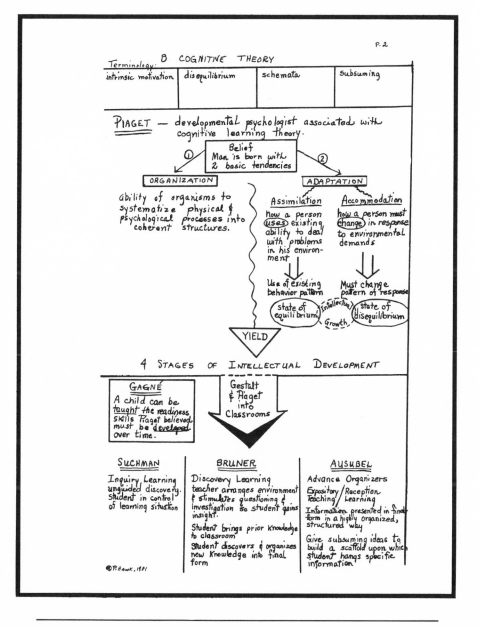

need to know what its purpose is and how to use it. Thus, the teacher informs the students that the organizer belongs to each of them and that it contains the framework of important facts and concepts for which they will be held responsible. Definitions will be written into the blocks and other important information filled in at appropriate times and places by each student.

Throughout the instruction related to the chapter, the instructor calls attention to specific points being discussed on the graphic organizer. During each class meeting, the teacher briefly reviews what has been taught on previous days and proceeds to the next section of material. This process, called integrative reconciliation by Ausubel, is essential to the success of any type of organizer. It not only provides review for the students, but also an opportunity for them to write down on their organizers any information they might have missed during previous class meetings.

Use of the graphic organizer does not change the pedagogy of the teacher. Whatever teaching styles the teacher uses—teaching centers, learner activities, field trips, etc.—are unaffected by using graphic organizers. Graphic organizers represent an adjunct instructional aid that provides additional structure to the material and provides advance notice of what is critical for the student to learn.

When a teacher uses a participatory type graphic organizer, he or she must check prior to any evaluation to see that the students' organizers do not contain misconceptions. The organizer ultimately provides the information to be learned in the final form. The process of providing feedback to the students on their organizers is usually done by the teacher during the chapter review session. This review session should be conducted during the class meeting prior to the test and should focus on the organizer, that is, let the organizer provide the structure for the review. Teachers should urge students to keep their graphic organizers for future review and study. This is particularly advantageous in settings where comprehensive exams are administered, since that type of an exam requires high-level integration and relation of ideas. The organizers will also function as effective retrieval cues.

Effectiveness of Graphic Organizers

The *traditional concept of graphic organizer* (structured overview) that reflects the structure of a chapter or passage in advance of that chapter or passage has received lukewarm support at best (Barron, 1980; Moore and Readance, 1983). The effectiveness of the organizers will be a function largely of how they are used. Recent research using traditional graphic organizers or structured overview has suggested that:

- Graphic organizers should not reflect the overall structure of the passage but should present a top-level structure (e.g., comparison-contrast) that is different from the passage structure, requiring learners to reorganize the material (Alvermann, 1981). For a further discussion of passage structure, see Meyer's chapter in this volume, especially Table 3.1.

- Graphic organizers are best at integrating multi-theme passages rather than single themes, so graphic organizers should be used at the chapter or unit level or higher (Dana, 1980).

- If you ask knowledge-level, detailed questions on your tests, do not expect graphic organizers to work. *They are contexts for assimilating ideas—not cues for specific facts.*

In studies using *graphic organizers, as represented in this chapter*, at the junior and senior high school levels, students who used graphic organizers scored significantly higher on 100-point teacher-made achievement tests than students who did not use graphic organizers (Hawk, McLeod, and Jeane, 1981). A sixth-month study, completed recently, conducted with 455 seventh graders enrolled in 14 classes of life science, reports that the seven classes who used graphic organizers scored significantly higher (p. .001) on a science achievement test than did students who did not receive organizers. This study showed graphic organizers to be beneficial for immediate achievement, one chapter at a time, and for retention, seven chapters over a five-month time span. Research also has been conducted using graphic organizers at the college level (Hawk and Jeane, 1983). In a study with 75 students in an Introduction to Geography course, findings showed a significant increase in the grades of students who used graphic organizers when compared to students who did not use graphic organizers. Other studies have indicated significant effects on immediate recall but no advantage for retention and no effects for either recall or transfer (Jonassen and Hawk, 1983).

Research results from this pictorial form of graphic organizer indicate that:

- Graphic organizers do facilitate retention of information, especially for younger learners, rather than older, skilled learners.
- Immediate recall appears to have been more consistently affected than longer-term retention of information, though recent support for the latter has been produced.
- Graphic organizers do provide cues for recall of specific facts and detail, whereas structured overviews do not, perhaps because pictures provide more lasting cues, as predicted by the encoding specificity hypothesis (Tulving and Thompson, 1973).
- Graphic organizers do facilitate retention of information.

It is important to note that all of these studies were carried out in the classroom under normal school conditions. While naturalistic studies of this sort lend ecological validity, experimental control of myriad intervening variables suffers. Therefore, empirical validation is incomplete. The use of graphic organizers is grounded in the most widely accepted theories in educational psychology and has now received some empirical support. We have concluded that graphic organizers, as described in this chapter, are capable of signaling content structure and key concepts as well as acting as retrieval cues; however, additional research is needed.

Probably the most constructive advantage of this process of preparing teachers to construct and use graphic organizers that we have found is that the teachers have become more involved and more systematic in their presentation of materials. They have consistently reported perceiving themselves as more organized and thorough in their preparation. Those benefits doubtlessly generalize to other areas of teaching, resulting in more productive teachers.

Future Research

A necessary direction for research to take concerns the probability of task treatment interactions. Transfer tasks and those requiring integration and synthesis of content structure should be more susceptible to organizer influence (Mayer, 1979). Yet, immediate recall has generated the largest effect sizes. The design of the organizer and the manner in which learners participate will surely affect transfer learning. The more generative the nature of student participation, the more likely it is that transfer and higher level learning will be affected. Having students construct their own graphic organizers or structured overviews after reading or studying has produced consistent support (Barron, 1980; Barron and Schwartz, 1979; Moore and Readance, 1983). Students who map content are forced to organize and interrelate key concepts in their own way, which understandably leads to greater comprehension. A potentially successful compromise may result from providing students with a structural map or graphic organizer of the content which identifies the links and having the learners fill in the concepts that define each node on the map, such as in "Ed Syke: the Frame Game," which accompanies Clifford's (1981) textbook. Rather than setting off vocabulary blocks in your organizer, include the blocks in the organizer diagram. A rule-of-thumb at this point is to design graphic organizers to be as participative as possible.

The use of graphic organizers must also be considered in light of individual differences. Advanced (verbal) organizers tend to benefit older, more skilled learners more than younger, less able learners (Hartley and Davies, 1976). In a comparison of verbal and graphic organizers, better readers benefited more from verbal organizers, while graphic organizers produced no differential effects (Jonassen and Hawk, 1983). The assumptions about the bi-modal advantages of graphic organizers bear scrutiny. For example, contrary to predicted advantages for low-verbal, high-spatial learners, diagrams (presumably processed similarly to graphic organizers, at least with respect to modality and sign type) seemed to help high-verbals (Winn and Holliday, 1982). Perhaps the organizational and integrative advantages of all organizers will accrue most to those who naturally do those things better.

Graphic Organizers and Electronic Text

Graphic organizers can potentially play a more important role in the design of computer courseware. Since computer-assisted instruction replaces student-teacher interaction with student-computer interaction, most of the functions of the teacher must be provided by the program, if the courseware is to achieve the stand-alone status most designers seek. Most courseware specializes in stimulating learner involvement and providing feedback, but neglects the organizational, structural, and preparatory functions that the teacher provides. Very little courseware that we have reviewed supplies any pre-instructional strategies. When we consider the restricted access structures available in most computer courses, advance organization becomes paramount. In print text, the reader can skim, preview, review, take notes, underline, and outline a passage—all strategies that help generate meaning. If a learner wishes to review a previous concept as a point of comparison to new information, he or she merely pages back to the location which may have been noted earlier. Since most computer courseware prescribes a sequence of learning which prevents the learner from reviewing or moving ahead without restarting an instructional sequence, most of the previously-mentioned strategies are precluded. While these restrictions in courseware design are changing, current, state-of-the-art software could use some pre-instructional structuring.

The use of graphic organizers with computer courseware can take two forms. A print version can be developed and provided for the student using the procedures and processes already outlined. That is, work through the software, noting terms and concepts. Analyze the lists, check the types of responses requested by the program, block the terms, and organize them into a graphic representation. These print organizers can then be previewed before working through a program and reviewed afterward. They may be included with a disk version of the program by using the plastic disk sleeves and a loose-leaf binder, providing a learning package that is shelvable and distributable. Related workbook activities also may be included in such a package.

If we are designing courseware or are able to amend existing courseware, we will want to include graphic organizers in the

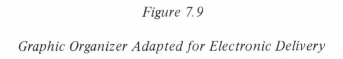

Figure 7.9

Graphic Organizer Adapted for Electronic Delivery

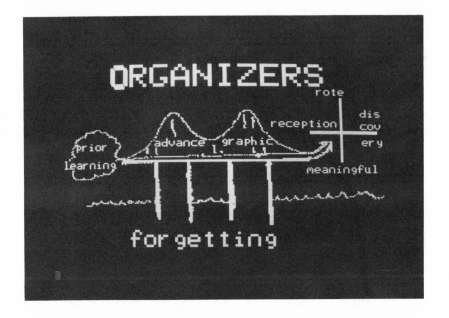

program. A graphics tablet is useful in constructing the organizer for screen display but by no means essential, especially for designs such as Figure 7.7 (shown earlier). Figure 7.9 was produced using a graphics tablet and is indicative of the type of display you can produce. Because of the limitations in a screen size and resolution, considerably less information can be reproduced at any time on the screen than can be put on paper. This will necessitate breaking up your print organizers into two or more sequential displays which should be linked for easy paging back and forth.

Graphic organizers can be placed in courseware in a variety of places with different access points. One option is to use the graphic organizer as a title page and create an auto-boot to make it the first screen. The same subroutine could be appended to the end of the program to automatically display the organizer for review. If your courseware is menu-driven, you may want to make the organizer the first option on the menu, calling it "overview" or "begin." At the end of chapters or units in the program, when the menu is displayed automatically, a prompt that recommends that the learner access the organizer might help. Whatever placement technique you build in, remember that organizers need to be periodically reviewed in order to accommodate the newly-presented information into it. In addition to adding graphic appeal to your software, graphic organizers should make them instructionally more effective.

Summary

A critical factor in student learning is the nature of teaching, including: (1) positive interpersonal skills, and (2) planning and organizational skills. This chapter is concerned with the second component most often associated with teacher effectiveness—organization.

The organizational process suggested is the graphic organizer, an expository teaching procedure that evolved from Ausubel's advance organizers and is an expansion of Barron's structured overviews. The graphic organizer enables the teacher to present efficiently subject material that requires moderate to large amounts of reading, either from text or in computer courseware. It is a strategy that provides structure to material and advance notice to the students of what is critical for them to learn.

There are two kinds of graphic organizers, participatory and final form. There is no definitive theoretical foundation for either type, although, when the teacher uses a participatory organizer, he or she must be aware that students have filled in their organizer, because ultimately the information should be in final form.

There are ten steps to follow in constructing a graphic organizer. When followed, a structural map of important concepts is available to aid students in learning and retrieving important material. The construction process requires training of the teachers and an investment of their time. The available research indicates, however, that it is time well spent.

References

Alvermann, D.E. The compensatory effects of graphic organizer instruction on text structure. Paper presented at the annual meeting of the American Educational Research Association, Los Angeles, April, 1981.

Ausubel, D.P. *The psychology of meaningful verbal learning.* New York: Grune and Stratton, 1963.

Ausubel, D.P. *Educational psychology: A cognitive view.* New York: Holt, Rinehart, and Winston, 1978.

Balch, P.M. The most effective instruction—what do students really want? *Kappa Delta Pi Record*, 1981, *17*(4), 107-108.

Barron, R.F. The use of vocabulary as an advance organizer. In H.L. Herber and P.L. Sanders (Eds.), *Research in reading in the content areas: First year report.* Syracuse University: Reading and Language Arts Center, 1969.

Barron, R.F. A systematic research procedure, organizers, and overviews: An historical perspective. Paper presented at the annual meeting of the National Reading Conference, San Diego, CA, December, 1980.

Barron, R.F., and Schwartz, R.M. Teacher acquisition of semantic relationships about reading instruction. Paper presented at the annual meeting of the National Reading Conference, San Antonio, TX, December, 1979.

Bruner, J. *The process of education.* Cambridge: Harvard University Press, 1960.

Bruner, J. *Toward a theory of instruction.* New York: Norton, 1969.

Clifford, M.M. *Practicing educational psychology.* Boston: Houghton Mifflin, 1981.

Dana, C.M. *The effect of using a graphic advance organizer before, during, and after reading on the comprehension of written text: A study conducted with sixth-grade students.* Madison: University of Wisconsin Research and Development Center for Individualized Schooling, 1980.

Duffy, T., and Waller, R. (Eds.) *Designing useable texts.* New York: Academic Press, in press.

Eggan, P.D., Kauchuk, D., and Kirk, S. The effect of hierarchical cues on the learning of concepts from prose materials. *Journal of Experimental Education*, 1978, *46*(4), 7-10.

Glynn, S.M., and DiVesta, F.J. Outline and hierarchical organization as aids for study and retrieval. *Journal of Educational Psychology*, 1977, *60*, 89-95.

Hall, J.W., and Pierce, J.W. Recognition and recall by children and adults as a function of variations in memory coding instructions. *Memory and Cognition*, 1974, *2*, 585-590.

Hartley, J., and Davies, I.K. Pre-instructional strategies: The role of pretests, behavioral objectives, overviews, and advance organizers. *Review of Educational Research*, 1976, *46*, 239-265.

Hawk, P., and Jeane, G. A study of graphic organizers with college level geography students. *Capstone Journal of Education*, 1983, *4*(1), 53-63.

Hawk, P. McLeod, N.P., and Jeane, K.L. Graphic organizers in initial learning and retention. *Carolina Journal of Educational Research*, 1981, *2*(2), 70-78.

Holliday, W.G., Brunner, L.L., and Donais, E.L. Differential cognitive and affective responses to flow diagrams. *Journal of Research in Science Teaching*, 1977, *14*, 129-138.

Jonassen, D.H. *Technology of text: Principles for structuring, designing, and displaying text.* Englewood Cliffs, NJ: Educational Technology Publications, 1982(a).

Jonassen, D.H. Advance organizers in text. In D.H. Jonassen (Ed.), *The Technology of text: Principles for structuring, designing, and displaying text.* Englewood Cliffs, NJ: Educational Technology Publications, 1982(b).

Jonassen, D.H., and Hawk, P. Using graphic organizers in instruction. *Information Design Journal*, 1983, *4*(1), 58-68.

Kolers, P.A., Wrolstad, M.E., and Bouma, H. *Processing of visible language*, Vol. 1. New York: Plenum Press, 1979.

Kolers, P.A., Wrolstad, M.E., and Bouma, H. *Processing of visible language*, Vol. 2. New York: Plenum Press, 1980.

Mayer, R.E. Can advance organizers influence meaningful learning? *Review of Educational Research*, 1979, *49*, 371-383.

Moore, D.W., and Readance, J.E. Meta-analysis of graphic organizer research. Paper presented at the annual meeting of the American Educational Research Association, Montreal, Quebec, Canada, April 11-15, 1983.

Ornstein, P.A., Trabasso, T, and Johnson-Laird, P.N. To organize is to remember. *Journal of Experimental Psychology*, 1974, *103*, 1014-1018.

Paivio, A. *Imagery and verbal processes.* New York: Holt, Rinehart, and Winston, 1971.

Sari, I.F., and Reigeluth, C.M. Writing and evaluating textbooks: Contributors from instructional theory. In D.H. Jonassen (Ed.), *The technology of text: Principles for structuring, designing, and displaying text.* Englewood Cliffs, NJ: Educational Technology Publications, 1982.

Tulving, E., and Thompson, D.M. Encoding specificity and retrieval processes in episodic memory. *Psychological Review*, 1973, *80*(5), 352-373.

Wileman, R.E. *Exercises in visual thinking.* New York: Hastings House, 1980.

Winn, W., and Holliday, W. Design principles for diagrams and charts. In D.H. Jonassen (Ed.), *The technology of text: Principles for structuring, designing, and displaying text.* Englewood Cliffs, NJ: Educational Technology Publications, 1982.

Wolpert, E.M. Modality and reading: A perspective. *Reading Teacher*, 1971, *14* 640-648.

Section IV

Providing Access to Information in Text

Introduction

The chapters in this section of the book describe text design techniques that function as *access structures* (Waller, 1979). Text, in its myriad forms and displays, performs a variety of roles based upon the information needs of the reader. That is, people access textual materials in different ways depending upon what they need to know. For instance, you search an airline schedule differently than you study a geometry textbook, because you have different information needs related to each. A frequent criticism of much of the research on reading relates to the way readers access text. Only in reading research, claims Macdonald-Ross (1979), do people sit down, read straight through a text, put it down, and ignore it until such time as they are required to recall the information they read. Rather, we access and read text or portions of text in a non-sequential manner in order to fill information needs. Text, however, is arranged sequentially. Text structure can provide the better reader with some clues regarding the location of information, but accessing text still requires some sequential searching. Therefore, text designers include a variety of typographic supplements to straight text that facilitate access to specific information in the text. As Waller explained in his chapter in Volume One of this series, "Using Typography to Improve Access and Understanding," these typographic access structures may improve either *global accessibility* using contents lists, summaries, and indexes, or *local accessibility* using headings, cuing, and layout.

187

The *access function* of typography shares some commonality with the text structuring techniques, such as signaling, discussed in the second section of this book, since they also function as *macro-punctuation* (Waller, 1982). That is, typography can also provide an overview of subject matter, lending a visual structure to an argument—the text as diagram notion that Waller discusses in his chapter in Section II.

While most of the techniques discussed in this section possess that dual role (as access structures and macro-punctuation), they have been combined here because of their access functions. The first three chapters are concerned with providing local accessibility to text information, that is, visually cuing the location of specific information contained in text. The most local accessibility is provided by *typographic cuing* (e.g., underlining, capital letters, flashing text), which uses typographic means for highlighting small units of text. Marginal information and headings are used to describe the information contained in larger units of text (e.g., paragraphs). Finally, in this section, we will look at the most common techniques for providing global access to text—contents lists and indexes. In addition to providing the most frequently used access points to text, they also function to structure the arguments presented in text and provide an overview of their organization.

As is evidenced by the title of the first chapter in this section, access structures exert some text control over the comprehension process. Since their major functions are to structure arguments and provide access to content, they can be classified as means for providing text control of content and process, according to our two-dimensional classification scheme. While deciding to access text is based upon learner needs and is, therefore, learner-controlled, access structures function to guide or control that access. Therefore, the purpose of the access function is text control of the information acquisition process. The macro-punctuation function, on the other hand, represents text control of content. It is the access and therefore the process concerns that are most considered by these chapters.

Typographic Cues in Text

In the first chapter in this section, Shawn M. Glynn, Bruce K. Britton, and Murray H. Tillman examine the practice of typographic cuing from a *human information processing* perspective. They justify the use of typographic cuing systems based upon limitations in working memory and the need to organize information in order to get it permanently encoded into long-term memory. The first is more of a process concern and the second a content concern. Typographic cuing is compared with verbal cuing systems, such as the signaling suggested by Meyer and Armbruster and Anderson in the second section of the book. The authors explain and exemplify the purposes for using typographic cues based upon their earlier information processing analysis. Finally, guidelines for using specific cuing systems are provided for text designers. The authors have provided us with a useful set of heuristics for using typographic cues in text that are easily comprehensible yet theory-based.

Marginalia

Philippe C. Duchastel again bridges C.P. Snow's two worlds by bringing his unique, scientific-artistic perspective to a discussion of how to best use margins in text. Concentrating on the use of marginal notes and marginal glossaries, he summarizes their access functions. The chapter also compares the value of marginal notes to typographic cuing discussed in the previous chapter and the value of a running, marginal glossary to an end-of-text glossary. Finally, he discusses the implications of marginalia for the design of print vs. electronic text. Perhaps most importantly, exemplary use of marginalia is made throughout the chapter.

Headings in Text

At a more global level of accessibility, headings provide access to larger chunks of text as well as performing more of a summarizing role. James Hartley and I describe the functions of headings in print and then electronic text. We further break down the subject by sequentially analyzing the *encoding* and comprehension functions of headings, followed by their *access functions*. This chapter could have appeared in the second section of the book, because of the structural effects of the encoding function of headings, but it was arbitrarily placed here because of their access functions, which are equally important and generally more reliable. In the chapter, we review the research related to the use of headings, such as their form (question vs. statement) and reader awareness of their purpose. We provide some guidelines for writing good headings in print text.

Because of screen limitations and the way people access electronic text, headings are bound to function differently than in print text. For instance, online access normally entails menus or tree structures to get at specific units of text, so the headings may play a more specific access role. Yet, headings play an entirely different role in computer courseware. We conclude with some simple heuristics on structuring and presenting headings in electronic text.

Contents Lists and Indexes

Every non-fiction text has a table of contents and an index, right? These global access tools are the key summaries of the organization of content in text. They are also the primary, initial *access points* in text, the places you go first to find out what a text is about. Yet, variations in quality are probably more evident in contents lists and especially indexes than any other part of a book, journal, or electronic text file. Kieth C. Wright draws on his extensive information design experience to provide us with a chapter full of instructions on how to structure, design, and display contents lists and indexes for print and electronic delivery. The most distinctive feature of the chapter derives from his ability to distill at least two books' worth of information into a chapter of readable text. The descriptions of the arrangements of indexes is especially useful to the uninitiated (which I assume that many readers of this volume are). And since indexing is probably one of the most arcane and esoteric academic pursuits, that is a significant accomplishment.

Summary

Information, in order to be useful, must be *found*. And, once found, it must be made memorable. That requires both an *emphasis plan* and attempts to relate it to the rest of the text being presented as well as to what the reader already knows. These are all primary access functions. They describe the purpose of the techniques reviewed in this section of the book.

Chapter 8

Typographical Cues in Text:
Management of the Reader's Attention

Shawn M. Glynn, Bruce K. Britton, and Murray H. Tillman

Overview

The comprehension of instructional text can be a cognitively demanding task. One of the arguments to be made in this chapter is that the author or courseware designer who plans potential typographical cues during manuscript production or computer software programming can often improve the comprehensibility of the final product. Typographical cues help readers to identify, organize, and interpret the most important content in a text or instructional program.

The author's purposes and the suggested cues for achieving them can be annotated directly on the manuscript, or they can be listed separately. In courseware, where the author has more control and responsibility, they need to be included in the program. If the author's purposes and suggestions are good ones, then the editorial and production staff of the publishing house should give them serious consideration. The editorial and production staff should not consider the author's input an intrusion into their domain of expertise—after all, it is the author who knows which content is the most important and which content is the most difficult to comprehend. If the staff takes the author's goals and suggestions into consideration, the resulting typographical design will satisfy both functional and aesthetic requirements.

At the same time, the author should realize that many suggested cues, even some that are fairly good ones, will be modified by the publishing house staff for a variety of production considerations, not the least of which is cost. Frequently, the cue redesigned by the publishing house staff will achieve the author's purpose with greater effectiveness and cost efficiency. The courseware designer who also programs has more authority and is less likely to be edited, except when working for a large publisher that revises the structure and appearance of software to comply with a product line. Other electronic text systems (e.g., teletext) generally have fairly rigid formulas for the extent and style of screen highlighting.

Another argument to be made in this chapter is that typographical cues should be used sparingly in a text. It is not necessary, or even desirable, for the author to cue every important idea in the text; it is only necessary for the author to cue some of the important ideas, just enough to help the reader judge the relative importance of the ideas that have not been cued. If typographical cues are used excessively, the purpose of the cues will be defeated. The cues will not only fail to increase the comprehensibility of the text, but in all likelihood, they will decrease it.

Cognitive Demands of Text Comprehension

The comprehension of instructional text is a formidable task because the reader must be able to call upon large bodies of relevant prior knowledge and *concurrently* carry out a variety of component comprehension processes. These component comprehension processes include: recognizing the words in the text and retrieving their meanings, parsing the sentences those words are in, identifying the important ideas in the text, organizing those ideas, and integrating those ideas with prior knowledge (for empirical studies of some of these processes, see Carpenter and Just, 1977; Thibadeau, Just, and Carpenter, 1982).

When these processes are carried out successfully, they produce the cognitive structures that are the desired end-products of text comprehension. On the other hand, when one or more of these processes are not carried out successfully, comprehension breaks down. When comprehension breaks down, the reader either fails to understand certain text ideas or misunderstands them.

Working Memory

The component comprehension processes and the relevant prior knowledge both compete for limited space in the reader's *working memory* system. In this system, information that is currently being attended to is maintained temporarily through the process of rehearsal. While maintaining this information, the reader operates on it in different ways (e.g., constructing images, performing computations, making associations, etc.) and integrates it with other bits of related knowledge that have been retrieved from the reader's *long-term memory* system. In a sense, then, the reader's working memory functions as a workbench. The novel products of the operations and integrations performed on this workbench are stored in the reader's long-term memory system.

Readers cope with the limited capacities of their working memories in a number of ways. One of the ways they cope is by allocating their attention differentially to text information, giving the most important information the most attention. Another way they cope is by organizing information into hierarchically-related conceptual categories.

Text Structure

Selective attention is possible, and indeed quite effective, because the ideas in an instructional text vary considerably in their importance. Authors intend for readers to attach more importance to some ideas than to others. Usually, the sequence of ideas within sections of a text approximates a *hierarchical organization*, with the most important ideas being at the top of the hierarchy.

Headings are particularly important items of information because they summarize in a few words the major themes of a text. Depending upon the author's purpose, however, any of the following items could be particularly important within a given section of text: principles, definitions, facts, and conclusions. The items that are low on the hierarchy are less important only in the sense that they are intended to support and extend the reader's comprehension of the items at the top.

Readers' Decision Criteria

Once readers have some insight into the hierarchical organization of the text, they allocate their attention differentially to ideas, with the most important ideas receiving the most attention. On the basis of cues provided directly or indirectly by the text author, readers formulate *decision criteria*, which they use to judge the relative importance of the text ideas that have not been cued by the author. Basically, the criteria help readers to decode the hierarchical organization of the text and to internalize it. The readers' criteria may be vague upon entering the text, but they become more sharply defined as the readers progress through the text and encounter the author's cues.

Management of the Reader's Attention

By cuing the reader's attention throughout the text, the author can help the reader to identify, organize, and interpret the most important ideas in a text. It is not necessary for the author to cue every important idea in the text. This would be counterproductive, in fact, for reasons that will be discussed later. It is only necessary for the author to cue some of the important ideas, just enough to help the reader construct and validate effective decision criteria.

Readers clearly find cues helpful during initial reading and later review sessions. In fact, when authors fail to provide cues, readers generate their own (see the generative processing chapter in the first section of this book). In a survey conducted by Fowler and Barker (1974) of 200 randomly selected used textbooks for sale in a college bookstore, about 92 percent were found to contain cues applied by the students who previously owned the texts. These cues included margin notes, underlining, highlighting in various colors, and boxes. The students also applied punctuation marks such as asterisks, parentheses, brackets, and exclamation points to their texts.

Since some readers have trouble identifying information of major importance, particularly on their first reading of a text, it is essential that authors provide readers with optimal cues. Readers can then supplement these optimal cues with cues of their own if they wish.

Text authors have two kinds of cuing systems at their disposal: *verbal* and *typographical*. In general, the author's intent in using either kind of cuing system is to alert the reader to something out of the ordinary. Usually, the author wants to point out a piece or body of information that is special and that should be distinguished from the other information in the immediate context.

Verbal Cuing Systems

Verbal cuing systems include short signal phrases that pave the way for important items of information. "It is noteworthy that," "The most important point is that," and "The bottom line is that" are examples of such phrases. Verbal cuing systems also include more formal devices such as adjunct questions, instructional objectives, advance organizers, outlines, headings, and margin notes. For information about the use and effects of these verbal cuing systems, please refer to the chapters by Meyer; Armbruster and Anderson; Linder and Rickards; Waller; Hartley and Jonassen; and Duchastel.

Typographical Cuing Systems

Typographical cuing systems are nonverbal devices for attracting and focusing the reader's attention. In print, *italic* type and **boldface** type are the most popular typographical cuing systems; in typewritten manuscripts, their use is denoted by underlining and wavy underlining, respectively. Color, arrows, and boxes are other examples of typographical cuing systems.

For present purposes, *white space* will also be considered a typographical cuing system. White space or vertical typography (Hartley, 1980) are terms used to describe horizontal or vertical blank space on a page, such as the blank space found in the margins, the blank space found between sections, and the blank space used to set off tables, figures, and boxed supporting materials such as biographies and detailed examples. If the author is working on a microcomputer and the final product will be in the form of a diskette rather than a book, then *inverse* or *flashing* can also be used as a typographical cue. Items of information can be made to flash on and off in order to attract attention. (In Volume One of *Technology of Text*, the design of electronic text is discussed in detail in chapters by Jonassen, Coke, Merrill, and Reynolds; see also the chapters by Eisele, and Lancaster and Warner, this volume).

There are few strict conventions for using typographical cues in an instructional text. In fact, unconventionality in the design and use of typographical cues is often the rule rather than the exception. If readers become too familiar with a cue, they adapt to its presence and the cue loses some of its power to attract the readers' attention. For this reason, new variations of familiar cues are developed every day. For example, imagine a children's book about the solar system that uses rocketships as pointers instead of the more conventional arrows. As this example suggests, the design and use of typographical cues can be an art as well as a technology.

Typographical cuing systems are frequently combined with verbal cuing systems. For example, headings are effective, in part, because of their spatial arrangement: center, side, and paragraph headings help the reader to decode the hierarchical organization of the ideas in the text.

Purposes for Using Typographical Cues

The use of typographical cues in a text frequently involves extra printing costs. These costs are justified, however, if the cues make it easier for readers to comprehend the meaning of the text.

Three of the major purposes for using typographical cues in instructional text are: (1) *to set off important items of information and enhance their recall,* (2) *to set off relatively large chunks of supporting information from the main body of the text,* and (3) *to simplify interpretation of complex tables and figures.* These three purposes and some cues for achieving them will be discussed in detail in the sections that follow.

There are, of course, purposes for using typographical cues in instructional text other than those listed above. For example, a graphic artist who wishes to decorate a text and make it more marketable might use color in a creative way. The present discussion, however, will be restricted to the purposes that directly enhance the readers' comprehension of the text content.

Identifying Important Information and Enhancing Its Recall

Headings summarize major themes and help readers decode the hierarchical structure of an instructional text. Because of their importance, headings are usually cued by means of boldface and type size.

Within a section of text, italics are conventionally used to indicate: the titles of books, periodicals, plays, motion pictures, long poems, long musical compositions, paintings, drawings, and sculpture; the actual names of particular ships, aircraft, and spaceships; foreign words and phrases; and words that are being considered as words (e.g., How many vowels does *typography* contain?). These conventional uses are discussed in detail in writing manuals such as Turabian's (1973) *A Manual for Writers.*

If a text is lengthy and densely packed with information, the author should also consider using italics (underlining) to cue some of the most important terms, facts, and principles within each section. Presumably, when readers encounter cued information, they pause and process this information extensively. The cued information can be processed extensively by rehearsing it, by integrating it with relevant prior knowledge, and by constructing visual images and verbal mnemonics for it. The readers probably carry the products of processing in their working memories for a time, using them to comprehend information that builds upon the cued information.

It is well-established that the provision of a cue such as underlining increases the learning of cued information (for literature reviews, see Glynn, 1978; Hartley, Bartlett, and Branthwaite, 1980). When study time is fixed, the cued information acquires its advantage at the expense of the noncued information (Fowler and Barker, 1974; Glynn and Di Vesta, 1979; Hershberger and Terry, 1965). The latter finding is consistent with the notion of a limited-capacity working memory.

Isolating a Chunk of Information from the Main Body of the Text

Frequently, the author seeks to extend the reader's comprehension of the main ideas in an instructional text by including supporting information such as examples, anecdotes, and biographies. However, if information of this kind is more than a paragraph or two, and if it is included in the text proper, it can cause some readers to lose track of the author's main line of thought. A common solution is to treat the information as a figure, using white space and a box to set it off from the main body of the text (see Figure 8.1). The boxed chunk of information will still be available to support the author's main ideas; however, it will now be less likely to interfere with the reader's comprehension of those ideas.

Another use for a box is to set off a list of important items that is too long to italicize. A boxed list of important principles, questions, etc., will get the attention that it deserves.

Simplify Interpretation of Complex Tables and Figures

Many readers experience difficulty when attempting to interpret a complex table, graph, diagram, flow chart, or map. Authors can help readers by using typographical cues that focus the readers' attention on the critical components of the stimulus array. For example, in the case of a table of numbers, authors could recommend that the most important numbers are identified by boldface or by an arrow (see Figure 8.2). Or, in the case of a graph or map, authors could recommend that shading or color be used to break the figure into its component parts and simplify its interpretation (see Figure 8.3).

Figure 8.1

BOX C ***Diagnostic picture of a student***
with minimal brain dysfunction

Larry M. Age: 9 years, 3 months
Full-scale IQ, 78; verbal IQ, 81; performance IQ, 79

Areas of minimal brain dysfunction:

1. Larry has not established a preferred hand. Sometimes he will switch from one hand to the other during the middle of a task. He is not proficient with either hand.

2. When asked to copy a triangle, Larry inverts the figure so that the base of the triangle is at the top (other reproductions are mirror images or reversals).

3. Drawing and writing are very poor. Letter reversals are common.

4. When presented with the outline of a picture, Larry cannot fill in the details. Often he even fails to recognize the picture on the basis of the outline.

5. Intersensory studies suggest a great deal of inadequacy. Specifically, Larry cannot feel an object (for example, a triangle) with his eyes blindfolded and then describe what he is feeling. He is unable to translate materials presented by touch into a concept. .

A detailed example set off from the main body of the text by white space and a box. (From Hudgins, Phye, Schau, Theisen, Ames, and Ames, 1983, p. 139. Reproduced by permission of the publisher, F.E. Peacock Publishers, Inc., Itasca, Illinois.)

Figure 8.2

EXAMPLE

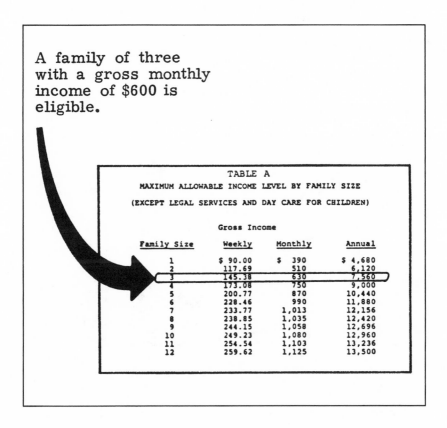

A family of three
with a gross monthly
income of $600 is
eligible.

TABLE A

MAXIMUM ALLOWABLE INCOME LEVEL BY FAMILY SIZE

(EXCEPT LEGAL SERVICES AND DAY CARE FOR CHILDREN)

Family Size	Gross Income		
	Weekly	Monthly	Annual
1	$ 90.00	$ 390	$ 4,680
2	117.69	510	6,120
3	145.38	630	7,560
4	173.08	750	9,000
5	200.77	870	10,440
6	228.46	990	11,880
7	233.77	1,013	12,156
8	238.85	1,035	12,420
9	244.15	1,058	12,696
10	249.23	1,080	12,960
11	254.54	1,103	13,236
12	259.62	1,125	13,500

In this example from a training manual, an arrow focuses the readers'
attention on the numbers under consideration. (From *Training Guide for
Title XX Eligibility Determination*, Omni Systems, Inc. Under a contract with
the Florida Department of Health and Rehabilitative Services, 1981, p. III-52.
Copyright © 1981 by Omni Systems, Inc. Reprinted with permission.)

Figure 8.3

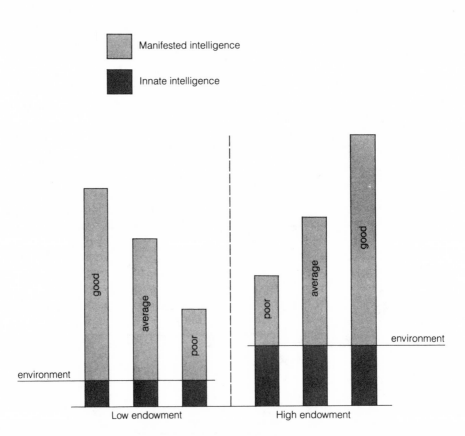

The Stern Hypothesis (individuals with different potentials for intellectual development—low and high genetic endowment—can manifest poor, average, or good intelligence as a function of environmental forces).

The shading in the above graph breaks the figure into its component parts. (From *Psychology for Teachers*, by Guy R. Lefrancois © 1982 by Wadsworth, Inc. Reprinted by permission of Wadsworth Publishing Company, Belmont, California 94002.)

Guidelines for Using Typographical Cues

Authors can ensure that their typographical cues achieve their intended purposes if they keep in mind three guidelines. First, use a cue only when its purpose is perfectly clear. Second, use a cue sparingly. And third, avoid a complicated cue. Each of these guidelines will be considered separately.

Use a Cue Only When Its Purpose Is Perfectly Clear

If authors are not sure that readers will understand the purpose of a particular typographical cue, then the purpose should be explained to readers before the cue is used. In order for the cue to facilitate comprehension, readers must know how to attend to it and how to use it. Readers should not have to guess the reason why information is being cued. Consider the example in Figure 8.4.

In the example in Figure 8.4, the purpose of the cue should have been explained before the experimental material was presented. If a reader fails to quickly comprehend a cue, then the author fails too, since the author's primary goal in using a cue is to improve the comprehensibility of the text.

Use a Cue Sparingly

It would be counterproductive for the author to cue every important item of information in a text. Since readers' conserve their limited processing capacities by being selective in their allocation of attention, excessive use of a particular cue could tax their processing capacities and cause their comprehension to break down.

Typographical cues should be used only when they can make a significant improvement in the comprehensibility of the text and only when the improvement cannot be easily obtained through the use of verbal cues alone. Thus, if typographical cues are used at all in a text, they should be used sparingly. The overuse of a typographical cue defeats its purpose.

Figure 8.4

A psychology student who participated in a selective-attention experiment heard the following words over his headphones:

> Vegetable gardeners all agree that *Family camping* homegrown vegetables *has attracted millions* are much better *of Americans.* than those purchased in supermarkets. *It was* Although it's fun to *once a summertime activity* grow vegetables in your *only for* backyard, you should not forget that *the young.* gardening requires a good deal of *Now both young people and* labor and time. *older, retired adults* Do not allow your springtime *camp on a year-round basis.* enthusiasm to get out *For the beginning camper,* of hand. *the best way* You might find that *to start is by borrowing or renting equipment.* you have bit off more vegetables *That way you can see if you* than you can chew. *like it without spending too much money.*

The student heard, alternately, the italicized words in his right ear and the non-italicized words in his left. After he heard all the words, he was instructed to recall only the words he heard in his right ear.

In the above example, the purpose of the italics should have been explained before the material was presented.

Italics and boldface. Frequently, authors overuse italics and boldface. There are two reasons for this. First, the presence of these cues can be easily indicated on a manuscript by using a straight underline and a wavy underline, respectively. And, second, some authors mistakenly believe that every important item of information should be cued. It is important to remember that the effectiveness of these cues decreases as the frequency of their use increases. For example, it would be clearly pointless to apply italics to more than 50 percent of the information in a selection of instructional text. Note that in Figure 8.5, where almost all of the words have been italicized, it is the *nonitalicized* words that perceptually stand out.

Italics or boldface should not be applied to too much content, or the recall advantage produced by these cues will be lost. As a rough rule-of-thumb, it is recommended that the application of these cues be limited to ten percent of the content on a page. This figure is based on Glynn and Di Vesta's (1979) study where a cue applied to about ten percent of the content in a text produced a recall advantage of 25 percent.

Color, boxes, and white space. A decision to use italics or boldface is much less expensive than a decision to use color. The addition of even one color to an instructional text can significantly increase the cost of publishing it. Boxes combined with white space can be expensive too when they increase the number of pages in a text and the time needed to design those pages. In general, if authors want to suggest the use of color and boxes to a publisher, they should have excellent reasons why they expect the use of these cues to improve the readers' comprehension of the text. Authors should also be prepared to explain to the publisher why other cues—particularly less expensive ones—cannot be used instead.

Avoid a Complicated Cue

When cues are complicated, they frequently fail to help readers identify, organize, or interpret important text ideas. One way to complicate a cue is to combine it with a variety of other cues. For example, Hershberger and Terry (1965) distinguished five categor-

Figure 8.5

JEAN PIAGET (1896-1980)

Jean Piaget, *was born in 1896, in Neuchatel, Switzerland, and by the age of twenty-one had received his doctorate in biological science at the University of Lausanne. Shortly thereafter, he became interested in psychology and went to Paris where he studied at the Sorbonne and worked in Alfred Binet's intellectual assessment laboratory. After completing his work in Paris, he accepted a position as director of research at the Jean Jacques Rousseau Institute in Geneva. Piaget wrote numerous books on intellectual development including* The Origins of Intelligence in Children (1952) *and* The Construction of Reality in the Child (1954). *He called his approach* genetic epistemology. *Epistemology is the study of how people acquire knowledge. Piaget remained in Geneva and, even in his eighties, maintained his remarkable level of scientific productivity.*

In the above biography, where most of the words have been italicized, it is the nonitalicized words that perceptually stand out.

ies of text content by combinations of underlining, variations in the size of type, and variations in color of ink. They found that the effect on recall of this combination of cues was equivalent to that of no cues at all. They concluded: "It seems likely that the complexity of the typography may befuddle the reader sufficiently to offset an advantage derived from the cuing" (p. 59).

Another way to complicate a cue is to apply it to too much information. For example, in Figure 8.6, the pencil cues are intended to help the reader identify relationships among major topics and chunks of subordinate information. This "graphic organizer" is difficult to comprehend, however, because it contains so much information, and because the information it contains is positioned irregularly. Many readers might not be willing or able to expend the time and effort required to comprehend the relationships among the topics and the subordinate information. In this instance, it might have been better for the author to split up the information, presenting it in two figures rather than one.

Summary

The comprehension of instructional text is a formidable task because component comprehension processes and relevant prior knowledge both compete for limited space in the readers' working memory systems. Readers cope with the limited capacities of their working memories by selecting the most important information for extensive processing and by organizing this information into hierarchically-related conceptual categories.

Typographical cues can help readers to identify, organize, and interpret the most important content in a text. The typographical cues discussed in this chapter included italics, boldface, arrows, color, boxes, and white space. These cues can be used to set off important items of information and enhance their recall, to set off relatively large chunks of supporting information from the main body of the text, and to simplify the interpretation of complex tables and figures.

Authors were encouraged to keep in mind three guidelines when planning their typographical cues: (1) use a cue only when its

Figure 8.6

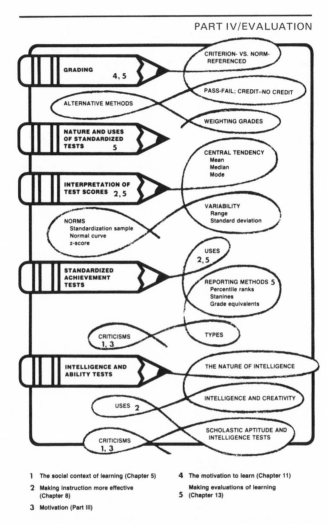

The amount of information in this figure, and the irregular positioning of the information, undermine the effectiveness of this "graphic organizer." (From Seifert, 1983, p. 424. Copyright © 1983 by Houghton Mifflin Company. Reprinted by permission.)

purpose is perfectly clear, (2) use a cue sparingly, and (3) avoid a complicated cue. These guidelines were discussed and illustrated.

References

Carpenter, P.A., and Just, M.A. Integrative processes in comprehension. In D. LaBerge and S.J. Samuels (Eds.), *Basic processes in reading.* Hillsdale, NJ: Lawrence Erlbaum Associates, 1977.

Fowler, R.L., and Barker, A.S. Effectiveness of highlighting for retention of text material. *Journal of Applied Psychology*, 1974, *59*, 358-364.

Glynn, S.M. Capturing readers' attention by means of typographical cuing strategies. *Educational Technology*, 1978, *18*(11), 7-12.

Glynn, S.M., and Di Vesta, F.J. Control of prose processing via instructional and typographical cues. *Journal of Educational Psychology*, 1979, *71*, 595-603.

Hartley, J. Spatial cues in text. *Visible Language*, 1980, *14*, 62-79.

Hartley, J., Bartlett, S., and Branthwaite, A. Underlining can make a difference—sometimes. *Journal of Educational Research*, 1980, *73*, 218-224.

Hershberger, W.A., and Terry, D.F. Typographical cuing in conventional and programmed texts. *Journal of Applied Psychology*, 1965, *40*, 55-60.

Hudgins, B.B., Phye, G.D., Schau, C.G., Theisen, G.L., Ames, C., and Ames, R. *Educational psychology.* Itasca, IL: Peacock, 1983.

Lefrancois, G.R. *Psychology for teaching* (4th Ed.). Belmont, CA: Wadsworth Publishing Company, 1982.

Seifert, K. *Educational psychology.* Boston: Houghton Mifflin, 1983.

Thibadeau, R., Just, M.A., and Carpenter, P.A. A model of the time course and content of reading. *Cognitive Science*, 1982, *6*, 157-203.

Training guide for Title XX eligibility determination. Florida Department of Health and Rehabilitative Services, July 1981.

Turabian, K.L. *A manual for writers.* (4th Ed.). Chicago: University of Chicago Press, 1973.

Chapter 9

Marginalia

Philippe C. Duchastel

1. Introduction

Marginalia: elements appearing in the margin, e.g., marginal notes and key definitions

Marginalia are text elements that appear in a book's margin. The marginal notes that run along the left-hand side of this page, for instance, are a form of marginalia. Key terms and technical definitions that appear alongside a text (see Figure 9.2) are also marginalia.

At first glance, one might assume that there is not much to be said about marginalia, and that they have rather secondary value in terms of a technology of text. This, I believe not to be the case.

A role in text processing

A role in text design

On the contrary, I believe that marginalia can play an important role for the student in processing a text, and furthermore that marginalia can play a part in the ongoing evolution of text design itself. These two aspects of marginalia are what this chapter will deal with.

2. Context

Not new

Marginalia are not new to the world of text design (see Figure 9.1), nor are they

Figure 9.1

159

De diſſectione partium corporis
humani, Liber ſecundus.

Prœmium.

Væ partes in humano corpore ſolidiores & exte= *Quid dictum*
riores erant,quæ´q; ipſam machinam potiſſimum *libro ſuperio-*
conſtituebant,ſatis iam explicatæ nobis videntur *re.*
libro ſuperiore.Sequitur,vt internas percurramus *Quid ſecun=*
quæ maximè pertinent ad vitam, & ad earum fa= *do libro dice-*
cultatum quibus incolumes viuimus conſeruatio= *tur.*
nem.In quo(quemadmodū inſtituimus) ſubſtan=
tia,ſitus,forma,numerus,cōnexio,earum partium
de quibus ſermo futurus eſt,breuiter exponenda.
Ad quod munus ſtatim aggrediemur,ſi pauca prius de inſtituto ac de iudi=
cio noſtro ſubiunxerimus.Q uanq̄ enim hic noſter in ſcribendo ac diſſecan
do labor,complures non modo in anatomes cognitione,ſed etiam in Gale *Purgatio ad-*
ni ſententiæ interpretatione iuuare poterit:tamen interdū veremur,ne qui= *nerſus eos,*
buſdam nomen hoc anatomicum ſit inuiſum : mirentúrq; in ea diſſectione *anatomes in-*
tantum nos operæ & temporis ponere: cum alioqui ab ijs qui nummorum *dagationem*
potius quàm artis aucupio dant operam facile negligatur.Atq; ita nobis oc *minus probat*
curritur,dum quærunt:ſatiſne conſtanter facere videamur,qui cum corpo=
ris humani partiū longiori indagationi ſtudemus , quæ magis ſunt vtilia,
imprimíſq; neceſſaria prætermittimus:ſatius eſſe affirmantes,eius rei cogni
tionem ſicco (vt aiūt)pede percurrere,in qua alia certa,alia incerta eſſe di=
cunt:alia probabilia,alia minus probabilia inueniri.Q uod certe dictum(ſi
qui tamen inueniantur qui hoc dicant) hominum mihi videtur parū con=
ſyderate loquentium:atq; in maximis rebus errantium. Q uibus vellem ſa=
tis cognita eſſet noſtra ſententia.Non enim(vt inquit quidā) ſūmus ij quo
rum vagetur animus errore : & incertis rebus demus operam,neque habea=
mus vnq̄ quod ſequamur . Q uid enim eſt,per deos,abſoluta anatomes co= *Anatomesco-*
gnitione optabilius? quid præſtantius?quid Medico vtilius?quid Chirurgo *gnitionis vti*
dignius? quá qui expetunt & adſequuntur,tundemū Medici ac Chirurgi di *litas & digni*
cendi ſunt:nec quicq̄ eſt aliud,quod Medicum aut Chirurgum magis com *tas.*
mendet,quàm ipſa anatome.Cuius ſtudium qui vituperat,haud ſanè intelli
go quidnam ſit quod laudādum in huiuſmodi viris aut artibus putet.Nam
ſiue oblectatio quæritur animi:quid æquè delectat,aut ingenuos animos af
ficit,atq; conditoris noſtri,in hoc microcoſmo procreando, diligenter per=
ſcrutatum artificium?ſiue perfectio,& abſoluta quædam ars petitur : certe
abſq; anatome,Medicina aut ars nō erit, aut nulla omnino.Itaque neceſſe
eſt,qui hæc omnia in quibus tantopere inſudamus, neglexerit:artem quoq;
ipſam,cuius humani corporis anatome ſine controuerſia fundamentum eſt

L.ij.

The use of marginal notes in a text published in 1545.

but still novel

new to the more specific design of textbooks (as illustrated by Figure 8.13 in the first volume in this series [p. 189], which represents a use of marginal notes in a 1923 textbook). However, they are generally considered novel, innovative even, in today's textbooks. Even if their use is still relatively infrequent, some would consider them to be a trend of the future (although some would undoubtedly also say that they are merely a catchy new trend, a notion which I hope to dispel in this chapter).

Marginalia can be defined too broadly

Marginalia are a class of elements that are ordinarily defined by their presence alongside the main body of the text itself (I shall, however, be elaborating an extended meaning of marginalia in Section 5 of this chapter). They thus include not only notes and technical terms, but also any other elements that can be positioned in the margin of a book, such as headings can be (see Hartley and Jonassen, this volume), or even section numbers, illustrations, running heads, and so on. Already, we see that the notion of marginalia as operationally defined in terms of a book's margin is overly broad, and could thus lead to ambiguity.

Our focus will be
—marginal notes
—running glossary

In this chapter, I shall concentrate only on two important forms of marginalia: marginal notes and key definitions in the form of a running glossary. In so doing, I shall consider these elements in terms of their book design context, by contrasting them with functional alternatives

... in the context
of the form/function
interplay

such as traditional summaries, footnotes, standard glossaries, and highlighting techniques. We will be dealing here in fact with the form/function interplay of text design, a topic which will be expanded in Section 5 of the chapter.

3. Marginal Notes

Infrequently used

The use of marginal notes is not at all widespread in modern textbooks (one could even say that they are positively rare), hence their connotation with novelty in design. Their instructional design potential was first brought to my own attention through an analysis made by Robert H. Waller (1977) at the Open University in Britain. Waller also provides a good illustration of marginal notes in Figure 7.8 in the first volume of this series (p. 153), an illustration taken from an Open University text.

Illustrated by
Waller

Two functions:
—access
—summary

Marginal notes serve two important text-processing functions for the student (Duchastel and Chen, 1980):

- they facilitate access;
- they summarize.

Indeed, one can view them as elaborated labels that facilitate access to the ideas discussed at length in the text, and one can view them as a running summary that replaces the end-of-chapter summary traditionally included in textbooks.

In general: they
facilitate text/
reader interaction

These two functions of marginal notes are embedded within the more global function of text design, namely to structure the text so as to facilitate the interaction between reader and text (this complex interaction being the juncture at which learning either optimally takes place or becomes problematic—a theme developed in my previous contribution of this series; see Duchastel, 1982).

within the context of elaborating a cognitive structure

Both the accessing and summarizing functions of marginal notes can be understood in terms of a conception of learning centered on the elaboration of cognitive structures (see Jonassen, 1982, for such an analysis of learning). It is only a figure of speech to say that a student *derives* knowledge of a topic from a text. In reality, a student *constructs* a representation of the topic in his or her mind through interaction with the resource which is the text (this is a rather involved topic which would take us too far afield if elaborated here, but which I hope to analyze in a further contribution to this series of volumes). In effect, then, at any point while processing a text, the student is assessing the relationship and value of encountered information in terms of his or her evolving representation of the topic.

Their access role: to characterize the related textual contents

Access devices of a certain kind, including marginal notes, play the specific role of identifying and characterizing the textual contents to which they are related. This specific role is what Waller, in the preceding series volume (1982), has identified as local accessibility, in contrast to global accessibility, which emphasizes a previewing/overviewing function (p. 144).

Access devices of this sort assist the reader in engaging in the following type on ongoing and automatic questioning, as he or she processes the text: "What will be treated in this paragraph? How does it fit into my current representation of the topic?" (See Brown, Campione, and Day, 1981, for an elaboration of this theme.)

in terms of
relevance and fit

Their role as
summary: helping
sort out the
essential

The summarizing function, on the other hand, responds to a different type of question involved in the same ongoing learning process: "What is essential here and what is secondary? How can I synthesize the elements presented here in a compact way which will not over-load my limited-capacity working mem-ory?" Learning meaningful information is in effect a process of summarizing, i.e., of constructing an underlying hierarchy of relevance and concentrating one's attention on the upper levels of that hierarchy (see Meyer, this volume).

An analysis such as the preceding one reveals how closely tied to learning mechanisms can be such textual design features as marginal notes (among other elements, of course).

How do they
compare
...

There remains the question of how marginal notes compare in terms of facilitation to alternate design options such as headings, typographical high-lighting, or end-of-chapter summaries.

l—to headings?

In their access device role, marginal notes can be viewed quite simply as

*They are richer
(more precise
access)*

elaborated sub-headings (in terms of local accessibility). Their role here overlaps with the role of headings, but goes further: it extends downward the level of detail involved in the access function, or to put it differently, it enriches the access structure operative in the book. Just as headings will enrich the access structure of a book initially devoid of headings (straight, continuous prose), so, too, marginal notes can enrich the access structure of a book involving only headings.

*2—to typographical
highlighting?*

No better?

A comparison with typographical highlighting of the kind employed in Chapters 8 and 17 of the preceding volume of this series is a more complex one. Typographical highlighting would seem to do all that marginal notes do: identifying, marking the relevance of, and synthesizing the information contained in a paragraph. Furthermore, from a publishing perspective, highlighting is much more economical of space, and hence of manufacturing cost as well (this last factor may indeed be the principal reason for the continued rarity of marginal notes in modern textbooks).

*Yes, more
articulate*

The main drawback of typographical highlighting (compared to marginal notes) lies in it being slightly less articulate: a summary composed of sentences simply lifted from the paragraph and concatenated (which is the functional equivalent of the student focusing on the highlighted sentences) is generally, although not always, less articulate than a rewritten summary (the functional equivalent of marginal notes).

All in all, whether one favors highlighting or marginal notes is a difficult design choice, subject not only to cost factors, but also surely to the nature of the material and to purely aesthetic factors (within the context of the art of book design). I would conclude that marginal notes are functionally better than highlighting, but perhaps not too much better, and therefore their use must be constrained by the particular publishing situation at hand. I realize this seems rather equivocal, but there are simply too many factors and trade-offs involved in any publishing situation for a general principle or prescription to be formulated in this matter.

generally, but perhaps not always

3—to an end-of-chapter summary

Marginal notes constitute a running summary of the text and are equivalent in these terms with an end-of-chapter summary. Their value over the latter is quite straightforward: they serve both a summarizing function (as the traditional summary does) and an accessing one as well (which the traditional summary does not).

Summary and access

The value of such comparisons is better analysis, not necessarily strong prescriptions for design

I take this opportunity to make a general point concerning design feature comparisons of the kind I have been making in the above section. I see the value of such comparisons mainly in helping us further analyze the characteristics of particular features (marginal notes in this case). I do not see this analysis-by-comparison being strongly informative in design decision-making. At a certain level, design remains an informed art (a skill) concerned with optimally combining design features into a total product. Trade-offs are constant (as we have seen in discussing highlighting), but one design solution need not preclude the utilization of multiple features in one book. Again prescription is of limited value in this context.

In concluding on marginal notes, I should just mention that we have been dealing here with one kind of notes: those, as illustrated in this chapter, which can have accessing and summarizing functions. What we have not been dealing with are footnotes, as traditionally conceived, even when such footnotes may occupy the margins of a book (as in the case illustrated by Waller in Figure 7.7 in the preceding volume of this series [p. 152]).

Marginal notes ≠
footnotes

4. Running Glossary

Technical term
definitions

We come now to the second form of marginalia to be considered in this chapter: the presence alongside a text of the definitions of the major technical terms which it contains (see Figure 9.2).

How does a running
glossary compare to
end-of-book
glossaries?

A running glossary is little more than a conventional glossary distributed throughout the book rather than collected as one element, as is customary, at the end of the book (or sometimes at the *beginning* of a book). We need to consid-

Figure 9.2

have a cone-shaped tip at their "business" end. (See Color Plate 12.)

Both the rods and cones contain chemicals that are very sensitive to light. When a beam of light strikes a rod, it causes the *bleaching* or breakdown of a chemical called **rhodopsin**, or visual purple (the Greek word *rhod* means "rose-colored"). In ways that we still don't entirely understand, this bleaching action causes the rod to respond electrically. This visual input message passes up through the lower centers of your brain and eventually reaches the occipital lobe (see Fig. 7.5). At this point, you become "consciously aware" that you have actually seen something.

Your rods are *color-blind*. They "see" the world in blacks and whites no matter how colorful the world actually is. Your rods respond much like a "fast but grainy" black and white film you might use in your camera responds. That is, they need less light to operate than the cones do, but they give a less detailed picture of the world than the colorful view provided by your cones.

For the most part, the rods are located in the outer reaches or **periphery** of the retina. There are about 120 million rods in each of your eyes.

Your cones contain several types of photosensitive chemicals which break down when struck by light waves. This chemical reaction triggers off an electrical response in your cones which passes along the optic nerve until it reaches the visual input area in your occipital lobes.

The cones are your *color receptors*. There are a few cones in the periphery of the retina, but most of the cones are bunched together in the center of your retina near the fovea. The fovea contains no rods at all, *only cones*. There are between six and seven million cones in each of your eyes.

Since your cones are located *primarily* in the center of your retina, this is the part of your eye that is *most sensitive to color*.

When you look at something straight on, the light waves coming from that object strike your fovea and stimulate the cones, giving you clear color vision. When the same object is at the outer edges (periphery) of your vision, the light waves from the object strike primarily the rods in the periphery of the retina. Since the rods are color-blind, you will see anything that appears at the edges of your visual world as lacking or very weak in color.

Structure of the Retina

If you were called upon to design the eyes for a NASA robot, the odds are that you would never think of making the robot's retina like yours.

Retina (RETT-tin-ah). The photo-sensitive inner surface of your eye. Contains the visual receptor organs.

Sclera (SKLAIR-ah). The tough outer layer of the eyeball.

Choroid membrane (KOR-oid). The dark, middle layer of the eyeball that contains blood vessels and pigment cells.

Fovea (FOE-vee-ah). The tiny "pit" or depression right at the center of your retina that contains only cones, and where your vision is at its clearest and sharpest.

Blind spot. That small part of the retina near the fovea where blood vessels and nerve pathways enter and exit from inside the eyeball. The blind spot contains no visual receptors.

Rods. The needle-shaped visual receptors that mediate black and white vision.

Cones. The visual receptors that mediate color vision. They also respond to black and white visual stimuli. Located primarily in and near the fovea.

Rhodopsin (ro-DOP-sin). From the Greek word meaning "reddish-purple." We get our words "rose" and "rhododendron" from this same Greek source. Rhodopsin is a purple-colored, photo-sensitive pigment found in the rods.

Periphery (pair-IF-er-ee). From the Greek word meaning "to move around the outside." The periphery is the outer edge of any closed surface, such as a circle.

Peripheral nervous system (pair-IF-er-al, or purr-RIF-er-al). Those neurons that lie at the outer edge of your body, such as your skin receptors.

To begin with, your retina has *ten distinct layers*, with the rods and cones making up the *back layer*. The tips of your rods and cones—which contain the photosensitive chemicals that react to light—are actually pointed *away* from the outside world. For light to strike your rods and cones, it must first pass through *all nine other layers of your retina* (see Color Plate 15).

The receptor cells in your *skin* are a part of your **peripheral nervous system**. That is, they are nerve cells which lie outside your brain and spinal cord. Since the retina evolved directly from the brain, however, it is considered by most authorities to be a part of the central nervous system.

The top layers of your retina contain a great many "large neurons" that are very similar in structure to those found in your cortex. These "large neurons" begin processing visual information right in the retina, before sending messages along to your visual cortex (in the occipital lobes at the back of your brain). Your retina is the *only receptor organ* in your body that processes inputs so extensively before sending them along to the cortex.

The top layers of your retina also contain the tiny blood vessels that serve the retina. Surprisingly enough, light must pass through these "large neurons" and the blood vessels before it can stimulate the rods and cones. Fortunately,

171
The Eye

The use of a running glossary in a contemporary textbook. From *Understanding Human Behavior*, 4th edition, by James McConnell. Copyright © 1983. Used with the permission of Holt, Rinehart, and Winston.

er the advantages and disadvantages of such an arrangement, and I shall therefore proceed by briefly examining a few forms of end-of-book glossaries before returning to the concept of running glossary itself.

The standard glossary: a specialized dictionary

A standard glossary is fairly straightforward. It simply contains a list of the technical terms contained in the book, along with a summary definition of each term. It is in fact a selective and specialized dictionary applicable to the book contents.

Its function: recovery of the meaning of a term

in an easy way

The main function of a glossary is to enable a student to easily recover the meaning of a term encountered earlier but which is forgotten or unclear at the moment. Without a glossary, the student would have to use the index and then attempt to recover the term's meaning through a possibly cumbersome search through the pages listed for that index term. A glossary is quick, easy, and hence useful.

Also, a summarizing function

A secondary advantage of a glossary lies in the conciseness of its definitions. Each entry is in fact a summary statement of the essential features of the meaning of the term being defined. The advantage of summary statements for the process of learning, which was discussed in the section on marginal notes, applies here as well. The conception of learning as synthesis is applicable not only to large bodies of knowledge, but to particular elements (including technical concepts) as well.

Some variants:
—the glossary-index

There are different forms of end-of-chapter glossaries. A variant to the traditional glossary is the glossary-index combination (see Figure 9.3). Yet another form is what can be considered a large-scale glossary in the form of a specialized mini-encyclopedia meant to accompany a textbook. Being extensive, the glossary in this case is bound separately from the text itself, and the text and encyclopedia together form a learning resource package for the student. This approach is exemplified in the textbook package titled *Economics '73-'74,* which was published by the Dushkin Group in the early 1970s.

—the encyclopedia

as part of a learning resource package

—the relational glossary

A further form of glossary, exciting for its potential, is the one developed by Zimmer (1981) at the Open University in Britain. This form of glossary, illustrated in Figure 9.4, is called a relational glossary. Its principal attribute is the fact that it spells outs the major logical relationships which connect each concept to the others in the topic. This type of glossary emphasizes the connectivity of the technical concepts in a field. In Figure 9.4, those concepts printed in bold type within an entry appear themselves elsewhere as entries in the glossary.

which spells out the logical relationships between entries

and has been found to be very useful

Such a relational glossary goes far beyond the traditional glossary both in the effort and time needed for its preparation and in its usefulness to the student (Zimmer, 1981, provides supportive data from an educational evaluation of this particular glossary).

Figure 9.3

dies, stamping, 176, 186, 348, 352. *The plates with which covers are stamped.*
   copy preparation for, 352
   embossing, 177
digitized codes, 48; *see also* coded tape
dimensions, indication of, 128–29
direct positives, 121–22
disc-operated machines, 35, 47–52
display type, 36, 40, 58, 77, 79–81, 82, 270. *Type used for headings, etc. Usually 18 pt. or larger.*
distortion of type, 58, 89
distributing type, 38. *Returning individual type characters or matrixes to their storage place after use.*
distribution, book,
   commercial analysis, 219–20
   problems, 11
distributor bar, 40, 41
doctor blade, 145
double column,
   penalty for, 194
doubledot halftone, 114
double-fold imposition, 166
double spread, 253, 291–92, 300–01, 304–07. *Two facing pages.*
dropout (highlight) halftone, 114, 115
dropped initials, 269
drum, 54
dry mounting, 127. *Adhering by means of a pressure-sensitive wax.*
dry offset (letterset), 133. *Offset printing in which the offset blanket is inked by letterpress.*
dull-coated paper, 121, 154. *Coated paper on which the surface has a matte rather than a glossy finish; see also* coated paper.
dummies, 61, 129–30, 293–95. *Blank sheets of the same size as the book pages (or jacket, etc.), on which rough proofs and sketches are placed to show position and general appearance.*
   for gravure printing, 331
   for letterpress printing, 331–32
   for lithography, 331
duotone, 114
duplicate plates, 37, 131. *Printing plates made from a mold of the type and/or cuts.*
duplicating machines, 69
Duroid, 184
Dwiggins, W. A., 6, 78
Dycril plates, 134
Dymo Pacesetter, 55

E

Econolin, 185
ECRM, 50
edge color, 171, 341, 351. *The colored stain or gold leaf applied to the edges of a book's pages, usually at top.*
editing, copy, *see* copy editing
editing devices, 47, 48, 51–52, 57
editor, *see* book editor

editorial analysis, 220–21
editor-in-chief, 384, 385
eggshell finish paper, 154
Egyptian typefaces, 75, 76, 80
Ektachrome film, 122
electrostatic printing, 132, 139, 147. *Transfer of an image by use of the attraction of electrically charged particles to those oppositely charged. Sometimes called* xerography.
electrotype plates (electros), 67, 134. *Duplicate plates made with copper deposited by electrolysis in a mold of type and/or cuts.*
Elements of Style (Strunk and White), 436
Elephant Hide, 184
elite typewriter, 211
elongated type, 29
em, 26. *The square of any type size.*
emage, 32. *The area of a block of text or a text page measured in terms of ems of its type size.*
   composition rates based on, 191–94
embossing, 162, 176, 177, 186, 348. *Stamping that produces an image raised above the surface.*
emphasis, in typography, 83
en, 26. *Half an em.*
end-feed casemaker, 173–74
endpapers, 154, 185–86, 198, 338, 350–51. *The paper pasted to the inside of the front and back covers of a casebound book. Sometimes called* end sheets, endleaves, *or* linings.
English (British) editorial style, 407
errors, *see* manuscript, errors
estimate. *A calculation of the cost of any work or material. A calculation of the number of pages a Ms will make.*
   of cost, *see* cost estimating
   of length, *see* copyfitting; number of pages
etching, 186
expanded type, 29
explanatory notes, 259
extended type, 29
extract, 258. *Quoted material that is set off typographically from the text.*
   character count, 213

F

fees, reproduction, 103–07
felt side of paper, 153
figures, 29, 278, 408. *Numerals. Sometimes used to mean illustrations.*
   superior, 260
filler, 152, 182
film, 63, 122
   assembly, 130
   font, 54
   masks, 116
   negatives, *see* makeup

Part of a glossary-index. Reprinted from *Bookmaking*, 2nd edition, with permission of the R.R. Bowker Company. Copyright © 1979 by Marshall Lee.

Figure 9.4

TERM	RELATIONSHIPS	UNIT	SECTION
SYNCHRONIZED CLOCKS at rest in any particular **inertial frame of reference**	can be thought of as all running at the same rate and reading the same instant in time no matter where they are. That is, they would all appear to read exactly the same instant in time for a hypothetical, *non-physical* being who could stand next to each and every clock at one and the same instant (i.e. who could be everywhere at once!). They are therefore exactly the same in concept *both* in Newtonian mechanics and in **Einstein's special theory of relativity**, *provided that* one thinks about them only within a *single* chosen inertial frame of reference.		
	in **Einstein's special theory of relativity**, will *not* appear to be synchronized when observed by an **observing system** which is moving relative to the frame in which they are at rest. (See the **relativity of simultaneity**.)	5	4.2
	in Newtonian mechanics, are *assumed* to appear synchronized *regardless* of the frame of reference from which they are observed.		
	in **Einstein's sepcial theory of relativity**, are embodied in a **space–time diagram** by the very *existence* of an *x*-axis or an *x'*-axis, i.e. by the fact that a straight line (the axis) can be used to represent the same measurable **instant** in **time** at all possible measurable **positions** in **space** within any one single inertial frame of reference S(x, ct) or S'(x', ct').	5 7	7 4
	can be set up, in **Einstein's special theory of relativity**, by a simple procedure which allows for the finite **speed of light** as it travels from one clock to another. This procedure makes use of the fact that the speed of light is always the same under all conditions within a given inertial frame of reference, i.e. is absolutely invariant.	5	4.3
	presumably can be obtained, in Newtonian mechanics, by a procedure which allows for the finite **speed of light** as it travels from one clock to another. This procedure would be complicated on account of the assumption that the speed of light would depend on the motion of the clocks with respect to the 'aether' and therefore also on the direction of propagation of light from one clock to another.		
	in *both* **Einstein's special theory of relativity** and Newtonian mechanics, will actually appear *un*synchronized at any given **instant** in **time**, to a *physical* data taker at rest at a *single* **position** in **space** in the given inertial frame. In both theories the **speed of light** is finite, and therefore the synchronized clocks will appear to him to read earlier and earlier instants in time, the farther away from him they are.	5	6
A TEST CHARGE	is a particle bearing a known *small* **charge** (usually called charge *q*) which is used to measure the **electric field** at a point in **space–time**. (The charge on it must be small so that its effects on the charge distributions or current distributions that give rise to the fields being measured can be considered negligible.)	4	2.2
The **THRESHOLD ENERGY** for a reaction	is the minimum **energy** required to start the reaction. This energy is usually supplied by the **relativistic energy** of an incoming particle.	7	6.5

Part of a relational glossary. From the course *Understanding Space and Time*, Copyright © 1980, The Open University Press. Reproduced by courtesy of Robert Zimmer and The Open University.

And the running glossary?

It can be combined with others

What can be said now for the concept of the running glossary? It is certain that it can never substitute for a relational glossary, but it can substitute for a traditional glossary or even appear in addition to it. The latter approach is exemplified in a recent economics textbook (illustrated in Figure 8.4 in the previous volume of this series [p. 172]), which combines three features to overcome the terminology problem: (1) highlighted terms in the text itself, (2) a running glossary in the margin, and (3) a traditional end-of-book glossary.

It can be "found"

The usefulness of a running glossary is well illustrated by the experience of James McConnell, who obtained student feedback on an early textbook he was using in his introductory psychology classes. Of particular concern to the students was "the fact that we used 'so many big words'." He goes on to say that "some 90 percent [of the students] either never discovered that there was a glossary at the end of the book or found it out too late to do them much good." His response to this situation was to include a running glossary in the margins of his own later best-selling textbook, *Understanding Human Behavior*, which is illustrated in Figure 9.2. (This experience was related by McConnell to P. Laffoon in an article in the magazine *Nutshell*, 1979-80.)

and therefore has a chance of being used

Just as it is certain that educators can teach students the proper use of a standard glossary in studying, it is also certain that some students will nevertheless not use such a glossary when one is provided. The running glossary overcomes this usage problem to some extent.

5. *Marginalia and Text Design*

The role of marginalia as innovative

I have indicated earlier that, despite an old history, marginalia portray something of an innovative character. I would like in this section to pursue this line of thinking and explore some of its ramifications within the ongoing evolution of text design.

Different types of writing have different styles

There are styles of text presentation which, in a given era, characterize different forms of writing. The novel for instance has its own style—descriptive prose interlaced with dialogue—as does the scientific paper, the scholarly book, and the textbook, each of the latter having its own typical style.

even among textbooks

Within the field of the textbook itself, distinctions in style are evident among the various educational levels, with the consequence that a primary school text is rather different in design than a university text.

whose features change over time

University texts grew out of the academic book tradition and have tended to preserve some of the flavor of that tradition, the main element of which is continuous expository prose. Textbooks of a few decades ago were indeed rather simple, by today's conventions, in terms of instructional text design (as illustrated by the changes which have occurred in the well-known Samuelson text over some 30 years—Figures 9.5 and 9.6).

The change lies in the breakdown of continuous prose

What has happened and continues to evolve is the gradual breakdown of continuous prose. Textbooks are becoming less bookish in an effort to be more responsive to the needs of the learner. That is, there is a growing awareness of the complex and interactive nature of the student-text relationship.

One radical attempt was PI

which failed as a general form of instruction

One radical attempt in this direction was, of course, the programmed text, which was a direct and forceful attempt to adapt text design to the theory of learning prevailing at mid-century. In retrospect, it is easy to see how this attempt was misguided in its ambition to be a generalized form of instruction. Programmed instruction was (and still is) useful within given situations, but fails in most situations which we think of as educational.

More traditional attempts involve the incorporation of various design features

Within the more traditional line, textbooks have evolved toward the inclusion of varied design features which are all aimed at supporting learning, be it in the realm of attention, comprehension, or retention (see Duchastel, 1982). Some of these features are implicit means of structuring text (within the prose itself), while others are explicit means of doing so (via graphic design)—see Jonassen, 1982, Introduction. Both types of feature contribute to the ongoing dissipa-

Figure 9.5

former directly impoverishes the British Isles. Fortunately, the United States has come out of the most costly war in all history with little impairment of capital equipment and external debt.

"We All Owe It to Ourselves."   If an internal debt is simultaneously owed and owned by Americans, why do some people think that the wartime creation of 250 billion dollars of government bonds makes the public more wealthy and more ready to spend? If we draw up a consolidated balance sheet for the nation as a whole, we see that the (internal) debt represents a kind of fictitious financial wealth, which cancels out as a liability and asset.

Even purely financial assets have important effects. Every citizen who owns government bonds includes them when drawing up his periodic balance sheet, along with his other assets. But he is a very rare man indeed if he also includes as a present liability the amount of *future* taxes which he may have to pay to finance government interest payments or debt retirement. He does not even have a way of estimating his share of these taxes. The result is that the internal debt, which as a liability should exactly cancel out itself as an asset, tends instead to be counted by people primarily as an asset. Given a nest egg of bonds which they can either sell or cash in, people *feel* richer and more secure and perhaps, therefore, tend to have a higher propensity to consume out of current income.

Debt Management and Monetary Policy.   The existence of a large outstanding public debt may also have an influence on the interest rate and on its use to fight the business cycle. Some writers fear that channeling investment funds into the purchase of government bonds will raise the rate of interest to private borrowers. Alexander Hamilton, the spokesman of the conservative Federalist party, had just the opposite opinion. He felt that, rightly managed and in the right amounts, a public debt would be "a national blessing" because it would provide a secure gilt-edge asset that would give businessmen an income and enable them to trade for smaller profits.

As was shown in Chap. 15 on Central Banking, the Federal reserve authorities have strong powers to regulate rates of interest on government bonds. Therefore, any undue upward or downward pressure of the debt upon interest rates can be offset by open-market purchases and sale of government securities. But, and this is an ironic paradox, the existence of the vast public debt, while it enhances their power, at the same time serves to inhibit the exercise of effective monetary and interest policy by the Federal Reserve Banks.

A page from a university-level textbook of 1948, illustrating the academic style common then. From *Economics*, 1st edition, by Paul Samuelson. Copyright © 1948. Used with the permission of McGraw-Hill Book Company.

Figure 9.6

CALCULATION OF MARGINAL COST

(1) QUANTITY PRODUCED q	(2) TOTAL COST TC	(3) MARGINAL COST MC
399	$15,960.05	
		$39.95
400	16,000.00	40.00
		40.05
401	16,040.05	

TABLE 23-1
Marginal (or extra) cost can be shown numerically by subtraction of successive items The difference in total dollar cost from producing an extra unit is found by subtracting adjacent items of total dollar cost in Column (2). At $q^* = 400$, $MC = \$40$ to a high degree of approximation (as shown by the light-orange average of dark-orange MC data).

ing or averaging over the trifling differences caused by the trifling lumpiness of units, we estimate $MC = \$40$.

Definition: Marginal Cost at any output level q is the extra cost of producing one extra unit more (or less);[1] it comes from subtracting total dollar costs of adjacent outputs.

Just as we can calculate MC for $q^* = 400$, we can calculate it for any and every q. Table 23-1 had put a microscope on cost behavior around 400 and 401 units. To see the big picture,[2] let us stand off and see how the Marginal Cost curve behaves at *all* levels of output.

Figure 23-2 and its table show that Marginal Cost is related to Total Cost in the same way that Fig. 22-3, page 409, related Marginal Utility to Total Utility. From Fig. 23-2(b), you will see this:

MC tends to be U-shaped: ultimately it rises even though there is an initial phase in which it falls.

[1] WARNING: *MC* is not the same as average cost per unit, which we get by dividing total cost by number of units produced: *MC* is extra, incremental, or differential cost. As we've seen from the use of the word "marginal" in connection with *extra* utility, the appropriate name is indeed Marginal Cost.
[2] Figure 23-2 and the accompanying table measure q in units of hundreds; hence, $q = 300, 399, 400, 401, 500$ in Table 23-1 would show in Fig. 23-2 as $q = 3, 3.99, 4, 4.01, 5$, etc.

Why can you expect Marginal Cost to be ultimately a rising curve? This takes us back to the law of diminishing returns of Chapter 2, pages 21 to 25. Behind the dollar costs of the firm lies the production relationship between the firm's output and the labor and other inputs it hires. This will be discussed in depth in Chapter 27, but here we can indicate the general logic of the situation.

Suppose some factor is held fixed in the short run we are considering: it could be fixed land or, in manufacturing, it could be fixed plant capacity. Suppose that we get our varying amounts of q by hiring varying amounts of some input such as labor. If we can always buy labor at the same wage per unit, the only reason our marginal or extra cost of getting more q should rise would be because the extra product added by each successive unit of labor is going down. Hence, if we do get diminishing returns to the varying labor factor, we shall certainly get increasing Marginal Cost.

Costs and productivity returns are merely opposite sides of the same relationship.

Why does *MC* often decline *at first*, as shown in Fig. 23-2(b)? Recall that the law of diminishing returns tends *ultimately* to hold. But at the beginning, it might be negated by a strong tendency toward *increasing* returns, owing to the economies of large-scale production associated with indivisibility of the process and chances to introduce more elaborate division of labor as scale expands. If at first we have strong *increasing* returns, Marginal Cost must at first be *declining*, rather than increasing.[3]

We can summarize the relationship holding between the productivity laws of returns and the laws of Marginal Cost:

[3] Later we shall examine the behavior of Marginal Cost in the long run. Suppose we consider so extended a period of time that nothing can be regarded as fixed. Old plants can wear out and be replaced. New plants can be designed and built. Old land obligations can expire. New land contracts can be made. And so forth. In the long run, as a small firm, we may be able to buy *all* the factors of production in balance at unchanged input prices. Now what will happen to long-run costs, particu-

A page from the same textbook in its updated edition of 1980. From *Economics*, 11th edition, by Paul Samuelson. Copyright © 1980. Used with the permission of McGraw-Hill Book Company.

tion of continuous prose as a textbook style.

Marginalia are separate but related

The importance of marginalia in this context lies in the emphasis they create in explicitly structuring text elements (be they marginal notes or a running glossary) as relating to, but not being within, the main text itself. This view of marginalia places them within the realm of adjunct aids (see Lindner and Rickards, this volume) or places them, more generally, within what has been called the supra-discourse structure of a text, as opposed to the discourse itself (Macdonald-Ross and Waller, 1975).

These conceptions of text are useful in conceptualizing and furthering the contemporary move away from unidimensional prose, but they do also tend to dichotomize the instructional text into (1) the main text itself, and (2) associated elements meant to facilitate processing of the main text. While useful in its time, this may now be a conceptual limitation within the current expansion of text forms.

and thus seem to emphasize bidimensional text

but there is a problem

The problem lies in considering the breakdown of traditional forms of unidimensional prose as consisting principally in the addition of adjunct elements to this prose, with the implicit subservience of such elements to the prose itself.

Marginalia are both subservient and central

Marginalia, however, are not so much adjunct elements as such, but rather a distinct level of discourse in themselves.

In other words, their principal role is not so much to help the student process the main text, as it is to serve as contents to be learned in their own right.

Text is being differentiated into levels of discourse, as is sometimes done by the use of footnotes

This conception of text differentiation in terms of levels of discourse is well exemplified by the academic style of writing in which heavy use is made of footnotes (see Figure 9.7). It is also found, although not graphically signaled, in implicit means of structuring text, as through elaboration theory (Sari and Reigeluth, 1982).

and is seen in design experimentation

The more experimental forms of text presentation, such as those of Horn and Showstack (both represented in the previous volume of this series) or that of Jewett (1981), each attempt in their own way to provide levels of discourse and graphically punctuate these levels. It is in association with such experiments in text design that marginalia carry an innovative flavor.

Marginalia defined as a level of dicourse

Marginalia may thus best be characterized not by their physical location on a text page (that was our working definition of marginalia in Section 2 of this chapter), but rather by their status as a distinct level of discourse within the book itself.

may be rather broad

This definition is a broad one and overlaps with other text features not considered in this chapter, or considered as contrastive (for instance, highlighting). Its advantage, however, lies precise-

but is creative in intent

Figure 9.7

« ET MOI JE VOUS DIS… »

Et Benni Lévy lui disait : « *Tu as, depuis longtemps, été sensible à cette idée qu'au fond l'individu est mandaté* […].* » Tout se passe comme si, de Freud à Monod, de Jankélévitch à Bloch, et à Sartre —Sartre étant le premier d'entre eux à la formuler—, tous constataient en l'homme la réclamation d'une connaissance intuitive, la présence d'une convocation irrésistible [1].

Ce qui nous conduit directement à la grande révélation-divulgation qu'apportait le Nazaréen. Elle tient en sept mots que l'on trouve à la fois en Luc (17,21) et dans l'un des *« logia »* de l'*Évangile selon Thomas.*

1. Toute une rumeur hostile s'est développée autour de ces paroles dernières, et remarquablement explicites, de Sartre. Olivier Todd s'est même permis à ce sujet des contre-vérités hargneuses et violentes, parlant d'« *escroquerie* », de « *montage* », de « *ramassis d'âneries* ». Ce qui inspira à Alain Finkielkraut (dans *le Nouvel Observateur* du 13 avril 1981) cette âpre et juste observation : Sartre aura donc connu *« l'étrange destin de mourir inécouté ».* Cependant la même semaine et dans *le Monde* du 17 avril 1981, Michel Contat, autrement sérieux qu'Olivier Todd et respectueux du vrai, tenait à constater publiquement que « *l'âge puis la mort* » auront « *empêché* » Sartre de réaliser le projet qui était le sien : *« réviser ses idées »* et « *fonder une morale* ».Ceux (et celles) que consternent les affirmations de J.-P. Sartre ont recouru à l'explication par la sénescence. Mais Marc Beigbeder —qui, comme moi, n'y croit guère— a fait observer, dans sa *Bouteille à la mer* du 3 décembre 1981, que ce que lui aurait prétendument « *extorqué* » Benni Lévy « *se trouve déjà* », pour l'essentiel, dans *les Mots*, à propos desquels il est difficile d'évoquer (ou d'invoquer) la sénilité.

97

A heavy use of footnotes in an academic text.

ly in undermining the traditional distinctions between text and adjuncts, between content and processes, and between form and function.

Being a skilled art, instructional text design must constantly operate within the interplay of these various dimensions. The further evolution of text design, if its current experiments are an indication of its orientation, will most likely involve combining such dimensions and perhaps the creation of new ones. Text will continue to become further differentiated, but in interrelated ways.

Text differentiation may be an emerging design style

6. Electronic Text

Severe display problems

lead to 2 emphases: —structured information —explicit interaction

The storage and presentation of information in electronic form is seen as a trend that will probably accelerate as it follows the ongoing computer revolution. The nature and current limitations of the display media (CRT or computer printer) can lead to a number of display problems, as illustrated by Merrill and by Reynolds in the preceding volume in this series. These limitations have also led, in videotex systems, to an emphasis on highly structured information rather than on text as traditionally conceived, and, in educational systems, to an emphasis on explicit interaction with the information rather than the implicit interaction found in text processing.

Eventually, electronic text will permit

As limitations are removed, however, experimentation with computer display *traditional text display*

and likely encourage text differentiation

systems will likely lead to a wide range of display and interaction options, including those we currently associate with printed texts. The power of the computer will not only enable such presentation diversity, but also will encourage attempts to overcome the limitations of the printed text itself. In doing so, it may well encourage the very differentiation of text discussed in the preceding section.

Issues become non-issues, e.g., the location of the glossary

The current interactive power of the computer (of its programs, actually) already render certain text issues meaningless when it comes to electronic display. For instance, the location of a glossary is no longer an issue when a glossary item can be called up on demand on a CRT screen. That is one text limitation which is easily overcome.

But not all, e.g., the discourse level issue

Current systems, however, are far from sophisticated enough to easily handle the "level of discourse" problems except through rather rigid branching procedures. This is a limitation which is still shared with texts.

Marginal note concerns do not generalize to electronic text

Unless the computer is simply used as a page-turner or as a text printer, the concerns about marginal notes which were discussed in this chapter do not readily generalize to electronic text.

Other potential solutions will be developed

The scope for differentiating text through selective presentation and interaction go far beyond such means. Efforts in this direction, such as the artificial intelligence research described by Collins and Grignetti (1975) are still quite lean compared to their potential, despite the fact that the problems are far from trivial, especially those of cognitive representation (Duchastel and Rahmlow, in preparation).

The media are different . . . and so are their potentials

The tentative conclusion one derives from the consideration of electronic text and its potential is that textual display issues may be rather different in this area than they are in traditional text. While the two media will certainly influence one another, their different limitations and respective potentials will undoubtedly encourage different design solutions. The pace of the computer revolution will also most likely quicken the pace of experimentation in text design itself.

References

Brown, A., Campione, J., and Day, J. Learning to learn: On training students to learn from texts. *Educational Researcher*, 1981, *10*(2), 14-21.

Collins, A., and Grignetti, M. *Intelligent CAI.* Final Report. Cambridge, MA: Bolt, Beranek, and Newman, Inc., 1975.

Duchastel, P. Textual display techniques. In D.H. Jonassen (Ed.) *The technology of text: Principles for structuring, designing, and displaying text.* Englewood Cliffs, NJ: Educational Technology Publications, 1982.

Duchastel, P., and Chen, Y-P. The use of marginal notes in text to assist learning. *Educational Technology*, 1980, *20*(11), 41-45.

Duchastel, P., and Rahmlow, H. Computer text access, in preparation.

Economics '73-'74. Guilford, CT: The Dushkin Publishing Group, Inc., 1973.

Jewett, D. Multi-level writing in theory and practice. *Visible Language*, 1981, *15*(1), 32-40.

Jonassen, D.H. Aptitude versus content-treatment interactions: Implications for instructional design. *Journal of Instructional Developmennt*, 1982 (a) *5*(4), 15-27.

Jonassen, D.H. *The technology of text: Principles for structuring, designing, and displaying text.* Englewood Cliffs, NJ: Educational Technology Publications, 1982 (b) (Volume 1 in this series).

Laffoon, P. Dawn of the undull: A best-selling professor battles the boring textbook. *Nutshell Magazine*, 1979-80, 93-97.

Macdonald-Ross, M., and Waller, R. *Open University texts: Criticisms and alternatives.* Milton Keynes, England: Institute of Educational Technology, The Open University, 1975.

Sari, F., and Reigeluth, C. Writing and

evaluating textbooks: Contributions from instructional theory. In D.H. Jonassen (Ed.), *The technology of text: Principles for structuring, designing, and displaying text.* Englewood Cliffs, NJ: Educational Technology Publications, 1982.

Waller, R. Marginal Notes. *Notes on transforming No. 3.* Milton Keynes, England: Institute of Educational Technology, The Open University, 1977.

Waller, R. Graphic aspects of complex texts: Typography as macro-punctuation. In P. Kolers, M. Wrolstad, and H. Bouma (Eds.) *Processing of visible language, 2.* New York: Plenum, 1980.

Waller, R. Text as diagram: Using typography to improve access and understanding. In D.H. Jonassen (Ed.), *The technology of text: Principles for structuring, designing, and displaying text.* Englewood Cliffs, NJ: Educational Technology Publications, 1982.

Zimmer, R. The relational glossary: For easier teaching and learning at a distance. *Aspects of Educational Technology*, Vol. 15. London: Kogan Page, 1981.

Chapter 10

The Role of Headings in Printed and Electronic Text

James Hartley and David H. Jonassen

Introduction

This chapter is divided into two parts. In the first part, we discuss headings in printed text. We consider their functions, and we report on research that has examined the effects of headings on recall, search, and retrieval. In the second part, we extend this discussion to headings in electronic text. We note here that headings are important for categorizing information. In addition, we also comment on the fact that the amount of text displayed at any one moment in electronic text is much smaller than that in printed text, and we discuss the implications of this point.

In writing about headings we have, of course, tried to practice what we preach and to use headings appropriately in this text. It is perhaps of interest to comment here on how research on headings contributed to decisions in this repect. Certainly, as we shall see below, the research suggests that headings can help readers perceive the organization of a piece of writing, and that this can help them find their way about it, retrieve information from it, and recall its content. But the research does not tell us much else. It does not tell us, for example, what kinds of headings are most effective, when we should use several and when few headings, whether headings are best cited in the margin or embedded in the text, or how we can denote different heading levels most effectively. Choices have to be made for all of these issues–choices guided by past experience and suggestions from research.

In the first draft of this chapter, we had more headings than we have now. Such an approach, as we shall see below, was probably more appropriate for electronic text than for printed text. We had fairly full main and secondary headings, embedded in the text, and we had shorter tertiary headings (often one for each paragraph) positioned in the margin. But this approach seemed like "overkill" for printed text with its double-page spread. So we finally settled (without too much confidence) for the traditional ways of presenting headings in a text of this nature. Thus, as readers can see, we have embedded all our headings in the text, and we have used different kinds of typography to denote their various levels.* A brief, but useful, discussion of possibilities open to writers and designers in this respect is given by Twyman (1981).

I. HEADINGS IN PRINTED TEXT

The functions of headings

If we wish to analyze the effectiveness of headings, we must first consider their functions, for without a functional context, we can only speculate as to why certain experiments produce certain results.

We believe that headings function in two different ways to help learners acquire knowledge from text. These are (1) during the initial *encoding* of the information from the text into memory—when headings help to organize and structure the incoming information and thus help recall, and (2) during *access* to the text—when headings help in locating desired information and facilitate retrieval from the text: this may occur when re-examining familiar text in order to find something that you know or think is there, and when searching through new text in order to

---

*This chapter includes headings at three levels:
A. Main capitals, centered.
B. Lower-case, spatially coded, flush left.
C. Lower-case, italic, run-on, beginning paragraphs.
These are printed in boldface capitals for A, boldface lower case for B, and italic lower case for C.

see what is there. These two functions are shown schematically in Figure 10.1.

Encoding

In order to make sense of what we read, we have to relate what we read to what we already know. Our memories contain interrelated networks of concepts (schemata or scripts) that represent objects, events, situations, and ideas. We use these networks to help us interpret and assign meaning to information in text, to make inferences, and to relate the new information to previously-acquired knowledge. The following example perhaps makes this point more clearly. This passage is presented by Bransford (1979):

> The procedure is actually quite simple. First you arrange items into different groups. Of course, one pile may be sufficient depending on how much there is to do. If you have to go somewhere else due to lack of facilities that is the next step; otherwise, you are pretty well set. It is important not to overdo things. That is, it is better to do too few things at once than too many. In the short run, this may not seem important, but complications can easily arise. A mistake can be expensive as well. At first, the whole procedure will seem complicated. Soon, however, it will become just another facet of life. It is difficult to foresee any end to the necessity for this task in the immediate future, but then, one never can tell. After the procedure is completed, one arranges the materials into different groups again. Then they can be put into their appropriate places. Eventually, they will be used once more and the whole cycle will then have to be repeated. However, that is part of life.

Bransford suggests that without an appropriate context this passage cannot be properly understood.

Headings can function as cuing devices to provide such a context. Headings can activate appropriate networks (schemata or scripts) which in turn act as a context for comprehending what is presented. The more novel, obscure, or ambiguous the text, the more comprehension and memory can be improved by simply inserting titles or headings (Bransford and Johnson, 1972; Dooling

Figure 10.1

**Graphic Heading on Information-
Processing Functions of Headings**

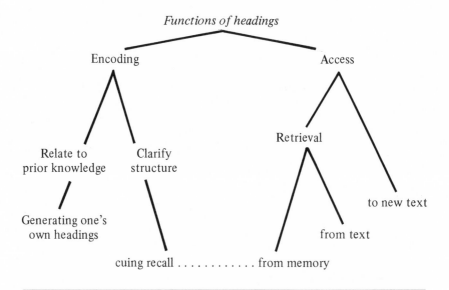

and Lachman, 1971). If we now tell you that the title of Bransford's passage presented above is "Washing Clothes," you may now re-read it with quite a different experience.

Context aids comprehension. So, the argument runs, headings cue the recall of appropriate knowledge structures which then aid comprehension. The context that is activated will determine the meaning that is assigned to the text. The more familiar the context, the more networks that are interrelated and available, the better a passage will be comprehended and remembered (Anderson, Spiro, and Anderson, 1978).

This theory provides a conceptual rationale for using headings. Nonetheless, the research that supports it employs intentionally ambiguous prose. The effectiveness of headings needs to be affirmed with natural, less ambiguous prose. The question is whether or not headings serve the same contextual function for prose that is well-organized and meaningful. Few studies have examined this question posed in this particular form. Schwarz and Flammer (1981) did find, however, that titles helped Swiss university students to recall Norwegian fairy tales. Most studies of *headings*, however, have simply asked whether or not headings aid the recall of information. It is to these studies that we now turn.

Research findings

Do headings aid recall? A number of studies have in fact found that headings produce no better recall than non-cued normal text.

- Robinson and Hall (1941) found no difference in the immediate recall of university students.
- Christensen and Stordahl (1955) found no difference in the immediate or delayed recall of Air Force basic trainees.
- Klare, Shuford, and Nichols (1958) found no main effects, but that low-aptitude learners (airmen) profited more.
- Snavely (1962) found no difference in the immediate recall of nine, ten, and 13-year-old children reading text with purpose statements or marginal notes.
- Landry (1967) found no difference in the immediate or delayed recall of 11-12-year-old pupils.
- Cole (1977) found no differences on an immediate recognition test of 15-16-year-old male pupils.
- Jonassen (1983) found no differences in two studies on probed recall or free recall of familiar content with university students.

However, some investigators have been more successful:

- Lee (1965) found in two studies that headings (with overviews, transitional paragraphs, and conclusions) aided male undergraduates to recall the main points of a passage but not within-paragraph details.
- Rickards (1975-76) found that superordinate sentence headings (organizers) appearing before text segments produced superior total recall, recall of general concepts, and subsumption of related as well as unrelated facts.

- Doctorow, Wittrock, and Marks (1978) found headings aided the recall of 10-12-year-old children on an immediate multiple-choice and a delayed (one week) cloze test.
- Hartley *et al.* (1980) found headings aided the recall of 12-13-year-old pupils both on immediate recall and 14 days later (short answer test).
- Holley *et al.* (1981) found headings aided the recall of students on both immediate recall and five days later (free recall).
- Brooks *et al.* (1983) found structural outline readings aided the long-term retention of students on four different recall measures given after five days in one study but not in a second one.
- Dee-Lucas and Di Vesta (1983) found headings (in the read-only conditions) produced the highest scores on each of three measures of recall for female university students, although these differences were not always significant.
- Hartley and Trueman (1983) found in each of three studies headings aided the immediate recall of 14-15-year-old children (short answer test).

In fact, Hartley and Trueman (1983) carried out nine related studies on headings. They argue, because of the differences between the studies listed above—differences in passages, measures, age groups, etc.—that there is a need for a *series* of studies to replicate, extend, and build on a set of findings. The argument, which has some force, is that such a research strategy is more likely to produce more dependable findings.

Another way to assess the overall impact of headings on recall is to pool the results from all those studies that provide sufficient data to enable one to carry out meta-analysis (Glass, McGaw, and Smith, 1981). We have carried out such an analysis and found the average effect-size to be 0.46. This figure indicates that the average size of improvement for the headings group is almost one half of a standard deviation above the mean of the control groups. This figure is undoubtedly inflated because of the omission of five of the eight studies showing neutral results (since they did not provide the data necessary to do the calculation). However, if one enters each of these studies into the calculation with an effect-size of zero, the overall effect-size is 0.27 (i.e., one-quarter of a standard deviation higher than the mean of the control groups).

What are the effects of different kinds of headings? There have been a number of studies looking at the effects of different kinds of headings upon recall. Thus, people have found that two-word headings are better than single-word ones (Doctorow *et al.*, 1978); that semantic headings organize information better than content markers (Jonassen, 1983); and that sentence outlines, used like headings, aid learning (Proger *et al.*, 1970, 1973).

One issue studied more than most is whether or not headings written in the form of questions produce better recall than headings written in the form of statements. The studies that have examined this question have not found, generally speaking, that headings in the form of questions produce any better recall (Christensen and Stordahl, 1955; Hartley *et al.*, 1980; Hartley and Trueman, 1983). There has, however, been some suggestion that headings in the form of questions aid the recall of less-able readers. This effect was found with 12-13-year-olds by Hartley *et al.* (1980) and with 15-16-year-old remedial learners by Hartley *et al.* (1981). The effect was present with 14-15-year-old learners but not significantly so in the studies reported by Hartley and Trueman (1983). But, in the most recent and thorough studies of this phenomenon, the effect had disappeared (Hartley *et al.*, 1984).

Do learners know how to use headings? The equivocal research findings related to recall from text with and without headings (reviewed above) has led some researchers to question whether or not many learners know how to use headings effectively. Robinson and Hall (1941), for instance, concluded their report by observing that students did not profit from headings, and that, "Obviously, such a lack of study skill indicates a definite instructional need." Other investigators have assumed that learners know intuitively that headings have an encoding function, and thus that they know how to relate them to the content and how to use them as retrieval cues. Hartley and Trueman (1983), for example, did not give the participants in their recall studies any guidance on how to use headings and yet the participants benefitted from their presence.

One way to test the assumption that learners intuitively know how to use headings is to present ambiguous or misleading headings and see if they are at all confused by headings which have no relation to the text, or which are in some way dissonant from the textual content. The little research that has been done along these lines has shown that biasing titles and headings does indeed affect comprehension (Kozminsky, 1977). Swarts, Flower, and Hayes (1980) showed that inappropriate headings in bureaucratic documents prevented readers from being able to predict information included in any section, thereby hindering comprehension of the document.

If readers are misled by inappropriate headings, then this implies that they do appreciate their encoding function and that headings do assume the role of anchoring points around which text is organized. But how—and when—is this knowledge acquired? There have been no systematic studies done (to our knowledge) with children of different ages to see how headings affect recall. One might expect at first that children would be unaware of the significance of headings, but that they would gradually become more aware of their significance (especially if taught to write their own). Eventually, however, this significance might depreciate with age, since general text processing strategies might be applied to all texts, irrespective of whether or not they had headings. In addition, of course, one might expect changes with ability as well as with age. Less-able children might profit from headings, as they will help them to process the text: more-able children might prefer to generate their own headings to help them to recall. Such ideas are at the moment speculations and, it must be admitted, there is as yet no clear support for them.

Four studies that trained learners to use headings report inconsistent findings.

- Cole (1977) compared the results of students trained to use a particular reading strategy with those not so trained on their recall of a passage with and without headings, but he found no significant differences in their performance.
- Holley *et al.* (1981) trained groups of students to attend to embedded headings and to actively attempt to tie the headings to information presented in the text. Another group was given topic outlines and trained to use the outlines to recall information presented in the text. Both kinds of training proved ineffective.

- Brooks *et al.* (1983) trained a group of students on how to use embedded headings to facilitate input, storage, and output. This training did prove effective.
- Taylor (1982) trained 11-12-year-old children to use a summarization strategy which involved headings when reading expository text. This training procedure proved effective in one study, but the findings were not replicated in a second study.

Encoding and recall

If one subscribes to the encoding hypothesis, then one believes that what gets encoded in memory will determine what cues will be effective for recalling the information that was encoded. The weight of the evidence seems to suggest that when readers intentionally memorize headings, they function best as retrieval cues, especially for low-level or subordinate information. Two studies support this conclusion.

- Brooks *et al.* (1983) argued that since elaborate training in the processing of headings resulted in better performance on non-cued tests, but that untrained readers performed just as well on cued tests (short answer, multiple-choice), headings could be inferred to have their greatest effects as retrieval aids.
- Doctorow *et al.* (1978) showed that when learners were asked to generate sentences from memory about each paragraph, they almost always included the headings–thus indicating that these headings were involved in retrieval.

What happens if learners write their own headings? The theory set forth at the beginning of this chapter argues that comprehension occurs when readers construct the meaning for text by activating appropriate prior knowledge during comprehension. Meaning is dependent upon the store of memories and distinctive experiences that a reader can apply to any text. So, the argument runs, if learners are stimulated to generate their own elaborations for text rather than relying on those provided by the author, recall should improve. Doctorow, Wittrock, and Marks (1978) found that when they gave 10-12-year-old children instructions to write sentences from memory about each paragraph they had read, the children comprehended better and recalled more than children who received only headings. They also found that when headings were added to this generative processing, that is, when the children had to write their descriptive sentences about the paragraphs with the headings provided in addition, then these headings functioned effectively as retrieval cues, improving the level of recall even more. Dee-Lucas and DiVesta (1983) found with university students that writing headings produced a greater recall of text structure, and facilitated the recall of subordinate (less important) information on a free-recall test.

The findings from these two studies support to some extent the arguments put forward by Robinson (1961) in his text, *Effective Study*. Robinson suggests that if a text that is being studied does not contain any headings, then readers should construct headings for themselves, and, in particular, that they should turn these headings into questions.

Such procedures may be appropriate for text with simple structures, but there may be limits to the levels of structure that can be generated by learners. Eggan, Kauchuk, and Kirk (1978) found that few 9-11-year-old learners were able to construct and add to a two-dimensional conceptual hierarchy unaided. However, when they were provided with hierarchical headings, they improved their ability to interrelate concepts and they obtained better comprehension of the passage in question. In this particular study, the headings facilitated the recall of high-level information, while providing no help with the recall of low-level information.

It would seem, therefore, that writing one's own headings may aid comprehension if the text is simple, but that hierarchically-structured headings may aid recall if the text structure is more complex.

Headings and access to the text

One of the most obvious functions of headings (and thus the least researched) relates to the fact that headings provide access to information in the text. Reading is normally a selective process, especially with non-narrative text, and devices such as contents pages, headings, and indexes aid this access (Waller, 1979). Headings, in addition to providing an overview of textual content, identify and characterize particular units of the text. Waller (1982) argues that the primary function of headings is to orient readers to the text, allowing them to locate the information that they need.

Headings can effectively signal the nature of the content of any part of the text, and thus facilitate retrieval from it. The specific role to be played by headings depends upon the nature of the document and the reader's degree of familiarity with it (Swarts *et al.*, 1980). Hartley and Trueman (1983) distinguished between (1) *retrieval* of information from *familiar* text, and (2) *searching* for information in *unfamiliar* text.

If headings in text facilitate *retrieval*, then readers should be able to locate information more quickly, and/or make fewer errors when using text with headings. The research support for this contention is not unanimous, but it is reasonably strong:

- Jonassen and Falk (1980) found that students found 50 percent more answers in the same time when using a mapped version of text, which included an extensive use of marginal headings.
- Charrow and Redish (1980) found that adult shoppers failed to retrieve information any more quickly or accurately when using short re-redesigned texts which included embedded headings.
- Jonassen (1983) found that students failed to retrieve information any more quickly or accurately from a text which had various types of headings.
- Hartley and Trueman (1983) found that 14-15-year-old participants retrieved information significantly faster from texts that had either marginal or embedded headings. (These findings were replicated on each of three occasions for both marginal and embedded headings.)

If headings facilitate *searching* unfamiliar text, then again, readers should be able to locate information more quickly and make fewer errors when searching text with headings. Search tasks, with headings, have not been widely researched:

- Hartley and Burnhill (1976) found that students made significantly less errors and found information more quickly when using a re-redesigned text which included marginal headings.
- Hartley and Trueman (1983) found that 14-15-year-old participants searched text which had either marginal or embedded headings significantly more quickly to find the answers to short-answer questions about the content of the text. These findings were replicated on each of three occasions with both the marginal and the embedded headings. No differences were found between the effects of the marginal and the embedded headings—both were equally successful.

The findings of Hartley and Trueman that headings aided search and retrieval are, of course, specific to the participants employed, and to the semi-technical passage used in these studies. It may be that there might be an advantage for marginal headings in more dense technical text, but this issue has yet to be explored.

What are the characteristics of good headings?

The access function of headings depends upon a meaningful, user-oriented construction of headings. Headings have to be written with both the readers' prior knowledge and the readers' needs in mind if they are to be effective in providing access to the text. In many texts, it seems that headings are rather vague and that they are often based on broad concepts rather than on users' specific needs (Swarts *et al.*, 1980). One reason for this might be that it is sometimes very difficult to know what the readers' needs will be, and another that it might be thought (by the author) better to go for a neutral, safe position when it is known that different readers will have different needs. In preparing this chapter, for example, we have been aware of this problem, and we have tried to provide broad overview headings that will meet the requirements of technical writers, editors, instructors, and psy-chologists—at least four of the different audiences that we hope will read this text.

Swarts *et al.* (1980) showed in their studies that when headings misled readers about the contents of a text, then the content was harder to predict and to reconcile to the readers' expectations based upon the headings. These authors, therefore, recommend that writers should pay particular attention to what they call the "scenario principle" when writing headings.

In their research on reading government regulations, Swarts *et al.* found that—in order to make sense of particular regulations— readers frequently turned the meaning of a section in the text into a condition/action sequence (If I do this . . . then that . . .)or created a dramatized scene or "scenario" in which somebody did something. For example, if the original text said something like, "No part of such financing shall be used to . . . .," the reader might turn this into "*If* a borrower has that money on hand . . . *then* we won't make her a loan so that she can use the money on hand to buy land or things like that." Thus, in order to interpret regulations, readers were creating circumstances in which they could see how a regulation might in fact operate—in effect, creating "scenarios." Headings following the "scenario principle," then, should contain an agent or action (e.g., Bransford and the encoding hypothesis) or should indicate that the text is likely to provide an answer to a question that the reader might well have in mind (e.g., What are the effects of headings?).

In addition, Swarts *et al.* (1980) recommend that in writing headings one should try to:

- anticipate readers' questions,
- clarify all the terms used, and
- use short, accurate, and specific headings.

Concluding comments to this section

An overview of the research on headings suggests that headings can aid recall, search, and retrieval, and that there are some plausible explanations as to why this might be so. It is possible that headings will be of particular benefit to younger, less-capable, and less-developed learners. Learners who are less-capable of organizing and structuring materials may gain more from headings which provide the necessary structural cues. That is, they may benefit more from text-driven strategies. Better-developed learners who prefer to impose their own organizational strategies on the comprehension process may, however, be deterred by headings that represent the author's structure. These learners are likely to benefit more from using their own conceptually-driven comprehension processes. As with so many areas of educational research, future research on headings may well be advised to de-emphasize the search for main effects and to concentrate more on interactions between age and ability and the use of various types of headings in various kinds of passages. Further work on how learners use and can be taught to use headings seems desirable.

II. HEADINGS IN ELECTRONIC TEXT

In discussing the role of headings in electronic text, we must first clarify the meaning of electronic text itself. Electronic text refers to documents, instructional programs, abstracts, or bibliographic information stored in databases on computers. The main purpose for storing such text in this way is to accelerate access to the information contained within it. The phenomenally high-speed matching capabilities of main-frame computers or even microcomputers allow us to supply the computer with a term (or string of characters) and to ask the computer to locate the term (or string) and all of the other information designated by or associated with that term in the database. The terms that we identify or associate with documents or collections of text in a database are—in effect—subject headings. The functions of such headings in electronic text are shown schematically in Figure 10.2.

Subject headings and document accession

Subject headings are used to reflect the organization and classification of knowledge in library and information systems, both in online and hardcopy catalogs. Classification systems seek to emulate the hierarchical arrangements (e.g., L.C., Dewey) or the categorical or faceted arrangements (e.g., colon) of knowledge in human memory. Information is readily accessible in memory only because it is chunked into categories that we can selectively access. So we do not need to do a sequential or linear search of all of the

Figure 10.2

Graphic Heading on Functions
of Headings in Electronic Text

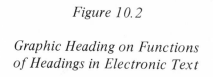

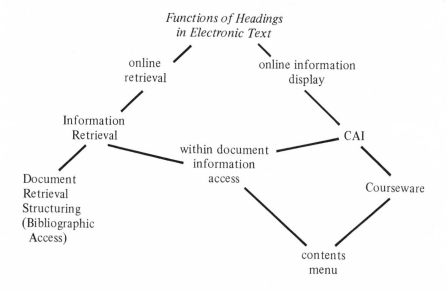

information contained in memory in order to access a specific information trace. Likewise, libraries and information systems facilitate access to information contained in them by allowing readers to do the same. Readers are not required to search sequentially every book in a collection or every entry in a bibliographic database in order to find a desired document. The primary route to fulfilling information needs is via what is usually called "subject-access."

Online retrieval

Subject access to documents is commonly provided by a *controlled vocabulary*, that is, by an accepted list of subject headings that are supposed to describe all of the information contained therein. In library catalogs, we index our collections by class labels to represent their subject matter. In online document retrieval systems, we use a *thesaurus* of descriptors to describe the subject matter of the documents contained in the databases. While controlled vocabularies offer the advantages of consistency and accessibility, they also have some distinctive disadvantages. The use of controlled vocabularies in database searches limits the precision of the search, especially when the appropriate or relevant descriptors are not available (Antony *et al.*, 1979). Also, preparing subject headings, especially for online access, increases the cost of preparing documents, since each document must be read by knowledgeable readers who then have to assign the descriptors to it (Heaps, 1978).

Controlled vocabulary subject heading searches can be supplemented by *free text* searches of titles, abstracts, or even full documents (Mandel, 1981). While free text searches will access a larger number of documents in most databases (Markey *et al.*, 1980), a rudimentary principle of retrieval systems predicts that as recall goes up, precision goes down. More searching produces more *false drops* (irrelevant documents retrieved). One way to increase the precision of online searches is to provide, online, interactive displays of the thesaurus terms or even the class labels. This procedure allows the user to change search strategies by using related, broader, or narrower terms (Mandel, 1980; Markey *et al.*, 1981). This ability to recombine subject terms on line, using a variety of Boolean connectors with terms, provides a large number of access routes to the desired information.

Nonetheless, a question remains: Can a subject headings list describe a document and its contents as well as the author can? Can controlled vocabularies provide enough access points to databases? A recent library users' study recommended that additional access points, including keywords in titles and *added subject headings describing the whole document and the sub-headings describing the units or chapters* would be a desirable feature of an online system (Kaske and Sanders, 1980). Thus, headings supplied by an author could not only improve access to information *within* a document, but also access *to* that document, if the headings were added to the entry as descriptors. Free text searches of these headings along with titles, in addition to free text searches of the document or its abstract, could provide a more precise method of online access. The implications for authors are obvious: We need to provide clear headings which describe the content of our document, possibly aiming at different readers' needs.

Access to information within documents

When we read non-narrative texts, especially scholarly or technical reports, we seldom start at the beginning and read steadily to the end. Indeed, we each employ individualized sets of cognitive strategies for extracting information from the text. Maurice Line (1982), for example, describes how for a research report he first reads the Abstract, then the Conclusions, next the Discussion section, and then scans the sub-headings and graphs, tables, keywords, etc. At any point, reading or scanning may cease if the information in the article is not germane to his information needs.

It is relatively easy to make such decisions about the usefulness of a report with printed text, but this may not be the case with electronic text. Gaining access to information in electronic displays presents a distinct set of problems that cannot be resolved by simply transforming a printed document into an online display. The act of scrolling through an electronic display of text is tedious and visually taxing compared with paging through a book or journal (Muter *et al.*, 1982). Also, since most databases are accessed on a time-charge basis, the reader may become anxious about the cost of obtaining information. Such anxiety is likely to affect adversely the processing of the document, thus making retrieval even more difficult.

Online information display

Headings provide obviously useful access points to electronic text displays. Essentially, articles designed for online display should be menu-driven, with a contents list of headings appearing at the beginning of the document. This list would provide the shortest route to the relevant portions of the document as well as serving an organizational function. The contents list of headings and sub-headings constitutes an overview which signals the structure of the document, and provides a useful organizer and retrieval function (Eggan, Kauchuk, and Kirk, 1978). Articles written in this format appear in the *British Electronic Journal* (Shackel, 1982), but as yet no data are available concerning how readers use the headings for these purposes.

Headings in computer courseware

Numerous authoring guides suggest a variety of user-oriented rules for sequencing and displaying text on the screen for computer courseware (e.g., CDC, 1977; MECC, 1977; Eisele, this volume). Suggestions include:
- Display only a limited amount of text on the screen.
- Let readers control the pace of presentation rather than use timing loops or scrolling.
- Use consistent responses for advancing the display.
- Provide help keys and allow the reader to escape to the menu at all times.

In addition, some excellent instructional design guidelines have appeared recently (Eisele, 1978; Gagné, 1981; Roblyer, 1981; Wager, 1982). These help us design meaningful courseware consistent with principles of learning and instructional design.

Unfortunately, to date, there have been virtually no typographic design principles for courseware development. This is a great pity for, as noted earlier, the display problems associated with computer courseware and online display of electronic text are different from those for printed text. The method of accession is different. The amount of information displayed is different. The fundamental design principles are different, since the screen is limited in many ways (e.g., with respect to print), yet has more possibilities in others (e.g., color).

One key problem arises from the change in size of the display. In a textbook of this kind, the display is a double-page spread. With electronic text, the screen size is typically much smaller. Davies (1982) provides the following illustration:

THIS PARAGRAPH IS WRITTEN IN THIS STYLE OF FOR-
MAT TO DEMONSTRATE THE MAXIMUM DISPLAY OF
TEXT AVAILABLE ON A NUMBER OF MACHINES. THE
MOST YOU CAN GET ONTO A LINE LIMITED TO FORTY
COLUMNS IS SHOWN HERE. THE MAXIMUM NUMBER OF
LINES ON DISPLAY AT ANY ONE TIME IS TWENTY FOUR.
BUT THAT IS ONLY IF YOU CAN ACCEPT THE LINES
RUNNING INTO EACH OTHER ABOVE AND BELOW. IF
YOU WISH TO SEPARATE THEM WITH SOME SPACING AS
USED HERE, YOU ONLY REALLY HAVE TWELVE USABLE
LINES.

It would take approximately ten of these "screen pages" to accommodate one double-page the size of this textbook!

One has to consider carefully, therefore, how best to display text in this new form. Hartley (1980a) commented on which features of printed text could be adapted easily to electronic text, and which could not. Others, too, have remarked on these issues (e.g., Bork, 1979; Bruce and Foster, 1982; Foster and Bruce, 1982a, 1982b; Reynolds, 1982). Clearly, the influence of spatial coding is important (Hartley, 1980b, 1981), but there is less room for maneuvering in this respect with electronic text. In Viewdata Systems, color coding is used in addition to, or as a replacement for, spatial denotation of text structure. One difficulty here, of course, is that readers do not intuitively appreciate a hierarchy of colors (unlike a spatial hierarchy).

As yet, there is little evidence available about the effectiveness of different design features for courseware development. It would be reasonable to suggest, however, in connection with headings, that headings should be displayed in the same position on each program page and in the same style. Some form of enhanced type or spatial cuing will be necessary to distinguish them from the rest of the text, but flashing type and other distractors are not recommended.

Three purposes for headings

The primary purposes of headings for computer courseware should be (1) to signal the structure of the program, (2) to provide pointers for accessing specific pages, and (3) to confirm that access has been made to appropriate pages.

The major concern in designing courseware is the structure of the program—how the instructional sequence should be put together. To signal that structure, CAI programs need to provide an index or table of contents of the lessons in the program (Spitler and Corgan, 1979) or an outline of topics (headings) (Alessi and Dennis, 1979).

Spitler and Corgan (1979) recommend that a fine index (a list of sub-headings) also be presented initially in addition to the program index. Such fine indexes would provide a structural overview of the course, offering options to the learners. Each learner can choose a heading from the index or contents list, and this choice accesses that page or segment of the program.

At the top of the page, the heading should be displayed that confirms the learners' choice of page, and lets them know that they have arrived at the right place in the program (Reynolds, 1982).

It may well be, of course, because of the exclusively instructional purpose of courseware, that headings may facilitate lesson completion and recall, especially when the courseware (such as TICCIT) provides higher levels of learner control (Merrill, Schneider, and Fletcher, 1974). However, this suggestion has not yet received empirical verification, although it is derived from accepted principles of courseware design.

Concluding remarks

Headings in electronic text displays are used for different purposes and in different ways from printed headings. In particular, headings serve a greater access and retrieval function in electronic displays. Authors find that in writing text for electronic text displays they have to use more headings. The principles that we outlined before for constructing headings still apply—only more so. These are:
  • Use *user-oriented* headings to help the user access relevant portions of a database or course.
  • Anticipate readers' questions.

- Make sure that the headings are short, accurate, and specific.

In addition, it may be helpful to pretest versions of the text in order to decide what the users' informational/instructional needs actually are in accessing a particular text, and how the headings can speed up or facilitate the retrieval process.

In conclusion, we reiterate that headings in electronic text need to be structurally-oriented in order to display the organization or sequence of lessons or pages in a document or program. Indexes to texts can be formed by combining the headings in databases/ courses, and these indexes will indicate the structure of the information contained in the text. This structure need not be—and, in fact, probably will not be—hierarchical, since few user needs are facilitated by a hierarchical retrieval scheme. However, the headings need to show clearly what is in all the parts and levels of the database/lesson and to indicate how the user can best get at the information. Learners need to have a mnemonic key to the index or menu available at all times that will enable them to break the program display and to get back to the headings list at any point in time (Merrill, 1982). The user who is simply browsing does not want to get locked into paging through lengthy sequences of program, unable to search and/or access different segments.

Acknowledgments

The preparation of this chapter has been assisted by Contract No. DAJA45-83-C-0033 from the U.S. Army Research for the Behavioral and Social Sciences through its European Liaison Office at the European Research Office of the U.S. Army, London, England. The opinions expressed are those of the authors and they do not necessarily represent those of the U.S. Army.

We are indebted to Alice Slaney for secretarial assistance.

References

Alessi, S.M., and Dennis, J.R. *Designing instruction for teaching with a computer*, Illinois Series on Educational Applications of

Computers, No. 3E. Urbana, IL: University of Illinois, Department of Secondary Education, 1979.

Anderson, R.C., Spiro, R.J., and Anderson, M.C. Schemata as scaffolding for the representation of information in discourse. *American Educational Research Journal,*, 1978, *15*, 433-440.

Antony, A., Weimer, S., and Eden, V. An examination of search strategy and an online bibliographic system pertaining to library and information sciences. *Special Libraries*, 1979, *70*, 127-134.

Bork, A. Tentative textual taxonomy. Discussion paper available from the author, Department of Physics, University of California, Irvine, California 29717, 1979.

Bransford, J.D. *Human cognition.* Belmont, CA: Wadsworth, 1979.

Bransford, J.D., and Johnson, M. Contextual prerequisites for understanding: Some investigations of comprehension and recall. *Journal of Verbal Learning and Verbal Behavior*, 1972, *11*, 717-726.

Brooks, L.W., Dansereau, D., Spurlin, J.E., and Holley, C.D. Effects of headings on text processing. *Journal of Educational Psychology*, 1983, *75*, 292-302.

Bruce, M., and Foster, J.J. The visibility of colored characters on colored backgrounds in Viewdata displays. *Visible Language*, 1982, *16*(4), 382-390.

CDC. *Author's Guide.* Minneapolis, MN: Control Data Corporation, 1977.

Charrow, V.R., and Redish, J.C. A Study of standardized headings for warranties. Tech. Report No. 6. Washington, DC: American Institutes for Research, Document Design Project, 1980. (ED 192 341)

Christensen, C.M., and Stordahl, K.E. The effect of organizational aids on comprehension and retention. *Journal of Educational Psychology*, 1955, *46*, 65-74.

Cole, J.N. The effects of non-prose textual characteristics on retention of major concepts and supporting details with and without specific instruction in their use. In D.P. Pearson and J. Hansen (Eds.), *Reading: Theory, research and practice* (26th Yearbook of the National Reading Conference), Clemson, South Carolina, Clemson University, 1977.

Davies, P. The primary curriculum/microcomputer interface. In R. Garland (Ed.), *Microcomputers and children in the primary school.* Lewes: Falmer Press (U.K.), 1982.

Dee-Lucas, D., and DiVesta, F.J. Learner generated organizational aids: Effects on learning from text. *Journal of Educational Psychology*, 1983, *75*, 304-311.

Doctorow, M.W., Wittrock, M.C., and Marks, C. Generative processes in reading comprehension. *Journal of Educational Psychology*, 1978, *70*, 109-118.

Dooling, D.J., and Lachman, R. Effects of comprehension on retention of prose. *Journal of Experimental Psychology*, 1971, *88*, 216-222.

Duchastel, P.C. Textual display techniques. In D.H. Jonassen (Ed.), *The Technology of text: Principles for structuring, designing, and displaying text.* Englewood Cliffs, NJ: Educational Technology Publications, 1982.

Eggan, P.D., Kauchuk, D., and Kirk, S. The effect of hierarchical cues on the learning concepts from prose materials. *Journal of Experimental Education*, 1978, *46*, 7-10.

Eisele, J. Design for Computer Based Instructional Systems. *Educational Technology*, 1978, *18*, 14-21.

Foster, J.J., and Bruce, M. Reading upper and lowercase on Viewdata. *Applied Ergonomics*, 1982(a), *13*(2), 145-149.

Foster, J.J., and Bruce, M. Looking for entries in videotex tables: A comparison of four color formats. *Journal of Applied Psychology*, 1982(b), *67*, 611-615.

Gagné, R.M. Planning and authoring computer-assisted instruction lessons. *Educational Technology*, 1981, *21*(9), 17-21.

Glass, G.V., McGaw, B., and Smith, M.L. *Meta-analysis in social research.* Beverly Hills: Sage, 1981.

Hartley, J. *Designing instructional text.* New York: Nichols, 1978.

Hartley, J. Introduction to Section 4. In J. Hartley (Ed.), *The psychology of written communication: Selected readings.* New York: Nichols, 1980(a).

Hartley, J. Space and structure in instructional text. In J. Hartley (Ed.), *The psychology of written communication: Selected readings.* New York: Nichols, 1980(b).

Hartley, J. Spatial cues in text. *Visible Language*, 1981, *14*, 62-79.

Hartley, J., and Burnhill, P. Explorations in space: A critique of

BPS publications. *Bulletin of the British Psychological Society*, 1976, *29*, 97-107.

Hartley, J., and Burnhill, P. Fifty guidelines for improving instructional text. In J. Hartley and I.K. Davies (Eds.), *Contributions to an educational technology*, Vol. 2. New York: Nichols, 1978.

Hartley, J., Kenely, J., Owen, G., and Trueman, M. The effect of headings on children's recall of prose text. *British Journal of Educational Psychology*, 1980, *50*, 304-307.

Hartley, J., Morris, P., and Trueman, M. Headings in text. *Remedial Education*, 1981, *16*(1), 5-7.

Hartley, J., and Trueman, M. The effects of headings in text on recall, search, and retrieval. *British Journal of Educational Psychology*, 1983, *53*(2), 205-214.

Hartley, J., Trueman, M., and Pigram, J. The effects of question or statement headings in text on the recall of low-ability pupils. Paper presented to the AERA Annual Convention, New Orleans, April, 1984.

Heaps, H.S. *Information retrieval: Computation and theoretical aspects.* New York: Academic Press, 1978.

Holley, C.D., Dansereau, D.F., Evans, S.H., Collins, K.W., Brooks, L.W., and Larson, D. Utilizing intact and embedded headings as processing aids with non-narrative text. *Contemporary Educational Psychology*, 1981, *6*, 227-236.

Jonassen, D.H. Blocking and types of headings in text: Effects on recall and retrieval. Paper presented at the annual meeting of the American Educational Research Association, Montreal, Quebec, Canada, April, 1983.

Jonassen, D.H., and Falk, L.M. Mapping and programming textual materials. *Programmed Learning and Educational Technology*, 1980, *17*(1), 19-26.

Jonassen, D.H., and Pace, A.J. Comparison of the effects of different forms of presentation on recall and retrieval of information. Paper presented at the annual meeting of the American Educational Research Association, New York, March, 1982.

Kaske, N.K., and Sanders, N.P. Evaluating the effectiveness of subject access: The view of the library patron. In *Communicat-*

ing information: Proceedings of ASIS annual meeting, 1980. White Plains, NY: Knowledge Industry Publications, 1980.

Klare, G.R., Shuford, E.H., and Nichols, W.H. The relation of format organization to learning. *Educational Research Bulletin*, 1958, *37*, 39-45.

Kozminsky, E. Altering comprehension: The effect of biasing titles on text comprehension. *Memory and Cognition*, 1977, *5*, 482-490.

Landry, D.L. The effects of organizational aids on reading comprehension. *Dissertation Abstracts International*, 1967, *27*(10), p. 3229.

Lee, W. Supra-paragraph prose structure: Its specification, perception, and effects on learning. *Psychological Reports*, 1965, *17*, 135-144.

Line, M. Redesigning journal articles for online viewing. In P.J. Hills (Ed.), *Trends in information transfer.* Westport, CT: Greenwood Press, 1982.

Mandel, C.A. *Subject access in the online catalog.* Washington, D.C.: Council on Library Resources, 1981. (ED 212 286)

Markey, K., Atherton, P., and Newton, C. An analysis of controlled vocabulary and free text search statements in online searches. *Online Review*, 1980, *4*, 225-236.

MECC. *A guide to developing instructional software for the Apple II computer.* St. Paul, MN: Minnesota Educational Computing Consortium, 1977.

Merrill, M.D., Schneider, E.W., and Fletcher, K.A. *TICCIT.* Englewood Cliffs, NJ: Educational Technology Publications, 1974.

Merrill, P.F. Displaying Text on Microcomputers. In D.H. Jonassen (Ed.), *The Technology of Text: Principles for structuring, designing, and displaying text.* Englewood Cliffs, NJ: Educational Technology Publications, 1982.

Muter, P., Latremouille, S.A., Treuniet, W.C., and Beam, P. Extended reading of continuous text on television screens. *Human Factors*, 1982, *24*(5), 501-508.

Proger, B.B., Carter, C.E., Mann, L., Taylor, R.G., and Bayuk, R.J. Advance concurrent organizers for detailed verbal passages used with elementary school pupils. *Journal of Educational Research*, 1973, *66*, 451-456.

Proger, B.B., Taylor, R.G., Mann, L., Taylor, R.G., and Bayuk, R.J. Conceptual pre-structuring for detailed verbal passages. *Journal of Educational Research*, 1970, *64*, 28-33.

Reynolds, L. Display problems for teletext. In D.H. Jonassen (Ed.), *The technology of text: Principles for structuring, designing, and displaying text.* Englewood Cliffs, NJ: Educational Technology Publications, 1982.

Rickards, J.P. Processing effects of advance organizers interspersed in text. *Reading Research Quarterly*, 1975-76, *4*, 599-622.

Robinson, F.P. *Effective study* (revised edition). New York: Harper and Row, 1961.

Robinson, F.P., and Hall, P. Studies of higher level reading abilities. *Journal of Educational Psychology*, 1941, *32*, 241-252.

Roblyer, M.D. Instructional design versus authoring of courseware: Some crucial differences. *AEDS Journal*, 1981, *81*, 173-181.

Schwarz, M.N.K., and Flammer, A. Text structure and title-effect on comprehension and recall. *Journal of Verbal Learning and Verbal Behavior*, 1981, *20*, 61-66.

Shackel, B. Plans and initial progress with BLEND—an electronic journal network communication experiment. *International Journal of Man-Machine Studies*, 1982, *17*, 225-233.

Snavely, A.E. The effectiveness of purpose statements and marginal notes as aids to reading comprehension. *Dissertation Abstracts International*, 1962, *22*(8), p. 2711.

Spitler, C.D., and Corgan, V.E. Rules for authoring computer-assisted instruction programs. *Educational Technology*, 1979, *19*(11).

Swarts, H., Flower, L., and Hayes, J. How headings in documents can mislead readers. Tech. Report No. 9. Washington, D.C.: American Institutes for Research, Document Design Project, 1980. (ED 192 344)

Taylor, B.M. Text structure and childrens' comprehension and memory for expository material. *Journal of Educational Psychology*, 1982, *74*, 323-340.

Twyman, M. Typography without words. *Visible Language*, 1981, *16*, 5-12.

Wager, W.W. Design considerations for instructional computing programs. *Journal of Educational Technology Systems*, 1982, *10*(3), 261-270.

Waller, R.H.W. Typographic access structures for educational texts. In P.A. Kolers and M.E. Wrolstad (Eds.), *Processing of visible language*, Vol. 1. New York: Plenum, 1979.

Waller, R.H.W. Text as diagram: Using typography to improve access and understanding. In D.H. Jonassen (Ed.), *The technology of text: Principles for structuring, designing, and displaying text.* Englewood Cliffs, NJ: Educational Technology Publications, 1982.

Chapter 11

Designing Contents Lists and Indexes for Access

Kieth C. Wright

> If the reader is, in fact, an active participant in the communica-
> tion process, we are challenged to investigate ways of presenting
> text that give readers a reliable basis for sensible sampling. If
> access is to be provided with headings, content lists, and so on,
> they need to be related logically and consistently to the structure
> of the text and to each other.
>
> (Waller, 1979, p. 184)

Contents lists and indexes *designed for access* must have certain characteristics if the reader is to have "sensible access" and if these lists and indexes are to have a logical and consistent relationship to one another, the text, and the needs of the reader. Pugh (1975) and Thomas (1976) noted that effective readers are not straight-through linear readers. Several of the effective reading techniques listed by Pugh are selective activities concerned with locating and making decisions about the content of a text. Observation of persons engaged in the study of text (as in "doing" a required reading) would seem to indicate that readers use contents lists and indexes as means of selective retrieval. Kintsch (1977) has summarized the various theories regarding selective attention.

This chapter will discuss various types of contents lists and indexes, discuss the factors that affect the display of a contents list or index, and give some indication of the impact of user access on the design of contents lists and indexes.

Contents Lists for Access

Typographic Design of Contents Lists

The display of a contents list or index is affected by type style, type size, line leading (space between lines), and proportional spacing, as well as the contrast and reflective qualities of particular ink-and-paper combinations. Type styles are usually classed as "serif" or "sans-serif," depending on whether the fine "serif" line is used to finish off various letters (these words are set in a serif type style). Several studies have shown that readers prefer serif type (Becker, Heinrich, Sichowsky, and Wendt, 1970; Paterson and Tinker, 1932). Type styles may also be used to differentiate certain text from the main body of the text as in the case of using *bold* or *italic* type (Paterson and Tinker, 1940). Hartley's (1979-1980) investigation of content page layouts found that italic style used for authors' names aided searchers in finding the text they wanted and ignoring the text they wished to ignore. Overuse of bold or italic type tends to defeat the highlighting purpose of emphasizing specific areas of text. Bold type is recommended for major sections of contents lists combined with a regular type face for sub-sections.

Type size is counted in points, which are 1/72 of an inch in height. A typical American newspaper is printed in 8-9 point type. This book is done primarily in 11 point type. Like highlighting, varying the size of type is used as a typographic cue to indicate portions of text which are important and relatively unimportant. Thus, main topical section headings in contents lists will be presented in larger type, and main headings in subject indexes are also often in larger type. Writers and editors should note that the opposite impressions can be given to the reader by the use of smaller type size: i.e., that the text is not important because the type size is so small. No text in the contents list should be smaller than 8-9 point, and major section headings should be at least 14 point.

Horizontal spacing between letters also affects the readability of the text of contents lists and indexes (Payne, 1967). Most typewritten text allows the same amount of space for all letters, assuming that letters like "i" should be given as much space as "w." Some typewriters and printers attached to computers allow for proportional spacing, depending on the actual size of the letter. Proportional spacing allows for increasing reading speed without a loss of understanding and decreases the cost of printed materials (Davenport and Smith, 1965). The type you are reading is proportionally spaced.

The selection of paper stock and ink can drastically affect the ease with which text can be read and therefore the ease with which a contents list or index can be read. Even carefully planned displays of contents lists and indexes can be frustrating to the reader because of the reflection factors of paper and ink. Traditionally, the black ink on white paper with a minimum of reflection from the ink and a maximum of reflection from the paper have been found to allow for greater reading speed and ease of reading at a distance (Paterson and Tinker, 1931; Taylor, 1924). Light reflected into the eye is measured in Munsell values (Munsell Color, Baltimore, Md.) or United States Government Printing Office values. The higher the number, the more light is reflected from the paper and ink into the eyes. About 70 percent reflectance of paper has been recommended for use with black ink (Tinker, 1963). Higher reflectance (lighter stock) is required for use with inks in other colors. Use of colored papers or inks should always take into account the fact that many people have color deficiencies because the cones of the eyes are not able to process some colors and see them as gray. Prior to making a commitment to a paper-and-ink color combination, it may be well to consider how readers will view the combination (Ralph, 1982). Reflectance and contrast levels for contents lists should be selected to allow rapid scanning of the contents list by the reader. Black ink combined with paper with at least a 70 percent reflectance should be the standard against which other options (different colors of ink, lighter paper stock) are judged.

Designing Contents Lists

A contents list functions as a linear display of the content of a text. The reader can use this list to scan rapidly the content of the text for sections which are important to that reader. Since the contents list is presented in the same linear order as the text itself and is an abbreviated representation of the text *in order*, the author and editor must use various typographic (varying type size and type intensity) as well as layout strategies (placement of text on the page) to indicate to the reader what portions of that linear display are most important.

Although the contents list is shorter than the text itself and may provide a means of showing major subject divisions or ideas, nevertheless, the display of a contents list mirrors the order of the text. The reader must proceed through that linear array to select the item of interest. Such a search takes considerably less time than paging through the whole text. As an outline of the topics of ideas of the text, a contents list allows for rapid, sequential search of the outline and finding a page reference to the appropriate section of the full text. Abstracts at the beginning of scientific and technical articles could provide the same type of access *if* phrases of the abstract were followed by page indicators. Unfortunately, this practice is not followed in most professional literature. The abstract of an article could contain page indicators as follows:

A study of reader receptivity to layout of contents lists. Forty-eight graduate students evaluated left ranging layouts, 23-24; right ranging layouts, 25-26; and a variety of run-on arrangements, 28-30. Results are presented indicating no measurable differences, 31; and some general conclusions are drawn, 32.

The necessity of a sequential search is complicated by an additional factor: contents lists are rarely specific enough for finding detailed information. Indeed, in many books and journals, the contents list appears to be simply a repetition of the chapter headings followed by chapter section headings as the subcontent display. For example, the illustration on "An Electronic Data Processing System" (p. 269) has a sub-section on "functional units." If the reader is interested in "central processing units," he or she must now enter the text and scan the section to see if information on that topic is included under the sub-section, or scan through the text of the entire contents list to see if "Central Processing Unit" or "CPU" is listed at any point.

On the other hand, if the contents list is very detailed, the

search for specific information becomes time-consuming. An
example of such detail is found in Fellows' *Cataloging Rules with
Explanations and Illustrations* (New York: Wilson, 1926):

> General Directions and Suggestions 8
> 1 Handwritten Cards
>   a. legibility
>   b. space between words
>   c. space between groups
>   d. other spacing
> 2 Typewritten Cards
>   a. space at top of card
>   b. cards evenly placed on roller
>   c. position with relation to vertical rules
>   d. space between lines
>   e. clear-cut impression
>   f. spacing in person's name when inverted

All of these references are to page eight. Fellows graciously
provided a "bird's-eye view" or summarized contents to his book
on the preceding page. Usually, editorial policy dictates that the
contents list be brief (one to two pages) and emphasize major
topics of the text. In detailed or technical publications, a strong
case should be made for extending the length of the contents list
in order to provide more detailed information to the reader.

Various layout and typographic techniques can be used to
highlight major items in the contents list. These typically include
larger and darker type for major headings which denote chapters
and smaller, lighter type to denote the contents of each chapter or
unit in the text. Spacing can also be used to highlight important
text. Often, appendices, lists of contributors, tables, etc., are also
displayed in the same smaller and lighter typeface. Where the
contents of major chapters of sections are listed in detail, the list
may be set out in an inverted style:

> MAJOR SECTION
>   subsection 1, subsection 2,
>   subsection 3, subsection 4

Such a display is preferable because it sets off the main section
from the related subsection and clearly defines the main section.

Page designations may follow subsections or may be set out so that each subsection takes a separate line:

ELECTRONIC DATA PROCESSING SYSTEMS 19
    Stored Programs 22
    Microcode 25
    Functional Units 26
    Peripherals 29

Burnhill, Hartley, and Davies (1977) found that the retrieval time in index displays was not related to ranging the display in the more traditional form (numbers ranged right) or to ranging the page numbers next to the subheadings (as above) or to arranging the entries with the subtopics run on:

ELECTRONIC DATA PROCESSING SYSTEMS 19
    Stored Programs 22; Microcode 25
    Functional Units 26; Peripherals 29

It is considerably cheaper (in terms of layout time) to use the run-on style in the display of contents lists.

Hartley (1979-1980) and Hartley and Guile (1979-1981) have investigated user preferences for various layouts of journal contents lists. Their experiments contrasted horizontal layouts (which placed authors' names on the left, centered titles, and had page references on the right) with vertical layouts in which page numbers were followed by title and author information in inverted paragraph style. The layout in horizontal style was found to be superior in assisting readers to retrieve significant information because that is the way in which readers of the English language learn to retrieve information (letting the eyes range left to right). The most appropriate length for horizontal displays and the use of different type styles need further research.

Vocabulary of the Reader

If the reader is considered to have an active role to play in the process of using contents lists, then the authors and editors of printed materials need to pay closer attention to the vocabulary of the reader. Since most contents lists derive from the author's chapter and section headings, it can be argued that these lists reflect the author's attempt to communicate the main structure of the passage to his or her potential readers. Still it cannot be assumed that there is a one-to-one relationship between the author's meaning and the reader's meaning even when they both use the same word or phrase to indicate a subject. Even the same concepts may be expressed in very different terminology. As will be noted below, the studies of subject indexing have concerned themselves for some time with the relationships of the varied vocabularies of indexers, authors, and readers. Careful studies of the ways in which readers use contents-list vocabularies are needed, and more exploration of the use of unambiguous terminology and control of synonyms and homographs is needed. If the reader is to use the contents list to select areas of text to attend to, then it is essential to provide the best possible guidance, in vocabulary that the reader understands. Following the principle of least effort, the more effort required to find the appropriate section of text, the less likely it is that the reader will expend the effort to find that text. Conversely, the easier it is for the reader to use his or her natural vocabulary to find appropriate sections of text, the more likely it is that the reader will use the text. Since contents lists are for the use of the reader, careful attention to the right amount of detail and the vocabulary of those lists seems essential.

Contents Lists in Computer Programming Menus

A related development in education and business applications of all computers—especially microcomputers—is the "menu-driven program." Such programs make use of the ability of programming languages such as BASIC or PASCAL to branch to particular functions on the basis of the program user's direction. In a typical program, a series of four to six options will be displayed on the screen with the instruction that the user is to indicate his or her choice by entering the number of the procedure wanted.

Such menus are contents lists to the various program functions that the user may access. Such programmed menus force the user to access and use the contents list, thereby constraining the opportunities for browsing. Access to text is more purposive. The same factors of layout, type size and display, and vocabulary apply to menus. In addition, menu displays can take advantage of the graphic and color capabilities of most microcomputers. The menu should be displayed in sufficient detail so that choices are obvious to the user. Of course, the same principles apply to the development of contents lists in printed materials. The user should not have to select an item and run the program in order to determine what the particular function does. In many menus, the user can press a key to view an abstract of a section of text. With teletext systems, the reader who inquiries about a topic is presented with a more detailed contents list of that section, providing a tree-structured access to information. In such tree-structured programs, the user should be able to return to any level of the structure with ease.

Often, current menus are *not* that clear. Where possible, the display of the menu should be in a larger type size for ease of reading and interpretation. In some microcomputer systems, it is possible to add graphic and color cues to the various choices, which will make choices easier for children and those with limited English language abilities. Programs can also be written that utilize a light pen to control the selection of items on a menu. Touching the light pen to the selected item on the menu causes control to pass to the appropriate section of the program. Once items on a menu are selected, their layout on the screen should be studied to determine the likely priority of user selection. The function most likely to be used should be listed first. Overall screen layout should be studied to eliminate irrelevant items or words that create "noise" for the user.

The primary difference between computer menus and print contents lists is the organization of information. While contents lists are linear, computer menus are often hierarchical. Often, major menus are created, which lead to submenus for other functions. This type of tree structure can be very useful if the logic of the creator is similar to the logic of the user. User testing of such tree-structured menus is important because the logic must not only make sense to the creator, but also to the user(s), who may not subdivide information in the same way that the creator does. Designers of tree-structured menus must consider the ways in which users will access needed information and attempt to develop tree structures that make sense to users.

A final factor in menu-driven computer program displays should be mentioned. Each menu program should be tested so as to be as "idiot proof" as possible. What happens when the user makes a numerical choice that is not displayed on the screen? What happens if the user decides not to use any of the listed functions (is there a way out beyond shutting off the machine)? Does the program allow for mistakes between the letter "l" and the number "1" (and zero and the letter "o")? Many commercially-available programs of this sort have obviously not given any thought to the ways in which menus should be designed, the capacities of the particular programs to give nontextual cues, and the large potential of the user to create alternatives that are unacceptable to the program. There are a variety of "error trapping" strategies that can be used to assist the user. The failure to respond with the appropriate type of response can cause another program section to be invoked which gives the user more guidance:

> "Do not use (o) (the letter)   for
>   (0) (the number)   "

> or

> "Bad signal, 'CAPS LOCK' key pushed down??"

Error messages should be as descriptive of the error made as possible and should avoid jargon such as "syntax error," or worse, "Error #4." The option of recovering from a mistaken decision ("Do you really want to delete your file?") or leaving the program ("Type ESCAPE to quit the program") should be included.

Indexes for Access

The Arrangement of Indexes

Indexes are designed to allow the reader access to information in a text without the necessity of following the linear organization of the text itself. Names and subjects are typically arranged in an arbitrary way that is familiar to everyone from using telephone books and other directories and encyclopedias: the alphabetical arrangement. This arrangement allows the reader to select a subject, look it up in the alphabetical display, and go directly to the page(s) where the information is to be found. Indexes provide selective access to the information contained in a text. Most modern subject indexes and index arrays utilize a computer program to follow that same procedure. The "inverted files" used in large database systems are typically arranged in an alphabetical display and can usually be accessed by a system command which will display a portion of the alphabetic arrangement prior to, and following, the entry word. An example from such a file might be (from the "expand" command of the DIALOG system of Lockheed Retrieval Service):

E1	APPEAL	234
E2	APPEALING	24
E3	APPEALINGLY	5
E4	APPEALS	15
E5	APPEAR	19
E6	APPEARED	3
E7	APPEARS	2

Inverted files are created by a program when textual materials are entered into the computer memory, usually on the basis of differentiating types of information in the text (for example, authors, title information, descriptors, various types of numerical coding, and the text of the abstract or article itself). Each differentiated item is separated from the record and filed in a separate file, which is later sorted and compared with current files of that type. The result of these operations is an alphabetical file of information in which authors, title words, descriptor words, and text words are arranged in an alphabetical display with indicators of location attached. Such "mapping" of text fields allows for searching of specific inverted files for information rather than a sequential search through the whole text. Thus, searching for a particular author does not require a search of each entry in the system memory, but only a search of the author inverted file, and a program-based reference to the appropriate entry(ies). Concordances are also arranged in this manner. Selecting index terms, regularizing vocabularies, and arranging index entries are covered in Borko and Bernier, 1978; Cleveland and Cleveland, 1983; and Knight, 1979. Standards for indexing have been developed in the United States (*Basic Criteria for Indexes*) and the United Kingdom (*Recommendations for the Preparation of Indexes of Books, Periodicals, and Other Publications*).

The two basic alphabetical arrangements are word-by-word and letter-by-letter filing. Word-by-word filing arranges all items having one word in order prior to filing the next word. Letter-by-letter filing treats the whole phrase as if there were no spaces in the string of characters and files on that basis. For example, the determination of where to file "Newark" will be affected by the type of filing. Letter-by-letter filing places "Newark" prior to words which begin with "New" followed by another word such as "Haven" or "York." Word-by-word filing places "Newark" after such words. Hartley, Davies, and Burnhill (1981) have conducted experimental studies of how university students and younger children arrange items in an alphabetical list. Students seem to use a variety of methods, mainly sense and meaning, to put words in order. No one method of arrangement seems better for retrieval purposes. It is important that the arrangement pattern chosen be evident to the reader of the index. In fact, the rules of arrangement should be described and illustrated at the beginning of the index. As the file grows in size, the addition of cross-reference notes to indicate the location of specific entries might be considered so that the user would not have to scan long series of entries to find the specific entry wanted.

Text Derivative Indexes

Indexes may be derived from the text with which they are associated. Examples of such indexes include (1) name indexes of persons, places, and/or events mentioned in the text, (2) author indexes in cumulated periodical indexes, and (3) title indexes in periodical indexes. Such derived type indexes may include subject indexes when the vocabulary is selected from the text itself, as in the case of free text indexing derived from the text without reference to a subject heading list or authority file (a listing of terms used in the indexing system). Various automated indexing schemes based on the frequency of occurrence or co-occurrence of words in a vocabulary of text are also totally text dependent. A related type of derivation is found in title derivative indexes (Feinburg, 1973; Luhn, 1962; Vorees, 1965), which utilize the text of titles of journal articles to create displays of subject terms derived from titles. All significant words in each title are arranged individually by computer program, sorted into an alphabetical array, and printed.

The two major types of title derivative indexes are: (1) Keyword in Context (KWIC) indexes and Keyword out of Context (KWOC) indexes, which will be discussed later. KWIC indexes use a computer program to shift each significant title word into a fixed indexing position and display the chosen word with the words of the title immediately surrounding it. After all of the titles in a particular indexing activity are shifted, they are sorted into an alphabetical display and printed with each item printed on one line. Some KWIC indexes select an index entry point near the center of the page and allow extra blank space at this point to create a column highlighting the alphabetical arrangement of selected terms. Other words in the title are "wrapped around" the selected word and the column space so that the reader receives more information about the whole title. An example may help:

Engineering report—rusty	tool	1191
Companies put new zip in old sales	tool (tech. report)	0100
The dictionary as a writer's	tool	0860
Language as a engineering	tool —preparatio	1699

KWIC indexes have been used as current awareness tools in a number of fields, and various methods of displaying the selected significant words in alphabetical order have been tried. The longer the entry line can be, the more full title information can be included and the better the opportunity for the reader to be able to "unrotate" the title and recreate the original title sense. Emphasized display of the entry word by bold type, arrangement on the page, and use of columns have also been used. KWIC indexes do not look like "regular" indexes and take some practice before they can be used effectively. The introductory information and example of a KWIC index are critical to reader success. Seeing a display of 120 characters, arbitrarily split into two columns near the center, with the journal identification number on the right takes some adjustment. The user does not begin reading on the left as experience would indicate, but begins to the right of the "gutter" created by the column.

Wright and Threlfall (1980) have looked at reader expectations as they affect the usability of indexes, noting that previous experience with indexes affects the way readers approach a new index. In the American scene, one can expect that the index format of Wilson Company indexes such as the *Reader's Guide to Periodical Literature* will be part of the experience of all readers. KWIC index forms present information to the reader in a non-traditional form. The reader enters the textual display in the middle of the page (or wherever the "gutter" space is provided), reads to the right finding the document citation, and then returns to the left margin to add more title information. Obviously, the *Reader's Guide* is not arranged in this way nor are the card catalogs of major libraries in schools and colleges. It may be possible to arrange index displays so that they are more useful than present back-of-the-book or periodical displays; but the burden of proof will remain with the innovator. KWIC indexes can be useful as current awareness tools or to provide access to previously unavailable information. KWIC index display of a contents list or of previously unindexed journal articles is relatively inexpensive to produce and can be easily generated within the context of a research and development organization's special library or a department of a large academic or research library. Because of its non-traditional appearance, some instruction in the use of the KWIC index should precede the text of the index itself.

The interest in having a more "normal" index display led to the development of keyword out of context (KWOC) indexes in which a computer program is used to process significant title words but displays these significant words as subject headings followed by each title containing that word. If the significant words are ordered alphabetically and titles arranged under each significant word, the arrangement looks like a typical back-of-the-book index. Some programs allow for the inclusion of cross-references in the display so that words which are not in the titles can be added to guide the reader to terms which occur in titles. An example might be:

```
LANGUAGE
    Comments on the relevance of language        1234
    A numerical notation for language systems    0987
    PL360 a programming language for 360 comput  1365
```

Not all title words are chosen for display by the computer program. Every program contains a list of "stopwords" which consist of articles, conjunctions, prepositions, pronouns, auxiliary verbs, some adjectives, and editorially-selected words judged to have no value as index terms such as "action," "theory," or "summary." This stoplist of words is checked each time the computer processes a word. If the word is found on the stoplist, that word is not processed as an entry point for the index. Often, such words are counted during processing to determine the number of words in titles which are not useful for indexing purposes.

KWIC and KWOC indexes provide rapid access to information, since they require less human effort in indexing because they are processed by computer program. Questions remain as to the quality of access provided, because index term selection and coordination are entirely dependent upon the author's selection of terms. Any attempt to attract attention by using "cute" titles or "jargon" will create nonsense for the reader. For example, an article on teaching of reading in China should not be given a title like, "There Are Only Three Dogs in China." I can remember a journal article with that title on that subject. All title derivative indexes require that the author and the reader be using similar vocabulary related to the subject of inquiry. Some indexing services have attempted to deal with this particular problem by having a professional indexer add terms to the title field prior to computer processing. Such activity increases the possibility of relevant access for the reader but increases the costs of indexing and delays the production of the printed index.

Where the vocabulary of the discipline is specific enough to eliminate multiple meanings of words and phrases and titles are written to give specific information about content of the article or paper, title derivative indexes can provide fast, inexpensive access for the members of that discipline. The more human intervention required for editing, adding words to titles, and dealing with problems of ambiguity, the more likely another form of index will be found to be more useful to readers and less expensive to the producers.

Coordinate Indexes

Coordinate indexes are created by assigning single index terms from an authority list (or controlled vocabulary list) to articles or documents and subsequently recombining these terms to create a specific index entry. Thus, "three," "little," and "pigs" might be index entries which could later be combined into "Three Little Pigs" for retrieval (Mooers, 1956; Taube and Wachell, 1953). Since single terms in a computer file can be manipulated with Boolean logic, many large indexing systems have developed coordinate indexing systems in which title words, subject descriptor words, and words from abstracts can be individually (or in combined groups) combined by the system user with the Boolean "and," "or," and "and not." With the exception of the Online Computer Library Center (OCLC), all major online bibliographic databases now available use such systems.

Coordination of single words (by computer or in a card file) proved inadequate to the amount of information indexed, so indexers began to introduce various multiword terms as well as role and link designators to avoid false combinations such as "Polish Cars" from "Cars" and "Polish" (or "Blind Venetians"). Artandi and Hines (1963) have pointed out the inevitable movement toward subject authority files in order to avoid ambiguity, synonymy, and to establish a cross-reference (or syndetic) structure.

User access is improved by coordinate indexing systems because of the ability of the *user* to form his or her own indexing phrases and search them in combinations not necessarily thought of by the original author or the publisher of the index or database. Such user access depends, however, on the ability of the user to manipulate the system to his or her own advantage. Use of the present-day computer-based coordinate indexing system requires training if the user is to be able to manipulate the system effectively.

Alternative Index Displays

Faceted indexes (Classification Research Group, 1955) are based on a prior set of decisions concerning all of the exclusive aspects (or facets) of a particular subject area, and indexing terms are pre-coordinated by the indexer. The display of a faceted index is often in classification order based upon a classification scheme rather than alphabetical order. Chain indexes were first used by Ranganathan in his Colon classification (Ranganathan, 1937, 1964). Such indexes use a similar pre-coordination to allow every concept to be linked (or chained) to every other related concept in a hierarchical system (Coates, 1973). The Preserved Context Index System (PRECIS) utilizes a computer program to display (for the patron and for printing) the possible set of concept relations among indexing terms. Terms are selected and arranged in a string with a program manipulable grammar of punctuation which allows the indexer to predetermine which concept relations are to be displayed and in what order (Austin, 1971; Richmond, 1981). Classified indexes arranged by classification scheme such as the Fiction Index (London: Association of Assistant Librarians, 1953-) have been produced in specialized situations.

The major advantage of faceted, chain, and classified indexes is that they allow for a conceptual search by putting related subjects together much as a classification scheme and its notation system bring like books together on the library's shelves. The major disadvantage is that such schemes require an alphabetical index for initial specific access to the classified display. The two displays usually mean that a reader must enter the system by means of a specific term (in the index), and then proceed to the classified array for browsing. Any time the creator of an index asks the reader to retrieve some term or number and then use that number to retrieve the full entry (as in the ERIC system), he or she is creating an index with built-in possibilities for errors of transcription or memory. Ease of access for the reader is not improved by a double look-up system. Not only is there the possibility of error multiplied, but the time involved in the look-up process is increased. In most situations of journal and book publishing, a single look-up alphabetical index is to be preferred over a faceted display. It can be argued that classified displays present a hierarchy of information which may be useful to the reader once he or she has gained entry into the display. The same argument is often heard about the value of browsing in an open stack library arranged by some classification scheme. Few reports are available on the actual utility of such browsing or the cost of such browsing in terms of reader time and effort. Research is needed on how readers actually use classified displays of index information. Various layouts of classed information (horizontal, vertical with indentions) also need research.

Citation Indexes

Citation indexes (Garfield, 1979) are arranged on the basis of the author of an original article with subarrangement under that article of all the authors of articles which cite that article. North American examples of citation indexes include the publications of the Institute for Scientific Information: *Science Citation Index* and *Social Science Citation Index*. Such indexing depends on citation and not on subject headings or index terms, although the Institute for Scientific Information does provide a title derivative index based on the co-occurrence of terms in titles in its various citation indexes. The citation index provides access to the "invisible college" of scholars who cite one another in written materials. Since the citation index provides access on the basis of citation rather than title words or indexer selected words, subject relationships among articles is assumed to be based on the fact that the author of an article cited someone else's work as he or she was writing. Citation indexes provide a type of access for the reader, which no other type of index provides: "who cites whom" information. For this reason, they are very important as retrieval tools, especially in the fields of instructional and information design. I am aware of no books published with citation indexes. Although the extended bibliographies in some publications are an attempt to identify all significant authors in the field, there is no attempt made to show the interrelationship among authors. Authors and editors might want to consider the value of citation indexing as an addition to the textual materials and references in a publication. Such citation indexing combined with a subject index derived from the titles of publications cited might be extremely useful to readers.

Problems in Subject Index Displays

Almost all forms of indexes in current use have some type of subject access either supplied by an indexer or derived from title or text information. Two major problems of all subject indexing are synonymity (the use of several different words to indicate the same content) and scattering of index entries (because "cats," "felines," and "tabbies" all refer to the same concept but file alphabetically in different locations). A controlled vocabulary list is one method of dealing with synonyms. In the vocabulary list or authority file, cross-references are made from all synonyms to the one term which is to be used in the index. The indexer selects the index entry on the basis of the vocabulary of that list. Particular attention must be paid to new terminology as it is added to the list in order to be sure that new terms are not merely synonyms to current terms. Otherwise, the cross-reference structure must be changed to make the new term the preferred term. Controlled vocabulary lists also define ambiguous terms and define the situations in which alternative terms may be used through scope notes (brief annotations defining usage in the index) and illustrations. Usually, the various homographs are distinguished with some form of special notation so that the specific application of a term is clear. Thus, the various uses of the word "base" might be distinguished with a parenthetical phrase or word: BASE(military), BASE(chemistry). Modern thesaurus lists also indicate the relationship among terms by the use of indicators for Broader Term (BT), Narrower Term (NT), and Related Term (RT). For example: Education NT Preschool Education.

Scattering of entries is caused by the way specific terminology is created in the English language. More specific indications of meaning are created by adding adjectives in front of the noun. "Cats" becomes "black cats" becomes "Large black cats" as terminology becomes more and more specific. Each of these entries about cats will file in a different place in an alphabetical array. One method of dealing with this scattering is to file entries on the noun with the adjective "inverted" behind the noun. As in this example:

> Cats, Black
> Cats, Domestic
> Cats, Wild

Another method is to utilize cross-references in the controlled vocabulary list in the display of the index. The reader can then use the index itself to find information on a particular topic either by page reference or cross-reference to another subject:

> Felines SEE Cats, domestic

All forms of subject indexes must deal effectively with the problems of synonymity (by use of a controlled vocabulary) and scattering of references (by use of inverted subject headings) if the reader is to have effective access to the text by means of the subject index. Too many different terms referring to the same subject and too many phrase headings cause the reader to miss information relevant to his or her interests. Access for the reader is improved by gathering all of the relevant information under one heading (and its subheadings). The other major consideration is the pattern of language use of the reader. If readers form more specific information requests on the basis of traditional English language patterns (as described above by adding specifying adjectives in front of nouns which name things), then indexes must make provisions for access on the basis of readers' expectations. In an inverted index display, such access can be created by phrase heading cross-references ("black cats SEE cats, black"). Careful study of the use of language among readers or among authors in a discipline can aid in the design of a subject index, which is then accessible to those particular users.

Summary

All contents lists and indexes are an attempt to indicate the content of a text in a language and format which will be useful to the potential reader of the text. Contents lists provide a brief summary outline of the contents of the text in sequential order. Indexes provide selective access to text on the basis of an alphabetical display of subject terms selected by an indexer, coordinated by a searcher using a database, or derived from a computer processing of title information. Not all index displays are arranged in alphabetical order, but classified displays, chain displays, and other hierarchical displays require some form of alphabetical index for effective use. A variety of layout and typographical signals may be used to emphasize (or de-emphasize) aspects of contents lists and indexes. It is important that authors and editors remember that the *content* of the display is probably more important than the display techniques used: nonsense well displayed is still nonsense. References even properly displayed which lead the reader to useless information or information different from that indicated in the display can only be frustrating. Relating the language of the author to the language of the intended reader will remain a major challenge in all contents lists and indexes. Obviously, the more we know about how the reader makes use of language as he or she processes information, the better able we will be to construct contents lists and indexes which are useful.

References

American National Standards Institute. *Basic criteria for indexes.* New York: ANSI, 1974.

Artandi, S., and Hines, T.C. Roles and links, or forward to Cutter. *American Documentation*, 1963, *14*, 74-77.

Austin, D. PRECIS indexing. *Information Scientist*, 1971, *5*, 95-113.

Becker, D., Heinrich, J., Schowsky, R.V., and Wendt, D. Reader preference for typeface and leading. *Journal of Typographic Research*, 1970, *4*, p. 61.

Borko, H., and Bernur, C.L. *Indexing concepts and Methods.* New York: Academic Press, 1978.

British Standard 3700. *Recommendations for the preparation of indexes of books, periodicals and other publications.* London: BSI, 1976.

Burnhill, P., Hartley, J., and Davies, L. Typographic decision making: The layout of indexes. *Applied Ergonomics,* 1977, *8,* 35-39.

Classification Research Group. Need for a faceted classification as a basis for all methods of information retrieval. *Library Association Record,* 1955, *57,* 262-268.

Cleveland, D.B., and Cleveland, A.D. *Introduction to indexing and abstracting.* Littleton, CO: Libraries Unlimited, 1983.

Coates, E.J. Some properties of relationships in the structure of indexing languages. *Journal of Documentation,* 1973, *29,* 390-404.

Davenport, J.S., and Smith, S.A. Effects of hyphenation, justification, and type size on readability. *Journalism Quarterly,* 1965, *42,* p. 381.

Feinberg, H. *Title derivative indexing techniques: A comparative study.* Metuchen, NJ: Scarecrow Press, 1973.

Garfield, E. *Citation indexing: Its theory and application in science, technology, and humanities.* New York: John Wiley and Sons, 1979.

Hartley, J. Designing journal content pages. The role of spatial and typographic cues. *Journal of Research Communication Studies,* 1979/1980, *2* 83-98.

Hartley, J., Davies, L., and Burnhill, P. Alphabetization in indexes: Experimental studies. The *Indexer,* 1981, *12,* 149-153.

Hartley, J., and Guile, G.A. Designing journal contents pages: Preference for horizontal and vertical layouts. *Journal of Research Communication Studies,* 1979/1981, *2,* 271-288.

Kintsch, W. *Memory and cognition.* New York: John Wiley and Sons, 1977.

Knight, G.N. *Indexing, the art of: A guide to the indexing of books and periodicals.* London: G. Allen and Unwin, 1979.

Luhn, H.P. Keyword-in-Context index for technical literature (KWIC index). *American Documentation,* 1962, *11,* 359-366.

Mooers, C.N. Datacoding applied to mechanical organization of knowledge. *American Documentation,* 1956, *2,* 20-52.

Paterson, D.G., and Tinker, M.A. Studies of typographical factors influencing speed of reading: VI. Black type versus white type. *Journal of Applied Psychology*, 1931, *15*, p. 241.

Paterson, D.G., and Tinker, M.A. Studies of typographical factors influencing speed of reading: X. Style of type face. *Journal of Applied Psychology*, 1932, *16*, p. 605.

Paterson, D.G., and Tinker, M.A. *How to make type readable.* New York: Harpers, 1940.

Payne, D.E. Readability of typewritten material: Proportional versus standard spacing. *Journal of Typographic Research*, 1967, *1*, p. 125.

Pugh, A.K. The development of silent reading. In W. Latham (Ed.), *The road to effective reading.* London: Wardlock, 1975.

Ralph, J.B. Handicapped by design: The need for printing and publishing guidelines. *American Rehabilitation*, March-April, 1982, 4-10.

Ranganathan, S.R. *Prolegomena to library classification.* Madras, India: Madras Library Association, 1937.

Ranganathan, S.R. Subject headings and facet analysis. *Journal of Documentation*, 1964, *20*, 109-119.

Richmond, P. *An Introduction to PRECIS for North American usage.* Littleton, Co: Libraries Unlimited, 1981.

Svenonius, E.F. Directions for research in indexing, classification and cataloging. *Library Resources and Technical Services*, 1981, *25*, 88-103.

Taube, M., and Wachell, I.S. The logical structure of coordinate indexing. *American Documentation*, 1953, *4*, 67-88.

Taylor, C.D. The relative legibility of black and white print. *Journal of Educational Psychology*, 1924, *25*, p. 561.

Thomas, L. The self-organized learner and the printed word. Center for the Study of Human Learning, Brunel University, 1976.

Tinker, M.A. *Legibility of Print.* Ames, IA: Iowa State University Press, 1963.

Vorees, H.E. Improvements in permutted title indexes. *American Documentation*, 1965, *16*, p. 99.

Waller, R.H. Typographical access structures for education text. In P.A. Kolers, M.E. Wrolstad, and H. Bouma, *Processing of visible language.* Volume I. New York: Plenum Press, 1979.

Wright, P., and Threlfall, M.S. Readers expectations about form influence the usability of an index. *Journal of Research Communication Studies*, 1980, *2*, 99-106.

Section V

Electronic Display of Text

Introduction

Electronic production, storage, and distribution of text are affecting not only what gets recorded, but also the roles of all the participants (including and especially the author) in the text production process. However, most affected by the transition to *electronic publication* of information are likely to be the users of text, for text is beginning to appear in novel forms, which are being accessed in novel ways.

The exponential growth of information is resulting in dramatic changes in the way that it is disseminated and the way it is used. One of the most significant problems associated with the growth of information is in gaining access to it. That is, simply finding what we want to know is often the most demanding step in solving a problem because of the voluminous amount of data through which we probably have to sift. Fifteen years ago, we might have spent a few hours manually searching indexes containing thousands of records in order to complete a literature review. Today, we have many more indexes with many times the quantity of information in each. So we use the computer, which requires but a few seconds to search many more databases containing millions of records. The growth of information has necessitated such high-speed computer searching.

The next set of *information retrieval* problems relates to how to sort through and deal with the voluminous amount of information that the computer has found for us. This process begins selectively with the search, where we use Boolean logic to extract only potentially relevant information. So, the information we get is pre-sorted. Accessing the information is only the first step. Next, we need to synthesize what we have come to know into meaningful conclusions and hypotheses. Such synthesis traditionally was dependent on the conceptual ability of the researcher, who read, interpreted, and inferred from what was known. However, as the amount of knowledge we access has grown proportionately with what is known, we are relying more on computer algorithms to sift through our data, draw our conclusions, and make our inferences. For instance, when we use a computer program to perform a meta-analysis of factorial research data, we are asking for a synthesis of a body of research. Virtually every piece of information returned from space from the myriad collection devices are received and interpreted by computers. Eventually, computers will be making value-laden decisions that affect all of our lives, such as whether or not to enter war or whose lives should be saved by medical research. In the pure and applied sciences and increasingly in the social sciences, computers are relied upon for determining and interpreting what we know.

An analogy to this process may be in order. In that neglected closet in the spare room which has for years been the repository of all those unclassifiable possessions, we find it difficult to locate what we are looking for because of its lack of organization and eclectic content. The databases we search are similar—eclectic collections of knowledge. The only difference is that the computer can search through all of the contents of its closet, arrange it, synthesize it, and deliver what we want to know before we can get the door to ours open. Its speed, accuracy, and volume of storage make it a natural search tool that is changing not only the way we do research but also the thought processes leading to and resulting from it. Electronic storage and publication of information affects the processes we use to gain access to and interpret information.

According to our classification scheme, electronic publication *controls* the *process* of text reception and comprehension. Yet, in another sense, we can say that electronic text provides greater *learner control* of the process. For instance, if we are reading an electronic display and want to review a concept, all we need to do is ask the computer to locate the information rather than trying to recall locational cues and sequentially scanning the text pages looking for them. Potentially, we can exercise extensive control over the text acquisition and comprehension process (see, for instance, the discussion of *hypertext* in the Lancaster and Warner chapter, this volume). That type of access is not yet common. Also, it is the text and its organization in computer readable form that provide that capability, so the processes are ultimately computer-controlled. This distinction is not so important as the process.

Electronic Publication

Although the history of electronic publication is short and technical, F.W. Lancaster and Amy Warner make it fascinating. They quickly take us from the advent of electronic typesetting to today's *electronic journal*. Of greater interest is their description of the transition from the present into the future (which may be the *present* by the time this book is published and the *past* by the time you read it). Capabilities such as printing on demand, rewritable books, videotex, user publishing, and computer conferencing will no doubt change the ways that text is generated and used.

They continue our journey into the future by discussing trends in text presentation, such as the decline of narrative text (such as this book) and the development of hypertext, the ultimate in learner control. The ability of the reader or learner to control not only the sequence of electronic text presentation but also the organization of the content being presented begins to accommodate what we know about human information processing and storage. Though the concept has been around for a decade, it is too *dynamic a learning tool* to explain using current notions of text delivery and computer-based instruction. Future electronic publications, claim the authors, will be truly interactive rather than the receptive display modes to which we are accustomed.

Authoring Systems

The previous chapter did not specifically consider the problems of schooling or the educational implications of electronic text, though they should have been obvious. Much has been written about educational applications in the past few years, especially regarding microcomputers. Virtually every school in the country has at least one microcomputer (though they need at least eight or ten per classroom to have a truly significant effect). An expansive cottage industry has emerged to produce thousands of pieces of "educational" software to begin to fill the demand for computer literacy and learning. Yet, there is a dearth of quality software to cover an ever-expanding curriculum.

One solution to part of this problem is through the expanded use by teachers of *authoring systems* to develop their own, tailored software. James E. Eisele provides an excellent introduction to the functions and processes of authoring systems. A strong case has been built against teacher-produced software using languages such as BASIC or Pascal, primarily because teachers are inadequate programmers, not properly versed in *computer logic*. What experienced teachers do know is *instructional logic*. Authoring systems exist to mediate the translation of instructional logic into computer logic. The purpose and organization of these is entirely different. One criticism of authoring systems is that the more sophisticated authoring languages can be as complex as lower-level languages such as BASIC, including numerous statements and rigid syntax. What is important, though, is that they are very high-level languages that are organized around instructional principles (which teachers understand best), not computer logic. It is not necessary for teachers to understand the range of I/O commands in order to prepare meaningful courseware. They simply need to apply years of experience in teaching students, using their ability to explain material, cite relevant examples, anticipate difficulties in understanding material, and adapt instruction to designing courseware (see the Komoski and Woodward chapter, this volume, for a discussion of some of these teacher mediational functions).

Consistent with the chronological approach taken by Lancaster and Warner, Eisele begins by considering authoring systems from an historical perspective. They represent some of the earliest endeavors in computer-based instruction (e.g., IBM's Coursewriter). He continues by defining authoring systems, describing how they work, and what they can produce. Most useful, perhaps, is his set of guidelines or capabilities that authoring systems should possess. These can be used as a set of selection criteria when evaluating alternative authoring systems. He concludes by providing a list of some *currently* available authoring systems. This list is not annotated, because Eisele convinced me that currency in any computer systems is an ephemeral concept. Since new software is constantly being developed and existing software updated, the list will be somewhat obsolete by the time this book is published (a testament to the flexibility of the electronic media when compared to the relative intransigence of print). A letter to the publishers of these systems will doubtlessly produce an avalanche of promotional literature (probably in print form). If you are interested in educational applications of computers, this may be the most important chapter in the book.

Summary

There are numerous design concerns related to electronic text that need to be considered. Most of the chapters in this book address at least one of them. As electronic publication becomes more prevalent, instructional and information designers will become more concerned with electronic displays, as will subsequent volumes in this series of books.

Chapter 12

Electronic Publication and Its Impact on the Presentation of Information

F.W. Lancaster and Amy Warner

The term "electronic publishing" may be broadly interpreted to mean the application of computers and other electronic devices to the publishing and distribution of information. An "electronic publication" is an information source that exists on some electronic medium (e.g., computer databases, videotex). This chapter discusses the presentation of information in electronic publications, dealing with three major issues:

(1) the way information is or could be presented;

(2) the impact of the presentation on both the authors and the users of electronic texts; and

(3) some limitations that must be overcome in presenting information in electronic form.

The Evolution of Electronic Publishing

It is now well accepted that computer technology tends to affect human activities in two stages. It first changes *how* things are done and later changes *what* is done. This certainly seems true of the electronic publishing situation, where the two main stages can be characterized as follows:

(1) a "simulation" stage in which electronic technology is used either to generate a conventional print-on-paper publication or to produce an electronic publication that is made to resemble print on paper; and

(2) a more "creative" stage in which the true capabilities of the electronic medium are exploited, and authors and publishers free themselves from the static limitations of the paper medium.

The first of these stages can be traced back approximately 20 years; the second seems just to be beginning.

Electronic publishing began in the early 1960s, when computers were first used to "set type" (i.e., photocompose) in order to generate a printed product. The first publications to be significantly affected were those, such as *Index Medicus*, that index or abstract the primary literature (e.g., as it appears in journals or reports). These publications, by virtue of their size, cost, and data manipulation requirements, had most to gain from automated production. Once such a publication was generated by computer, the magnetic tape used in the publication process became available for other applications. Thus, in effect, two versions existed: the conventional print on paper and the equivalent machine-readable format, the latter being an "electronic publication."

The appearance of completely new publications solely in electronic form began soon afterwards. Initially, these were mostly collections of data—numerical, statistical, chemical, physical—but other types, including new indexing services and state-of-the-art compilations, emerged somewhat later. The new science journal in electronic form is just now emerging (Broad, 1982). The next logical step in this evolution would be the gradual *replacement* of existing print-on-paper publications by their electronic counterparts or competitors. This step has not quite been reached yet, although we may be on the threshold of it. There is already some evidence of a "migration" from the use of paper publications to the use of electronic forms: some libraries have begun to cancel subscriptions to certain publications in favor of online access on demand, while some other, newer libraries have by-passed the print-on-paper stage and moved exclusively to electronic access for those publications available in this way.

In the short history of electronic publication, it is possible to discern several dimensions of a rapid but orderly spread of use and influence. First, various types of publications seem to go through the several steps of conversion to electronics in a logical sequence. The news media—newspapers and popular magazines—were affected after the indexing/abstracting services, with other forms being influenced later. The scholarly journal has felt significant effects only recently, and certain types of publication, notably imaginative works, have hardly yet been influenced at all.

As different types of publication have been affected, the amount of information provided has increased: bibliographic references only, references plus abstracts, data compilations and, finally, complete text. The full text of large bodies of legal material has been available in machine-readable form for about 20 years. That of certain newspapers and popular magazines became accessible online somewhat later. Accessibility of the full text of scholarly journals online is a more recent development and very few are so far available in this way. Nevertheless, plans are under way to make many more such journals accessible in one electronic format or another. A few reference books, such as directories and encyclopedias, are also accessible in full text form online and many more are likely to become so accessible in the future.

It is possible that electronic printing on demand may be an important interim step in the evolution from print on paper to electronics (Starr, 1983). Some publishers are already using laser printers to generate a copy of a publication when ordered: 124 pages can be printed and ready for binding in 62 seconds. This has led some to suggest that future bookstores will display a single copy of each item and generate sale copies only when requested.

With printing on demand, a user could search and retrieve items from some computer-controlled document filing system (e.g., on optical disk). The document store interfaces with a computer-assisted makeup and imaging system, which generates paper copy according to the user's specifications for type face and for size and kind of paper. An obvious advantage is that the text can easily be updated so that the user always gets the latest version printed out.

Some believe that, in principle, re-usable ("multitime") paper could be developed for use with electronic printing. They visualize a folder of loose sheets that can be "inserted" into some terminal. Anything that can be displayed on the screen can be printed on the sheets, which can be carried away by the user and re-arranged at leisure. At a later time, the same sheets can be re-used in much the same way that one records over videotape (Maurer *et al*, 1982). A somewhat similar notion is a "blank book," which can be inserted into a slot in a terminal connected to some electronic library. Text and illustrations are transmitted electronically and reproduced on the pages of the book, which are, in effect, "blank visual tapes of sorts" (Shneour, 1983).

Using a computer to print on paper, while an important step in the evolution from paper to electronics, has little effect on the way information is presented. The distribution of a publication in electronic form, on the other hand, has more profound implications. Undoubtedly, the most important dimension of the evolution of electronic publishing relates to the form in which the product is distributed or otherwise made accessible. At first, such publications were available only as magnetic tape to a rather small number of organizations that were owners of large mainframe computers and that would use a source frequently enough to justify the expense of leasing the tapes from the publisher. Later, most sources became more accessible through computer centers (typically in universities) that entered into licensing agreements with publishers and sold services to other organizations or individuals. Since about 1970, the accessibility of electronic information sources has increased by orders of magnitude as more and more have been made available online.

More recently, other media for electronic publication have emerged. Some forms of publication are already put into the home through interactive television (i.e., videotex), some are distributed as tape cassettes or other media for use with personal computers, some have been produced on optical disks, and it seems reasonable to assume that new electronic forms may appear in the near future.

Impact of Electronics

A publication distributed electronically could be substantially different from one printed on paper. In point of fact, however, existing electronic publications, for the most part, are little more than print on paper displayed on a screen. The full text of several popular magazines and scholarly journals can now be accessed through online networks, and the text of some encyclopedias can be accessed through such networks or through interactive television. While this does offer certain advantages (for example, the ability to perform a computer search on the words in the text itself), it also has undoubted disadvantages: legibility may suffer and browsing, at least in the conventional sense, is more difficult. The fact is that these are not "true" electronic publications. The authors did not write for the electronic medium; nor did the publishers design their products for it. To take print on paper and distribute it electronically does not produce a real electronic publication, since the full capabilities of the medium are not being exploited. Regrettably, it is difficult to free our minds of the *limitations of the printed book*. For example, experiments with completely new electronic journals have been conducted (Senders, 1980; Shackel, 1982), but even these seem intent on producing a product that closely resembles print on paper. Electronic publishing is still in an embryonic state; certainly, it has not matured beyond the simulation stage identified earlier.

It is clear, however, that electronic technology can have a significant effect on many facets of the production and distribution of information: how authors work, what they produce, how they interact with referees and publishers, how information is packaged and distributed, and how it is used.

Coke (1982) has reviewed the various computer aids available to help an author in writing text: word processing systems, spelling aids, and programs to calculate readability, to evaluate word choice, and to assess writing style.

Some authors are beginning to compose on a microcomputer, to submit paper copy to the publisher, to modify the stored text as a result of editorial review, and to submit a final version in machine-readable form, perhaps floppy disk, that can interface with a publisher's photocomposition system (Armbruster and Yates, 1982). In other cases (Shotwell, 1982), authors are using telecommunications facilities to transmit from their microcomputers to others in the publishers' offices.

One feature of The Source (Source Telecomputing Corporation), a service designed primarily for microcomputer users, is known as User Publishing; it permits the author to become his or her own publisher. A manuscript, composed on a microcomputer, is transmitted electronically to an editor at The Source, the author being charged for online input time. If approved by the editor, it goes into the User Publishing database and is listed on the system's public menu. Each time accessed, the author/publisher receives a nine percent royalty on the access charges. Science fiction stories and "practical" items (such as "Be your own lawyer") are among the types of publications that have been issued in this way. The Source has plans to tie in with a cable television network in order to reach a wider consumer market (Pocker, 1982).

Thus, we see that microcomputer technology can aid the publisher, can aid the author, can facilitate interaction between authors and publishers, and can allow the author and publisher roles to be combined. More of this can be expected in the future.

Computer conferencing can greatly facilitate collaborative authorship. In particular, it allows the generation of new state-of-knowledge compilations. As an example, the Hepatitis Knowledge Base, developed by the National Library of Medicine (Bernstein *et al.*, 1980) was created and is kept current through the achievement of a group consensus, among specialists in this field, achieved via computer conferencing (Siegel, 1979).

The packaging and marketing of information could also change considerably. In an electronic world, it would make no sense to subscribe to a single journal. Instead, a subscription would allow one's interest profile to be matched against the contributions accepted into a wide range of electronic databases.

Ultimately, then, electronics may be used in all phases of the publication process. King and Roderer (1978) give outlines of a system, which they refer to as the Electronic Alternative, in which electronics would be used in article preparation by the author, in review by editors and referees, and finally, in the dissemination of full text articles to the community of users. Similarly, Roistacher (1978) describes a virtual journal in which all articles submitted are potentially publishable based on the decision of each individual author, but where the:

> inclusion of reader and reviewer evaluations as information retrieval terms would preserve the quality of publication despite the unlimited page capacity of the virtual journal. (p. 23)

Alternatively, Shackel *et al.* (1983) describe the BLEND-LINC project, which enters papers electronically into an "archive" which, they stress, has the status of pre-publication drafts only.

King and Roderer (1978) emphasize that a system such as the Electronic Alternative should be introduced gradually to participants and that it could eventually change the publication industry from a dependence on subscription income to income based on use. All of this, however, depends on ability to overcome technological barriers, such as the need for standards for word processing and text-editing, reduced costs, and higher quality graphics capabilities.

The Presentation of Information

It is the presentation of information within electronic "packages," however, that is the main concern of this chapter. As more publications are designed *ab initio* for electronic distribution, it seems certain that changes will take place in the way text is presented. Perhaps more importantly, it may also mean that *narrative text declines in importance as a means of communicating information.*

One concern, of course, is simply that of the readability of electronically displayed text and graphics. Some guidelines on display techniques, particularly microcomputer display, have been presented by Merrill (1982), who deals with the formatting of material on a screen, paging techniques, possibilities for user interaction with the text, and ease of use factors. Reynolds (1982) discusses factors affecting the readability of information displayed by videotex methods. She stresses that information cannot be transferred directly from a printed document to electronic display without extensive editing. The design problems are similar to those faced in the design of print on paper in that one must find ways of effectively relating, dividing, and emphasizing items of information. With videotex, of course, the available means for doing this are rather different; for example, color variations may be used in place of typographic variations.

While Reynolds seems mostly concerned with the transfer of information from print on paper to the electronic medium, Nisenholtz (1982), drawing on experience from the Alternate Media Center, deals more directly with the design of new publications for videotex presentation. Since display limitations necessitate that each "message" be brief, editors and designers use graphics to "strengthen and highlight" portions of the text. If properly used, Nisenholtz points out, graphics can: clarify or highlight text, enhance it through some form of decoration (e.g., a cartoon or caricature), replace long text strings by pictorial symbols to express ideas or feelings, and "provide a sense of stylistic consistency in and across content areas."

Maurer and Sebestyen (1982) make a useful distinction between videotex pages designed to be read and those designed merely to be glanced at (i.e., pages intended to "route" a reader elsewhere). They contend that, while the former must not be overloaded with text, the latter "could and should contain densely packed information to avoid too many routing paths."

Many other writers have contributed to the discussion on the more technical aspects of display technology as it affects electronic publication, including Crowell (1982) on the use of graphics on videodisc and Whelan (1982) on designing for videotex. Greenagel (1981) discusses the design of an encyclopedia for electronic distribution (e.g., on videodisc), and some more general aspects of the differences between print on paper and electronic publication are presented by Katzen (1982).

Much of the literature relating to differences between electronics and print on paper seems to concentrate on current technological limitations of electronic media, such as poor screen resolution and the need to design pages differently for electronic texts to compensate for the limited display capability of a typical terminal. With technological improvements, one might expect that electronic publishers will both exploit the medium more effectively and create displays more psychologically appealing to the reader.

Line (1982a) has discussed factors involved in "redesigning" journal articles for online viewing. His ideas contributed to a pilot research project (Hills *et al.*, 1983), the aim of which is to:

> test the feasibility of providing readers of electronic journals with the means of undertaking some form of analogue to the browsing process. . . . The hypothesis was that the resources of a computer could be used to provide the reader with a means of performing reading strategies, by making available a breakdown of the contents of an article together with a series of brief summaries of each section. The reader should be able to call up this material in

his or her own preferred order, and thus be able to simulate to
some extent browsing and scanning. (pp. 6, 8)

The perceptions of readers were obtained regarding restructured
articles with summaries versus original articles without restructur-
ing. In addition, ability to jump around within an article was
provided in both restructured and non-restructured texts. Users
seemed to have no preference between full texts and texts plus
summaries; however, they did express enthusiasm for the ability to
jump around in the text.

The importance of this study lies not so much in its alterations
of text to exploit the electronic medium, but in its direct
consideration of user preferences in the design of electronic
publications. The alterations to the text seem more cosmetic than
fundamental in character, although Line (1982b) himself has
elsewhere hinted at a more basic change in the way information is
presented and used:

Electronic transmission could have an effect on writing and
reading, not only by encouraging the writing of marketable
material, but by favouring smaller units of information. The
shorter the article, the better for identification and transmission;
better still, the information in it can be broken up into small
blocks, like articles in a concise encyclopaedia. The user would
have then to piece together his own packages from the blocks:
the original writer then becomes a brickmaker, and the user a
builder, perhaps even an architect. (p. 145)

Line hints at, but does not explicitly mention, the possibility of
some form of "hypertext" capability.

Hypertext (Nelson, 1974, 1978, 1981) consists of a text
presentation system that gives the user freedom to direct its
movement in a way that is logical to him or her, rather than
confining the user to movement that is logical to the author. It
combines flexibility of access, ability to comment in context, and
ease of locally modifying the text to make it highly specific to
individual needs and specifications. More specifically, Nelson
speaks of making rapid, arbitrary jumps, where material stored in
one place may offer a link, much like a footnote, to material
stored in another place, in either the same or a different

document. Such an arrangement is highly dynamic, since the reader can pursue various pathways through the text and can make various comments or annotations as he or she proceeds. In addition, the text can be constantly updated by means of computer conferencing among a group of subject specialists, the authors of the text. Thus, this form of presentation is not pre-specified, but transforms the organization of its contents into a more useful form for each individual reader (Weyer, 1982).

Thursh and Mabry (1980) have developed an electronic text-book using the hypertext principle. An electronic textbook can look much different from one printed on paper. It need not be designed to be read in one particular sequence. It may allow many alternative reading pathways or be capable of reorganization into various sequences to meet the needs of different instructors, courses, or students. At any point in such a text, a student may enter an annotation, a comment, or a question to an instructor. Instructor responses can also be incorporated and, for any portion of the text, a student could get access to the questions and comments of other students and/or the responses of several instructors. Even the bibliography for such a text does not need to be static. Indeed, the text could be interfaced with an online retrieval system in such a way that the reader can get virtually immediate access to citations representing the latest literature on any topic discussed in the text. Furthermore, the text itself can be constantly updated by means of computer conferencing. A change or addition to the text is made as the result of a consensus, among the authors, achieved through the conferencing facilities.

In the same vein, one can visualize an electronic encyclopedia that is re-organizable under the control of the reader. For example, information on James Joyce could be dispersed through-out various volumes and pages of a conventional encyclopedia. Not only would the electronic encyclopedia allow the reader to bring all relevant passages together, but it would also allow him or her to preserve all these passages on some local storage medium such as a floppy disk.

The key feature of hypertext is that it is not static, unlike text in printed book form, which is entirely so—neither re-organizable by the user nor easily updated.

Electronic publication, then, can affect the presentation of narrative text, both by promoting conciseness and by creating a more dynamic presentation whose sequence can be changed and expanded by the reader.

Weyer (1982) has discussed the dynamic book in some detail. He sees the major difference between the electronic book and the conventional book as being the ease with which the former can be searched for specific passages or factual information.

The designers of electronic publications must continue to seek innovative ways of presenting textual information if they are to demonstrate conclusively the superiority of the electronic medium. This point was made forcefully in an announcement concerning the research project (Hills *et al.*, 1983) which investigated the re-design of journal articles for online viewing:

> The extent to which electronic journals supersede or merely appear alongside conventional printed publications will probably be influenced by the structure of online text and the ease with which scanning and browsing can be achieved compared with reading print on paper. (*British Library, R&D Newsletter*, 1981, p. 10).

While text can be made dynamic and re-organizable, narrative text might be much less important in electronic publications in which animation, electronic models, moving pictures, and sound can be employed by the author.

Several electronic forms, including optical disk and interactive television, offer the possibility of incorporating sound to supplement or reinforce the use of text and graphics. In fact, Greenagel (1981) has pointed out that, when the television set becomes the readers' terminal, sound is actually expected:

> The research also revealed that people reading an article on their TV screen expected that a noise of some sort should also come from that set; they have been conditioned to expect sound as well as video, and were somewhat disconcerted by the silence—'sensory deprivation' is what psychologists would term it. (p. 179)

The advantages of being able to use sound within a publication, of course, have already been recognized. For example, a guide to the identification of birds, incorporating both sound and motion pictures, is now being marketed on optical disks.

The graphics capabilities of electronics are even more exciting. However good the quality of an illustration in a printed book, this illustration is entirely static. This makes little difference when a static object is depicted, as in the reproduction of a famous painting, but it is a definite restriction when an author is trying to describe how something works. Electronic publications can include, not only static illustrations, but motion picture segments as well as animation or electronic analog models.

Anyone who has used a sophisticated computer-aided instruction system, such as PLATO, will know that a system of this type can incorporate very effective analog models. It is possible to build such a model of a scientific experiment, in, say, chemistry or physics, as well as analog working models of various types of equipment. It is not difficult to realize that electronic publications need not be restricted to the static properties of the printed page. The true capabilities of electronics in publishing will be reached when completely new and dynamic publications emerge. Visualize an electronic encyclopedia that incorporates dynamic analog models of equipment and experiments. In an encyclopedia for children, for example, a rather lenghty narrative description of what makes an airplane fly, accompanied by a few static diagrams, could be replaced by an electronic model that the child can manipulate. The reader is allowed to vary the forces and loads and immediately sees the effects on the electronic model of the plane. This type of publication would be truly interactive and the "reader" would become, in effect, an active participant in the publication. In fact, such a publication might closely resemble what we now think of as an electronic game.

The same capabilities could be extended to more "serious" publications. Consider the capabilities of future journals in scientific/technical fields. Rather than describing what happens when stresses of a particular type are applied to some structure, a journal in applied mechanics could demonstrate these effects. Moreover, since computer programs can be incorporated into a contribution to an electronic journal, the reader could actually perform new data manipulations, varying the loads or stresses, for example, and observing the effects. Future publications can be truly interactive. The possibilities are limited only by the imagination.

The ability to combine textual information, visual images (static and moving), and sound into an interactive system has stimulated work on what Negroponte (1979) has referred to as books without pages. In Negroponte's system, developed at MIT, the reader sits in a chair whose arms are fitted with a joystick and touch-sensitive pad. These facilities can generate whole-wall displays (including a zoom capability) of text or graphic information as well as sound. Moreover, the reader can move the material around and, as it were, browse in an "information space." Different sources (i.e., data-bases) can be brought together on separate but adjacent screens, and the reader is given some capability to annotate and store in an electronic notebook. A working version of the system, known as Dataland, is in place in the White House and the Pentagon. At least two commercial versions, of varying levels of sophistication, have been developed.

A derivation of Negroponte's work is the Spatial Data Management System (SDMS), based on optical disk technology, which is said to store static and moving pictorial information in a "spatial location," allowing the user to search, browse, and retrieve in an "information space." The basic system, produced by the Interactive Television Corporation, comprises two monitors (one color and one monochrome), a microcomputer, and an industrial disk player. One capability of SDMS is "vicarious travel": a user can take a simulated trip through a selected geographic area using a joystick to control the speed and direction of the travel. This feature is now being used, within the U.S. Army, to teach spatial orientation and navigation skills. Such interactive optical disk technology is considered to have great potential in a variety of instructional applications (Instructional Applications, 1982).

While imaginative works have been little affected by electronics up to now, there is no reason to suppose they will remain unaffected. At least one electronic novel already exists (Electronic Novel, 1983). Titled *Blind Pharaoh*, and authored by Burke Campbell at the Art Culture Resource Centre in Toronto, the 19-chapter novel can be read online by subscribers to The Source. It can also be downloaded onto a personal computer disk or printed out locally. Henry Kisor, book editor of the *Chicago Sun-Times*, is reported to have reviewed the book (Electronic Novel, 1983):

Writing a 20,000 word novel on a computer in 72 hours is a stunt, but Burke Campbell pulled it off handsomely. The result, "Blind Pharaoh," is rough-edged as one would expect, but its splended narrative drive makes up for that. I enjoyed it very much.

More important, perhaps, is its proof that videotex is a going concern as an alternative to the printed book. The technology is here already; all that is needed is a larger audience. And that will come; the only question is when. (p. 121)

Krueger (1983) has given a rather detailed discussion on some of the possibilities for creative writing in electronic form. One is kinetic poetry (expression through the animation of words). In this form, poetry becomes a kind of dance:

The words and letters could constantly be in a state of flux, moving around the screen, juxtaposing with other words, transforming themselves into new words, picking up new letters and disbanding—in ways limited only by the imagination of the programmer poet. A sequence of such interactions would constitute a poem. (p. 198)

Interactive poetry and interactive novels are other possibilities. Krueger suggests the possibility that, in interactive poetry, the words could even travel around the reader ("participant") through, for example, holographic projection:

Words displayed on a lighted graphic floor could follow the participant or be chased by the participant . . . Allowing a word to interact physically with a participant is a symbolic statement, for the word is then no longer a vehicle for communicating meaning, but an entity behaving on its own. Given the impact of television and film, and the fact that computers are slowly acquiring the ability to speak and understand speech, the written word may one day be obviated. Thus, it seems appropriate to give it life, allow it to leave the page, interact with the person who wrote it, and leave the scene. (p. 199)

The electronic novel may merely be one with alternative story paths or it could be one in which the narrative is actually generated by computer, perhaps under the direction of the individual reader (an artificial intelligence system, TALE-SPIN, as described by Meeker (1976), already approaches such capabilities). Krueger suggests that the adventure games now available on home computers may resemble the electronic novels of the future.

Some experimental publications of the general type that Krueger discusses do exist. Nisenholtz (1982), for example, has described ongoing experience with such prototypes at the Alternate Media Center, New York University.

Conclusion

Electronic publications of the future, then, may be much different from the publications of today. Indeed, it seems entirely possible that the electronic medium could do more than change the form of existing publication types; it could change the types themselves. To mention an obvious case, there is no reason to suppose that people will still be writing what we now think of as novels a century from now.

While many have discussed the possibilities, few have done so as concisely as Krueger:

> The computer provides alternatives. It can represent and present knowledge not in rigidly formatted pages, but in a collage of images, text, and aural representation that can be assembled to make maximal use of a person's visual field and the spatial organization of their memory. (p. 213)

Ten years ago, Von Foerster (1972) referred to the printed book as the "bottleneck in man's communication channels." While the printed book still has many virtues, not least of which are its aesthetic appeal and relative portability, there may be a lot of truth in Von Foerster's claim. Electronics seem to offer the potential for removing this bottleneck. Let us hope the medium is used wisely as well as imaginatively.

References

Armbruster, D., and Yates, D. Saving keystrokes. *Scholarly Publishing*, 1982, *14*, 35-37.

Bernstein, L.M., Siegel, E.R., and Goldstein, C.M. The Hepatitis Knowledge Base. *Annals of Internal Medicine*, July 1980, Part 2, *93*, 169-181.

British Library R&D Newsletter, 1982, (25), p. 10.

Broad, W.J. Journals: Fearing the electronic future. *Science*, May 28, 1982, *216*, 964-968.

Coke, E.U. Computer aids for writing text. In D.H. Jonassen (Ed.), *The technology of text: Principles for structuring, designing, and displaying text.* Englewood Cliffs, NJ: Educational Technology Publications, Inc., 1982, 383-399.

Crowell, P. Using graphics on videodisc. *Videodisc/Videotex*, 1982, *2*, 216-221.

Electronic novel. *Information Technology & Libraries*, 1983, *2*, 120-121.

Greenagel, F.L. Aretê–a 3000-year-old word for the latest in electronic publishing. *Electronic Publishing Review*, 1981, *1*, 177-182.

Hills, P. *et al. An experiment on the redesign of journal articles for on-line viewing.* Leicester: University of Leicester, Primary Communications Research Centre, April, 1983.

Instructional applications of spatial data management. *Videodisc/Videotex*, 1982, *2*, 181-187.

Katzen, M. The impact of new technologies on scholarly communication. In M. Katzen (Ed.), *Multi-media communications.* Westport, CT: Greenwood Press, 1982, 16-50.

King, D., and Roderer, N. The electronic alternative to communication through paper-based journals. *Proceedings of the American Society for Information Science*, 1978, *15*, 180-183.

Krueger, M.W. *Artificial reality.* Reading, MA: Addison-Wesley, 1983.

Line, M.B. Redesigning journal articles for on-line viewing. In P.J. Hills (Ed.), *Trends in Information Transfer.* London: Frances Pinter, 1982(a), 31-46.

Line, M.B. The production and dissemination of information: Some general observations. In M. Katzen (Ed.), *Multi-media communications.* Westport, CT: Greenwood Press, 1982(b), 138-146.

Maurer, H.A., and Sebestyen, I. One-way versus two-way videotex. *Electronic Publishing Review*, 1982, *2*, 279-295.

Maurer, H.A. *et al.* Printing without paper. *Electronic Publishing Review*, 1982, *2*, 151-161.

Meeker, J.R. *The metanovel: Writing stories by computer.* New Haven, CT: Yale University, 1976.

Merrill, P.F. Displaying text on microcomputers. In D.H. Jonassen (Ed.), *The technology of text: Principles for structuring, designing, and displaying text.* Englewood Cliffs, NJ: Educational Technology Publications, Inc., 1982, 401-414.

Negroponte, N. Books without pages. *Conference Record*, pp. 56.1.1 to 56.1.8. IEEE International Conference on Communications, Boston, June 10-14, 1979.

Nelson, T.H. *Dream machines: New freedoms through computer screens—A minority report.* Chicago: Hugo's Book Service, 1974.

Nelson, T.H. Electronic publishing and electronic literature. In E.C. DeLand (Ed.), *Information technology in health science education.* New York: Plenum Press, 1978, 211-216.

Nelson, T.H. *Literary machines.* Swarthmore, PA: Author, 1981.

Nisenholtz, M. Designing for teletext and videotex: Two case studies. *Electronic Publishing Review*, 1982, *2*, 199-209.

Pocker, B.B. User publishing: A new concept in electronic access. *Publishers Weekly*, 1982, *221*(16), 38-39.

Reynolds, L. Display problems for teletext. In D.H. Jonassen (Ed.), *The technology of text: Principles for structuring, designing, and displaying text.* Englewood Cliffs, NJ: Educational Technology Publications, Inc., 1982, 415-437.

Roistacher, R.C. The virtual journal. *Computer Networks*, 1978, *2*, 18-24.

Senders, J.W. The electronic journal. In L.J. Anthony (Ed.), *EURIM 4.* London: Aslib, 1980, 14-16.

Shackel, B. The BLEND system: Programme for the study of some "electronic journals." *Computer Journal*, 1982, *25*, 161-168.

Shackel, B. *et al.* The BLEND-LINC project on "electronic journals" after two years. *Aslib Proceedings*, 1983, *35*, 77-91.

Shneour, E.A. A look into the book of the future. *Publishers Weekly*, 1983, *223*(3), p. 48.

Shotwell, R. How publishers can use personal computers. *Publishers Weekly*, 1982, *221*(5), 284-285.

Siegel, E.R. Validating and updating the NLM's hepatitis data base: The role of computer conferencing. *Proceedings of the American Society for Information Science*, 1979, *16*, 124-130.

Starr, P. The electronic reader. *Daedalus*, Winter, 1983, *112*, 143-156.

Thursh, D., and Mabry, F. An interactive hyper-text of pathology. *Proceedings of the Fourth Annual Symposium on Computer Applications in Medical Care*, 1980, 1820-1825.

Von Foerster, H. *Technology: What will it mean to librarians? (A response)*. Urbana: University of Illinois, Department of Electrical Engineering, 1972.

Weyer, S.A. The design of a dynamic book for information search. *International Journal of Man-Machine Studies*, 1982, *17*, 87-107.

Whelan, H. Designing for Prestel. In M. Katzen (Ed.), *Multi-media communications.* Westport, CT: Greenwood Press, 1982, 114-137.

Chapter 13

Computer-Based Authoring Systems

James E. Eisele

Introduction

The use of computers for generating and displaying text is not a revolutionary breakthrough of this decade. Word processing systems have been around for some time and have been extensively used for creating various kinds of reports based upon existing databases and input data. Indeed, major document production has been done by computer for 20 years or more. However, the tools that have been available for this purpose for a relatively long time have also been available to only a very few users—most often those who worked in computing or data processing centers. Today these tools are available to almost every user and prospective user. Not only are computers more readily accessible, but software has become available that provides even further assistance to the user who needs to create and display text in almost any form.

The entire history of computers can be viewed as the efforts of human beings trying to create better ways to serve other human beings (and themselves, of course) through the use of science and technology. The same people who pioneered early computer hardware were not satisfied with the difficulty of use of programming aids. Some readers will remember the days when "programming" computers meant switching wires on a large panel to create "programmed" circuits in a computer. There has been, in short, an ever-present effort to make computers easier to use as well as more powerful and versatile for serving human needs.

Therefore, although computers could only be programmed through adjustments in their circuitry, languages that could be more easily used by humans and interpreted by computers have been available for many years. However, even these languages were difficult for many people to learn and, so, more languages were developed, which were thought to be more easily learned. The result of these efforts is the availability of "languages" at three levels of difficulty of use.

At the lowest level of languages are those that are most readily "understood" by computers but most difficult to learn by humans, such as binary number codes or machine languages.

The next level of languages, which are less readily "understood" by computers but are easier to learn by humans, are called higher-level languages, such as FORTRAN, COBOL, BASIC, PL/1, and Pascal. These and other languages all have a precisely-defined structure and command words, which the user must learn to use in a predefined way.

The third level of languages consists of special-purpose packages, which are designed to perform specific functions such as statistical analysis, word processing, and report generation. These packages are usually not even referred to as languages but are called application packages, although many of them contain a unique language in which programs can be written. While these packages are usually quite easy for the user to grasp, they require considerable interpretation before a computer's electronic circuitry can respond in the desired way. It is the function of the software to make this interpretation for the computer.

The aids for generating and/or displaying text described in this chapter are at the cutting edge of a new, and fourth, level of computer programming "languages." While the applications discussed have most of the characteristics of the highest level described above, they also contain elements that are even more user-oriented than anything else up to this time, resulting in a new phrase to describe these applications as "user-friendly." Indeed, these applications are becoming more "user-friendly" all the time. That is, they are easier to learn to use (often requiring no *new* learning at all), more conversational in interacting with the user, more powerful in the number and kind of functions performed for the user, and more often completely independent of any other software packages. In view of the history of rapid development in this direction, the trend toward ease of use and increased power of various kinds of authoring aids should continue, making speculation about the tools that will be available to the prospective author in the near future quite interesting. I will attempt a very brief discussion of some possible results.

There are so many unique ways in which authoring aids assist in creating or generating text that I must limit the scope of this chapter to only a small number of the possibilities. I will, therefore, concentrate on one very specialized type of aid, that which is available for assisting with the development of *computer-based education systems*.

Authoring Systems

A description of how authoring systems aid the generation and/or displaying of text is of primary importance. First, however, I must clarify the term, "authoring system." Next, I will discuss the essential capabilities of any authoring system, followed by the identification of several of the systems currently available.

What Is an Authoring System?

To many professionals today, the term, "authoring system," refers to computer software designed to aid in the creation of computer-based instructional materials. Why this terminology was chosen is unimportant. The important point is that computer-based instructional materials are often composed extensively of text and that instruction is one unique purpose for which text is often used. At any rate, what I will refer to as authoring systems are those that are designed for the purpose of presenting text-based instructional materials.

> The phrase, "Authoring System," is used in a variety of contexts, with each context giving the phrase a different meaning. The broadest use of the phrase is to encompass the entire process of developing instructional materials for the computer, beginning

with the educational process of identifying the learning needs of a target population and ending with the computer process of programming the lesson in a computer language and testing it to verify that it functions as the author intended. (Pogue, 1980, p. 57)

Since authoring systems aid in the generation and/or display of computer-based instructional materials, they focus heavily on those aspects of instruction to which text is most necessary. Typically, this includes the actual material the learner is to view, the prompts for eliciting the learner's response, and the feedback informing the learner of the adequacy of the response and what might be done next. These form the elements for most instruction.

Authoring systems usually aid in the process of creating computer-based instruction by prompting the writer to type the desired text at appropriate locations in the instructional system. Since there are many specific approaches to instruction, authoring systems often begin by asking the author to identify the type of lesson he or she would like to create. Choices at this point might include drill and practice, tutorial, simulation, or some other specific type of lesson. This selection will determine, to some extent, the types of text that the author will be prompted to enter next. Often, the next prompt will ask for the objective of the lesson. Another prompt will ask for the entry of the instructional material itself in the form of a question, information, concepts, etc., and, even, sometimes allows for the creation of graphics for this purpose. Another prompt might ask for entry of all possible appropriate responses, although this text will not be displayed but will be used to judge the response of the learner using the lesson. Another prompt will ask for the feedback, usually text, which is to be displayed for each possible appropriate response. Another prompt will ask for possible inappropriate responses where they can be specified, and still another will request feedback to be displayed for each of these inappropriate responses. A typical drill and practice session might look as follows:

What type of lesson do you want to author?

A. Drill and practice
B. Tutorial

C. Simulation
D. Problem-solving
E. Multiple-choice test
(Make your selection and press return)

? a

Very good. You have chosen to author a *drill and practice* lesson. If this is not what you wanted, press "N" and return; otherwise press return *only*, and you will be prompted to enter the content for your lesson.

? <return>

OK. Let's get on with the lesson.

Enter your first frame of text:

? What is the longest river in the United States?

Now enter the correct answer:

? Mississippi

Enter the response to this answer:

? Very good. You are exactly right.

Enter the frame number for next:

? 5

Enter incorrect responses separated by commas:

? Amazon, Ohio, Savannah, Missouri

Enter the response for these answers:

? No, you missed that time! Try again.

Enter the frame number for next:

? 1

Enter response for any other answer:

? I don't understand you, answer again.

Enter frame number for next:

? 1

A partial sample of how an authoring system might prompt the creation of a more complex or powerful lesson, such as a tutorial, might resemble the following:

What type of lesson do you want to author?

    A. Drill and practice
    B. Tutorial
    C. Simulation
    D. Problem-solving
    E. Multiple-choice test
(Make your selection and press return)

? b

Very good. You have chosen to author a *tutorial* lesson. If this is not what you wanted, press "N" and return, otherwise press return *only*, and you will be prompted to enter the content for your lesson.

? <return>

OK. Let's get on with the lesson.

You may enter text, questions, graphics, or a combination of these. Which do you want?

? <text>

Very good. Enter text. (press return twice when finished)

Frame #1
? Today we are going to learn to write an "interrogative' sentence. You will recall that we learned about "declarative" sentences earlier. <returnXreturn>

You may enter text, questions, graphics, or a combination of these. Which do you want?

? <question>

Enter question.

? Do you remember the purpose of a "declarative" sentence? <returnXreturn>

Enter first possible answer(s):

? yes, y

Enter the response to this(these) answer(s):

? Good, then we can get on with our discussion of "interrogative" sentences.

Enter the frame for next:

? 2

Enter next possible answer(s):

? no, n, maybe, sort of

Enter the response to this(these) answer(s):

? OK, let's review "declarative" sentences before we move on to interrogative" sentences.

Enter the frame for next:

? 20

Enter next possible answer(s):

? <return>

You may enter text, questions, graphics, or a combination of these. Which do you want?

? <text>

Very good. Enter text. (press return twice when finished)

Frame #2
? An "interrogative" sentence is one which asks a question. You may have heard the expression, "He was interrogated by the police." Interrogated means he was asked questions by the police, in this sentence. <returnXreturn>

You may enter text, questions, graphics, or a combination of these. Which do you want?

? <question>

Enter question.

? What kind of sentences would the police use to interrogate a suspect? <return>

Enter first possible answer(s):

Through the use of these prompts, the author does not need to know a computer language to assign specific functions to various text. Once all the essential text is entered by the author, the computer assembles, compiles, or condenses the text into a program that is displayed to a learner in the way the author intended it to be used. These aids have been found to be extremely useful in that they allow the educator with no computer knowledge to create computer programs for displaying instructional material with considerable ease and with practically no training other than in good instruction. In fact, authoring systems have brought to every educator the power to create computer-based instruction with little more than minimal typing skills.

What Capabilities Should Authoring Systems Include?

Sometimes authoring systems provide additional aids for editing text, once entered, through the addition of some kind of word processor, and for creating graphics in place of, or supplemental to, text for instruction. However, their most common feature is to prompt appropriate segments of text and to assemble that text into a program that functions as a lesson.

In selecting an authoring system, you must be sure to examine carefully the functions the system will perform. A system that purports to be an "authoring system" but does not prompt the author for specific types of lesson designs, or allows for the production of only graphics or only text in traditional conversational form will not aid the author of computer-based instructional materials much more than traditional programming languages or word processing packages. What one must look for in an authoring system is an underlying theory of the organization of elements of communication *for the purpose of facilitating learning.*

Based upon this underlying theory, authoring systems should perform certain minimal functions in order to distinguish themselves from other computer applications. At a minimum, these functions should include a unique language, which is called an authoring language, authoring prompts, graphics, a language translator, courseware libraries, a student mode, and records, statistics, and reports. Each of these will be discussed in brief.

Authoring Language

As with any computer language, an authoring language must have a set of instructions (command words) that can be understood by a computer and a set of rules for using these command words. Since authoring languages are high-level languages (easy to use), they should use command words that are very much like natural language statements. The computer language, BASIC, for example, uses the command word "PRINT" to instruct the computer to print whatever follows the command word. Authoring languages use command words that specify functions related to teaching, such as "answer" to allow for student response and "right" to specify the desired student response.

Rules for using the command words in an authoring language should be consistent with the overall function of the language but also should be somewhat flexible. That is, a command word such as "ANSWER" should be permitted only as a means of allowing student input in the student mode and, therefore, should always follow some other instruction. However, "answer" should be flexible enough to allow for a variety of student input depending upon the type of lesson being delivered. This variety should include varying length responses as well as a variety of sources of responses.

The authoring language should be capable of being used to write lessons that can be entered into a computer from a keyboard and be immediately executed as a program. Not all users will want to employ this capability, but for the author who wants to create an original type of lesson, or to modify an existing one, such a capability is essential.

Authoring Prompts

A second necessary characteristic of an authoring system is that the system will prompt a user to enter text (lesson content) to which the system will automatically assign the appropriate command words for the authors. For example, following a question the author has entered, the system would next prompt the author by displaying: "Please enter the correct response(s) to the previous question." Upon entering the correct response or responses, the computer structures the text in an appropriate format and precedes it with a command word such as "answers," all independently of the author.

An authoring system must provide not only the prompting feature but also the ability to alter the way in which prompts are displayed in keeping with the type of lesson to be developed. A drill and practice lesson, for example, would prompt the author to enter text as follows:

Question: (Enter text as student should see it.)

Correct Answer   :
    Feedback   :
    Next   :

Wrong Answer   :
    Feedback   :
    Next   :

Otherwise Do   :

Prompts provided by the system for a simulation might look more like this:

Situation   : (Enter text or picture.)

```
Options              :

Consequence 1        :
   Feedback          :
   Next              :

Consequence 2        :
   Feedback          :
   Next              :

Consequence n        :
   Feedback          :
   Next              :
```

And so forth. These prompts often use what are called *templates* for known lesson formats. Typically, there will be templates for drill and practice, simulation, tutorial, and multiple-choice tests. An author merely identifies the type of lesson desired, and the system selects the appropriate template to prompt the entry of lesson content. In addition, however, the authoring system should allow the user to create an original template whenever desired. Otherwise, the creative abilities of the author, not to mention the potential quality of the lesson, are severely limited.

Graphics

Because of the frequent use of pictures, charts, graphs, and animation in good instructional materials, the capability of producing graphics adds greatly to the value of any authoring system. Producing graphics for computer display can be a very arduous and time-consuming task if they are done by writing programs. Instead, software can be provided which allows the author to simply draw pictures on the screen from the keyboard, plotting dots and drawing lines where desired. Use of more than one color should be available and, if possible, the ability to create the appearance of animation.

A Language Translator

Another desirable feature of authoring systems is the ability to convert a program written under one system or language into another system or language. A wealth of instructional material already exists that may run on only one or two computer systems. At present, efforts are under way to manually translate existing programs from one language to another. The immensity of this task is overwhelming. Automatic translators, on the other hand, would offer the capability of acquiring courseware and making it run on your own system.

Courseware Libraries

There must be a means of saving lessons that have been created or acquired. Once the number of available lessons exceeds two, the management of those lessons becomes complicated. Just as libraries must be managed for acquisition, storage, retrieval, check-out, and return, so must courseware libraries be so managed. The authoring system should provide the necessary software for establishing such a management system.

A Student Mode

The authoring system should permit access to the system by students as well as authors. Therefore, there must be a student mode, which accords certain privileges, but not others, to student users. There must be a security system to protect some files from unauthorized access but which will allow users to access authorized files. This access might allow students to examine their own records of progress, the list of lessons they have completed, and the directory of remaining lessons available to them.

Records, Statistics, Reports

Finally, an authoring system should provide the capability of automatically collecting a wide variety of student and lesson performance data, to analyze these data in a variety of ways, and to generate reports for students, parents, teachers, and administrators. There should also exist the capability of *turning off* the recordkeeping mode as well, where the authorized user decides that such records are not needed or wanted.

Summary of Desired Capabilities of Authoring Systems

The purpose of authoring systems is to provide a powerful and easy-to-use system of developing and delivering computer-based instructional materials. To accomplish this purpose, certain minimal functions must be provided in the system. These functions must include (1) an authoring language, (2) authoring prompts, (3) graphics, (4) a language translator, (5) courseware libraries, (6) a student mode, and (7) records, statistics, and reports. Without at least these major components, the system is not complete. On the other hand, the individual user of an authoring system may choose to use only some parts of the system for specific lessons.

Some Currently Available Authoring Systems

Authoring systems have grown in popularity in recent years so that one is available for almost any major computer system. Not all available authoring systems, including those listed here, offer all the capabilities described above. The following list cites some representative systems with which I am currently familiar. I make no attempt here to evaluate those listed, and omission is not intended to imply disapproval.

Main Frame Computer-Based Education Systems

Courseware Authoring System
Digital Equipment Corporation
Marlborough, MA 01752

Interactive Instructional System
International Business Machines Corp.
White Plains, NY 10604

Microcomputer Authoring Systems

Blocks
Softswap
San Mateo County Office of Education
333 Main Street
Redwood Cify, CA 94063
    (for Apple)

CAIWare
MicroGnome
Fireside Computing, Inc.
5843 Montgomery Road
Elkridge, MD 21227
    (for Radio Shack)

Edugrammer
Roklan Corporation
10600 W. Higgens Road
Suite 200-1
Rosemont, IL 60018
    (for Atari)

GENIS
Bell and Howell
7100 N. McCormick Road
Chicago, IL 60645
    (for Apple)

PASS
Bell and Howell
7100 N. McCormick Road
Chicago, IL 60645
    (for Apple)

Pilot
Micropi, Inc.
2445 N. Nugent Street
Lumni Island, WA 98262
    (for Apple, Atari, Radio Shack)

Trainer 3000
Computer Systems Research
1644 Tullie Circle, N.E.
Atlanta, GA 30329
    (for IBM)

Z.E.S.
Avante-Garde Creations
P.O. Box 30161
Eugene, OR 97403
(for Apple)

Conclusion

In this chapter, I have attempted to provide a broad overview of authoring systems, hopefully replete with practical information for the prospective user. Some background about how authoring systems came into existence is necessary in order to understand how they differ from programming languages. I have also attempted to describe how authoring systems work to facilitate the development of computer-based instructional applications. This included a discussion of several capabilities that are essential for maximum utility of any authoring system. For convenience, a partial listing of available authoring systems has been provided.

Authoring systems will likely provide the vehicle to develop computer-based instructional materials in the quantity needed for the public schools. Authoring systems bring the power of computer programming to the novice who wants to develop instructional materials without learning computer programming.

References

Coburn, P. *et al. Computers in Education.* Reading, MA: Addison-Wesley Publishing Company, 1982.

Lutus, P., and Finstad, L. *Applewriter operating manual.* Cupertino, CA: Apple Computer, Inc., undated.

Pogue, R.E. The authoring system: Interface between author and computer. *Journal of Research and Development in Education.* Fall, 1980, *14*(1), 57-67.

Section VI

Designing Special Purpose Text

Introduction

The proportion of instructional time in schools devoted to reading text or text-related activities varies. Some claim that as much as 90 percent of instructional time is text-based (see Komoski and Woodward, this volume, for discussion). There is little question that text materials, textbooks, and, more recently, microcomputer courseware, provide a primary instructional focus in schools, both in terms of structuring content for learners and occupying time on instructional tasks. Students spend most of their time using textual materials in some way.

Schools are not, however, the only text-based learning systems. Alternative, non-traditional educational settings are often more text-oriented than schools. That is, they rely more on textual materials to assume the primary or solitary instructional role. Because of the independent nature of instruction or the often specialized nature of the content, the text that learners use needs to be especially effective in controlling either the process of learning or the content to be learned, or both. The design of the text needs to go beyond a simple exposition of subject matter.

In this section of the book, we will look first at the use of text to control the process of learning in distance education texts. Then we will examine design requirements for preparing technical material, first for engineers and then for the military. Scientific/technical writing was chosen because it most frequently employs text designers. Also, technical content for engineers and for the military entails a different process as well as a different instructional process. The major functions of the engineering/military text designer require accurately reflecting the structure of content as well as controlling the process necessary for acquiring that specific content.

The primary purpose of this section of the book is to provide examples of the text design process being discussed in the other chapters in this and the first volume of the series. Consistent with fundamental instructional design principles, adequate and appropriate instantiation is essential to learning the concepts and principles with which these chapters are replete.

Distance Education Text

One of the most notable examples of alternative educational settings is distance education, about which John F. Carter discourses in his chapter. Since students pursuing distance education ("correspondence" education) do not interact with teachers, we find that textual materials, often supplemented with television, radio, or teleconferencing, must provide not only all or most of the instruction but also all of the directional and meta-instructional activities normally assumed by the teacher. So, text design for distance education is as concerned with controlling the *process* of instruction as the content. Learners in distance education settings are obligated to follow the lead of the text, so it must do more than display content. The textual materials must display an instructional logic. In his chapter, Carter discusses the instructional design implications of and processes for designing self-study texts. He concludes that they should be personalized as much as possible and foster learning-to-learn as well as learning-of-content. Distance education texts are a unique type of text because of their purpose and use.

Technical Text

The next two chapters deal with preparing technical text, first for engineers and then, in the final chapter in this section, for the military. Rudy J. Joenk begins the process of preparing texts for engineers by considering the characteristics of his target audience—engineers. This should be an initial step in any text design process, but too often it is neglected in deference to content coverage. The function of engineers in the scientific community engenders a unique set of information acquisition habits which in turn result in specific information needs. For example, engineers interact best with materials prepared using a very systematic approach to design and development, claims Joenk. Therefore, texts for engineers should include objectives, learner verification (see Komoski and Woodward chapter, this volume), and information retrieval mechanisms so that texts may also be used for reference. Other important criteria include appropriate language, usability, and availability. Engineers, like all scientists and social scientists today, are inundated with information, so making the textual material easy to use is also an important criterion. That means including adequate access structures (see the fourth section of this volume). The text requirements and design process that Joenk describes provide us with an excellent example of the technology of text design.

Military Technical Manuals

For those readers who are occasionally frustrated by the bureaucratic encumbrances affecting their positions that simply will not let them function efficiently, Thomas M. Duffy's chapter should provide some comparative relief. The military produces more technical manuals than many industries combined—totaling in the hundreds of millions of pages. But Duffy claims that despite a wealth of research-based recommendations on how to design technical manuals and a lot of expert personnel, the process is subverted by the management of manual preparation. The procedure for preparing manuals is multi-layered and complex. Because of this, the manuals are not as easily usable as they should be, resulting in direct costs to the military in the billions of dollars. See, good text design *does* make a difference.

While most of us do not deal on the size scale of the military, we can all profit from his admonitions about the deficiencies in the process as well as his suggestions on how to improve it. Those suggestions are consistent with the ones expostulated in other chapters in this book. Therefore, this chapter, too, represents a good example of the technology of text. Duffy's major (no pun intended) concern is with developing user-oriented materials. This means that in technical manuals, the structure of the content presentation should be procedural rather than descriptive or conceptual (an engineering focus) as they so often are. He points out that the learner verification process (see Komoski and Woodward chapter, this volume) is even more essential to the design of user-oriented text than traditional instructional text. Because it represents an expensive delay to the military, however, it is too often neglected—to the financial and operational detriment of the military (and, ultimately, to the citizens who support it). Finally, he recommends a team effort, which includes a technology of text, to ensure that the interests of the manual's users are considered. That, after all, is the point of this book.

Chapter 14

Considerations in the Development of Distance Education Texts

John F. Carter

Distance education is hardly a new phenomenon. Under the rubric of "correspondence education," it has been in existence in the United States for approximately 90 years, providing educational programs to as many as 50 million students (Fowler, 1981). However, its acceptance within the general educational community has been limited by a bias favoring residential face-to-face instructional forms and questions about the practices of some correspondence institutions in previous years (e.g., Mitford, 1970). For the most part, it has been viewed as a second-choice and second-class educational approach.

The recent success of the British Open University, however, has focused new attention on distance education, and heightened awareness that in many situations nonresidential study can provide a quality educational experience which produces outcomes that rival or surpass those of traditional programs (Henderson and Nathenson, 1984). Indeed, in many parts of the world, especially in developing countries, distance education has been identified as the only viable means of providing educational programs to the vast majority of adult learners. Even in developed countries, there are individuals and publics who, because of age, location, or occupational circumstances, are not adequately served by campus-based programs.

But the development of distance education materials and programs is not a weekend and evening endeavor. It entails complexities which go beyond those involved in the design of instruction for the classroom, or the preparation of standard academic texts. In this chapter, I will explore a number of these issues and describe their implications for designing texts for distance use. To lay a groundwork, a definition and rationale for distance education will be presented and its role in providing educational services described. Next, I will emphasize the special characteristics of distance education which must be accommodated in text design. And, finally, I will touch on the need for learning and instructional research focusing on the distance education context.

What Is Distance Education?

There have been a number of attempts to develop a list of the critical attributes in a definition of distance education. This has sometimes produced a vigorous debate (e.g., Bååth, 1981; Keegan, 1980). In general, however, there is agreement that distance education involves a form of study in which students are physically separated from teachers (the element of distance) and which depends largely on written, mechanical, electronic, or other noncontiguous forms of two-way communication (Holmberg, 1979). Over the years, the most common form of two-way communication in distance education has been postal (the correspondence education model), but in recent years, systems employing radio, television, newspapers, audiocassette tapes, telephones, and computer-based components have been developed. On balance, though, it is fair to say that postal two-way communication is still the predominant means employed in systems of distance education and training, and the printed study guide the predominant means of structuring the study process. In this regard, it is important to understand that the "texts" of distance education are *instructional* texts. Their purpose is not only to communicate knowledge in an effective way, but to lead the student to an adequate understanding of the knowledge presented through a structured study process. The design of distance texts, therefore, is an instructional design process.

One of the characteristics that has been emphasized by some writers is the tendency for distance education to be an "industrialized" form of education (Keegan, 1980; Peters, 1971). By this is meant that the development and administration of distance education programs are generally characterized by the methodologies of mass production. This is possible because distance study programs are designed to be replicable over large numbers of individuals and are usually presented in some "hard copy" form. Consequently, there are economies of scale which tend to yield cost and efficiency benefits. Of course, there may also be negative trade-offs in an industrialized approach, such as a loss of personalization and the ability to respond in a unique way to student questions and concerns. More will be said on this point later in the chapter.

Why Educate at a Distance

I suppose it is fair to ask why distance education programs and institutions have come into existence and in what way they serve publics different from those served by conventional institutions. In so doing, we can establish a framework for considering the challenges to be met in the design of instructional texts for distance education.

Perhaps the most commonly recognized reason why persons select distance learning programs relates to their desire for an educational opportunity not available from traditional sources or not pursuable because of time and space constraints. Many students pursue distance education programs in order to acquire skills needed for career advancement and development without interrupting an existing profession. Because distance education provides flexibility in timing and location of study not typically available with traditional study programs, these individuals may find the distance approach to be the best way to achieve academic goals at the least sacrifice of personal life style. The genius of distance study is that students can stay where they are, doing what they are doing in life, and still attain educational goals.

Bonani (1980) has suggested that distance study may attract students who have experienced failure in previous educational undertakings. He characterized this as a form of "scholastic recuperation" for students who are seeking to rectify educational deficiencies, but are past the normal schooling age. This may be an especially important role for distance education in societies where there is a high secondary school drop-out rate. However, providing educational programs to such a population involves a special challenge. Distance programs may be more convenient, but there is no reason to believe that they are "easier," especially for students who may not have done well in previous schooling.

For many of these situations, there is a tendency to view distance education as the alternative of second choice—the one chosen only when no traditional program is available. However, for certain individuals, distance education may be the selection of first choice. Reasons for choosing a distance education program over an available conventional program may include flexibility in pacing, greater freedom of choice in selecting goals, greater personal autonomy, access to the unique expertise of a course writer, availability of special media combinations or program features made possible by the generally greater concentration of resources in course development, and so on. Moreover, some research suggests that students who choose distance education programs may be of a different sort than those who select campus-based programs. Moore (1976) found that distance education attracted students who were more autonomous as a cognitive style characteristic than those who chose to study in classroom settings.

Finally, there is the factor of cost. For instance, Daniel and Stroud (1981) reviewed published studies on costs for the British Open University and concluded that "no matter how the analysis was done the Open University provided education at a substantially lower cost than conventional universities" (p. 149). This should not be particularly surprising given the economies of scale available to a distance education system. These economies are usually reflected in lower tuition charges to students.

No doubt there are those who would claim that all of the above notwithstanding, there is still no substitute for the warm body of a truly knowledgeable teacher holding forth before an assembly of enraptured students as a truly first-rate educational experience. In this vision, the students are all paying close attention, the teacher is able to explain every point with clarity and enthusiasm (unfettered by notes, of course), and every question raised by a student results from his or her attempt to analyze, synthesize, and evaluate the course lecture material. Although some instances of classroom instruction may approximate this ideal, it is questionable whether most do. Moreover, there is no evidence that classroom instruction generally provides an increment in measurable learning outcomes beyond those obtained in a distance education system. If there is some unique contribution made by educational endeavors of the face-to-face variety, researchers have not been able to document it. Both Childs (1971) and Macken, van den Heuvel, Suppes, and Suppes (1976) concluded after a review of research comparing correspondence and other forms of instruction that correspondence students achieve as much as students studying in other ways and when there is a difference, it tended to favor the correspondence study method.

Summary

Distance education, especially in the form of correspondence study, has been around for a long time, but the success of the British Open University has caused a renewed interest in it in many parts of the world. Distance education programs have been developed to respond to a variety of societal and educational situations for which traditional classroom-based approaches are less feasible. They may also be preferred over classroom programs by students for whom flexibility, freedom, and autonomy are important. Moreover, the available evidence suggests that students who pursue distance education studies achieve at least as much as those who pursue study programs of the traditional variety.

Although programs of distance study may produce achievement levels equivalent to those obtainable through conventional means, they do represent a different approach. Designers of instruction to be delivered at a distance must accommodate a number of variables which are not normally encountered by designers of materials for teacher-centered programs. It is these special characteristics which we will consider in the next section.

Instructional Design Considerations in Distance Education

In many respects, programs of distance education are a form of individualized study similar to the Keller approach (Keller, 1968), the audio-tutorial method (Postlethwait, 1969), and programmed instruction in its various forms. Instructional design for a distance education program, therefore, would be similar to that for any systematically designed program, and would include concern for needs assessment, prespecified objectives, criterion-referenced testing, and instructional feedback. In addition, there are several other factors which enter into the situation. These include the distance aspect, the need for personalization, the teaching process, the instructional support system, and the design/development process.

The Distance Aspect

Probably the most salient characteristic of distance education is the distance aspect itself. Unlike most other forms of instruction, the student is assumed to be physically separated from the teacher/tutor. Moreover, communication between them is mediated through some written, mechanical, or electronic device, as mentioned earlier. Thus, the need for carefully thought-out instructional sequences is paramount.

Since the opportunity for students to obtain clarification of poorly-understood material may be hampered by a communication time-lag measured in days or weeks, it behooves the instructional design system to minimize the need for such interactions. The developer must make the "Murphyesque" assumption that "what can be misconstrued, will be misconstrued" and plan accordingly. Childs (1962) pointed out that the correspondence writer "must learn not only to express himself so that he may be understood but also in such a way that he may not possibly be misunderstood" (p. 18). Obviously, this implies a level of instructional clarity beyond that required for textbooks, most classroom situations, or those forms of individualized study which assume the presence of a teacher or tutor at some not-too-distant location. In fact, the distance student can seldom benefit from even that level of instructional assistance which can be gained from other students since they are also not conveniently at hand. There is probably no instructional situation which places a greater demand on the instructional design system to produce acceptable stand-alone instructional sequences than a distance education approach.

The Need for Personalization

A major concern for any distance education system is how to maintain a degree of personalization in the study process. Holmberg (1979) has formulated a theory of distance education as a "guided didactic conversation." In his view, the interaction between a teacher and student through printed, telephonic, and/or audio-visual media constitutes a "conversation" which can attain a personalized quality. This personalization "is created by an easily readable and reasonably colloquial style of presentation and . . . characterized by, for instance, the author using personal pronouns for self-reference (*I* or *we*) and the student being referred to as *you*" (p. 20).

Going somewhat further, Bäath (1979) suggested the possibility of applying to distance education aspects of the nondirective approach advocated by Carl Rogers (1969). In this approach, the teacher is assumed to be a facilitator of learning who seeks to aid the student to pursue his or her own goals. In essence, this view is an extension of Rogers' approach to psychotherapy. It emphasizes the importance of the relationship between the teacher and learner, and the freedom of the learner to define the learning outcomes. On the surface, such an approach would seem far removed from that employed in most distance study programs, with their prescriptive and highly-structured formats. However, Bäath suggested ways in which distance texts and programs could take on aspects of a Rogerian model in order to create a greater sense of relationship between the student and distance teacher. Interestingly, Bäath and Mansson (1977) reported the successful use of computer-generated personalized responses in which 76 percent of the students indicated a preference for this mode of interaction over hand-written responses from tutors. Thus, it appears that it may even be possible to use impersonal methods to achieve personalized instruction.

It is fair to ask whether there is any empirical evidence to support the desirability of personalizing distance study courses. I have been unable to locate any published experimental study which directly manipulated this variable. The justification for the practice, which is widely held among distance educators (Bäath, 1979), seems to be mainly theoretical and intuitive.

The Teaching Process

Distance education involves "teaching," not just the provision of an opportunity to learn. By this I mean it is necessary for designers of distance study materials and programs to take seriously the proposition that if a student who fits within the profile of the intended audience conscientiously completes study assignments and finds the program insufficient to produce the intended outcomes, then *it is the fault of the study program rather than the student.* This proposition, of course, is basic to the mastery learning approach to instruction (e.g., Block, 1971). It takes on added significance in a distance education setting because in addition to facing the usual demands of the learning situation, students must do so using a study method which is probably unfamiliar.

This suggests that the learning-to-learn process is a particularly important one in distance education. One reason the drop-out rates for distance study are usually large may be because insufficient attention has been given to this problem. Students who have spent 12 years, more or less, learning under the direct guidance of a teacher and educational system which closely supervise the pace and sequence of study are suddenly faced with a good deal more independence and personal control over the study process than they have ever before had. The need for considerable self-initiative and discipline is obvious. Moreover, they must learn how to make the system of two-way communication, however "personalized," work for them.

Studies have shown that the students most likely to follow through with a distance education program are those who submit their first lessons soon after receiving them (Macken *et al.*, 1976). It is at this point that they are usually considered to be a "starter." This suggests the importance of assisting students to get started properly by providing for helps and motivational devices within the course materials or associated instructional support system.

It must be noted that distance teaching institutions, especially private correspondence schools, have not always developed instructional systems which sought to maximize course completion rates. Sometimes there is greater profitability with high enrollments and low completions. Mitford (1970) highlighted problems of this kind. Since then, legislation and the efforts of accrediting bodies have ameliorated these problems (Fowler, 1981). It is even possible to conceive of systems where the economic incentives are structured to encourage course completions. Government-subsidized programs in some European countries, for instance, have this characteristic.

But these are economic and ethical issues rather than instructional ones. It is clear that the instructional problem is to develop a system that encourages both the starting and completing of distance courses. In this regard, distance educators have been particularly innovative in designing instructional systems and materials which provide support for the study process. Some of these approaches reintroduce an aspect of direct contact between students and teachers. Periodic face-to-face teaching/discussion sessions, telephone tutoring, regional study centers for student-teacher and student-student encounters, electronic mail, etc., have all been used. Efforts such as these tend to have the primary effect of increasing the proportion of individuals who begin and bring to completion their study programs (Bäath, 1981).

Earlier, I mentioned the importance of providing a thoroughly thought-out instructional sequence. Elements in such a sequence are normally considered to include statements of instructional objectives, advance organizers, content outlines, segments of content written with special attention to concreteness and clarity, study questions and exercises, self-tests, etc. These instructional features are well described in texts on instructional design (e.g., Gagné and Briggs, 1974) and need not be detailed here. In addition, there is the need for ample procedural directions and explanations to see that the student can move easily from activity to activity. These constitute the "glue" which holds the other elements together and ensures that students can proceed efficiently through the course.

One function that can be served by procedural instructions is to provide students with guidance in individualizing their own study. There have been many attempts to design instructional sequences of the branching sort described by Crowder (1963). Although theoretically appealing, instructional sequences with branching capabilities have not been found to have sufficient practicality for

general use. The basic problem is the extensive development work
needed to produce sequences which only a few students may need.
As an alternative, designers of distance study programs could
provide guidance to students on how to monitor and evaluate their
own performance while studying, and what to do about it. The
CADE (Computer-Assisted Distance Education) system described
by Bäath and Mansson (1977) does this to some degree using a
computer for personalized comments on student exercises. However, it is also desirable to build remediation prescriptions and
devices into the actual course materials so students can pursue
self-tailored study routines without the time-lag inherent in most
distance education communication systems. In some measure, this
can help to solve the problem of how to accommodate individual
differences encountered with all forms of standardized, pre-pack-
aged instruction.

The Instructional Support System

Designers of distance courses cannot content themselves with
the development of narrowly-conceived self-contained instructional sequences. Distance courses exist within a complex instructional
system that may have as much or more to do with student success
than the materials being studied. It is the instructional support
system that determines how much freedom students will have to
select program objectives; whether or not their study will operate
within a self-imposed or externally-imposed time frame; the
opportunity for tutorial consultation and guidance in academic
planning and problem-solving; what sort of communication system
will be used, and how to make it work so as to reduce the inherent
discontinuity in the communication process; whether there is an
opportunity for face-to-face, telphonic, or other forms of direct
interactive contact with teachers; etc. These are aspects of the
general instructional system with which designers have to deal in
course planning. Ideally, many of these factors can be specifically
determined as part of the course design process, but sometimes
they are already fixed by the institutional makeup. If this is the
case, they will need to enter into consideration as parameters to be
accommodated in course design. Even then, designers should seek

ways to vary aspects of an instructional support/management system to the advantage of the student wherever possible.

The major challenge, as pointed out by Daniel and Stroud (1981), is to achieve a balance between those activities a student can perform independently and those which are facilitated by interaction with others in the system. In terms of the cost to produce distance study materials, there are advantages to a system "lean" in instructional support mechanisms. In terms of instructional effectiveness, however, the advantages generally lie with a "rich" system. In my view, the role of the instructional designer is to be an advocate of those features which will make the materials instructionally effective, while recognizing the reality and necessity of working within economic constraints in regard to design alternatives.

The Design/Development Process

Not only does instructional design for distance education face the need to accommodate a set of special characteristics, but also it must cope with a particular set of dynamics concerning the role and function of those involved in developing the materials. A central concern in any distance education undertaking is how best to organize the process of designing and developing the instructional materials and systems to be used. A very common approach to this is to contract with teachers of a subject matter to produce a course. This includes both the course content and teaching components. In this situation, the teacher/writer is usually not a permanent staff member of the distance education institution. However, the institution does employ editors to work with the materials prior to publication and teachers or tutors to grade lessons and interact with students as they pursue their studies.

Other patterns involve a team-based approach. This is the strategy followed by the British Open University, and according to Perry (1977) represents "the most important single contribution of the Open University to teaching practice at a tertiary level" (p. 91). In this approach, course developers are full-time university staff members assisted by educational technologists and radio or television producers. Perry points out that the role of various members of the team tends to vary as a function of course subject area. Humanities and Social Sciences courses tend toward individual development by the discipline-oriented faculty members with the other team members serving a consulting role, while Math and Science courses tend to be developed more through collective effort. Whether this is a function of a greater degree of consensus concerning the underlying structure of the subject matter on the part of Math and Science faculty or is due to other factors is not clear. It has been suggested that the role of the educational technologist in this system has become somewhat problematical as content-oriented academic staff have gained skill in instructional development and depend less on the assistance of the technologists.

There are many possible variations of the two approaches described above. For instance, at the International Correspondence Institute (ICI) in Brussels, Belgium, where I have worked, the approach is somewhere in between the two. ICI employs part-time writers as content experts whose primary responsibility is for subject content, and uses an in-house instructional development staff to produce study exercises, testing, and other instructional components of the course. Thus, the subject matter, and the instructional process used to teach it, are largely the responsibility of different individuals. Although this is also a team-oriented approach, it reserves the primary role for the instructional developer.

All of this is to say that in distance education there are various roles and relationships among those responsible for course development which have to be sorted out. This is especially true in regard to those whose primary experience has been in teaching in a traditional institution or writing traditional academic textbooks. Teachers are used to delivering "content" and handling the educational process in a more or less *ad hoc* manner. They may not be sufficiently sensitive to the instructional dynamics involved in distance study. As Erdos (1975) put it, "The main difficulty in teaching by correspondence is that many writers feel they have only to write uninterrupted pages of factual content" (p. 21). Moreover, Perry (1977) has alluded to the reduction in individual academic freedom which results from a team-oriented development approach. Add to this the problem of effectively positioning the instructional development expertise of an educational technologist and marrying all this with production line techniques and schedules, and the network of relationships, roles, and functions becomes exceedingly complex.

Adding even more complexity are the emerging electronic and computer-based technologies which will eventually take their place as part of distance learning systems. These hold out the prospect that not only will course development teams need content experts, educational technologists, and media producers, but specialists in computer and videodisc technologies as well. Instructional software development will become more and more difficult as these technology options become available and new professional roles and relationships are integrated into the development process. Those most comfortable with the paper, pencil, and postage-stamp technologies of the past may find the transition a traumatic one.

Summary

In this section, I have tried to describe some of the distinctive characteristics of distance learning systems which present a particular challenge to an instructional design process. Probably the most salient of these is the distance aspect, but the need for personalization, an effective teaching-learning approach tailored to the distance situation, and the special dynamics of the distance course development process are all aspects to be considered. They combine to produce a complex and challenging setting in which to examine and apply educational theory.

Educational Research and Distance Education

As everyone who has pursued the course of learning research over the past two decades knows, there has been a shift from a behavioral to a cognitive approach. Recent reviews by Greeno (1980) and Calfee (1981) have detailed this transition. Moreover, this has had an effect upon the way researchers are thinking about education and instructional design (e.g., Gallagher, 1979; Merrill, Kelety, and Wilson, 1981; Wittrock, 1979).

Nevertheless, I believe it is fair to say that the imprint of behavioral psychology has been, and still is, broadly apparent. For instance, despite the reservations expressed by some researchers concerning behavioral objectives (e.g., Macdonald-Ross, 1973), they are still widely used in distance education (Holmberg, 1979). Other behavioristic practices, such as the requirement for student responding and provision of corrective feedback, are also prevalent. Although cognitive research has begun to provide better insights into the role various kinds of instructional activities can play in the formation of knowledge structures, until now it has produced relatively minor changes on a terrain which has derived its primary features from behaviorism. Not only is this true for the learning systems being developed but also for the processes used to develop them.

But there is no question that the influence of cognitive theory will grow. Probably the greatest strides thus far have been made toward an understanding of knowledge structures and their relationship to subject matter organization (see Jonassen's chapter, this volume, on generative strategies). This is a necessary element in the development of a theory of instruction (Glaser, 1976). Unfortunately, sophisticated schemes for mapping conceptual relationships in subject matter are difficult for even individuals trained in cognitive psychology and psycholinguistics to apply. For the instructional text designer, they are well-nigh impossible to apply. Thus, it seems to me that it is in the explication of how various task demand requirements affect cognitive processing and the consequent development of cognitive structures and skills which has the broader general application to design/development practice. We need a comprehensive taxonomy of these activity-outcome relationships at a sufficiently detailed level to give guidance to practitioners who are not themselves cognitive scientists. Moreover, these relationships need to be represented in algorithmic form if they are to be useful. If they can be computer-based, all the better.

Toward this end, it would be helpful if cognitive researchers gave greater attention to the practical implications of their work. I would suggest that distance education presents a likely setting for applied research on instruction, since many of the variables which are problematic in classroom research are controllable due to the highly structured nature of distance study.

Consider, for example, the instructional model presented recently by Rothkopf (1981). Six variables were described which were thought to influence the probability that a particular instructional event or event sequence will be successful. These variables were described as:

   —the number of redundant instructional events;
   —attendance to instruction and compliance with assignments;
   —disparity between the instructive event and the learning goal;
   —experience of student relevant to instruction;
   —likelihood of sufficient mathemagenic processing by student; and
   —retrievability of learned information or competence.

It should be fairly obvious that such a model maps rather nicely upon the kinds of instructional sequences that characterize distance study. Because the events of instruction are represented objectively and concretely in either the instructional materials given to students or the two-way communication system, it should be relatively easy to manipulate the variables outlined by Rothkopf in a systematic manner, more so than for most teacher-dependent instructional systems.

Distance education represents fertile ground for both theory-oriented and practice-oriented research on instructional processes. However, educational researchers in this country have largely ignored this context. This may be to the detriment of our understanding of "real world" learning.

In any event, recent developments in learning and instructional theory hold forth great promise for the advancement of instructional design science. What is needed is an orderly means for the translation of this knowledge into the kinds of rules, procedures, and guidelines which can inform practice. If this happens, it will be to the benefit of teachers, text designers, and instructional designers of all kinds.

References

Bääth, J. *Correspondence education in the light of a number of contemporary teaching models.* Malmo: Liber Hermods, 1979.

Bäath, J. On the nature of distance education. *Distance Education,* 1981, *2,* 212-219.

Bäath, J., and Mansson, N. *CADE—A system for computer-assisted distance education.* Malmo: Hermods Skola, 1977.

Block, J. (Ed.) *Mastery learning: Theory and practice.* New York: Holt, Rinehart, and Winston, 1971.

Bonani, G. Correspondence teaching: Second choice or second class? Paper presented at the Spring Workshop of the European Home Study Council, Bled, Yugoslavia, May, 1980.

Calfee, R. Cognitive psychology and educational practice. In D. Berliner, (Ed.), *Review of research in education* (Vol. 9). Washington, DC: American Educational Research Association, 1981.

Childs, G. Problems of teaching by correspondence study. In *Application of new communication media in correspondence study.* Austin: University of Texas, Division of Extension, 1962.

Childs, G. Recent research developments in correspondence instruction. In O. MacKenzie and E. Christensen (Eds.), *The changing world of correspondence study.* University Park: Pennsylvania State University, 1971.

Crowder, N. On the differences between linear and intrinsic programming. *Phi Delta Kappan,* 1963, *44,* 250-254.

Daniel, J., and Stroud, M. Distance education: A reassessment for the 1980s. *Distance Education,* 1981, *3,* 146-163.

Erdos, R. *Establishing an institution teaching by correspondence.* Paris: The Unesco Press, 1975.

Fowler, W. The National Home Study Council: Distance education leadership for five decades. *Distance Education,* 1981, *2,* 234-239.

Gagné, R., and Briggs, L. Principles of instructional design. New York: Holt, Rinehart, and Winston, 1974.

Gallagher, J. Cognitive/information processing psychology and instruction: Reviewing recent theory and practice. *Instructional Science,* 1979, *8,* 393-414.

Glaser, R. Components of a psychology of instruction: Toward a science of design. *Review of Educational Research,* 1976, *46,* 1-24.

Greeno, J. Psychology of learning, 1960-1980. One participant's observations. *American Psychologist,* 1980, *35,* 713-728.

Henderson, E.S., and Nathenson, M.B. *Independent learning in higher education.* Englewood Cliffs, NJ: Educational Technology Publications, 1984.

Holmberg, B. Practice in distance education: A conceptual framework. *Canadian Journal of University Continuing Education*, 1979, *6*, 18-30.

Keegan, D. On defining distance education. *Distance Education*, 1980, *1*, 13-36.

Keller, F. Good-bye teacher. *Journal of Applied Behavior Analysis*, 1968, *1*, 79-88.

MacDonald-Ross, M. Behavioral objectives: A critical review. *Instructional Science*, 1973, *2*, 1-52.

Macken, E., van den Heuvel, R., Suppes, P., and Suppes, T. *Home-based education: Needs and opportunities.* Washington, DC: National Institute of Education, 1976.

Merrill, M.D., Kelety, J., and Wilson, B. Elaboration theory and cognitive psychology. *Instructional Science*, 1981, *10*, 217-235.

Mitford, J. Let us now appraise famous authors. *Atlantic Monthly*, 1970, *226*, 45-54.

Moore, M. *Investigation of the interaction between the cognitive style of field independence and attitudes to independent study among adult learners who use correspondence study and self-directed independent study.* Unpublished doctoral dissertation, University of Wisconsin, 1976.

Perry, W. *The Open University.* San Francisco: Jossey-Bass, 1977.

Peters, O. Theoretical aspects of correspondence instruction. In O. MacKenzie and E. Christensen (Eds.), *The changing world of correspondence study.* University Park: Pennsylvania State University, 1971.

Postlethwait, S. *The audio-tutorial system* (2nd Ed.). Minneapolis: Burgess, 1969.

Rogers, C. *Freedom to learn.* Columbus, OH: Charles Merrill, 1969.

Rothkopf, E. A macroscopic model of instruction and purposive learning: An overview. *Instructional Science*, 1981, *10*, 105-122.

Wittrock, M. The cognitive movement in education. *Educational Researcher*, 1979, *8*, 5-11.

Chapter 15

Engineering Text for Engineers

R.J. Joenk

> With information becoming more important than ever before, the
> new civilization will restructure education, redefine scientific
> research and, above all, reorganize the media of communication.
> Alvin Toffler, *The Third Wave*

Information is *the* megatrend of the '80s. Because diversity,
specialization, and personalization characterize our increasingly
information-oriented society, more publications are covering
narrower portions of the technology spectrum for smaller segments of the technical population.

Three important characteristics distinguish technical text from
literary text:

- *First, technical text must be written with the audience in
  mind.* The writer of a novel or a short story can be
  successful without considering whether the readers will be
  engineers or chauffeurs, secretaries or doctors, college
  professors or day laborers. The technical author, however,
  must engineer information specifically to the level of the
  audience.

- *Second, technical text is instructional*; it is writing to
  inform rather than to entertain. If it has style, if it is
  attention-holding, if it is amusing or entertaining, however,
  it may accomplish its purpose better than instructional
  text without these features. Gleason (1982) describes
  several effective uses of humor in technical text.

- *Third, technical text must be clear and unambiguous*; its
  language must be precise. Consequently, it is usually more
  conservative and less "flowery" than other forms of
  literature.

"Ellis, don't you think we ought to have more bookcases built so we'll be ready for the megashift from an industrial to an informational society?"

Reprinted with permission of Tribune Co. Syndicate.

This chapter has two purposes: to characterize engineers as an audience and to suggest how to engineer or tailor your information for them. The three attributes—audience, instruction, and language—are reviewed; recommendations are given for making your technical text more usable; and two benefits of electronic text are cited.

This is not a treatise on teaching technical writing to engineers. It is advice for educators and authors who are not engineers themselves but whose intended audience is engineers. The bibliography includes several books on the elements of technical writing, useful for both engineers and non-engineers.

Engineers Are Not Scientists

Casual writers and survey takers often categorize everyone with a technical background as a scientist, or they loosely equate scientists and engineers. Why should an educator or author be concerned about this?

Your goal in writing is information transfer. To accomplish this, you have to trigger some reaction in your readers, not merely display your accumulated wisdom. Your audience's characteristics, if you do not take them into account, may cause your message to be misunderstood or ignored.

The world of technical literature is flavored by science. Science has a popular history of, say, 3000 years, engineering about 300. Thus, professional scientific societies generally predate—and serve as the models for—engineering organizations. The "publish or perish" syndrome, however, is paramount in scientific activity but not in engineering. Scientists are very concerned with communicating, mostly to obtain recognition and acknowledgment of their work *outside* their organizations; engineers are more concerned with achievement and recognition *within* their organizations.

This primary difference between engineers and scientists leads to different philosophies and habits not only about contributing to technical literature but also about using technical literature and other sources of information.

Engineers' goals differ from those of scientists. Engineering students, for example, prefer career success to independence by a margin of nearly 2:1, whereas science students choose independence over success by a small margin (Krulee and Nadler, 1960). Although the students generally agree on some of the qualities essential for success, the engineering students rate practical knowledge above basic theoretical knowledge, whereas the science students hold the opposite view.

Because such values and goals differentiate engineers from scientists even in the early stages of their training, conscientious technical educators and authors must recognize that they need to modify, often significantly, the pervasive image of scientist if they really want to communicate with engineers.

What happens after graduation? Currently, there are nearly equal numbers of engineers and scientists in the United States, about 1.3 million each (U.S. Bureau of the Census, 1981). Private industry employs three-fourths of the engineers and only one-fourth of the scientists. In academic institutions, however, scientists outnumber engineers almost 9:1.

Although some of the work of the engineers and scientists is indistinguishable on a day-to-day basis, there are differences in their creative processes and in their creative products (Blade, 1963; italics added):

- Engineers engage in *problem-solving for practical operating results*; scientists seek a result for its own ends.
- Engineers seek to *develop and make things*; scientists search for theories and principles.
- Engineers *use and exploit nature*; scientists attempt to discover and explain nature.

Another example of goal differences is found among engineers and scientists in industry (Ritti, 1971): Engineers choose helping the company increase its profits as their most important work goal 2.5 times as frequently as scientists, whereas scientists' most popular work goal, by a ratio of nearly 6:1 over engineers, is publishing technical articles. This polarized attitude about publishing, coupled with the academic socialization inherent in the process of obtaining advanced degrees (which most scientists do and most engineers do not), accounts for significant differences between the literature of the two fields and between the information-gathering and -use habits of the two professions.

Generally, the engineer's contribution—and basis of recognition—is physical, not verbal. Not writing or publishing as much, the engineer tends to depend less than the scientist on written material as a source of information. The primary alternative to written communication is personal communication. Engineers prefer and rely most on this in their job-related and technical- and business-information gathering.

In large, multi-site and multi-national corporations, however, there is a form of internal communication, often called the "technical report," that helps prevent reinventing technological "wheels" within the organization. These technical reports are part of engineering's informal communication network. When they do not contain proprietary information, these reports even move across industry lines.

Engineers' Reading Habits

Engineers and their managers regard reading as very important to their jobs, their careers, and their self-development. "Technical people read to analyze problems, propose solutions, and carry out research. Managers and supervisors read to review, advise, assign, develop organizational procedures and policies, and so on" (Miller, 1982). Miller's survey of 28 high-technology people at Sperry Univac reported 15 to 20 hours per week spent on technical reading.

At RCA, the attitudes are essentially the same (Jenny, 1978a). According to a survey of more than 3,000 (75 percent) of RCA's engineers, nearly half of the information they received was from reading (Jenny, 1978b). Eleven to 16 hours per week are spent on reading (Table 15.1), about 54 percent of it at work and the rest at home.

Table 15.1

Time Spent Reading*
(Hours per Week)

	Engineers	Leaders	Managers
Technical—job	5.0	6.0	6.4
Technical—other	3.0	2.9	2.6
Professional	1.5	1.4	1.9
Business—other	1.1	1.6	1.9
Business—RCA	0.9	2.0	3.3
Total	11.4	13.9	16.0

*Jenny, 1978, b.

Printed information is either formal or informal. The formal sources are textbooks, reference books, handbooks, professional society journals, and trade magazines—media that are generally available to the public. The informal source is primarily the intra-organization technical report that is seldom published or available outside. These two forms are used with about equal frequency (Allen, 1977). The formal sources are usually consulted for specific information; the informal ones are often read or studied in greater depth. Thus, on the average, more than twice as much time is spent on an informal report as on a formal reference. Time devoted to a textbook in *classroom* use is not part of these results.

Among the formal sources, Allen found that textbooks are the most frequently used items, about 28 percent of the uses in a set of technical-project studies. Trade magazines and controlled circulation journals are next with about 20 percent each. These three items account for about two-thirds of an engineer's printed information sources. Journals of the professional engineering societies are used less, about ten percent, presumably because they are patterned after the scientific society journals and are usually produced by the small portion of engineers in academic work, whose writing is more theoretical and mathematical than serves the industrial engineer's needs and mathematical abilities.

Table 15.2 is a list of technical trade journals serving a broad range of engineering. Almost by definition these journals are supported by advertising, even if they are also subsidized by the sponsoring organization. In contrast, professional engineering journals such as *AIChE Journal, Proceedings of the IEEE*, and *Transactions of the ASME* usually have little or no advertising.

Another interesting contrast with scientists is that engineers tend to obtain books from their company libraries but maintain their own office collection of periodicals, which often are free. Scientists, on the other hand, accumulate books during their longer education period but use periodicals in the library because of high subscription costs.

A supplementary observation is that, through book reviews, science-oriented periodicals expose their readers to considerably more new technical material than do engineering periodicals. During 1982, for example, 15 science publications published an

Table 15.2

Technical Trade Journals and Magazines

Title	Publisher	Circulation
Association Publications—Membership or Paid Subscription		
Agricultural Engineering	Amer. Soc. Agr. Eng.	13,000
ASHRAE Journal	Amer. Soc. Heating, Refrigerating and Air-Conditioning Engineers	42,000
Chemical Engineering Progress	Amer. Inst. Chem. Eng.	40,000
Civil Engineering	Amer. Soc. Civil Eng.	85,000
IEEE Spectrum	Inst. Elec. and Elec. Eng.	220,000*
Industrial Engineering	Inst. Industrial Eng.	38,000
Mechanical Engineering	Amer. Soc. Mech. Eng.	80,000
Metal Progress	Amer. Soc. Metals	53,000
Robotics Today	Soc. Manufacturing Eng.	6,000
Simulation	Soc. Computer Simulation	3,500
Standardization News	Amer. Soc. Testing and Materials	23,000
Tappi Journal	Tech. Assoc. Pulp and Paper Industry	28,000
Water Pollution Control Federation Journal	Water Pollution Control Federation	32,000
Commercial Publications—Paid Subscription		
Chemical Engineering	McGraw-Hill, Inc.	75,000*
Communications	Cardiff Publishing Co.	20,000
Electrical World	McGraw-Hill, Inc.	24,000
Electronics	McGraw-Hill, Inc.	98,000
Petroleum Engineer International	Harcourt Brace Jovanovich Publications	20,000
Power	McGraw-Hill, Inc.	52,000
Solid State Technology	Technical Publishing Co.	18,000
Solid Wastes Management	Communication Channels, Inc.	23,000

Table 15.2 (Continued)

Title	Publisher	Circulation
Commercial Publications–Free, Controlled Circulation and Paid Subscription		
American Machinist	McGraw-Hill, Inc.	68,000
Computer Design	Computer Design Publishing Co.	86,000
EDN Magazine	Cahners Publishing Co.	117,000
Electronic Design	Hayden Publishing Co.	125,000*
Industrial Research and Development	Technical Publishing Co.	105,000*
Infosystems	Hitchcock Publishing Co.	110,000
Instruments and Control Systems	Chilton Co.	75,000
Machine Design	Penton/IPC	155,000
Materials Engineering	Penton/IPC	61,000
Microwave Journal	Horizon House/Microwave, Inc.	45,000*
Mini-Micro Systems	Cahners Publishing Co.	100,000
Plastics Technology	Bill Communications, Inc.	38,000
Production Engineering	Penton/IPC	95,000
Quality	Hitchcock Publishing Co.	63,000
Telecommunications	Horizon House/Microwave, Inc.	61,000*
World Oil	Gulf Publishing Co.	35,000

*1983 data; other values, 1981-82.

average each issue of almost nine signed, critical reviews of new technical books, while 15 of the more book-oriented engineering publications averaged only two reviews per month (Joenk, 1983).

Textbooks and Instructional Materials

The 1970s were prolific years for research in the design and delivery of instruction (Braden, 1981). The methods evolving in instructional systems development (ISD) use some activities basic to the practice of engineering, though not common to the practice of engineering education: systems analysis, design of instruction, and optimization. These procedures do not guarantee success, but their judicious application makes sense in designing text for engineers.

Systems Analysis

A textbook, a course, or a training procedure rarely stands alone. Rather, it is part of a relevant system or environment, e.g., a junior-year course in a four-year curriculum or a local engineering-education department in a multi-national corporation. The educator or author must determine where the proposed work fits in: why it is needed, exactly what is needed, how it will complement the rest of the system, what constraints exist, and what resources are available. The idea is to create a peg that fits the hole; it should neither rattle nor have to be forced into place. As obvious as this may seem, many books and training courses are simply a result of the author's accumulated knowledge.

Explicit learning objectives must be established in advance; they must be expressed in terms of the students' performance; they must be measurable; and the students must be informed of them in advance. Start by thinking of the final test questions or activities: What must the students ultimately know or do? Then track backward: What intermediate, auxiliary, or prior knowledge and skills are required? Does the rest of the system provide any or all of it?

To avoid being another memory-dump author, analyze the

content of your proposed textbook or course or even journal article as suggested by the decision diagram in Figure 15.1. The analysis can be adapted to differential levels of content, e.g., in a text on VLSI (very large scale integration) circuits, from a short section on the solution of a different equation used in circuit analysis to a longer one covering the principles of thermal conduction to a full chapter on methods used in manufacturing VLSI chips. Conscious decisions like these help focus the information on knowledge and skills that (1) are critical to the students' or engineers' performance, (2) will be used frequently, and (3) are needed soon.

Design of Instruction

Next, consider the medium. Is a textbook really appropriate for all the objectives? What levels of learning are involved? Will a lecturer supplement the text with visual aids? Must the students have access to a computer? And so on. ISD emphasizes choosing the most effective method of instructional delivery (within the constraints of the system) for each learning task.

Delivering the instruction in a useful sequence is another consideration. Instead of an obvious "first things first" order, another sequence may encourage greater student or reader motivation, more opportunity for practice, or better reinforcement for remembering. For example, presenting the most difficult or most important element first highlights its status and provides the most practice time. Early hands-on experience is usually more realistic and satisfying than academic, verbal input.

Overall, the design of usable and effective instructional material results from teamwork—the integration of three skills: subject-matter expertise, educational technology, and "technology of text" (as exemplified by the content of these volumes).

Optimization

If you have ever followed an editor's advice to put your just-finished technical paper in a drawer for 30 days before

Figure 15.1

Decision Diagram

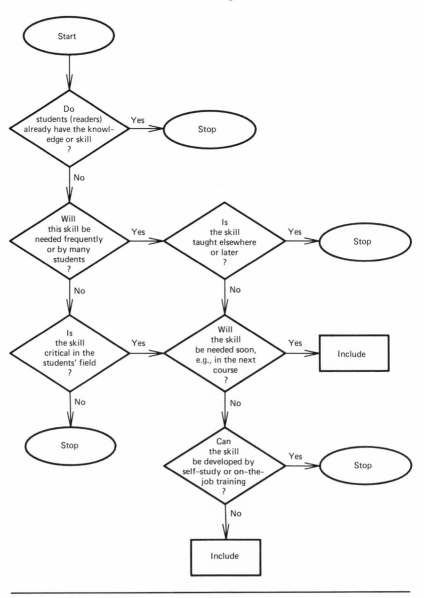

deciding to submit it, you were probably surprised and pleased at the improvements you could make after the delayed rereading. Similarly, instructors who use and revise class notes several times before completing a textbook have taken a giant step toward optimizing their work.

In other words, effective instructional systems include user testing in the development process, followed by revision or modification in the areas where the instruction proved ineffective (Al-Awar, Chapanis, and Ford, 1981). The question should be simply, "Did the students attain the objectives?" In the Al-Awar work, a computer-based tutorial was tested and reprogrammed repeatedly until its users responded correctly.

The intent is to compare each student's performance to pre-established criteria, not to compare one student's performance to another's performance. This is one of the major departures of ISD from traditional instruction. Closely related is a switch from "constant time, variable learning" to "constant learning, variable time" so that all students master the subject. Obviously, traditional textbooks must change if the instructional system does. The differences between traditional and systematic instruction are elaborated by Hannum and Briggs (1982).

Textbooks are also used as a formal source of information by engineers *after* graduation. Two features that enhance their value in this mode, as well as in course work, are:

- examples and exercises that use realistic engineering applications to clarify theory (rather than theoretical problems); and
- embedded information-retrieval mechanisms, such as typographic and layout cues, structuring, multi-level writing, and a detailed index.

A recent study of engineering students' attitudes toward their careers suggests that engineering educators and textbook producers might usefully structure their *technical* courses to additionally serve the *professional* needs of their students (Krowne and Covington, 1982). Being technically indoctrinated, the students generally have little knowledge about their professional responsibilities—how they will be called on to perform on the job and what the day-to-day responsibilities, tasks, and procedures will be. Much of that activity is communication-oriented, both written and oral.

Simulating professional activity in the technical classroom could be synergistic. Krowne and Covington recommend (1) requiring in-class oral reports related to the content of the course (let them preach what they practice!) and written reports analogous to organization technical reports, including recommendations; and (2) putting problem and design assignments in a realistic industrial context.

Technically Write! is a textbook on writing rather than engineering (see the bibliography) which accomplishes those goals by developing a fictional consulting-engineering company. The book personalizes the key officials and relates all of the course assignments to the activities and needs of that organization.

Another way to increase the value of engineering texts is to integrate discussion and examples that create an awareness of the effects of technology on society. In many areas today (e.g., the environment, public safety, and telecommunications), the technical problems and the social issues are closely connected. Policy making in those areas is hampered because of the lack of common ground between engineers, who *own* the technical problems, and policy makers, who *control* the problems. As a result, the study of technology and public policy issues is evolving into an important degree area for hybrid engineers (Bereiter, 1983). Graduates who have studied economics, political science, and policy analysis, for example, as well as engineering, are better equipped to deal with engineers on technical matters and with policy makers on policy matters.

Language

Language is the third important concern in technical text. Even among and between engineers and scientists, there are language barriers. Technology is often defined in words and phrases that defy translation into conventional or widely understood terms. Everyday language, and even current technical language, often lacks the necessary precision and explicitness to describe emerging concepts. In other words, the specialized vocabularies (jargon) of the various technologies *are* useful and necessary. Conscientious educators and authors must either be absolutely certain that their audience already understands the language or they must surmount the language barrier.

The language barrier can be surmounted in two ways. One is literally to translate the technical language, consciously deciding on an acceptable trade-off between technical precision and effective communication. Consulting with technical experts coupled with user testing can effect this translation (see, for example, Johnson, Garrard, and Hausman, 1982). Such writing is not *down* to the audience but *for* the audience. Seldom does simple, clear writing offend or alienate even an interested, highly educated reader.

The other method is to explicitly relate the underlying concepts and principles of the new technology to the audience's knowledge in other areas and contexts, such as those in a prerequisite course or phase of training (see, for example, Dunkle and Jackson, 1982). These two techniques, of course, are not mutually exclusive; they work well together.

Once you have introduced and defined a technical term, use it consistently. Resist using synonyms merely to avoid repetition or to "improve" style.

Usable Text

Usability is sometimes a subjective evaluation—it depends on what you want—but *objective* human factors engineering is showing its value in the marketplace. For example, consider the competition for hardware and software sales among video-game and personal-computer makers. Ultimately, usability of the instructional *information* accompanying those products will be the deciding factor when two or more offer the same functions.

For technical information to be usable in a larger sense, it must (a) be available, (b) fit a need, (c) be easy to use in a specific sense, and (d) leave the reader with a feeling of accomplishment.

Availability

Availability is an obvious necessity. Unless you are consciously writing for a very limited audience, do not bury your work in an obscure publication. Data from 500 Bendix Research Laboratory engineers and scientists confirm that source availability and ease of use are the leading determinants of use of a particular source (Chakrabarti, Feineman, and Fuentevilla, 1983). Although engineers prefer informal channels of communication, i.e., getting information orally from colleagues, they do tend to collect trade journals and magazines (Table 15.2), particularly those that are supported by advertising and offered free to qualified subscribers.

Even though it may take longer to locate printed information, colleagues are an effective channel for engineers, especially when those colleagues are in the "gatekeeper" class (Allen, 1977; Shuchman, 1981). Gatekeepers are individuals in an industrial organization who, more than most, communicate outside their organization—by reading a variety of technical literature, including the more academic journals; by participating in meetings and conferences; and by talking with and writing to technical people in other organizations.

Whether the audience receives your information directly or second- or third-hand, you can make it easier for all concerned by (1) providing effective titles and abstracts (see **Ease of Use**, pp. 361-365) and (2) choosing a publication that is indexed or abstracted by well-known retrieval services, such as the *Engineering Index* and the *Applied Science and Technology Index*, particularly those that are computer-based and available on information networks, e.g., Lockheed's *DIALOG®* Information Retrieval Service, SDC Search Service's *ORBIT®*, and Bibliographic Retrieval Service's *BRS*.

You can also improve availability by changing the physical location of instructions, for example, those for operating an electromechanical device. A possible solution for hand-held calculators, for example, has been to minimize the instructions and reduce the type size until the instructions contained in the booklet can be displayed in the calculator case, making the instructions readily available. Can similar improvements in availability be made for instructional manuals? For these larger items, the solution is usually less onerous than that for hand-held calculators.

Fitting a Need

Most engineers explain that they read "to keep current in their own field" (Shuchman, 1981). Seventy percent of a survey sample said this was the most important reason, and another 26 percent regarded it as moderately important. In more specific contexts, the two principal reasons that engineers *search* the literature are to generate ideas and to help define, or refine, their problems (Allen, 1977). This second category involves comparing and evaluating alternative problem-solving strategies and methods.

Trade and controlled-circulation journals are most used for "keeping abreast of developments in one's own field," "browsing that results in significant discovery," and "keeping abreast of developments on related or competing systems." Publications like *Scientific American* and sometimes the professional society technical journals are used for broadening interests and learning new specialties. Texts and handbooks, as well as professional journals, are most used for specific help in directly solving a problem, e.g., for an analytical procedure or a calculation.

Based on responses from 1,300 engineers, Shuchman (1981) prioritized 16 categories of technical information used in engineering work (Figure 15.2). The clear leaders are (1) basic knowledge in science and technology, needed by 82 percent of the respondents, and (2) proprietary technical data, needed by 72 percent. Although in-house data can be supplied only by technical reports and colleagues, many formal print media provide new technical knowledge as well as physical data, new-product characteristics, design methods, etc.

Thus, your writing for engineers is more likely to succeed if you (a) address *their* needs and (b) choose the right medium. To paraphrase Fitzgerald, do not write because you want to say something, write because you have something (useful) to say.

Ease of Use

Like most professionals today, engineers are inundated with information—and starved for knowledge. The Sperry Univac engineers in Miller's survey (1982) suggested that as much as half of their considerable reading time was inefficient. The complex material they try to read is often too dense, lacks structure, has no table of contents, assumes too much background and terminology knowledge, uses too many acronyms, and so on.

Figure 15.2

Categories of Technical Information Used in Engineering Work

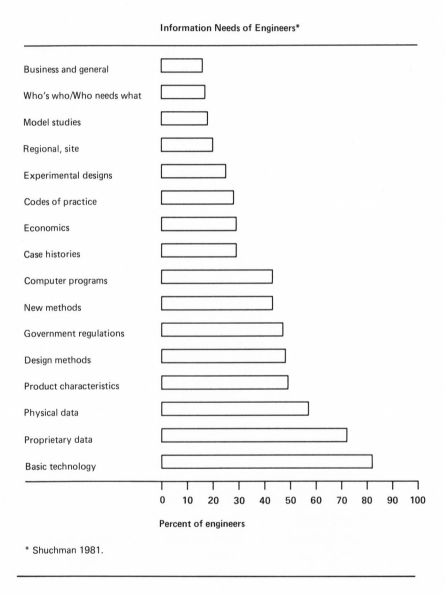

Information Needs of Engineers*

Business and general

Who's who/Who needs what

Model studies

Regional, site

Experimental designs

Codes of practice

Economics

Case histories

Computer programs

New methods

Government regulations

Design methods

Product characteristics

Physical data

Proprietary data

Basic technology

0   10   20   30   40   50   60   70   80   90   100

Percent of engineers

* Shuchman 1981.

From necessity or self-defense, one of the first things efficient readers learn is to scan and filter the sea of information. If your article or text does not pass that preliminary review, it will not matter whether you had something significant to say.

The importance and breadth and implementation of "ease of use" are only hinted at here. The bibliography complements this brief section.

Title. To pass the scanning test, the title, abstract, and section headings must be carefully developed. Enke (1978) maintains that the title should be written first: "The writing will lack direction and focus until a title is found that defines the theme." A technical-article title should be as short as possible, and it should use key words that will "respond" to an online information search. There sometimes is merit if the title arouses the reader's curiosity or if the imagination that went into it can be detected; however, in technical material, this is secondary.

The basic criterion for a title is that it clearly state the specific subject of the article, without resorting to jargon. It should promise only what the article delivers. Rathbone (1972) tests a title with these four questions: Is it correct? Is it complete? Is it comprehensible? Is it concise?

Abstract. As an author, you should be well acquainted with prior literature and work in your field so that in your abstract or introduction you can clearly describe the place of your contribution and what new information you are presenting.

The abstract can compensate for the brevity of the title, but it must be understandable without referring the reader to the body of the paper. It, too, should use key words that will respond to an information search. These should be recognizable terms, not new ones defined in the paper. Abstract-like paragraphs make good precis for book chapters.

Headings. Burma-Shave was skilled at giving messages to readers traveling 50 miles per hour (see box). But that speed is fast compared to the eye's ability to scan a page of text. Section headings are to the technical reader what road signs are to a traveler. They define where the paper is going and mark principal changes of direction, e.g., from theory to experiment to data analysis to interpretation. Like the title, section headings should be short and descriptive, and they should stand out from the text.

> If you dislike
> Big traffic fines
> Slow down
> 'Till you
> Can read these signs
> *Burma-Shave*

Burma-Shave sign, 1939.

Graphics. Figures are more important to technical articles and books than they are to most other writing. Figures intrinsically communicate trends and correlations and comparisons better than words, they help people visualize concepts, and they can increase the efficiency of scanning technical text.

Graphic images convey elements of information in parallel; text conveys them serially. When figures appear in a sea of text, they naturally attract the eye. Thus, pictorial information can often be processed faster and used more readily than verbal information. Accompanied by a well-written caption, an illustration properly chosen and carefully designed may be *the* decisive factor in rating your text "usable."

Spatial cues. Typographic cues are another aid to reader understanding. Examples are contrasting fonts such as **boldface** and *italic* that stand out from the text font; placement of headings; lists; boxes; lines (or rules) and borders; color; indention; white space; the sequence or structure of information in references—in short, almost any visual stimulus that helps the mind locate, identify, organize, and assign relative value to the input it is receiving.

These cues may be used only once in an entire article or a few times in an entire text—for example, a sidebar, which is a boxed unit of auxiliary information, can be read at any time to supplement the text without disrupting its natural flow—or cues can be used repeatedly in text to establish its structure. For example, boldface headings can highlight primary aspects of the topic; italic headings, secondary aspects; and so on.

Organization. Overall, start to finish, organization is the key to communicating technical information. Logical organization is more than the mere assembling of chapters or sections—it should permeate the development of each section and paragraph and even sentence. The organization must consider the audience and the purpose of the communication. For example, background information or technical prerequisites may appear first in some communications but in an appendix in others. Recommendations may logically be last in some peer-oriented technical reports but should be first, or nearly so, in management-oriented reports. The books on technical writing in the bibliography offer some useful thoughts on suiting textual organization to its purpose.

Index. Although most journal articles and technical reports are not long enough to warrant an index, the use of a textbook or a handbook demands a good index. Even moderate length—but extremely valuable—survey and review articles are enhanced by a modest index or an extensive table of contents.

Synonyms are key to making an index usable. Recognize that a person who has not read your book from cover to cover may not use the same terminology as you. And so you should seriously consider including alternative index entries that may not be as precise as your technical terms but which can link users to other references in your field or establish entry points to your text for engineers, and even laypersons, from other fields. See Wright's chapter, this volume, on indexes and contents lists for a more detailed discussion of this topic.

Satisfaction

"Happy is the man who reads . . ." begins the third verse of the Revelation of John (*New English Bible*). Seldom is that result achieved with technical writing because, to paraphrase Sheridan, easy reading's curst hard writing.

Students may be forced to penetrate ponderous texts, but they are not obligated to keep, use, and recommend them later as reference material. Similarly, equipment operators may have to use "unfriendly" instructions but, likely, at the cost of efficient learning.

Satisfaction of students, operators, and any technical reader derives from (a) being written *to*, not down to or above; (b) being able to locate and understand the desired information; and (c) being able, unembarrassingly, to recover from errors.

The tone and style of your writing greatly affect its reception and effectiveness. Developing a tone and style is an individual, experiential process, and it is an art rather than a science. When in doubt, however, *short, simple, direct,* and *active* are preferred writing characteristics. But these are only a beginning; practice (revising) makes perfect. You may enjoy Williams' (1981) chapter, "A Touch of Class."

Electronic Text

A short novel, *The Blind Pharaoh*, was written and published electronically in November, 1982. It is available to computer users who subscribe to the information utility known as *The Source*^{TM}. So, electronic publishing has arrived. Although not likely to replace paper for a long time, electronics offers two significant benefits that will be further advanced by the personal computer explosion (see the Lancaster and Warner chapter, this volume, for a detailed discussion of these topics).

The more direct benefit is the potential for better writing. Extensive revision is the key to good writing. By eliminating *drudgery*, electronic text processors give writers the opportunity to spend more time on critically important rewriting. Many of these devices can check spelling, and some can provide a sophisticated style analysis. This analysis can offer (1) synonyms for uncommon words; (2) suggested improvements for awkward phrases or misused words; (3) numerical data and comparative statistics on use of passive and other verb forms, length of sentences, capitalization, reading-grade level, etc.; and (4) reference information.

The time saved by these flick-of-a-key activities can be applied to the intellectual tasks of writing; ultimately, the reader benefits. Keep in mind, however, that the final step—proofing—must remain a personal activity, not left to a machine, because a document can *read* logically and still be inaccurate.

The second benefit to accrue from electronics is the ability to retrieve specialized information. Known generically as videotex, encyclopedic databases such as *BRS, DIALOG®,* and *ORBIT®* use time-sharing networks to allow individual subscribers to access millions of pages of information stored in large, remote computers. This industry will be nourished by competition among computer and communication equipment manufacturers, by the expansion of long-distance telephone services, and by the widespread installation of cable TV.

More than most people, engineers are "computer literate," and they are interested in more than playing games and balancing checkbooks with personal computers. They will use videotex services because they are interested in technical information to keep them current in their field and in techniques and data to help them solve problems (Figure 15.2). Therefore, authors—since stored text will continue to be primarily abstracts, summaries, and indexes rather than full documents—have good reason to work hard on abstracts, titles, key words, and headings; to make clear statements with jargon-free, unambiguous, information-laden content; *and* to choose their publication media wisely.

References

Al-Awar, J., Chapanis, A., and Ford, W.R. Tutorials for the first-time computer user. *IEEE Transactions on Professional Communication*, March, 1981, *24*(1), 30-37.

Allen, T.J. *Managing the flow of technology.* Cambridge, MA: Massachusetts Institute of Technology Press, 1977; chapters 3-7.

Bereiter, S. Engineers with a difference. *IEEE Spectrum*, February, 1983, *20*(2), 63-66.

Blade, M.F. Creativity in engineering. In M.A. Coler (Ed.), *Essays on creativity in the sciences.* New York: New York University Press, 1963.

Braden, R.A. One hundred book titles: A twelve-foot shelf of basic references for instructional design and development. *Educational Technology*, September, 1981, *21*(9), 41-45.

Chakrabarti, A.K., Feineman, S., and Fuentevilla, W. Characteristics of sources, channels, and contents for scientific and technical information systems in industrial R and D. *IEEE Transactions on Engineering Management*, May, 1983, *30*(2), 83-88.

Dunkle, S.B., and Jackson, P.M. Information structuring: Relating old and new knowledge. *IEEE Transactions on Professional Communication*, December, 1982, *25*(4), 175-177.

Enke, C.G. Scientific writing: One scientist's perspective. *English Journal*, April, 1978, *67*(4), 40-43.

Gleason, J.P. Humor can improve your technical presentations. *IEEE Transactions on Professional Communication*, June, 1982, *25*(2), 86-90.

Hannum, W.H., and Briggs, L.J. How does instructional systems design differ from traditional instruction? *Educational Technology*, January, 1982, *22*(1), 9-14.

Jenny, H.K. Heavy readers are heavy hitters. *IEEE Spectrum*, September, 1978(a), *15*(9), 66-68.

Jenny, H.K. Engineering Information Survey Results. Cherry Hill, NJ: RCA Corporation, 1978(b).

Joenk, R.J. Do scientists read more? *Abstracts of Papers, AAAS 149th National Meeting*, Detroit, MI; 26-31 May, 1982. Publ. 83-2; Arthur Herschman, Ed. Washington, DC: American Association for the Advancement of Science; 1983; Abstract 201: 123-124.

Johnson, P.H., Garrard, J., and Hausman, W. A method for translating technical to nontechnical prose. *IEEE Transactions on Professional Communication*, December, 1982, *25*(4), 182-185.

Krowne, C.M., and Covington, D.H. A survey of technical communication students: Some implications for engineering educators. *Engineering Education*, December, 1982, *22*(12), 247-251.

Krulee, G.K., and Nadler, E.B. Studies of education for science and engineering: Student values and curriculum choice. *IRE Transactions on Engineering Management*, December, 1960, *7*(4), 146-158.

Miller, P.A. Reading demands in a high-technology industry. *Journal of Reading*, November, 1982, *26*(2), 109-115.

Rathbone, R.R. *Communicating technical information.* Rev. Ed. Reading, MA: Addison-Wesley Publishing Co., 1972, p. 10.

Ritti, R.R. *The engineering in the industrial corporation.* New York: Columbia University Press, 1971, chapter 3.

Shuchman, H.L. *Information transfer in engineering.* Glastonbury, CT: The Futures Group, 1981.

U.S. Bureau of the Census. *Statistical abstract of the United States: 1981.* 102nd Ed. Washington, DC: U.S. Government Printing Office, 1981, section 21.

Williams, J.M. *Style: Ten lessons in clarity and grace.* Glenview, IL: Scott, Foresman and Co., 1981, lesson 8.

Bibliography

Bailey, R.W. *Human performance engineering.* Englewood Cliffs, NJ: Prentice-Hall, 1982, chapter 19, "Printed Instructions."

Blicq, R.S. *Technically-Write!* (2nd Ed.). Englewood Cliffs, NJ: Prentice-Hall, 1981.

Chandler, H.E. *Technical writer's handbook.* Metals Park, OH: American Society for Metals, 1983.

Gowers, Sir E. *The complete plain words.* Baltimore, MD: Penguin Books, 1962.

Hartley, J., and Burnhill, P. (Eds.) Special issue: "The Spatial Arrangement of Text." *Visible Language*, 1981, *15*(1).

Joenk, R.J. (Ed.) Special issue: "Making Information Usable." *IEEE Transactions on Professional Communication*, March, 1981, *24*(1).

Joenk, R.J. (Ed.) Special issue: "Making Information More Usable Through Graphics." *IEEE Transactions on Professional Communication*, June, 1982, *25*(2).

Jonassen, D.H. (Ed.) *The technology of text: Principles for structuring, designing, and displaying text.* Englewood Cliffs, NJ: Educational Technology Publications, 1982, section 2, "Explicit Techniques for Structuring Text."

MacGregor, A.J. *Graphics simplified.* Toronto: University of Toronto Press, 1979.

Mambert, W.A. *Presenting technical ideas.* New York: John Wiley and Sons, 1968.

Mandel, S. *Writing for science and technology.* New York: Dell, 1970.

Michaelson, H.B. *How to write and publish engineering papers and reports.* Philadelphia, PA: ISI Press, 1982.

Strunk, W., Jr., and White, E.B. *The elements of style.* 3rd Ed. New York: Macmillan, 1979.

White, J.V. *Editing by design* (2nd Ed.). New York: R.R. Bowker, 1982.

Chapter 16

Preparing Technical Manuals: Specifications and Guidelines

Thomas M. Duffy

The military has made a greater effort than perhaps any other segment of our society to apply educational technology to the development of texts. Rules, guidelines, task analysis procedures, summative and formative evaluation procedures, as well as specific strategies for organizing and formatting information have been developed, evaluated, and documented in detail (Hatterick and Price, 1981a; Joyce, Chenzoff, Mulligan, and Mallory, 1973; Military Specification, MIL-M-24100B, 1974). Yet, the military still faces severe shortcomings in the usability of its manuals (Booher, 1977).

In this chapter, I will first describe the efforts the military has made to improve the usability of its manuals. This will include a brief look at the research on job performance aids but will focus primarily on how these and other research findings as well as our experientially derived knowledge are implemented in the actual production of text. After that I will discuss what I consider to be the primary reasons why, after all of our efforts, military manuals are still considered to be inadequate. The basic conclusion I will reach is that we have considerable expertise in defining how text should be prepared.

Numerous projects have demonstrated effective text designs (e.g., Johnson, Thomas, and Martin, 1977; Martin, 1975; Shriver and Trexler, 1966). Thus, the educational technology is there, and the skill and knowledge are available in the operational world for the transfer of that technology. What is still required for the successful implementation is an overhauling of the management process and an adjustment of the management objectives in preparing the manuals.

This chapter only addresses technical manuals (TMs), i.e., manuals used on the job. I will not address the development of instructional texts. There are three reasons for this. First, most of the research on document design in the military has focused on TMs. Second, since TMs are almost always developed under contract, the organization of the publication process and the rules and requirements for designing the manual are well-specified. Finally, because of the contractual nature of the effort, the production team—writers, illustrators, editors, etc.,—are considered to be professionals in their particular discipline.

The Use of Technical Manuals

The primary mission of the military substantially involves the operation and maintenance of very complex weapons systems. The TMs are the primary, and frequently the only, source of system documentation available for use in carrying out these activities. The Navy alone had an estimated 25 million pages of TMs in 1975 and was adding and revising 400,000 pages yearly (Sulit and Fuller, 1976). Across the services there are 131,000 aviation maintenance manuals alone, containing an estimated 13 million pages (General Accounting Office, 1979). Today the per page development cost is estimated at $250 for a standard manual and up to three times that for user-oriented manuals (Hatterick and Price, 1981b).

While the manuals are costly to develop, deficiencies in their usability on the job could have far greater cost consequences. Shriver and Hart (1975), based on a review of the research evaluating technical manual design strategies, estimated the effect of the TM design on the life cycle costs of the equipment the manuals support. Life cycle costs are simply all of those costs associated with using the equipment—including operation and maintenance costs. They estimated that the use of a well-designed manual (as compared to the typical manual) could save the U.S. Army $830 million through the reduction in the time required to successfully complete maintenance activities and in the reduction in false removals of functioning parts. They further estimate a savings of $900 million in reduced training requirements if the manuals were fully proceduralized. So you can see that the development of TMs is an important issue to the military and deserving of the considerable attention it has received.

Technical Manual Research

Technical manuals, like textbooks, are information texts, and therefore most of the research on text comprehension is relevant to the design of TMs. The main difference is one of focus. The TM comprehension task is reading-to-do rather than reading-to-learn-about (Sticht, Fox, Hauke, and Welty-Zapf, 1977). As we shall see in the next section, much of what we know about effective typography, format, writing style, illustrations, etc., has been implemented, or at least stated as a requirement, in the TM production process.

Since the 1950s, the focus of research specifically addressing the development of TMs has been on: (1) techniques and procedures to insure that the presentation of the information in the manual is oriented to the user's requirements on the job; and, (2) providing detailed instructions on how to display the information (Foley, 1978; Lobel and Mulligan, 1980; Shriver, 1977). In contrast to the research approach, the organization of the information in the TM has traditionally been based on an engineering design perspective, i.e., written for engineers by engineers. In the traditional, and still most common design, the theory of operation is fully described and the organization is based on the physical components of the equipment. The contrast is between an organization based on system functions rather than hardware components and a presentation oriented toward the job tasks rather than toward the engineering theory.

Foley (1978) describes several effects of this engineering orientation. First, since the manual is not organized to support maintenance activity, the technician must jump around the physical component organization to get functional information. Second, the engineering approach results in a prevalence of narrative text from which the maintainer must infer the maintenance steps. Third, because of the difference in focus, some irrelevant information will be included and relevant information excluded. In particular, information required for troubleshooting tends to be excluded. Finally, there are no standards for the level of detail to be provided, for the pictorial support required, or for the length, complexity, or vocabulary to be used in the description. The result is a text which is theoretically oriented and written at a high level of difficulty, both of which will require a high aptitude user.

Hatterick and Price (1981a) describe over one hundred user-oriented formatting techniques which have been developed since the 1950s in response to the inadequacies of the traditional manual. These techniques are not for the design of the entire technical manual but rather address the display of specific kinds of information, e.g., troubleshooting instructions. Typically, a technique involves the specification of the type of information to be presented, how it should be sequenced, and how the text and graphics should be prepared and interrelated. Hatterick and Price (1981a) also describe six design systems which apply to the development of an entire TM. The systems include requirements for task analysis (detailed specification and description of job tasks) and detailed instructions for organizing the information, for writing, for illustrating, and for formatting.

As might be expected, the experimental evaluations which have been conducted strongly support the effectiveness of the user-oriented designs. For example, Potter and Thomas (1976) evaluated a fully proceduralized job performance aid (FPJPA) relative to the traditional manual in terms of the ability to troubleshoot. Both experienced and novice technicians scored 95 percent using the FPJPA, while the scores were 79 percent and 61 percent, respectively, using the traditional manual. Similarly, Elliott and Joyce (1968) found that high school students with only 12 hours of training in using the FPJPA had a 93 percent troubleshooting score while experienced technicians using the traditional manual had a score of only 84 percent. This literature is fully reviewed by Hatterick and Price (1981b), Foley (1978), and Shriver and Hart (1975).

Producing a TM

It is one thing to develop design procedures in a research context, and it is quite another to implement that procedure in a publication system. The procedures must be thoroughly and unambiguously described in a way that the production personnel (writers, illustrators, designers, etc.) can understand and use. Furthermore, there must be checks during the publication process to insure that the directions are being executed properly. In this section, I will describe the primary characteristics of the TM production effort which are relevant to the control of usability.

Production Phases

There are eight critical factors in the publication process. The importance of each of these factors to the success of the process will first be described. This is basically a "how the system *should* work" viewpoint. Then we will discuss how shortcomings related to these factors contribute to the deficiencies actually experienced in the design of technical manuals.

1. Funding. When a new piece of hardware is being developed, funds are provided for the design of the hardware, the development of the engineering data needed to operate and maintain the hardware (called the "logistics support analysis"), the manufacture of the hardware, and the production of the manual. Thus, the TM is one line item in the budget for producing the equipment. That budget is administered by a government program management office.

2. Contracts and Specifications. The government will then let a contract for the development of the manual. The contract may or may not be with the company developing the equipment. A number of specifications are cited in the contract. These are the directions given to the contractor as to how he or she is to develop the manual, what the manual should look like, and how it will be evaluated. These specifications are the legally binding agreement between government and contractor, and, therefore, they must be sufficiently explicit and detailed to be enforceable. Standards may also be cited. This is less explicit information provided to the contractor as guidance. For example, a government writing style guide is typically cited as a standard. Only extremely flagrant violations of the standard can be contested.

It is through specifications and standards that our cognitive, educational, and TM research gets implemented into the production system. The specifications will identify a particular font and point typeset to be used, the number of columns per page, the writing style, etc. It will also identify the organization of the manual, the level of detail to be provided, restrictions in the use of nouns and verbs, the amount of information to be presented in any graphic, etc.

The job-performance-aid formats that I discussed earlier have almost all been prepared as specifications ready for use by the program manager and the contractor. In fact, the Air Force has supplemented their specification for the fully proceduralized job performance aid with a detailed guide for the production manager and a guide and instructions on how to carry out the necessary task analysis (Joyce, Chenzoff, Mulligan, and Mallory, 1973). Let me quote a few lines from that specification to give you an idea of the amount of detail provided.

> Task analyses shall be prepared . . . [with] the following intermediate products [eleven intermediate documents are listed with detailed instructions for preparation] . . . The second person imperative shall be used for maintenance instructions . . . The third person indicative mood shall be used primarily in Notes, Cautions, and Warnings . . . Consistency shall be maintained between the first and subsequent occurrences of each item of nomenclature . . . Each maintenance step shall contain no more than three sentences and no more than thirty words . . . . Steps for an assistant shall be written exactly as those for the primary technician except they will be introduced by the phrase 'request that assistant. . .' . . . Each time a part is mentioned in text it shall be followed by a locator number used on the accompanying illustration. . . The illustration in a frame shall present only the

> equipment to which the actions in the frame refers, plus
> [orienting information] . . . [and] shall be drawn only from the
> angle of view of the technician . . . Arrows leading away from a
> locator to an enlarged view shall be unnumbered, tapered, and
> with a solid white body (Joyce *et al.*, 1973).

That particular specification is 140 pages long and incorporates
three other specifications. As you can see, the instructions are
detailed and comprehensive. Researchers have long advocated the
use of writing guidelines to aid the writer (Hartley, 1978, 1981;
Kirschner, 1981). These specifications are the ultimate of
guidelines. Not only are they detailed and comprehensive, but
they are also contractually required and, in the case of the
user-oriented specifications, are based on research.

3. Quality Assurance. One of the first products typically
required by the government is a quality assurance plan. This is the
contractor's statement as to what type of people will review the
drafts of the manual for compliance with the specifications, at
what points in the production the review will occur, and how the
results of the reviews will be documented. The quality assurance
review will include engineering reviews, editing, text proofing, and
a check on the art work. Most of the reviewing is done by
personnel who are part of the writing/editing team and thus are
under the same supervisor (Deardorff, Hageman, Hehs, and
Norton, 1979).

4. Book Plan and Draft. The contractor then prepares a book
plan or outline, which is submitted to the government for
approval. In the case of large systems, the unit of evaluation and
approval will likely be the chapter rather than the entire manual.
A draft of the manual is prepared after approval. During the
preparation of the draft(s), the documentation is reviewed in
accordance with the quality.

5. Validation. The draft is then validated by the contractor
personnel. Validation is part of the quality assurance system and is
accomplished by the contractor's subject matter experts. They
check the entire TM, line by line, to insure that all of the technical
data are accurate and consistent with the latest engineering data
and to insure that all of the operation and maintenance instructions are accurate and understandable (Tilly, 1971).

6. Verification. After corrections are made, reproducible masters are prepared and submitted to the government for verification. Verification is similar to validation, except that it is conducted by the government, and the procedures are performed on the actual equipment (if available) by a technician not previously involved in the preparation of the manual (Tilly, 1971). Some specifications call for the technician to be selected from the user population.

7. Follow-Up. After final corrections are made, the manual is reproduced and distributed. A comment sheet is included in the manual for personnel to provide feedback on deficiencies and errors. It is not uncommon for change pages, correcting errors in the manual, to be distributed to all users for years after the manual is introduced.

Personnel

All of the controls and specifications would be of little use if the production personnel did not have the expertise to understand the requirements and procedures. Imagine the university professor writing his or her first book to a specification as detailed as the military specifications! It is very difficult to define expertise, but we can say that virtually all of the production personnel are highly experienced, and most have made a career in the area of technical publications. There is a Society of Technical Writers which publishes a journal presenting theory and research relevant to technical writing. When a TM contract is received, contractors capitalize on this professional base by looking for writers who have experience writing in the same technical area (on the same system, if possible) and experience in writing to the particular specification that is being imposed.

Effectiveness

Clearly, we have the technology, the expertise is available, and we have the mechanisms for producing highly usable TMs. Indeed, all of this has been available for some time. However, an evaluation of the manuals actually in use indicates that the system has been far from successful in producing effective TMs (Booher, 1977; King and Duva, 1975). Foley (1976) reports little if any improvement in the quality of our TMs from 1966 to 1976, despite the introduction and demonstration of many effective development and design strategies during that time.

A General Accounting Office report (GAO, 1979) illustrates just how deficient our TMs are. For example, they report that to diagnose and repair one C141 aircraft radar malfunction required the technician to refer to 165 pages in eight documents and to look at 41 difrerent places in those documents. Foley (1975) estimated that the time spent in just such searching activity costs the Air Force $630 million yearly. Once the information is found, there is no guarantee that the technician will find it usable. Curran and Mecherikoff (1978) found many examples of graphics which were incomprehensible at least in part because of the complexity of the labeling system. For example, an exploded diagram with over 100 parts would have a numeric label or callout attached to each of the parts. The sequencing of the numeric labels was random in terms of the graphic display, thus making it a "hide-and-seek" task to find any particular part. A survey of Navy users has identified numerous other shortcomings of the TMs (Hughes Aircraft Company, 1978). These shortcomings are a likely basis for the fact that technicians tend not to use TMs, despite the fact that it is estimated that the average technician can successfully perform only 65 percent of the non-troubleshooting maintenance activities. The problem has been such that the Navy has funded a multi-year, multi-million dollar effort to totally redesign the TM system (Sulit and Fuller, 1976).

Deficiencies

Why is it that with so many controls and so much expertise involved in the publication of our TMs, that we still have so many problems? I would like to suggest that there are two general management factors that operate to short-circuit our best attempts to control the comprehensibility and accessibility of the information in the manuals. These two factors are: (1) the control and allocation of TM funds; and, (2) the engineering design focus of the personnel involved in the publication. I would now like to reanalyze the production process outlined previously in terms of these two problem areas. The first step in the process, acquiring funding, will be concerned only with the funding problem. However, the remaining steps will consider both the funding and the focus concerns.

1. Funding

In discussing the management of an equipment publication effort, Wolf and Kleinman describe the supervisor as first comparing, ". . . the budget with the estimate and decid[ing] if he has to make any adjustments [in the development procedures]. It seems to be fairly normal for the budget to be less than the estimate and we assume that to be the case" (1971, p. 154). How does the shortage of funds occur? The problem lies primarily with the fact that the publication and the equipment design and manufacture are tied to the same budget. Both the contractor and the government program manager have as a primary interest the particular piece of equipment. The focus, not unreasonably, will be on the quality and capability of the equipment. Thus, the contractor, in bidding, will propose the equipment with the maximum capability and the lowest possible price. The quality of the proposed TM simply will not win the equipment contract. However, because the manual is part of the equipment bid, bidding the full cost of a high quality, usable manual could cost him or her the contract. Thus, in preparing the bid, the cost estimate (and hence, the budget) for the TM will be pared to a minimum. An additional source of TM fund shortage can arise during the equipment manufacture. In design and production, there will almost certainly be additional cost increments for an added feature, a modified feature, or simply due to inflation. Unless the program manager can obtain additional funds, he or she will have to cut back elsewhere to obtain the modification. The cutback will more than likely be in the stringency of the requirements and hence in the cost of the TM. Thus, both the government manager and the contractor can and do affect the availability of funds for the TM.

The response to a fund shortage will be to cut back on the least important publication aspects. This obviously will involve a value judgment of what is important. The engineering focus in TM production, quite rightly, places very high value on the accuracy and completeness of the data. Indeed, this has been a major problem in the usability of TMs. The assumption is that the equipment cannot be repaired or operated if the information in the manual is inaccurate or sufficient data are not provided for the particular task. It is not that these usability issues are wrong, it is that they present an incomplete picture. The engineering focus pays little attention to defining the information the user requires and to assuring that the information is accessible and comprehensible (Booher, 1977, 1978; Foley, 1978). Therefore, with a fund limitation it is these usability factors—comprehensibility and accessibility—that will receive reduced attention.

Fund allocation is only the first step in the publication process. I would now like to go through the rest of the steps in the production process and discuss how both the cost and the engineering focus can operate to counteract each of the controls. All of the factors I will be discussing are seldom in full play within the development of a single manual. However, they are all very important factors, having a high frequency of occurrence.

2. Contract Specification

While specifications designed to make TMs highly usable and easily comprehended are available for use in contracts, these specifications are seldom called out in the procurement of TMs. While available, the systems are not utilized (Post, 1977). One reason proposed for the low utilization has been the lack of systematic instructions for the manager as to when each of the various systems applies. To fill this need, guides to aid the manager have recently been developed (Booher, 1978; Hatterick and Price, 1981a). I would hypothesize, however, that such guides will not increase the utilization because of a second, more dominant factor in the application of user-oriented specifications. Cost!

The user-oriented design approaches are labor-intensive and can increase the cost of the manual by a factor of three or four—from

$200 per page to $800 per page (Duffy, 1982; Hatterick and Price, 1981b). The extra cost is due to the requirements for task and job analysis, more intensive quality assurance, and more complex page layouts. Under the traditional specification, the writer can rely primarily on the logistics data collected during the engineering design. Task analysis requirements are minimized, and in fact are typically not even shown in a flowchart of a publication design process (see, e.g., Deardorff, *et al.*, 1979; Patterson, 1971; Wolf and Kleinman, 1971). Thus, the imposition of a requirement for a job task analysis, especially when detailed job descriptions are required, results in a large increase in cost. From an engineering perspective, the provision for information retrieval to support users in operational task performance is an unnecessary luxury. It is simpler, and less costly, to describe the equipment as designed. Simply developing the page layouts is also costly. Wolf and Kleinman had the following comments regarding one particular user-oriented specification: "The preparation of the pages requires the closest cooperation possible between writers, illustrators, and printers. Its future use is uncertain because of the page costs involved in its preparation" (1971, p. 125).

3. Quality Assurance

The next step in the publication system is the development of a quality assurance system. The focus of the quality assurance (QA) plan is on the compliance with the specification and on the usability of the TM. Because of the engineering perspective, however, the QA review is typically performed by subject matter experts, judging whether the maintenance instructions are consistent with the latest engineering data. Little attention is given to the ease with which the inexperienced technician will be able to follow the instructions (Deardorff *et al.*, 1979; Wolf and Klein-man, 1971).

Also because of the engineering perspective, there is little if any quality assurance control in the early development stages. Wolf and Kleinman (1971) indicate that the first quality assurance review typically begins after the writer's outline is completed. Deardorff, Hageman, Hehs, and Norton (1979) came to a similar conclusion after reviewing the production of U.S. Navy TMs. They found that 80 percent of the QA effort occurs after the first draft is completed, and *no* formal quality assurance occurs during the definition of the technical information. This is entirely reasonable from an engineering perspective, since most checking for accuracy and completeness requires a completed document for review. However, from an instructional or a user orientation it is precisely at the stage of content specification that a quality assurance review is most critical.

4. Book Plan and Draft

In preparing the draft and final copy of the TM, the primary focus is compliance with the specification. Therefore, it is essential that the writer be thoroughly versed in the details of the specification. While I do not have evidence for this, I suspect that attending to the detailed rules results in not seeing the forest for the trees—or the "ease of use" for the "details of design and layout." For example, all specifications state that text should be clear and easy to understand. However, these requirements are very difficult to enforce contractually. Therefore, most specifications today have been modified to include a readability formula score requirement (Duffy, in press). The specification will state, for example, that the text must be written to the tenth grade levels as assessed by some particular formula. It will provide details as to how text is to be sampled and the formula is to be applied. Having talked to contractors, I find the focus of their efforts not on how easy it is for the reader to comprehend the materials but on meeting the requirements of limiting the average word and sentence length. They focus on the syntactic requirement and pay little attention to the semantic issue underlying the requirement in the first place!

Cost savings is also a significant concern during the preparation of the text. In order to reduce costs, the writer and illustrator will attempt to use existing materials whenever possible. The existing materials may be engineering drawings prepared for the engineers during the equipment design, they may be text and graphics from sales brochures, and engineering drawings, schematics, and line drawings from the design disclosure data (Jordan and Shimberg, 1971). It is not that all of these materials will necessarily be less than adequate from a job task viewpoint. However, since the material was designed for other purposes, much of it *will be inadequate*; but with a concern for saving money, the tendency will be to use it anyway. The cost savings orientation also enters into the resolution of conflicting requirements. For example, two common requirements in specifications are: (1) minimize white space, and (2) place an illustration on the same page as the text in which it is discussed. When there is a conflict, reduction of white space wins out because it influences production cost. As a consequence, it is not uncommon to find manuals in which an illustration can be displaced from the reference discussion in the text by ten or more pages.

5. Validation

Virtually the sole focus of the validation process is to insure the accuracy and completeness of the data in the TM. Large manuals are developed over many years. Since the equipment is being developed at the same time, it is not unusual for many of the engineering specifications to change during that time. Thus, the validation is essential. However, because it is performed by subject matter experts, there is virtually no attention given to clarity or ease of use by the less knowledgeable. Indeed, the typical validation process will involve a review by either engineers involved in the equipment design or by the actual individual who wrote the chapter. While validation should be performed by carrying out the tasks on the actual equipment, the equipment is seldom available and therefore a "desk-top" review is carried out (Wolf and Kleinman, 1971).

6. Verification

In verification, a naive user is supposed to perform the tasks using the manuals. If this were done, we certainly would be able to determine those parts of the TM which were difficult to use.

However, this sort of verification is seldom conducted because it is expensive, time-consuming, and requires the availability of both the equipment and a representative user. Instead, as with the validation, a desk-top review is performed, and this is typically carried out by subject matter experts. Thus, the focus once again is on accuracy and completeness.

One might think that if a proper verification is not conducted as part of the contract, a verification of sorts will occur when the TM is placed in actual use. However, the contractor provides a training course on the new equipment for the initial cadre of personnel, thus guiding them through the manual and the equipment operation. Additionally, when the equipment first goes into use, technical representatives are present to clarify any question the technicians might have. A colleague of mine described his experiences on board a ship when a new manual and equipment were being introduced. Basically, there were as many contractor representatives on board as there were sailors. Any time a manual was being used a representative was right there to guide the user through the text. The contractors wanted to insure that the technical data were correct. If the sailor was having a problem, they would simply explain the solution to him and show him that the answer was available in the TM. Thus, the TM is okay and the problem is with the sailor. Of course, that behavior obviated any evaluation of the ease of use of the TM.

7. Follow-Up

The final phase in the production process is follow-up or feedback. Since it is a *post hoc* corrective method, I do not want to discuss it further here, where our focus is the initial publication.

What Now?

My discussion thus far sounds like a strong indictment of the military TM system. However, I suggest that the problems are similar and perhaps more severe in the world of commercial publications. There is a special issue of *Information Design Journal*

(1981) devoted to the discussion of those problems. Wright (1978, 1981) and Felker (1980) also provide extensive discussion of the problems in designing commercial documents and text.

I discussed two major negative factors affecting the implementation of effective TM design strategies: costs and the engineering focus. The problem of costs is an important problem that confronts commercial publishers as well. Everyone wants and needs to minimize costs. The problem of the engineering focus may also exist with commercial textbooks. How often is the object of a textbook to "cover" the topic area thoroughly and accurately, with only minimal concern for the interests, needs, and abilities of the *user*? The engineering focus can also be translated to the "sales" or the "artistic" focus in the area of commercial texts. That is, effective design, in many cases, is compromised by the desire for something that "looks pretty" or is "catchy" and therefore will attract sales. The basis for the purchase of a book, even a textbook, is typically a brief scan of the contents. Hardly enough time to effectively assess usability but certainly enough time to be affected by the attractive and the catchy features.

While the military and the commercial publishers have similar problems, I suggest that the military has made more progress toward producing effective texts than have the commercial publishers. Effective designs may not have been implemented as effectively as they could be. But, the military has contributed to the development of specifications for effective designs and has attempted to implement them and to obtain compliance from the contractor. Commercial publishers have not! Where else are the design requirements and the writing guidance provided in such explicit detail? Finally, I suggest that no commercial publishers attempt to achieve the consistency of design across books produced for the same purpose nor provide the detailed rationale for the design that the military has for their designs (ineffective as some of them may be).

The military experience amply demonstrates that while technology and expertise are necessary ingredients in the publication system, they are not sufficient by themselves to yield effective, comprehensible documents. Guidelines and instructions have been viewed by some as a primary tool for achieving effective design (Hartley, 1978, 1981; Kirschner, 1981). Our experience, however, indicates that rules alone—even when they are "good" rules and are contractually required—will not necessarily yield usable texts.

There must be a concern to produce manuals that support task performance, and there must be an understanding of the importance of clarity of presentation for that purpose. This desire and understanding must be present at the level of both management and the working developer. Without these ingredients, the application of information design technology will continue to be subverted.

How are we to develop the necessary attitude and understanding? It is unclear for the commercial world, since the bottom line is profit and usability is a cost burden and is, at best, only weakly related to sales. Rather than working with the publication houses, we may be better off addressing the training, and thus the orientation, the front line workers bring to their job. Consider, for example, the responsibilities versus the training of the graphic arts people. Typographers, graphic designers, and illustrators are responsible not only for the graphics but for the entire page layout. They have the final input on the relationship of prose and graphics, the use of headings, the font and column design, and the techniques for highlighting (Jordan and Shimberg, 1971; Rice, 1978)—all key elements in effective communication. One free lance graphic designer working for a publisher on an encyclopedia type of text told me that he was handed the prose text, with space requirements for graphics identified, and the companies' picture file. His job was to select pictures from the file that fit the semantic content and the space available. All of his selections were accepted, even though the selections reflected his political bias and required him to rewrite some of the text. While the graphic arts personnel have considerable input on the functional design of the text, their formal training involves little, if any, course work in functional analysis. Graphic designers and typographers are trained in schools of art where the focus is almost exclusively on aesthetics. It is unusual to find even a single functional design course—a course emphasizing the use of the text or graphic—in a school of art (Waller, 1980; Thomas, 1982).

The picture is not quite so bad for the writers; there is an emphasis on understanding the audience and on writing "clearly." However, in general, there seems to be little instruction on how to analyze the user's information requirements or how to determine the organization and sequencing that would best meet the user's needs. Furthermore, there is a focus on traditional prose communication rather than identifying other formatting strategies, e.g., flow charting, (Lewis, *et al.*, 1967), Information Mapping (Horn, 1976), and other techniques (Chapanis, 1965; Waller, 1977; Wright, 1981), which would facilitate use in particular circumstances.

Introducing appropriate courses in the training program would provide the graphics people and the writers with an understanding of the need to analyze the communication requirements, provide the skills for carrying out such an analysis, and provide some user-oriented design techniques. I would propose that such a course, or even a sequence of courses, be derived from our work in educational technology and specifically in instructional technology. Even if our text is for use on the job rather than a learning text, there is still a need for task analysis, the specification of objectives, and the appropriate sequencing of information, all of which are well-developed topics in instructional systems design and in human factors engineering.

I think that there needs to be greater recognition within the publication system that educational technology and the human factoring of information is a discipline in and of itself, just as writing, illustrating, and typography are disciplines. It is unreasonable to assume that one person can be an expert in the subject matter area, in writing or illustrating, and in educational technology or human factors of information. The training courses I propose, whether given in the schools or as part of the job, are necessary to produce an understanding and appreciation of the communication issues. However, we cannot expect the writer and illustrators to become experts in the area. Just as the review for accuracy requires a line by line reading by a subject matter expert, the review for comprehensibility requires a line by line reading by an educational technologist or a human factors expert. Macdonald-Ross and Waller (1975) have argued that there is a need for a representative of the reader in the publication system; someone to watch out for the reader's interests. They call this function the transformer function, as it involves transforming the text into a user-oriented product. I would propose that it is only with the development of the transformer function in the publication system that we will begin to see major improvements in texts. This is especially true for the military. As I discussed earlier, we have had numerous demonstration projects of effective TM development (see, e.g., Booher, 1977; Hatterick and Price, 1981). These projects are successful simply because the objective of the project is to attend to the user needs. Thus, personnel on the project fulfill the transformer role. Talk to anyone who has been involved in such a project and they will tell you it is a full-time job requiring constant review and interaction with the production group. Without the "demonstration project" orientation, the control reverts back to the hardware community, and the engineering focus returns. The preparation of a TM is already a team effort. These demonstration projects simply indicate that with the addition of one more person or office to the team, i.e., the transformer, the development of usable manuals on a regular basis can be realized.

Potentially, computer-aided editing and authoring could be used to reduce some of the manpower requirements in the publication process. The saved manpower could then be redirected to the performance of the transformer function. For example, many of the editing functions could be computerized, and the role of the editor could be transformed into the educational/human factors design function. Carter, in his chapter, reports on a demonstration of the potential effectiveness of this redesigned editing role.

The "air" component of the Navy has taken a different tack in approaching the transformer function. They have created an office (Naval Air Technical Support Facility) which has responsibility for overseeing the acquisition of all air system technical manuals. The office is staffed by human factors and educational technologists as well as by technical subject matter experts. This office is responsible for identifying the specification to govern the development of the manual, monitoring the development process, and carrying out verification. The primary restriction on their activities is financial. The program manager for the equipment is responsible for the budget and hence establishes the budgetary guidelines for the publication. Nonetheless, the shift to centralized control of the development function with an emphasis on human factors has led to the wide recognition of the "air" manuals as the best manuals produced by the Navy.

References

Booher, H.R. *Symposium proceedings: Invitational conference on status of job-performance-aid technology.* (NPRDC TR 77-33) San Diego, CA: Navy Personnel R&D Center, May, 1977.

Booher, H.R. *Job performance aids: Research and technology state of the art.* (NPRDC TR 78-26) San Diego, CA: Navy Personnel R&D Center, July, 1978.

Chapanis, A. Words, words, words. *Human Factors*, 1965, *7*, 1-17.

Curran, T., and Mecherikoff, M. *Quantification of technical manual graphics comprehensibility.* (NPRDC TN 78-2) San Diego, CA: Navy Personnel R&D Center, January, 1978.

Deardorff, D., Hageman, K., Hehs, W., and Norton, J. *Development of a quality assurance methodology for the technical information generation subsystem of NTIPS.* (NAVAIRSYSCOM-78-C-0175-0003) Bethesda, MD: Naval Air Systems Command, June, 1979.

Duffy, T.M. Organizing and utilizing document design options. *Information Design Journal*, 1982, *2*, 256-266.

Duffy, T.M. Readability formulas: What is the use? In T.M. Duffy and R. Waller (Eds.), *Usable texts: Theory and practice.* New York: Academic Press, in press.

Duffy, T.M., and Kabance, P. Testing a readable writing approach to text revision. *Journal of Educational Psychology*, 1982, *74*, 733-748.

Elliott, T.K., and Joyce, R.P. *An experimental comparison of procedural and conventional electronics troubleshooting.* (AFHRL TR-68-1) Wright-Patterson AFB, OH: Air Force Human Resources Laboratory, November, 1968 (AD 681-510).

Felker, D.B. (Ed.) *Document design: A review of relevant research.* (TR 75002-4/80) Washington, DC: American Institutes for Research, April, 1980.

Foley, J.P., Jr. *A proposed modified technical order system and its impact on maintenance, personnel and training.* (AFHRL TR 75-82) Wright-Patterson AFB, OH: Air Force Human Resources Laboratory, December, 1975 (AD A022-252).

Foley, J.P., Jr. *Hard data sources concerning more cost effective maintenance.* (AFHRL TR 76-58) Wright-Patterson AFB, OH: Air Force Human Resources Laboratory, July, 1976.

Foley, J.P., Jr. *Impact of advanced maintenance data and task oriented training technologies on maintenance, personnel and training systems.* (AFHRL TR-78-25) Wright-Patterson AFB, OH: Air Force Human Resources Research Laboratory, September, 1978 (AD A063-277).

General Accounting Office. *Improved management of maintenance manuals needed in DOD.* LCD-79-105. Washington, DC: U.S. General Accounting Office, July 10, 1979.

Hartley, J. *Designing instructional texts.* London: Kogan Page, 1978.

Hartley, J. Eighty ways of improving instructional text. *IEEE Transactions on Improving Professional Communication*, 1981, *24*, 17-27.

Hatterick, G.R., and Price, H.E. *Technical order management and acquisition.* (AFHRL TR 80-50) Wright-Patterson AFB, OH: Air Force Human Resources Laboratory, May 1981a.

Hatterick, G.R., and Price, H.E. *Technical order managers reference data.* (AFHRL TR 80-51) Wright-Patterson AFB, OH: Air Force Human Resources Laboratory, May, 1981b.

Horn, R. *How to write information mapping.* Lexington, MA: Information Resources, Inc., 1976.

Hughes Aircraft Company. *NTIPP fleet survey of technical manual users.* Bethesda, MD: David Taylor Naval Ship R&D Center, January, 1978.

Information Design Journal, 1981, *2*(213).

Johnson, R., Thomas, D., and Martin, D. *User acceptance and usability of the C-141 job guide technical order system.* (AFHRL TR-77-31) Wright-Patterson AFB, OH: Air Force Human Resources Laboratory, June, 1977 (AD A044-001).

Jordan, S., and Shimberg, H.L. Estimating and cost control. In S. Jordan, J. Kleinman, and H.L. Shimberg (Eds.), *Handbook of technical writing practices.* Vol. 2. New York: John Wiley and Sons, 1971.

Joyce, R.P., Chenzoff, A.P., Mulligan, W., and Mallory, W. *Fully proceduralized job performance aids. Vols. I, II, and III.* (AFHRL TR-73-43) Wright-Patterson AFB, OH: Air Force Human Resources Laboratory, December, 1973 (AD 775-702, 775-705, 775-706).

King, W., and Duva, J. (Eds.) *New concepts in maintenance*

trainers and performance aids. (TR NAVTRAEQUIPCEN IH-255) Orlando, Fl: Naval Training Equipment Center, October, 1975.

Kirschner, P. Manual for editors and authors. Paper presented at the annual meeting of the American Educational Research Association, Los Angeles, 1981.

Lewis, B., Horabin, I., and Gane, C. *Flow charts, logic trees, and algorithms for rules and regulations.* London: Her Majesty's Stationary Office, 1967.

Lobel, A., and Mulligan, J. *Maintenance task identification and analysis: Organizational and intermediate maintenance.* (AFHRL TR-79-50) Wright-Patterson AFB, OH: Air Force Human Resources Laboratory, January, 1980.

Macdonald-Ross, M., and Waller, R. The transformer. *The Penrose Annual*, 1976, *69*, 141-152.

Martin, A.C. *Relative merits of SIMM/FOMM and JPA/JPM.* In T.C. Rowan (Ed.), Proceedings of the invitational conference on improved information aids for technicians. Arlington, VA: Logistics Management Institute, May, 1975.

Military Specification MIL-M-24100B. *Manuals, technical: Functionally oriented maintenance manuals (FOMM) for equipment and systems.* Washington, DC: Government Printing Office. January 2, 1974.

Patterson, T. Data Processing. In S. Jordan, J. Kleinman, and H.L. Shimberg (Eds.), *Handbook of technical writing practices,* Vol. 2. New York: John Wiley and Sons, 1971.

Post, T. Selection of formats and media presenting maintenance information. In H. Booher (Ed.), *Symposium proceedings: Invitational conference on status of job performance aids technologies.* (NPRDC TR-77-33) San Diego, CA: Navy Personnel R&D Center, May, 1977.

Potter, N.R., and Thomas, D.L. *Evaluation of three types of technical data for troubleshooting.* (AFHRL TR-76-74) Wright-Patterson AFB, OH: Air Force Human Resources Laboratory, September, 1976 (AD A035-303).

Rice, S. *Book design: Text format models.* Ann Arbor, MI: Bowker, 1978.

Shriver, E. New directions for information transfer research in maintenance jobs. In H. Booher (Ed.), *Symposium proceedings:*

Invitational conference on the status of job performance aid technologies. (NPRDC TR-77-33) San Diego, CA: Navy Personnel R&D Center, May, 1977.

Shriver, E., and Hart, F. *Study and proposal for the improvement of military technical information transfer methods.* Aberdeen Proving Grounds, MD: U.S. Army Human Engineering Laboratory, December, 1975.

Shriver, E., and Trexler, R. *A description and analytic discussion of ten new concepts for electronic maintenance.* (HumRRO TR-66-23) Washington, DC: Human Resources Research Organization, December, 1966 (AD 647-229).

Sticht, T., Fox, L., Hauke, R., and Welty-Zapf, D. *The role of reading in the Navy.* (NPRDC TR-77-40) San Diego, CA: Navy Personnel R&D Center, September, 1977 (AD A044 228/5).

Sulit, R., and Fuller, J. *Navy technical manual system (NTMS) program summary* (TM-186-76-1). Bethesda, MD: Naval Ship Research and Development Center, March, 1976.

Thomas, D. Personal communication, January, 1982.

Tilly, V. Quality Assurance and control. In S. Jordan, J. Kleinman, and H.L. Shimberg (Eds.), *Handbook of technical writing practices,* Vol. 2. New York: John Wiley and Sons, 1971.

Waller, R. *Typographic access structures for educational texts.* Milton Keynes, England: Institute of Educational Technology, Open University, 1977.

Waller, R. Personal communication, November, 1980.

Wolf, I., and Kleinman, J. Equipment instruction manuals—military and government. In S. Jordan, J. Kleinman, and H.L. Shimberg (Eds.), *Handbook of technical writing practices,* Vol. 1. New York: John Wiley and Sons, 1971.

Wright, P. Feeding the information eaters: Suggestions for integrating pure and applied research on language comprehension. *Instructional Science,* 1978, 7, 249-312.

Wright, P. Informed design for forms. *Information Design Journal,* 1981, 2, 151-178.

Section VII

Evaluating Textual Materials

Introduction

Probably the most foundational concept in instructional development is evaluation. Its many manifestations, such as instructional product validation, formative evaluation of learning systems, and verification of instructional processes, are central to the practice of instructional development. Every design model reviewed by Andrews and Goodson (1980) included evaluation processes. Almost everyone included formative evaluation, learner verification, or a similar technique. The notion of accountability is at the heart of the instructional design process. Evaluation is a postulate of educational technology as well as the technology of text. The evaluation procedure is essential to the text design process. For instance, when designing self-instructional or user-oriented text, verification that it fulfills its stated goals is critical, since the user or learner cannot count on an instructor to mediate meaning or solve problems. The text, in those cases, should be able to stand alone.

This final section of the book, like the previous one, does not focus specifically on controlling processes or signaling the structure of text. Evaluation is a process that is applicable to both. These chapters represent a conclusion to the book, just as evaluation normally represents a conclusion to the design process. The intent of text design, be it signaling top-level structure or stimulating mathemagenic behaviors, should be evaluated in some way. For example, if the text designer were hoping to supplant or stimulate in the learner an elaboration strategy by graphing overall passage structure (e.g., pattern notes, entailment structures, or concept maps), then he or she needs to assess what learning occurred, *vis.* the degree of integration of main ideas rather than recall of details. The various sections of this book have promoted different perspectives on and procedures for designing text. It is incumbent on the designer using any of them to evaluate their effectiveness, for as any researcher knows, the most conceptually-sound theories often produce the most disappointing results.

Nowhere in this book is the contrast between ideas presented within a section more obvious than within this one. The first chapter presents the evaluation process from a classical instructional design perspective. The second points out the potential fallacies in such an approach—the myths of evaluation, as it were. In doing so, Patricia Wright questions the inevitability implied by proponents of all the processes in the book. This sort of reflection provides a valuable and fitting conclusion to the book.

Learner Verification and Revision

One of the best established materials evaluation processes is that of learner verification and subsequent revision, a process that P. Kenneth Komoski has been promoting for a decade. In their chapter, he and Arthur Woodward illustrate some of the problems resulting from neglecting this evaluation process in designing both print and computer-based text. They justify the process based upon the reliance of instructional systems on textual materials and, like Duffy's rationale for military expenditures, the costs associated with failing to perform it. Komoski and Woodward then present their rationale for and description of LVR. The process is summarized by the guidelines for LVR established by the Educational Products Information Exchange. Finally, the authors look back on the extent of its application and look forward to the future of LVR, a future that may be improving with the shift to computer-based text.

Myths of Evaluation

Evaluation should not be the final, inevitable check on text design, according to Patricia Wright. To do so is to perhaps lose sight of some important concerns, most importantly, the purpose for which you are evaluating. This forest-vs.-trees concern shows how analytical we all frequently become in the application of our respective pet theories. Evaluation should be a contextual process. Who the user is (their respective ontology) and how the user wishes to use the text should not be (but often is) excluded from the trees part of evaluation. Rules for designing text, conceptually-generated and empirically-validated, are formal and connote inevitability: Every rule can be justifiably broken according to Wright. And what good is a theory of text comprehension without considering *why* users are accessing text? Text assessment techniques, which she incisively reviews, need to consider the context in which the text will be used—the importance of clearly communicated information—as well as the nature of the text. The most important perspective that she brings to the text design process is that evaluation of a text's effectiveness, like the other technologies of text design, are not as exact as we would like them to be. This conclusion is not meant to compromise the rest of the book but rather to challenge its authors and all text designers to greater clarity of purpose and process.

Reference

Andrews, D.H., and Goodson, L.A. A comparative analysis of models of instructional design. *Journal of Instructional Development*, 1980, *3*(4), 2-16.

Chapter 17

The Continuing Need for
the Learner Verification and Revision
of Textual Material

P. Kenneth Komoski and Arthur Woodward

A Rationale for LVR

Learner Verification and Revision (LVR) is not a novel or, necessarily, a technical process. For if we think back to our own school experience, we can quickly identify the effective teachers we encountered during our years of schooling. Although these teachers had many notable qualities, perhaps the most notable was their ability to help us learn, interpret, and mediate the text and to impart an enthusiasm into what seemed like difficult subject matter. And it was precisely the teacher's ability to mediate and interpret the text that seemed to ensure a smooth flowing, coherent lesson; a lesson from which we learned something of value. Through experience, these teachers had learned the specific pitfalls in a material, the dependable confusions, and the sections that always needed supplementing. Thus, the poorly-drawn concept was made clearer with additional examples and nonexamples, the awkward transition from one sub-topic to another made smoother, and those exclusively factual questions at the end of each unit that tested only recall of facts were supplemented with questions and assignments that forced the use of logical, problem-solving, and reflective thinking skills.

We would expect that all "good teaching" includes this sort of subtle teacher-mediated matching of materials to the needs and abilities of students. For it would be unreasonable to expect that textbooks or computer courseware, given their large development, marketing, and production costs and their necessarily broad target audience, could hope to meet *all* the needs of *all* learners in *all* teaching situations. However, what can be expected is that any text material—in any specific subject matter in any format—that finds its way into the classroom has been subject to systematic learner-based testing that ensures that teachers and learners are not going to have to deal with textual and contextual difficulties that could have been eliminated as a result of having verified the text's ability to communicate effectively with individual learners and having revised the text, where necessary, based on that feedback from learners. In other words, testing the text and improving it to ensure that any material has a better chance of doing what the publisher implies it will do, and what teachers expect it will do. The need for this testing is equally important, though less prevalent, in today's microcomputer courseware. This process—commonly called Learner Verification and Revision (LVR)—is an effective means of ensuring an effective fit of materials to students and teachers (see Nathensen and Henderson, 1980, for discussion of the efficacy of the process of improving the instructional effectiveness of text material through feedback from learners).

The consequences of publishers not building LVR into their development and revision process can be severe. Likewise, the consequences of integrating LVR into the process can produce an instructional material that is a more effective teaching and learning tool.

LVR: Definition and Examples

Learner Verification and Revision (LVR) is not an arcane theory that purports to "improve" instructional materials and learning. Rather, it is a common-sense approach for ensuring that the textbook or floppy disk that ends up in the hands of students and teachers has, based on the results of systematic trials with students, none of the unclear questions, confusing directions, and mystifying content that are often scattered throughout textbooks and surprisingly prevalent in computer courseware—waiting to interrupt the flow of learning.

A useful way of illustrating the widespread need for LVR among present-day text materials is through the following example, taken from a widely-used fourth-grade basal text.

- *Medley Unit 15*
  Post-Assessment Text 34
  Noting Correct Sequences—Clue Words

- (Directions to students, which each student must read silently before taking a self-administered test at the end of the lesson.) You should understand that recognizing certain clue words in a story will help you to determine the time and the order in which events take place.

- In each of the numbered sentences below, two things are said to have happened. In some sentences, one thing is said to have happened before the other. In other sentences, the two things are said to have happened at the same time. Read each sentence carefully. Then draw one line under the event that happened first, and draw two lines under the event that happened second.

- In sentences where both events were said to have happened at the same time, draw one line under both events. Draw a line around the clue word that lets you know the correct order. The starred example has been done for you.

As the reader has just discovered, these directions are not easy for an adult to follow, and not unexpectedly, fourth-grade students had considerable difficulty in following the directions as well. In one documented experiment, typical fourth-grade students were unable to proceed with the exercise as a self-directed unit of work, and teacher intervention was required for each student before he or she could proceed to take the "self-administered" test.

Microcomputer courseware can also benefit from systematic student testing. Although companies such as Children's Television Workshop (CTW) do test their courseware prior to production, the vast majority of courseware companies do not. To take a somewhat obvious example, in a courseware program on telling time, the objective was for elementary school students to practice telling time with the aid of a graphic clockface. Analysis found the clockface misproportioned and the clock hands misaligned. Indeed, the clock graphics were so crude that students would be unable to discern what the time was, even if they had mastered telling time. In this case, the problems of the program seemed obvious. Yet, if the developers had tested the program with students, they would have seen these obvious problems and rectified them. For those schools that purchased this program in order to reinforce student learning, they were certain to be disappointed; the students who tried the program were certain to be confused and frustrated.

Clearly, a little LVR would have gone a long way toward alleviating the very real problems students and teachers encountered in both the above examples. Indeed, the efficacy—and the relative ease—of using LVR can be demonstrated in the following example taken from EDL/McGraw-Hill materials:

Nineteen students were given four audio directions for the illustrated page (see Figure 17.1).

The research record (see Figure 17.2) showed that for the first direction to the students, "Underline the man behind the man with the drum," only ten students identified the correct figure, although 16 understood the direction "underline." Direction number 2 to the students was "Put an X on the dog next to the garage pail." Again there was some confusion as to which figure was meant, but students did not understand the direction "Put an X on." In direction number 3, students were asked to "Circle the man in front of the man with the horn." Only ten students identified the correct figure, and six students did not even attempt the problem. The last direction was as follows: "There is a dog behind the garbage pail. Circle the dog behind." Sixteen students identified the correct response; 17 students made the correct mark.

As a result of the student reaction to the original format of the material, the publisher simplified the drawing and made all the directions similar in structure. The revised directions were as follows (see Figure 17.3):

1. Look at the dogs. Point to the dog behind the garbage pail. But an X on the dog behind the garbage pail.

Figure 17.1

Original Format

2. Now look at the dog next to the garbage pail. Underline the dog next to the garbage pail.
3. Look below at the people who play music in the parade. Point to the lady with the horn. Now point to the one in front of the lady.
4. Point to the boy playing the drum. Now point to the one behind the boy. Underline the one behind the boy.

It is important to stress that the examples described above are not uncommon ones, and it is only the outstanding or experienced teacher who can easily manipulate the text to ensure that a lesson is free from text-based interruptions and confusions. Indeed, our

Figure 17.2

Research Record

extensive observations of elementary classrooms reveal that at least one element in student time-off-task behavior is the failure of the teacher to compensate for text-based confusions. The same occurs in advanced text materials as well. Clearly, we are not talking about the rather subtle change teachers must and should make in their instructional materials to accommodate individual differences. Rather, what is at issue is the inappropriateness of *basic* elements in instructional materials—be they in student directions, vocabularly, passage topic and difficulty, questions, and so on. And that is an issue that can and should be addressed by the publishers' systematic application of the Learner Verifica-

Figure 17.3

Revised Format

tion and Revision process to their instructional materials development and revision procedures.

Importance of LVR

Reliance on Text

The imperative for LVR becomes even greater when we consider the dependence of many of our teachers on instructional materials, the nature of those materials, and the decreasing amount of each education dollar used to purchase instructional materials. We all know of the teacher who uses a variety of materials culled from many sources and collected over many years, and we know from conversations with teachers that few will admit the degree to which they are dependent on the textbook. Dependence on computer-based courseware is more recent. Its prevalence is now a matter of availability of machines and software. While in 1983, most elementary schools had only one microcomputer and high schools fewer than five—providing limited numbers of students 20 minutes (elementary) and 45 minutes (secondary) of computer time each per week, availability and access are growing at exponential rates (Johns Hopkins, 1983). The teacher who does not rely on the textbook and soon the microcomputer is rare. Surveys by the EPIE Institute (1976) and Frymier, Davis, and Clinefelter (1977) and qualitative data of Stake and Easely (1979) indicate that as much as 90 to 95 per-cent of instructional time is spent using some kind of instructional material. Perhaps it is because of this increasing text-dependent teaching that textbook material, over the years, has become more and more complex and elaborate, especially at the elementary and junior high school levels. For example, a typical reading basal series consists of a multi-level, multi-volume set of textbooks, each accompanied by workbooks, skill books, pretests, unit tests, and assessment tests. Similar organizational patterns are developing as an integral part of microcomputer courseware. The actual text-book, often organized in a "magazine" format, intersperses fiction, poetry, and nonfiction with skill lessons and reinforce-ment and enrichment exercises. Individual disks of courseware are usually organized in similar lessons and tests, etc., oriented by a "menu." Assumed in the basal approach is that the class will be divided into two or three ability groups each engaged in appropriately difficult tasks. Microcomputer courseware is pri-marily individualized, though study groups often emerge. In these situations, it is not surprising that the teachers' manual is especially important and extensively relied upon, and that untested material can cause serious cases of learner time-off-task not only for individual students involved, but for the whole class.

Cost Factors

The evolution of texts into elaborate series has brought with it a concomitant increase in cost and—in an era of economic uncertainty—less money to buy them. For example, in 1966, 1.4 percent of the school budget (or ten dollars per student) was spent on instructional materials; in 1976, one percent of the budget (or $17 per student) was spent on instructional materials; and in 1983, 7/10 percent of the school budget (or $20.63 per student) was spent on instructional materials. Thus, if 7/10 percent of the school budget supports 90-95 percent of instructional time, then it seems reasonable that the instructional materials perform the task for which they are designed. And it therefore seems reasonable that publishers ensure that that is, in fact, the case through the systematic gathering of learner feedback during the product development period, as well as during the period they are engaged in preparing a new edition of materials. Unfortunately, the extent to which publishers have, heretofore, practiced Learner Verification and Revision has been disappointing. In a survey of publishers' use of LVR in their development of junior high school science and U.S. History textbooks (*EPIE Materials Report,* 1980), only a few of the 28 programs had been subject to any identifiable LVR. Publishers of ten programs made no claims to have conducted LVR, and many of the remainder provided a range of evidence, including general statements of intent, observations, and student interviews as evidence of LVR. Based on EPIE's extensive analysis of instructional materials, there is no evidence to suggest that the scope of quality of LVR has improved; rather it seems likely that it may, in fact, have declined.

At this time it seems, in the face of increasingly sophisticated instructional materials, declining budgets, a continuing and inevitable reliance on textual materials, and the vocal demands for the improvement in the quality of instructional materials (see National Commission on Excellence in Education, 1983), the need for Learner Verification and Revision of text materials is clear. If anything, this need is clearer than it was over a decade ago when EPIE Institute (Komoski, 1971) reported to a subcommittee of the U.S. Congress that 99 percent of all instructional materials used in U.S. classrooms had never been put through the sort of learner feedback and improvement process advocated by EPIE, that is, Learner Verification and Revision (EPIE, 1971).

The Theory and Practice of LVR

Formative/Summative Evaluation and LVR

For some years, there has been confusion between the terms formative and summative evaluation and learner verification and revision. Indeed, researchers, such as Nathensen and Hendersen (1980), have gone as far as to subsume LVR into formative evaluation. However, the distinction that has been made, and we make, between formative evaluation and LVR seems both functional and clear.

Formative evaluation, to quote Bloom (1971), can be defined as "the use of systematic evaluation in the process of curriculum construction, teaching, and learning for the purpose of improving any of these three processes," thus formative evaluation (and its "end-product", summative evaluation) draws upon a variety of sources and methods to evaluate both fluid and static situations. It is both in the broad range of areas that formative evaluation can be applied and in the scope of the data that can inform the evaluation process that distinctions can be drawn between formative evaluation and learner verification and revision.

The qualitative and quantitative data sources that can inform formative evaluation can range from analyses and review of materials by subject matter experts, authorities in pedagogy, administrators, editors, writers, parents, and salespeople to the quantitative data collected by questionnaires, structured interviews, and observations. Formative evaluation may be employed at any point in the instructional materials development process— from the evaluation of an idea for a textbook to the summative evaluation of a finished product. Thus, content experts may advise as to the subject matter merit and scholarship of a text, professional educators to its pedagogical approach, practitioners to its classroom usefulness and attractiveness, editors to its fluency and appropriateness, and salespeople to its place in the market and its potential success against competing materials. The input into the development process by these "interest groups" often leads to the time-honored practice of editorial-review-and-revision, salesperson/marketing-review-and-revision and, to a lesser extent, teacher-review-and-revision.

Sources of Input

The quality of the revision process outcomes that are the end-product of formative evaluation can vary widely. The editorial revision process may well improve the instructional quality of instructional materials. Indeed, the expertise of particular editors in fashioning an effective material is legend. But the increasing trend in the instructional materials industry toward mass-produced instead of individually developed texts means that the impact of individual editors on a particular text is seriously diluted. The trend in educational publishing is toward a team approach. No longer can the school-oriented publishing industry be characterized by the basic "no frills" texts of earlier days. Gone is the standard format, colorless, with a simple presentation of content, especially in computer materials. Gone, also is the ease with which editors—and writers—can affect the instructional design of their texts. It is well-known that salespersons and marketing directors often have greater influence. For now, text materials employ elaborate designs, imaginative and varied presentation of content and activities, and perhaps most important, an expectation on the part of schools that students will learn more. With this increased sophistication and complexity of the once simple textbook, the role of the editor has changed from the leader of a small ensemble to conductor of a full orchestra consisting of multiple authors, actual writers, sub-editors, designers, sub-contractors, and so on. The computer courseware industry is rapidly assuming this production model as more publishers become involved. The transition (at least in the educational market) from single programmer cottage industries to production team seems inevitable, especially since more powerful equipment is providing the opportunity and requirement for more sophisticated programming. In this changed world of text design (medium and format), the editor is the coordinator, manager, and conciliator. The job is simply too large to assume that learner-based revision takes place, and if it does take place, that it is done systematically for all instructional materials.

It has been the feedback from salespeople, rather than from learners, that has traditionally been part of the development and revision process of instructional materials. Clearly, the information the salesperson brings to the design of a text can be crucial to a textbook's commercial success. The salesperson can assess what a new text must be like if it is to compete against rival products. Thus, the salesperson's contribution to textbook review and revision must, of necessity, reflect a special perception of the text in which sales and teacher reactions are prime considerations.

It is not necessary to enumerate the kind of product review and revision input that various parties will be concerned with or to point out the special interest instructional evaluators (it is unusual for publishers to have in-house research departments that conduct research on a material's instructional effectiveness). For as Thompson (1982) has argued in her discussion of the ecology of the world of instructional materials, it is natural that competing interest groups should exist and contribute to the tension of the instructional materials development process. It is a tension of competing needs and interests and the end-product—the text-book—or, in newer circumstances, the instructional disk—is supposed to be an appropriate and somehow effective compromise between those competing interest groups. This seems a realistic analysis of the world of instructional development as it exists. However, the analysis seldom questions how the learner (the ultimate "beneficiary" of this competition and compromise) actually benefits from this process.

Clearly, the contributions of various parties to review and revision is a conceptually legitimate part of formative evaluation. Yet, it seems to us that too often the emphasis or rationale for much of the review and revision practices that shape learning materials is to make the materials more acceptable to the purchaser and not necessarily more instructionally effective for the learner. This is the crucial distinction between formative evaluation and learner verification and revision.

The Process of LVR

Learner verification and revision is concerned only with assessing and improving the instructional effectiveness of text in terms of the learner. Hence, LVR is a narrowly drawn, restrictive process that concentrates only on the instructional materials, contextual materials, such as Teachers' Guide and teacher training materials, and *the learner*. It uses the process and some of the methods used by "good" teachers as they modify and mediate their textbooks or translate computer program logic and systematically apply those techniques to study. It studies the interaction of specific students who are within the text's target population with specific portions of print or program text, assesses instructional effectiveness, and supplies data upon which specific textual modifications and improvements can be based.

At this point, it might also be useful to mention a further distinction between formative evaluation and LVR. Not only does LVR specifically represent the learner (arguably the most important, but least represented, special interest group in the educational constellation), but it also extends the learner-feedback and revision process beyond the publication of a textbook or program. Formative evaluation, that conducted during the development or (formative) pre-publication stage of an instructional material's life, differs in scope from LVR. LVR is a continuous process that is designed to affect the reality of publishing and use over time. Increasingly, instructional materials are subject to periodic updating and reissuing in the form of new editions. In many respects, these new editions are simply established books in new bindings. Such is the imperative for currency of copyright date that textbooks are now routinely and periodically reissued. Since most microcomputer courseware is so new, this revision process (in any form) has yet to occur to any significant degree. Here lies a fundamental difference between formative evaluation and LVR. As a continuous process, publishers should use LVR to collect student data during the instructional life of a textbook or program and integrate the changes that are needed into the new edition of the material. It is our contention that in so far as any instructional materials are concerned, the concept of summative evaluation is less than useful. It can too easily lead to a false belief that because a large group of learners has been tested after using a particular text or other materials, it remains effective in subsequent editions. Publishers should improve and demonstrate the increasing instructional effectiveness of each of its textbook's succeeding editions based upon the revisions made.

While a time lag of up to five years is not unusual between the publication of a textbook and its new edition, no such time constraints affect the producers of microcomputer courseware. While development costs of high-quality computers are commensurately high, production costs are relatively low when compared with the production of a textbook; changes are relatively easy to make on a master disk, and thus the promise implicit in LVR of a continuous loop of development-production-use-revision-and-improvement can be readily built into the market life of computer courseware. In fact, many publishers provide updated versions of instructional courseware or computer utilities to original purchasers at a nominal cost.

Textual/Contextual LVR

Although LVR prescribes no one method for ascertaining the clarity and "learnability" of materials, it seems that a combination of classroom observation and criterion-referenced testing of learners, supplemented with interviews with both learners and their teachers, might be an optimum combination.

Data collected through interviews or questionnaire responses keyed to specific elements of the material being used and administered shortly after student/teacher completion can indicate specific areas for improvement. Interviews or questionnaire responses from a reasonable sampling of individual students from the instructional material's target group can help in verifying the specific portions of a material that need to be improved. Criterion-referenced tests can also be used to good effect. For example, if particular items on a unit test are missed by a majority of students, a materials developer has an obvious guide as to where to look toward improving the material in question.

The specific process publishers employ as they carry out LVR with their materials will vary; there is no standard way to conduct

LVR, and circumstances may influence the degree to which classroom observations or interviews are possible. However, in order to ensure that educators can both interpret LVR evidence and compare it to that of other companies, certain protocols must be followed. The guidelines established by a National Task Force (1976) provide a useful framework from which to work (see Table 17.1). These guidelines thus serve as an organizer for the publisher as they implement LVR and as a model to follow in presenting LVR data to educators.

Application of LVR

Although the rationale for learner verification and revision seems clear and its theoretical and practical utility quite obvious, LVR has had a chequered history. The enthusiasm that initially greeted the prospect of producing instructional materials based on systematic trials with students dissipated in the face of educators' apathy and publishers' resistance. And as with many educational innovations or movements, all interested parties were eager to jump onto the LVR bandwagon and, not unexpectedly, just as eager to jump off again as the instructional, economic, and political implications of LVR became clear.

After Komoski (1971) testified before Congress advocating the systematic use of LVR in preparing instructional materials, interest was intense. Many states considered adopting LVR legislation that would require publishers to submit evidence of learner verification and revision of their texts; failure to do so would mean automatic elimination from textbook selection lists. In the end, only two states enacted such legislation. State teachers associations advocated the use of LVR, and publishers indicated a willingness to use the LVR process in their development of materials and to participate in a task force to determine LVR guidelines.

As a major adoption state, much hope was placed on California's enactment of LVR legislation in 1973. For if California required publishers to submit evidence of LVR, then all publishers who wished to gain access to that major portion of the educational market would also have to comply with the ripple effect across

Table 17.1

National Task Force LVR Guidelines*

• Descriptive Information on Product

The "Catalog" information on the product, such as title, authors, copyright, medium or media involved, kinds of supplementary components, and so on. The "product" is any kind of material offered for adoption consideration as an instructional material.

• Instructional Design

The "instructional design" or overall *learning plan* for the product. The design should be described and the underlying *rationale for that design* should be stated.

• Intended Learner Outcomes to Be Investigated

A statement of *what the publisher intends the product to accomplish* when used with integrity with learners.

• Conditions of Use of Product

The instructional setting intended for the product, including a description of the *"target population"* and a noting of the kinds and extent of *"teacher preparation."* The target population is simply the kinds of learners for whom the product is intended. Characteristics which may or may not be relevant are: grades students are assigned to because of their maturity, not achievement, levels; actual grade levels, particularly with respect to reading achievement; ethnic backgrounds; family and community socioeconomic levels; and so on. Teacher preparation involves such teacher-related matters as supplementary teacher materials, inservice teacher education, and classroom preparation.

• Techniques for Gathering Feedback

Techniques used for gathering feedback from learners may include *classroom observations, interviews, questionnaires, and criterion-referenced tests.* These techniques should be designed to gather data both on direct learning effects and on affective reactions of learners.

• Description of Learners Used in LVR Process

The learners in the LVR Process are not to be confused with a scientifically drawn "national sample" of students required for the

Table 17.1 (Continued)

validation of standardized tests and for attempts at validation of other materials.

Conditions of a classroom setting suggest both "textual" and "contextual" characteristics. Textual characteristics are characteristics of the materials themselves which learners use (goals and objectives; scope and sequence; provisions for evaluation; and so on); contextual characteristics are characteristics of the setting in which the materials are used (the presence or absence of teacher's editions or manuals, or certain other supplementary resources; the teaching/management plan; and so on).

(In summation, the publisher should report: *(1) the procedure for selecting learners, (2) the relevant characteristics of these learners, and (3) the rationale for this step.*

• Analysis of Findings

The answers of the findings in a LVR Report should include *as much specificity as prudence allows—the kinds of trouble spots identified both within the materials used by learners and in the overall teaching/management plan.*

• Specific Improvements Made

Improvements can involve aspects relating to learner materials (textual), such as verbal or visual communications, manageability, appeal to learners, goals and objectives, scope and sequence, various kinds of bias, motivational elements, directions to learners, activities for learners, and the congruence of product elements. Improvements can relate to teaching aspects (contextual), such as classroom preparation, record-keeping provisions, teaching design, and inservice education.

As an ideal component of a LVR Report, the very in-house record of changes compiled by the publisher—including, perhaps, an annotated version of the product used with the selection of learners—might be made available by the publisher, on special request, for examination by an adoption committee.

• Background and Future of Product

The publisher should briefly describe any part of the product's history that might be relevant and helpful to a full understanding of the publisher's LVR efforts with the product. Also, the publisher may want to describe *plans for future LVR efforts with the product.*

*Condensed version of guidelines, reprinted with permission by the Educational Products Information Exchange.

the nation. However, implementation of the legislation was hampered by loose wording of the statutes, a faulty interpretation of what was meant by learner verification "proof," and an absence of state board leadership.

State education officials blamed publishers, teachers, and each other for the lack of action on LVR. However, one observer of the LVR situation charged that it was the state's educators, and not publishers, who balked at implementing the LVR legislation. Few of California's key educational personnel supported the LVR concept. By 1977, LVR was apparently a dead issue in the state. The California Textbook Commission dismissed the LVR statutes as being of little use, and while the commission did not flaunt the letter of the law continuing to ask producers for an LVR plan and reports, there was no evidence that they were examined or that they affected textbook adoption decisions.

In Florida, legislation and guidelines for implementing LVR contained none of the vague wording that characterized the California legislation. Before enacting legislation requiring LVR for instructional materials in order to be approved for adoption by the State of Florida, testimony was heard from both the Association of American Publishers and from EPIE Institute. As a result, publishers were given a grace period during which they could produce a "plan" to comply with the law. In addition, a set of guidelines was issued (the same as those of the national task force) to help educators and publishers meet the letter and spirit of the law. Internal opposition meant that little "education" work was done to inform Florida educators about LVR and no follow-up occurred to make sure publishers followed the LVR guidelines. LVR seemed a set of dead letters (Rousch, 1979).

Prospects

There are two appropriate phrases we would use to characterize the future of instructional improvement of text through the use of learner feedback. They are "guarded optimism" and "healthy skepticism." Optimism is in order because the new technology of electronic editing can reduce the time and cost of textual revision—especially for revising and improving microcomputer courseware. However, given the long-established lack of attention to the improvement of instructional effectiveness once an instructional product has been published—it seems wise to temper one's optimism with a healthy skepticism as to whether the instructional materials industry will take full advantage of the potential of electronic editing as a way of facilitating the instructional improvement of all types of text.

This potential is, we think, much greater than most people realize. But the actualization of this unrealized potential will depend to a very great extent on a new and uncharacteristic flexibility on the part of those who make and market instructional materials. The chance that such uncharacteristic behavior will develop among the producers of the traditional textbook and its related print and audio-visual supplements does seem unlikely in light of the small impact that LVR has had on the publishers of textbooks to date. However, as of 1983, there has been a new and vigorous initiative by the Florida State Department of Education to enforce Florida's eight-year-old Learner Verification and Revision legislation. New state guidelines for publisher compliance to that legislation were issued in the summer of 1983 and, according to State Department of Education officials, the initial response from some publishers has been encouraging. Whether publishers in general will meet the *spirit* as well as the letter of the law remains to be seen. Nevertheless, the Florida Department of Education deserves a good deal of credit for its perseverance, after almost a decade, to get publishers to recognize that the original Florida LVR guidelines allowed any publisher, who wished to, to avoid meeting the spirit of that state's LVR legislation by simply offering "a plan" to conduct LVR, but not necessarily ever actually carrying out that plan. The 1983 Florida guidelines for LVR closed the "plan" loophole and required publishers to document their actual learner verification procedures, including examples of primary data gathered directly from learners and teachers, as well as the textual revisions made on the basis of the publisher's analysis of those data.

The extent to which Florida and other large purchasers of instructional materials—printed textbooks and electronic learning materials—provide similar evidence of materials improvement through learner feedback remains to be seen. However, as noted earlier, it is in the area of this new technology that we believe the greatest progress toward learner-based improvement in instructional quality can be achieved. The degree to which this achievement will be realized, it seems to us, will depend largely on two things: (1) the willingness of the developers of computerized instruction to fully exploit the potential of the computer-as-instructional medium for constantly updating and improving instructional communications, and (2) the willingness of consumers of micro-computer products to demand that the instructional quality of these products be consistently improved by those who produce and market them.

It also seems to us that substantial strides toward instructional improvement of microcomputer products could be made through the cooperative efforts of producers and consumers if producers and marketers would adopt a policy of openly communicating to consumers the specific improvements that need to be made in a microcomputing product in order to better communicate with learners.

Because of the nature of microcomputer courseware, in particular, it would be possible for individual consumers, given appropriate directions, permission, and encouragement from pro-ducers, to actually modify specific portions of a particular microcomputer courseware product they had purchased, in ways that would incorporate the producers' findings regarding needed instructional improvements. Specifically, a producer, having ascer-tained through learner feedback that a particular learning se-quence, example, graphic, or procedure was confusing, or less than effective with learners, could make the necessary revisions and then communicate those specific revisions to each purchaser of the program in question, in the form of precise computer program-ming changes that the purchaser would be directed to make electronically in each copy of the program that had been purchased. (At present, many producers have created programs that enable teachers to "get inside" and modify or add certain types of examples or to make instructionally relevant changes in other program parameters.) Other publishers will provide up-dated versions to purchasers who return the original disk and pay a nominal fee. It seems to us that, were producers of computerized learning materials to undertake such a policy of cooperative revision, they would end up building a grateful consumer constituency as well as building better and better instructional products. If such a cooperative relationship could be developed between those who have purchased a specific product and those who produced that product, we believe that substantial strides toward the constant improvement of microcomputing courseware could be made on an ongoing basis.

We suggest this as one of many ways in which the flexibility of the electronic technology may be applied to the improvement of instruction and learning. We feel certain that there are other ideas and other strategies that might exploit the potential of this technology even more effectively. It is this flexibility that makes us guardedly optimistic about the future of learner feedback as a means of improving instructional texts of all types. However, the inertia and long-established habits of the instructional materials industry keeps healthy our skepticism about whether all of this potential for positive change will ever be realized.

References

Bloom, B.S. *et al. Handbook on formative and summative evaluation of student learning.* New York: Longman, Inc., 1971.

Education USA. Budget axes falling hard on textbook purchases. *Education USA*, May 23, 1983, *25*(39).

EPIE Institute. Micro-courseware PRO/FILES: Evaluation service of EPIE Institute, 1982.

EPIE Institute. *National study of the nature and the quality of instructional materials most used by teachers and learners.* EPIE Institute, Report Number 76, 1976.

EPIE Materials Report. *Deciphering L.V.R.: A key for consumers and publishers.* Report Number 92m, EPIE Institute, 1980.

Frymier, J.R., Davis, D.L., and Clinefelter, D. Curriculum materials used by eleven-year-old pupils. Paper presented at the annual meeting of the American Educational Research Association, 1977.

Komoski, P.K. Testimony. Washington, DC: U.S. House of Representatives, House Select Committee on Education and Labor, May 11, 1971.

Komoski, P.K. An imbalance of product quantity and instructional quality: The imperative of empiricism. *AV Communications Review*, Winter, 1974, *22*(4).

Komoski, P.K. Affecting the system through product evaluation. Paper presented at the annual meeting of the American Educational Research Association, New York, 1982.

Nathenson, M.B., and Henderson, E.S. *Using student feedback to improve learning materials.* London: Croom Helm, 1980.

National Commission on Excellence in Education. *A nation at risk: The imperative for educational reform.* Washington, DC: U.S. Government Printing Office, 1983.

Rousch, M.D. *A status report on the Florida instructional materials adoption procedures.* Tallahassee, FL: Florida State University, 1979.

Stake, R.E., and Easley, J.A. *Case studies in science education.* Washington, DC: U.S. Government Printing Office, 1979.

Thompson, P.J. *The textbooks niche in the ecology of education: The Cronbach Study after twenty-five years.* Unpublished dissertation, Columbia University, 1982.

Chapter 18

Is Evaluation a Myth?
Assessing Text Assessment Procedures

Patricia Wright

Introduction

This chapter will suggest that there are a number of myths surrounding the concept of evaluation. These myths relate to the perceived need for evaluation, the procedures involved in evaluation, and the overall adequacy of the evaluated text. Although there is a growing realization that procedures for troubleshooting a text are an important component of the production of non-fiction materials, the objectives and methods of evaluation are not always considered in detail. It is not appropriate to think of the objective of evaluating a text as being akin to "seeing if it works" or "seeing if readers understand it." Different procedures are best suited to detecting different problems. Without serious thought being given to the multiplicity of ways in which a specific text can succeed or fail, the choice of assessment procedure may inadvertently preclude diagnosing certain classes of poor communication that might be crucial for that text. If the choice is dictated by the capricious logistic constraints of time or budget, this outcome would seem inevitable. While it may be true that almost any evaluation is better than none, it by no means follows that any evaluation will be good enough for attaining the specific objective.

It might be illuminating to think of evaluation procedures as various kinds of filter which will strain out the lumps in a text. Such an analogy is helpful because it forces consideration of choosing the appropriate size of mesh for this filter. Such choices are critically determined by the purpose of evaluation. For example, if the aim of evaluation is to *optimize* the documentation, then the mesh will need to be chosen so as to catch all the lumps no matter how small. On the other hand, if the aim of evaluation is to avoid catastrophes within the documentation, then there is need only to remove the very large lumps. Different assessment procedures will be appropriate for these different objectives.

An alternative aim of text evaluation might be to provide various kinds of input for subsequent document design decisions. That is to say, the evaluator may wish to know not simply what are the shortcomings of the present text but how to avoid such shortcomings in other texts. For example, one might wish to have as a by-product of the evaluation process details of how to explain certain procedures to the target audience, or how to ask certain kinds of questions on forms, or, even more general still, one might wish to develop aspects of an improved design methodology. Procedures for accomplishing these various aims are seldom compatible. For example, deriving generalizable principles from evaluation may require contrastive testing between alternative texts, whereas detecting catastrophes does not. So an early decision has to be made about the precise aim of the evaluation.

Most analogies, however, have their limitations. It can be misleading to think of evaluation as a filter because this may encourage the mistaken conclusion that if problems have not been detected, then they cannot be present. Yet there are some kinds of problem that people have with documentation that are not easily found. It may be very difficult to diagnose omissions in the *content* itself if the assessment focuses on the *comprehensibility* of the text. A common complaint with documents that are frequently updated (e.g., manuals and leaflets accompanying consumer products) is that insufficient attention is given both to the substance and the sequencing of the content. Readers may be faced with picking their own circuitous route through relevant paragraphs. Since evaluation procedures are usually applied to the text in its original form, it is scarcely surprising that evaluators can easily overlook the need to plan further ahead.

Another aspect of the text that can be overlooked during

evaluation concerns the access structures provided for readers. These are the textual adjuncts such as contents pages, indexes, running headings, etc. (see Section IV of this volume for further discussion). Insensitive handling of these structures can result in readers becoming irritated or perhaps confused. During a brief evaluation study, the participants may feel it unnecessary to report their irritation. Nor will their confusion be easily detected if the evaluation tasks take them through the text in a linear fashion. The problem of moving about within a text in order to locate material of interest can be particularly onerous in an electronic medium, e.g., where the text is displayed on a CRT screen (Moray, 1980; Senders, 1977; Shackel, 1982).

There remains one other reason why thinking of evaluation as a filter can be misleading. In the physical world, once lumps have been strained out they can simply be thrown away. For textual materials, however, there remain a number of problems concerning what to do with the lumps after you have caught them. Their removal may require subtle expertise because the causes of a reader's difficulties can be extremely diverse. Knowing that certain information in the text is being misinterpreted will not necessarily indicate how the text should be revised. The author may have made wrong assumptions about the reader's knowledge or the reader's way of using the text. In this sense, "evaluation" needs to start at the very early stages of text design by finding out relevant characteristics of the readership. But that is not to suggest that it is an easy matter to know what these relevant characteristics will be or how to measure them. Nevertheless, the important point is that there are major advantages in considering text assessment as a recurrent part of the design process, rather than as a final stage akin to proofreading.

Approaches to Design and Evaluation

For our present purposes, it will be convenient to consider three broad categories of approach to the process of design: theories, guidelines, and procedures. These are not mutually exclusive categories, merely convenient groupings, but each category has implications for the aims and techniques of text assessment as well as for the ways in which the product of the evaluation procedures will be regarded.

THEORIES: Few theories of text design exist. Some have been based closely on models of comprehension derived from studies of readers of narrative or expository texts (e.g., Kieras, 1980). Such models, through their analysis of the propositional structure of text, have considerable potential for addressing issues, both at the level of individual sentences and at the level of the thematic organization of paragraphs. Textual revisions that reduce propositional complexity are perceived by readers as clarifying the content of the text (Frase, 1981). Increasingly, such models are taking account of the variation that exists in reading strategies (e.g., Meyer and Rice, 1982). There are a variety of ways in which text grammars can be constructed, and at present it is not clear which are the most useful with respect to their design implications. But all techniques of discourse analysis would seem to have limitations in bridging the gap between the language and its physical realization on the page. For example, Frase (1981) found that the clarity of the text was enhanced by certain typographic variables, such as numbering meaningful units within the text and listing such units vertically. In one study, Frase reports that the segmented text was read 18 percent faster than a conventional paragraph display.

There are a great many ways of implementing the notion of typographic segmentation (e.g., contrast the formats of Jewett, 1981; Jonassen, 1981; and Shebilske and Rotondo, 1981). At the moment, the absence of a theoretical framework for exploring these typographic variables makes it difficult to map with confidence a path between the realms of discourse analysis and typograhic options. However, recently there have been proposals for the development of notational devices for talking about typography (e.g., Twyman, 1981), as well as careful exposition of theoretical concepts relating to the macro-punctuation of text (e.g., Waller, 1982) and the domain of verbal graphic communication (Twyman, 1982). Such advances give grounds for optimism in anticipating the development of useful theoretical frameworks for text design. Furthering such development may come to be seen as one of the most useful by-products of text evaluation.

Apart from specific theories of text design, there have also been general discussions of classes of design theory. Such discussions yield insights of relevance to document design. For example,

Malhotra, Thomas, Carroll, and Miller (1980) suggested several broad classes of model, all of which have their uses and shortcomings when applied to text. For example, one class of model concerns theories which are specific to a particular application. Here everything hinges on the breadth of the word *specific*. If the application is a particular text, then such models, once devised, may be very useful. Within the model space, there is room for alternative evaluation aims such as optimizing the presentation, reducing the costs, or avoiding catastrophes. One advantage of these specific models is that they can be made to address issues relating to design options which are meaningful for that particular text. If the application is broad-based, such as teaching music to 13-year-olds, then models may be much harder to develop because of the numerous interactions among factors such as content, readers' knowledge, and design options. The limitation of highly-specific models concerns the cost-benefit of developing them if they have no generality to other texts. Such value judgments will in turn depend upon the characteristics of the text and the target audience.

A second class of model proposed by Malhotra *et al.* were those related to underlying psychological processes. One limitation of such models is that there may be no simple mapping between the psychological insights and the design solution. For example, psychologists may be able to explain why a particular passage of text is difficult for readers to understand. What the writer needs to know is how the information can be presented in order to communicate more successfully. This may mean abandoning paragraph prose style altogether, but such an option is likely to be outside the predictive scope of the explanatory model.

A rather different use of psychological theory has been advocated by Wright (1980), who suggested that much of the reader's interaction with technical documents can be characterized in terms of the kinds of psychological processes that are involved. Working from a very simplistic framework, concerning the way readers formulate their goals for interacting with documentation and the plans that readers use for achieving these goals, it seems possible to create a heuristic that enables a diagnostic assessment of a particular document. The heuristic recursively asks what the reader will do during the course of achieving whatever goals have been set. These questions are answered at the level of component psychological processes (e.g., pattern recognition, memory, comprehension, etc.). The design implications arise from seeking to reduce the number and/or complexity of these psychological processes. Some examples of the application of this heuristic are given in Wright (1981). One advantage that this approach has is that it can be addressed to many levels of the text. At the macro-level, it can reveal deficiencies in overall organization; at the micro-level, it can highlight problems with particular paragraphs, tables, or diagrams. Its chief disadvantage appears to be that it may only be a viable design tool for those who already have a background knowledge of cognitive psychology. Since most texts are designed by people without such expertise, this is a serious limitation. It is in sharp contrast to the detailed knowledge required by theoretical approaches that guidelines and procedures appear to offer more immediate assistance to authors and document designers.

GUIDELINES: There are various formalisms which permit the assistance of automation to be introduced at certain stages of the design process. Readability formulae would be one example of this at a simplistic level (Klare, 1976); text grammars are an example at a more complex level. The increasing use of word processing facilities means that such assistance can readily be made available and easily implemented without costly training programs (Lefrere, 1982).

The drawback associated with all such formalisms is that they tend to be exclusively text-based. That is to say, they usually have no mechanism for taking into account the ways in which the reader will be wanting to use the text, although the development of an expert systems approach may be one way around this limitation (Lefrere, Waller, and Whalley, 1980). Text-based analyses will ignore the ways in which the meaning of the text may be subtly altered by the extra-linguistic context in which the information is being used. Even revising a text to meet readability criteria is no guarantee of successful communication (e.g., Davison and Kantor, 1982), and numerous accounts of the shortcomings of readability formulae can be found (e.g., Bruce, Rubin, and Starr, 1981; Klare, 1976; Plung, 1981; Redish, 1981).

Nevertheless, automation can provide useful assistance to writers (Coke, 1982). A good example of this is the development of the computer-based writer's workbench at Bell Laboratories (Frase, Keenan, and Denver, 1980). Here various programs are available which will draw the author's attention to specific points in the text and ask the author to consider options at those points. The important factor contributing to the success of these programs would seem to be that they offer *assistance*. The automation does not override the intelligence of the author.

A rather different set of formalisms are those embodied in verbal guidelines. Not only are there qualitatively different kinds of guidelines, but for each kind there is a mixture of pros and cons. For example, there are high-level guidelines (e.g., write clearly). The number of such high-level guidelines that need to be given to an author is not very many. So they can either be remembered or listed in a way that can be easily referred to. Their major shortcoming is that they offer no explanation of how the author is to carry out the recommendations. In contrast, there are low-level, detailed guidelines. Not only do these become too long to be memorized (e.g., Hartley, 1981, lists 80 recommendations), but also they have numerous exceptions. There are very few rules about writing text that are not legitimately broken. Steinmann (1982) quotes the following sentence from Jonathan Swift to illustrate that long sentences are sometimes easily understood: "Therefore let no man talk to me of other expedients: of taxing our absentees at five shillings a pound; of using neither clothes nor household furniture except what is of our own growth and manufacture; of utterly rejecting the materials and instruments that promote foreign luxury; of aiming the expensiveness of pride, variety, idleness and gaining in our women; . . . ."

The exceptions to the rules could be stated but, in order to reduce the length of the guidelines, these exceptions are often ignored. Even so, the writer tends to be faced with a formidable problem when wanting to retrieve and consult a specific guideline within the overall listing. It is possible that some kinds of checklists, particularly those formulated as questions rather than as statements, may be helpful in trouble-shooting a document (Wright, 1981). But here the help consists mainly in the extent to which such lists assist in a "consciousness-raising" function and so aid the detection of textual problems. Removing the trouble-spots will require other sorts of information.

Another reason why formalisms and firm, detailed guidelines are of limited value is that research has shown there is no universally correct way of presenting information. Even when presenting the same content to the same readership, slight variation in the way people consult the text can mean that certain ways of presenting the information will make things easier for readers than other ways (Wright and Reid, 1973). Therefore, it becomes essential to develop techniques for analyzing how readers will interact with the documentation. In this sense, pretesting is again to be seen as part of the evaluation process. Indeed, as a contributory part of the evaluation process, guidelines and other formalisms can undoubtedly play a useful role. But it must be realized that they are not sufficient on their own, nor in principle can they be, as the sole means of evaluating a text.

PROCEDURES: Probably the most frequently used evaluation procedure is to give the text to someone else and to ask for comments. Macdonald-Ross and Waller (1975) have shown how valuable informed criticism can be for educational texts. Lefrere (1981) has discussed how the editorial role might change in an electronic medium.

Obviously, editorial comments can come from a range of experts (experts in the subject matter, experts with a flair for writing, experts with a flair for typographic display). The comments received can be extremely valuable, both in indicating where there are problems within the text and in suggesting ways in which the text can be revised. However, it is very likely, perhaps inevitable, that if a text is circulated to a variety of editors, then they will tend to comment on rather different aspects of the text (Wright, 1984). It is therefore quite conceivable that the recommendations received may not be wholly consistent with each other. For example, the subject matter expert may feel that a particular section needs expanding in order to make it clearer, whereas someone reading on behalf of the target audience may feel the same section needs eliminating because it did not make any sense. Reconciling such conflicts clearly becomes a matter for the writer's judgment. Similar conflicts may arise as a result of empirical testing.

Several recent proposals concerning text design have explicitly incorporated empirical testing into several of the design stages that are specified (e.g., Duffy, 1981; Redish, Felker, and Rose, 1981). Such testing is not reserved for the time at which the draft is nearing completion. Much earlier, even before beginning the first draft, considerable emphasis is placed on the analysis of target audience characteristics and the need to determine the ways in which that audience will interact with the documentation. It has already been mentioned that the findings from such pre-design analysis can later assist in the interpretation of the results of post-design evaluations.

Post-Design Testing

There are two broad classes of evaluation procedure. On the one hand, there are text-based techniques and, on the other, there are task-based assessments. As with theories and guidelines, most of these evaluation techniques have limitations. Considering first text-based techniques, the use of readability formulae has already been mentioned. Although very cheap and convenient to use, such formulae ignore the meaning of the text. A rather different technique, which captures at least local meaning, is the Cloze text. This is a procedure whereby blanks are left in the text every *n* words, and the reader is invited to complete these blanks. Difficulties in interpreting the text are indicated by wrong completions. This technique is more appropriate for paragraphs than for shorter texts such as occur on forms or in instruction leaflets, because readers are relying on thematic continuity in order to fill in the missing words. Klare (1981) recommends that every fifth word should be deleted from the text. Deleting more risks the completion of a given blank being too dependent on the completion of previous blanks; deleting fewer risks missing trouble-spots in the text. Cloze responses are usually scored as correct only if there is a verbatim match with the original text, so the whole procedure can be administered and analyzed by computer-based systems. This removes much of the tedium of using Cloze as a text assessment procedure. Less easily circumvented are suggestions that Cloze techniques are insensitive to thematic coherence across sentence boundaries (Shanahan, Kamil, and Tobin, 1982).

A quite different technique, and one that does not require long passages of continuous prose, is to apply rating techniques to the assessment of the relative difficulty of different sections of a document (e.g., Frase, 1981; Hartley, 1982). For a description of this assessment procedure being applied to the elements on forms, see Wright (1983). The essence of the procedure is that people record their judgments about various parts of the text using a five- or seven-point scale (e.g., ranging from "very easy to understand" to "very difficult to understand"). These assessments can then be pooled across a number of raters and what emerges is a profile showing where the consensus view considered the text to be difficult.

Rating techniques have the advantage of being simpler to administer and to score than Cloze tests, unless the latter are computerized. But ratings have the disadvantage of yielding data which do not clearly indicate whether the most difficult points are in fact so difficult that they need to have anything done about them, or whether even the relatively easy parts of the text are actually too difficult for the target audience.

Perhaps the most conventional text-assessment technique is to use some form of question-and-answer procedure (e.g., Hirsch and Harrington, 1981). For this method to succeed, everything depends upon the skill with which the questions have been devised. It will defeat the aim of evaluation if answers can be generated from particular phrases in the text without there being any necessity for those phrases to have been understood by the reader. Nevertheless, question-and-answer techniques are extremely versatile and enable an examination of the higher thematic levels of the text as well as the additional inferences that readers may draw from the text. Matthews, Jacobson, and Jones (1982) used extended interviews to evaluate a revised government form. Indeed, as an assessment procedure, question-and-answer techniques can be adapted to both text-based and task-based analyses.

Related to the use of question-and-answer interviews as an assessment technique is the use of surveys. These can be used to check whether the target audience would be familiar with particular terminology or with particular concepts. One potential limitation of such techniques is that they may ignore the kinds of context effects that all too often generate ambiguities for the reader. For example, words like *family* and *income* may well be recognized and identified appropriately by members of the target audience under survey conditions. Unfortunately, in a particular context (say a government form), the fuzzy boundaries that such concepts can have may create difficulties for the reader. Surveys are useful for what they detect in the way of knowledge gaps or misconceptions on the part of the target audience, but one needs to be cautious about what they fail to detect.

Existence of limitations for each of the assessment techniques discussed so far should not be taken to imply that these procedures are best avoided. Many of the techniques are quick, cheap, and informative. The intention underlying the repeated emphasis that all the techniques have limitations is to stress that the output from such techniques should always be interpreted with caution because the techniques themselves are not fail-safe. That is to say, if the techniques indicate difficulties, then these difficulties need some attention by the author. However, if the techniques do not highlight any trouble-spots, it does not follow that readers will find the text easy.

Moving from text-based techniques to task-based assessments does not change the assymmetry just noted. Task-based assessments are most appropriate for materials such as forms and instruction manuals. They are also vital when information is presented in a medium other than print (e.g., presented electronically on a visual display screen). These techniques can be divided into two major categories, one using field observations and the other using performance monitored under more rigorous, but artificial, laboratory conditions. Consider first the pros and cons of field observations. These may be conducted either unobtrusively by observers who seek to play the role of a fly on the wall, or intrusively by observers who deliberately interact with the person being observed. Technological advances, such as devices for monitoring page turning (Whally, 1982), have increased the scope of relatively unobtrusive observation. However, one limitation of unobtrusive procedures is that they may make it difficult for the observer to infer the precise nature of the reader's problems with the text. A subsequent debriefing session with the reader can sometimes be a way around this problem, but they rely on readers remembering and accurately reconstructing their interaction with the text. Debriefing sessions can also be valuable for providing more information about readers, their background knowledge relating to the content of the text, their reading purposes and strategies, etc.

A different way of collecting field observations in a relatively unobtrusive way is through questionnaires completed after reading the text. This can be an inexpensive means of collecting data, but it relies on the reader knowing what was wrong with the text or at least being able to remember and identify where confusions occurred. If having just read a chapter you felt that you did not understand the concepts that the author was trying to explain, then you may not be in a very good position to respond to a detailed questionnaire. Another difficulty with using such questionnaires is that readers may tend to assume that any misunderstandings are their own fault and so be reluctant to report where these difficulties occurred. Sometimes it may be possible to get around this problem by inviting comments about points in the text where *other* readers might experience difficulties.

If the observer is able to ask questions of the reader (or vice versa), then the causes of the reader's difficulties with the text are easier to diagnose. However, intrusive procedures also have drawbacks. They run the risk that the observer may inadvertently train the reader to understand the documentation, perhaps by pointing out how the text is organized. The assessment of the adequacy of the text will then be faulty. Another risk is that the observer may provide the reader with information early in the interview, which fortuitously eliminates subsequent confusions that would have arisen. Since the target audience will not have this helpful observer on hand to provide the extra information needed, the assessment may again be faulty and problems can go undetected at the evaluation stage. These risks may be greater when the documentation is presented in an unfamiliar medium (e.g., electronically), because the reader may need to be given information about text manipulation in addition to being provided with the text itself.

Field testing cannot be carried out for some texts, e.g., the documentation accompanying a product which has not yet been released onto the market. Here laboratory-based testing is valuable, sometimes essential. There are several varieties of laboratory-based task-testing. For texts which involve a great deal of procedural information, such as handbooks, it may be possible to simulate the appropriate procedural environment and to invite volunteers to use the text in this simulated context. Again the behavior can be monitored either unobtrusively or intrusively. Clearly, this technique is very dependent upon the faithfulness of the simulation. One limitation of artificial tasks is that they may change the presuppositions which users adopt, and this may mask ambiguities in the text.

One advantage of laboratory-based testing over field testing is that laboratory techniques are more easily made contrastive, in the sense that the investigation will provide a relative evaluation between design alternatives. Such contrasts can be made at either a global or a micro level. For example, the design options for a computer manual might be between a text electronically displayed on the screen, and a conventional printed text. It is a major drawback of such contrastive global evaluations that the results may have no generality to other kinds of texts or even to similar contents if presented in just slightly different ways within each medium. When the contrastive approach is concerned at the micro level with specific details within a text, the problems of generalizability are rather different. Now the difficulty is knowing whether all the small details can be pinned together to make an effective text. For example, the advantage of consistency throughout the text may conflict with the solutions arrived at by piecemeal testing.

Having reviewed a range of techniques and shown that all have limitations of one sort or another, the question then arises as to which techniques to choose for evaluating a particular text. Clearly, it is necessary to use several convergent techniques in order to circumvent the limitations of any one. But details of how many and in which order are extremely difficult to answer in the abstract. Much depends on the nature of the text, the extent to which the clear communication of certain information within the text is of critical importance, and the likelihood of related texts being produced subsequently. If further similar texts are going to be produced, then it may be a very good investment to have a thorough evaluation of the first text(s) in order that lessons can be learned which can be applied to the texts which will follow. Such thinking would also motivate the use of contrastive techniques whose findings could contribute to the development of design theories.

Results of Evaluation

No matter how the assessment is done, the result will be a frequency distribution of trouble-spots within the text. That is to say, at some locations no one will have encountered problems, at other locations, a few people may have experienced difficulties, and at some points there may have been many people who had trouble. Revision will tend to follow this frequency distribution, starting at the most frequently encountered trouble-spots.

Deciding when to terminate the revision process is inevitably arbitrary if time does not permit the examination of all the reported difficulties. It may not be appropriate to define the criterion for termination solely by reference to numbers, e.g., by suggesting that at all locations the error-rate should be less than five percent of readers (or two percent, or whatever). Instead, it may be necessary to classify passages of text in terms of the tolerance of misunderstanding: that will be accepted. For example, some safety instructions may require a stiff criterion that everyone tested shows a correct understanding. In contrast, some background explanation might not warrant, in cost-effectiveness terms, a reduction of the error rate below 20 percent.

Not only is there no magical figure that can be pinned on a text as some "seal of approval," but it is clearly meaningless to look at average figures for the total text. In particular, it should be noted that there can be very different re-design implications underlying a statement, such as, "Only five percent of people tested had any problems with the text." If all those five percent had trouble in the same place, then reducing the errors by revising the text at that point would seem highly cost-effective. On the other hand, if the five percent errors were distributed throughout the text then effective re-design might be a very lengthy process.

Although the immediate results of evaluation are simply diagnostic for that specific text, there is a long-term advantage to be gained from characterizing those faults in a way that will enable the problem to be avoided in subsequent texts. Such characterization is made difficult by the fact that any instance of faulty communication can have its cause in a variety of factors (e.g., content, language, or display factors). Some of these causes may not relate to any general principles which can be used subsequently. Others, particularly those relating to language and display factors, might repay consideration in the light of the various theoretical developments mentioned earlier.

In conclusion, it is a myth to expect evaluation procedures to be easy, fail-safe, and to require no theoretical support. Certainly, some procedures are easy to implement, but these are not necessarily the most informative assessments. No evaluation procedure is fail-safe, because each is sensitive to a particular dimension of readers' problems. So all methods of assessment risk failing to detect difficulties lying on other dimensions. The use of a variety of procedures is much safer than relying on any single technique. Knowing which techniques to select, and how to adapt or improve them for specific documents, is scarcely more than guesswork in the absence of adequate theoretical motivation. Often, the choice of techniques will vary with document factors such as content, importance, and longevity, since from a management viewpoint, these are the factors most clearly related to the cost-effectiveness of the evaluation. However, from a design standpoint, the choice of assessment procedures needs to be related both to the various dimensions of user difficulty (dimensions such as linguistic comprehension, display interpretation, readers' prior knowledge, ways of using the document) and to the development of a more systematic formulation of design practice. Without such development, no matter what evaluation procedures are used, interpreting the results will rely on the skill and caution exercised by the writing and evaluating team. To counteract this dependence on subjective interpretation, ideally the results of evaluation will have implications that go beyond the location of trouble-spots in the evaluated text.

References

Bruce, B., Rubin, A., and Starr, K. Why readability formulas fail.

IEEE Transactions on Professional Communication, 1981, *24*, 50-52.

Coke, E.U. Computer aids for writing text. In D.H. Jonassen (Ed.), *The technology of text: Principles for structuring, designing, and displaying text.* Englewood Cliffs, NJ: Educational Technology Publications, 1982.

Davison, A., and Kantor, R.N. On the failure of readability formulas to define readable texts: A case study from adaptations. *Reading Research Quarterly*, 1982, *17*, 187-209.

Duffy, T.M. Organizing and utilizing document design options. *Information Design Journal*, 1981, *2*, 256-266.

Frase, L.T. Writing, text, and the reader. In C.H. Frederiksen and J.F. Dominic (Eds.), *Writing: The nature, development, and teaching of written communication. Vol. 2: Process, development and communication.* Hillsdale, NJ: Lawrence Erlbaum Associates, 1981.

Frase, L.T., Keenan, S.A., and Dever, J.J. Human performance in computer aided writing and documentation. In P.A. Kolers, M.E. Wrolstad, and H. Bouma (Eds.), *Processing of visible language 2.* New York: Plenum Press, 1980.

Hartley, J. Eighty ways of improving instructional text. *IEEE Transactions on Professional Communication*, 1981, *24*, 17-27.

Hartley, J. Designing instructional text. In D.H. Jonassen (Ed.), *The Technology of Text: Principles for structuring, designing, and displaying text.* Englewood Cliffs, NJ: Educational Technology Publications, 1982.

Hirsch, E.D., and Harrington, D.P. Measuring the communication effectiveness of prose. In C.H. Frederiksen and J.F. Dominic (Eds.), *Writing: The nature, development, and teaching of written communication. Vol 2: Process, development, and communication.* Hillsdale, NJ: Lawrence Erlbaum Associates, 1981.

Jewett, D.L. Multi-level writing in theory and practice. *Visible Language*, 1981, *15*, 32-40.

Jonassen, D.H. Information mapping: A description, rationale, and comparison with programmed instruction. *Visible Language*, 1981, *15*, 55-66.

Kieras, D.E. How readers abstract main ideas from technical prose: Some implications for document design. Paper presented at a

Document Design Colloquium, American Institute for Research, Washington, DC, November 17, 1980.

Klare, G.R. A second look at the validity of readability formulae. *Journal of Reading Behavior*, 1976, *8*, 129-152.

Klare, G.R. Practical aspects of readability. Open University, Milton Keynes: Institute of Educational Technology, 1981.

Lefrere, P. Editors' roles in on-line journals. *Journal of Research Communication Studies*, 1981, *3*, 157-167.

Lefrere, P. Beyond word-processing: Human and artificial intelligence in document preparation and use. In P.J. Hills (Ed.), *Trends in information transfer.* London: Frances Pinter, 1982.

Lefrere, P., Waller, R.H., and Whalley, P. "Expert systems" in educational technology? In L. Evans and R. Winterburn (Eds.), *Aspects of educational technology XIV.* London: Kogan Page, 1980, 338-343.

Macdonald-Ross, M., and Waller, R. Criticism, alternatives, and tests: A conceptual framework for improving typography. *Programmed Learning and Educational Technology*, 1975, *12*, 75-83.

Malhotra, A., Thomas, J.C., Carroll, J.M., and Miller, L.A. Cognitive processes in design. *International Journal of Man-Machine Studies*, 1980, *12*, 119-140.

Matthews, C., Jacobson, M., and Jones, R. Common sense, skill, and research in forms design. *Information Design Journal*, 1982, *3*, 87-95.

Meyer, B.J.F., and Rice, G.E. The interaction of reader strategies and the organisation of text. *Text*, 1982, *2*, 155-192.

Moray, N. Towards an electronic journal. In P. Kolers, M.E. Wrolstad, and H. Bouma (Eds.), *Processing of visible language 2.* New York: Plenum Press, 1980.

Plung, D.L. Readability formulas and technical communication. *IEEE Transactions on Professional Communication*, 1981, *24*, 52-54.

Redish, J.C. Understanding the limitations of readability formulas. *IEEE Transactions on Professional Communication*, 1981, *24*, 46-48.

Redish, J.C., Felker, D.B., and Rose, A.M. Evaluating the effects of document design principles. *Information Design Journal*, 1981, *2*, 236-243.

Senders, J. An on-line journal. *The Information Scientist*, 1977, *11*, 3-9.

Shackel, B. The BLEND system: Programme for the study of some electronic journals. *Ergonomics*, 1982, *25*, 269-284.

Shanahan, T., Kamil, M.L., and Tobin, A.W. Cloze as a measure of intersentential comprehension. *Reading Research Quarterly*, 1982, *17*, 229-255.

Shebilske, W.L., and Rotondo, J.A. Typographical and spatial cues that facilitate learning from textbooks. *Visible Language*, 1981, *15*, 41-54.

Steinmann, M. Speech-act theory and writing. In M. Nystrand (Ed.), *What writers know: The language, process, and structure of written discourse.* New York: Academic Press, 1982.

Twyman, M. Typography without words. *Visible Language*, 1981, *15*, 5-12.

Twyman, M. The graphic presentation of language. *Information Design Journal*, 1982, *3*, 2-22.

Waller, R.H. Text as diagram: Using typography to improve access and understanding. In D.H. Jonassen (Ed.), *The Technology of Text: Principles for structuring, designing, and displaying text.* Englewood Cliffs, NJ: Educational Technology Publications, 1982.

Whalley, P. Argument in text and the reading process. In A. Flammer and W. Kintsch (Eds.), *Discourse processing.* Amsterdam: North Holland, 1982.

Wright, P. Usability: The criterion for designing written information. In P.A. Kolers, M.E. Wrolstad, and H. Bouma (Eds.), *Processing of visible language 2.* New York: Plenum Press, 1980.

Wright, P. Informed design for forms. *Information Design Journal*, 1981, *2*, 151-178.

Wright, P. Editing policies and processes. In T. Duffy and R. Waller (Eds.), *Designing usable texts.* New York: Academic Press, 1984.

Wright, P., and Reid, F. Written information: Some alternatives to prose for expressing the outcomes of complex contingencies. *Journal of Applied Psychology*, 1973, *57*, 160-166.

Index

Abstracts, 363
Access structures, 187
Achievement treatment interaction, 19
Adjunct questions, 36, 131-154
  artificiallity of paradigm, 145
  backward effects, 136-137
  cognitive analysis of, 151
  forward effects, 137-138
  frequency of questions, 134
  future paradigm, 150-151
  individual differences, 143-144
  level of processing, 134, 138-142
  level of questions, 146
  limitations of research, 145-148
  methodological concerns, 148-149
  paradigm, 132
  position of questions, 133
  reviews of research, 133-135
  theoretical orientation, 132-133
Application level questions, 140
Assimilation encoding theory, 16-17
Attention theory, 24
Ausubel's theory, 16
Authoring systems, 289-291, 310-324
  authoring language, 318-319
  authoring prompts, 319-320
  capabilities of, 317-322
  courseware libraries, 321
  currently available, 322-324
  defined, 312-317
  graphics in, 320-321

  language translator, 321
  record keeping, 321-322
  student mode, 321

Blank book, 294-295
BLEND-LINC, 297
Boldface, 205, 364,
Boxes, 205

Chain indexes, 279
Citation indexes, 280-281
Classified indexes, 279
Cognitive learning strategies
  elaborational strategies, 28-29
  imagery, 29
  organizational strategies, 29-30
  student generated questions, 27-28
Cognitive structures, 193
Cognitive theory, 342
Color, 205
Comprehensibility of text, 419
Comprehension and context, 240-241
Computer Assisted Distance Education, 338
Computer based instruction, 310-320
Computer based text, ix-x
Computer conferencing, 297
Computer languages, 311
Computer menu designs, 270-272
Concordances, 273-274
Contents lists, 190, 265-272
  designing, 266-269

in computer menus, 270-272
level of detail, 267-269
typographic design of, 265-266
vocabulary of readers, 269-270
Contracts and specifications, 374-375, 380-381
Controlled vocabulary, 252
Conversation
between writers and readers, 64-66
Coordinate indexes, 278-279
Correspondence education
SEE distance education
Courseware
learner verification of, 398-399, 408-416
reliance on, 403
Cramming, 24
Cueing systems
typographic, 196-197
verbal, 196

Design and evaluation
approaches to, 420-426
Diagrams, 106
Directed attention hypothesis, 139
Directed strategy hypothesis, 140
Discourse analysis, 421
Discourse organization, 71-74
Distance education
design/development process, 339-341
defined, 330-331
distance aspect, 334
instructional design considera-tion, 333-341
instructional support system, 338-339
personalization of, 335
rationale, 331-333
teaching process, 336-338
Distance education texts, 326, 329-345
Drill and practice, 313-314

Dual coding hypothesis, 164-166
Dynamic book, 302

Educational system
computer based, 312
Elaborational strategies, 28-29
design implications of, 37-38
Electronic encyclopedia, 299, 303
Electronic journal, 289
Electronic novel, 304-306
Electronic photocomposition, 296
Electronic publication, 287-289
history, 292-309
Electronic text, 232-234, 287-291, 366-367
readability of, 298
Electronic textbook, 301
Engineering text, 346-369
Engineers
characteristics of, 347-349
reading habits of, 350-354
Evaluation of text, 418-435
aims, 418-419
as a filter, 418-420
principles of, 395
procedures, 425-426
results of, 431-432
task-based, 428-431
text-based techniques, 426-428
Examples
in text, 358

Faceted indexes, 279
Factual level questions, 140
Formative evaluation, 405
Frames, 91-97
dynamic, 92
goal-action-outcome, 95
problem-solution, 95-96
science/technology, 92-94
social studies/history, 94-97
static, 92
Funding, 374, 379-380

General backward process, 135
General forward process, 135
Generative learning, 9-45
Generative model
  definition, 10-11
  processes, 15-16
  purpose, 13-14
  rationale, 16-19
Generative processing vs. mathemagenic processing, 4-6
Generative text stragegies
  accessing prior knowledge, 34-36
  organizing information, 36-37
  producing distinctive memories, 33-34
Glossary
  functions of, 220
  types of, 221
Graphic organizers, 161-185
  effectiveness of, 177-178
  final form, 168
  future research, 179
  in electronic text, 180-182
  participatory, 166, 168
  rationale, 161-166
  utilizing, 170-176
  vs. structured overviews, 163-164
  procedures for developing, 168-170
Graphics, 320-321, 364

Headings, 237-263, 363
  access functions, 246-248
  access within documents, 253
  and document accession, 250-251
  characteristics of good, 248-249
  effects on retrieval, 247
  effects on searching, 247-248
  encoding effects on recall, 245-246
  encoding functions of, 239-246
  functions of, 238-241

in computer courseware, 254-255
in electronic text, 250-256
in printed text, 189-190, 238-249
kinds of, 243
purposes of, 255-256
reader generated, 245-246
research findings, 241-250
Horizontal spacing, 265
Hypertext, 300-302

Imagery, 29, 33-34
Incidental learning, 131
Index Medicus, 293
Indexes, 190, 272-283, 365
  coordinate, 278-279
  citation, 280-281
  KWIC, 275-278
  text derivative, 274-278
Individual differences, 143-144
  incidental learning, 144
  intentional questions, 144
Inferential questions, 144
  SEE adjunct questions
Instructional design, 355
Instructional text
  defined, 47-48
Intentional learning, 131
Interactive poetry, 305
Interactive television, 302
Inverted files, 273
Italics, 205, 265, 364

Journal articles
  redesigning, 299-300

KWIC indexes, 275-278
Knowledge structures, 11, 16

Learner verification/revision, 394, 396-417
  application of, 410-413
  cost factors of, 404-405

examples of, 398-402
guidelines for conducting, 412-413
importance of, 402-407
potential of, 414
process of, 408-409
sources of input, 406-407
Learning systems
text-based, 325
Learning to learn, 6, 46-55
designing self-conscious text, 53-55
Lessons
templates for, 320
Levels of processing, 17, 138-142

Macro-processing of text, 4
Macro-punctuation, 421
Macro-propositions, 76
Macro-propositions
of book, x-xiii
Macro-structure
of text, 59-60
Marginal notes, 213-218
as headings, 215-216
as summaries, 215
compared to typographic cueing, 216
functions of, 213, 214
Marginalia, 189, 210-236
as level of discourse, 230, 232
defined, 210-212
in electronic text, 232-234
running glossary, 218-225
Mathemagenic behaviors, 14
Mathemagenic hypothesis, 9
Mathemagenic model
definition, 10
processes, 14-15, 50-51
purpose, 12-13
Mathemagenic processing vs. generative processing, 4-6
Meaningful learning, 134
Meta-processing of text, 4

Metacognition, 48-49
Metacognitive skills
training, 49-50
Metacognitive strategies
reader generated questions, 51-53
Micro-processing of text, 3
Mnemonics, 34-36
Node Acquisition/Integration, 30
Notetaking
encoding hypothesis, 24-25
external storage hypothesis, 23-24
generative, 25-26

Online information display 253-254
Online retrieval, 251-253
Optical videodisc, 302
Organization of text, 364-365
Organizational strategies, 29-30
Outlining, 37

PLATO, 303
Paper stock, 266
Plans
writing, 64-70
Printing on demand, 294
Programmed instruction 226
Psychological processes, 423

Quality assurance, 376, 381-382

Reader generated questions, 51-53
Reader's attention
management of, 195-197
Reader's plan, 422
Realistic learning situations, 146
Representation hypothesis, 142
Retrieval hypothesis, 136
Running glossary
advantages, 224
functions of, 220

Schemata, 17-19
Scripts, 17-19
Selective attention, 194
Signaling
    effects of, 79-84
    pointer words, 77-78
    preview statements, 77
    specifying structure of relation-
        ships, 76-77
    summary statements, 77
Slots, 91-97
Spatial cues, 364
Spatial Data Management System,
    304
Specific backward process, 135
Specific forward process, 135
Storage hypothesis, 136
Structural maps, 36-37
Structure of text
    signaling of, 60-61
Structured overviews, 163-164
Student generated questions, 27-28
Subject headings, 250
Subject index displays
    problems in, 281-282
Summative evaluation, 405
Systems analysis, 354-355

Table of contents
    SEE contents lists
Technical manuals
    deficiencies in process, 378-384
    effectiveness of, 377-378
    production phases, 374-377
    recommendations, 384-388
    research on, 372-374
    use of, 371-372
Technical manuals, 327-328,
    370-392
Technical text, 326-327
    characteristics of, 346
    compared with literary text, 346
    language in, 358-359
    usability, 359

Text assessment
    field observations, 428-429
    field test, 429-430
    question-and-answer procedure,
        427
    readability formulae, 426
Text characteristics
    experimentor-provided, 20
    learner-generated, 20
Text comprehension
    cognitive demands of, 193-195
Text derivative indexes, 274-278
Text design
    theories of, 421-423
    automation of, 423-424
    contents lists, 265-272
    engineering orientation, 373
    generative learning principles,
        31-33
    guidelines, 423-425
    indexes, 272-283
    marginalia, 225
    mediational strategies, 31-33
    reader based approach, 46-47
    suggestions for signaling, 85
    user orientation, 373
    using frames in, 97-98
Text processing
    generative learning, 9-45
    mathemagenic control, 9-15
    student's role, 158-160
    teacher's role, 160
Text processing strategies, 19-37
Text structures
    causation, 73
    collection, 71-72
    comparison, 73
    content dependent, 91-97
    description, 73
    problem/solution, 73
Text structure
    and text comprehension,
        194-195
    as evidence of planning, 70-76

content-dependent, 61
signaling of, 61, 64-89, 98-101,
    105-125
Text
    as diagram, 105-123
Text-based analysis, 423
Textbooks, 160-161, 226-228
    reliance on, 402-404
Textual materials
    evaluation of, 393-395
Titles, 363
Topic
    as network of ideas, 66-68
Tutorial, 315-316
Type size, 265
Typographic cueing, 188-189,
    192-209
Typographical cues
    guidelines for using, 203-207
    identifying important informa-
        tion, 198-199
    isolating information, 199
    purposes for using, 197-202
    simplifying tables and figures,
        199-200

Typography
    access functions of, 188, 190
    as discourse, 108
    as macro-punctuation, 188, 190

Underlining
    as generative strategy, 21-23
    as typographic cuing, 20-21
Usability
    retrieval, 360
Usable text
    availability, 359-360
    ease of use, 361-365
    fitting needs, 360-361
    satisfaction, 365-366
User publishing, 297

Validation, 376-377, 383
Verification, 377, 383-384
Videotex, 295, 298-299

White space, 205
Working memory
    and text comprehension, 194